W9-BRE-566

Critical Acclaim for *Observing the User Experience!*

Wow! So many of the user experience research methods we have refined and used over the years are now organized and described in detail in one book. It is an essential reference for any practitioner.
—**Christian Rohrer,** Manager, User Experience Research, Yahoo!

I love *Observing the User Experience!* This comprehensive guide approaches user experience research like never before, and is well-written, easy-to-read, and quite user friendly. It provides a real-world example of how research is done in just enough detail that it can both inform a CEO of the role of usability research as well as introduce methodology to someone starting out in the field. Bravo!
—**Kelly Braun,** Usability Manager, Ebay

You'll like Mike Kuniavsky's broad selection of practical user research methods—presented clearly and usably. And you'll like his timing too: while recent books focus on the whys of *user* experience, many are now ready for the *hows*. *Observing the User Experience* does just that: It demonstrates how to discover what is in users' heads, and suggests how we might balance those considerations with business objectives.
—**Lou Rosenfeld,** co-author of *Information Architecture for the World Wide Web*

Observing the User Experience provides the reader with a wealth of information. We now have a guideline that can be used to gain insight into those mysterious figures . . . our users. Knowing who our users are, what they need, and how they might use the things we build for them is the most important part of any product development cycle. Mike Kuniavsky's focus on this book is on the user experience as it relates to online interfaces, but ANYONE who builds ANYTHING can gain valuable knowledge from reading this book.
—**David Hoffer,** Senior User Interface Designer, CTB/McGraw-Hill

Mike Kuniavsky offers many practical procedures to conduct and analyze the results of your own custom usability tests. He shares lots of personal stories from the trenches, many of which are painfully ironic. The hope is that his knowledge will help spare you the pain of making the same mistakes others have made before you.
—from the forward by **Lynda Weinman,** Author and Founder, lynda.com, Inc.

Observing the User Experience

A Practitioner's Guide to User Research

The Morgan Kaufmann Series in Interactive Technologies

Series Editors:
- Stuart Card, PARC
- Jonathan Grudin, Microsoft
- Jakob Nielsen, Nielsen Norman Group

Observing the User Experience: A Practitioner's Guide to User Research
Mike Kuniavsky

Getting the Work Right: Interaction Design for Complex Problem Solving
Barbara Mirel

The Craft of Information Visualization: Readings and Reflections
Edited by Ben Bederson and Ben Shneiderman

HCI Models, Theories, and Frameworks: Towards a Multidisciplinary Science
Edited by John M. Carroll

Web Bloopers: 60 Common Web Design Mistakes, and How to Avoid Them
Jeff Johnson

Paper Prototyping: The Fast and Easy Way to Design and Refine User Interfaces
Carolyn Snyder

Persuasive Technology: Using Computers to Change What We Think and Do
B.J. Fogg

Coordinating User Interfaces for Consistency
Edited by Jakob Nielsen

Usability for the Web: Designing Web Sites that Work
Tom Brinck, Darren Gergle, and Scott D. Wood

Usability Engineering: Scenario-Based Development of Human-Computer Interaction
Mary Beth Rosson and John M. Carroll

Your Wish is My Command: Programming by Example
Edited by Henry Lieberman

GUI Bloopers: Don'ts and Dos for Software Developers and Web Designers
Jeff Johnson

Information Visualization: Perception for Design
Colin Ware

Robots for Kids: Exploring New Technologies for Learning
Edited by Allison Druin and James Hendler

Information Appliances and Beyond: Interaction Design for Consumer Products
Edited by Eric Bergman

Readings in Information Visualization: Using Vision to Think
Written and edited by Stuart K. Card, Jock D. Mackinlay, and Ben Shneiderman

The Design of Children's Technology
Edited by Allison Druin

Web Site Usability: A Designer's Guide
Jared M. Spool, Tara Scanlon, Will Schroeder, Carolyn Snyder, and Terri DeAngelo

The Usability Engineering Lifecycle: A Practitioner's Handbook for User Interface Design
Deborah J. Mayhew

Contextual Design: Defining Customer-Centered Systems
Hugh Beyer and Karen Holtzblatt

Human-Computer Interface Design: Success Stories, Emerging Methods, and Real World Context
Edited by Marianne Rudisill, Clayton Lewis, Peter P. Polson, and Timothy D. McKay

Observing the User Experience

A Practitioner's Guide to User Research

Mike Kuniavsky

MORGAN KAUFMANN PUBLISHERS

AN IMPRINT OF ELSEVIER

SAN FRANCISCO   SAN DIEGO   NEW YORK   BOSTON
LONDON   SYDNEY   TOKYO

Publishing Director	Diane D. Cerra
Assistant Publishing Services Manager	Simon Crump
Senior Project Manager	Julio Esperas
Editorial Assistant	Mona Buehler
Design	Frances Baca Design
Illustrations	Dartmouth Publishers
Project Management and Composition	Top Graphics
Cover Design	Yvo Riezbos Design
Copyeditor	Robert Fiske
Proofreader	Jennifer McClain
Indexer	Ty Koontz
Printer	The Maple-Vail Book Manufacturing Group
Cover Printer	Phoenix Color
Cover Image	Viewing binoculars, Golden Gate Bridge in background (B&W), The Image Bank, Bill Helsel

Designations used by companies to distinguish their products are often claimed as trademarks or registered trademarks. In all instances in which Morgan Kaufmann Publishers is aware of a claim, the product names appear in initial capital or all capital letters. Readers, however, should contact the appropriate companies for more complete information regarding trademarks and registration.

Morgan Kaufmann Publishers
An Imprint of Elsevier
340 Pine Street, Sixth Floor
San Francisco, CA 94104-3205, USA
www.mkp.com

07   06   5 4 3

Library of Congress Control Number: 2002115471

ISBN-13: 978-1-55860-923-5
ISBN-10: 1-55860-923-7

This book is printed on acid-free paper.

Foreword

Lynda Weinman
Author and Founder
lynda.com, inc.

Mike Kuniavsky and I met in 1994 when I was conducting research for my first book, *Designing Web Graphics*. I had found a web site called hothothot.com that I wanted to profile because of it's great concept, execution, and beauty. It was actually quite rare in those days to find a site that had any aesthetic merit whatsoever! Little did I know after finding this random nice site on the Internet that hothothot.com's web design company was practically around the corner from me. Mike and I met in person and began what has continued to be a professional kinship and friendship. Mike moved away to the bay area while I stayed in Southern California, but we've stayed in touch throughout the highs and lows of these long web years. I had never read anything Mike had written before receiving this manuscript in the mail. I was a little concerned that I might not like his book because this topic has been written about before and there are even some good books on it. I wasn't sure if it was going to be a "me too" kind of book, or if it had something original to say.

After reading the book, I can attest that there is no other book like this on the market. And I mean that in the best possible way! It is written in a conversational style, as if Mike is sitting right beside you. The good thing about having him there is that he's had tons of real-world experience testing and researching the usability of web sites. Most other authors out there market themselves as consultants or experts, but haven't really run their own projects like Mike has. He doesn't come at you as the all-knowing dogmatic "expert," but rather as seasoned veteran willing to share his war stories and victories.

Mike offers many practical procedures to conduct and analyze the results of your own custom usability tests. He shares lots of personal stories from the trenches, many of which are painfully ironic. The hope is that his knowledge will help spare you the pain of making the same mistakes others have made before you.

This book is wonderful. I know you might think I'm biased, but I liked Mike from the beginning for a reason—he knows his stuff and he shares what he knows with humor, generosity, and wisdom.

Contents

Preface

Why This Book?

You've picked up this book for a reason. You think it's important to know who is using the products you're making. And, you know, you're right. Finding out who your customers are, what they want, and what they need is the start of figuring out how to give it to them. Your customers are not you. They don't look like you, they don't think like you, they don't do the things that you do, they don't have your expectations or assumptions. If they did, they wouldn't be your customers; they'd be your competitors.

This book is designed to help you bridge the gap between what you think you know about your users and who they really are. It's not an academic treatise. It's a toolbox of ideas with which you can understand how people are going to experience the environment you're creating for them. The techniques—taken from the worlds of human–computer interaction, marketing, and many of the social sciences—help you know who your users are, to walk in their shoes for a bit.

In addition, the book is about the business of creating usable products. It acknowledges that product development exists within the complexities of a business venture, where the push and pull of real-world constraints do not always allow for an ideal solution. Usability is a dirty business, full of complexities, uncertainties, and politics. This book will, if it serves its purpose, help you tame some of that chaos and gain some clarity and insight into how to make the world a little better by making something a little easier to use than it was before.

Who Are You?

This book was written for people who are responsible, in some way, for the user experience their product provides. In today's software and Web development world, this could be any number of people in the trenches, and in fact, the responsibility may shift from person to person as a project progresses. Basically, if you've ever found yourself in a position where you are answering for how the end users are going to see the thing you're making, or how they're going to interact with it—or even what they're supposed to do with it—this book is for you.

This means that you could be

- A program manager who wants to know how to spec out the next version of the software
- An interface designer who needs to know how to make people best understand the task you're designing for them
- A marketing manager who wants to know what people find most valuable in your products
- An information architect who needs to know which organizational scheme works
- A programmer creating a user interface, trying to interpret an ambiguous spec
- A consultant trying to make your clients' products better

Regardless of your title, you're someone who wants to know how the people who use the product you're making perceive it, what they expect from it, what they need from it, and whether they can use what you've made for them.

What's in this book?

This book is divided into three major sections. The first section (Chapters 1 though 4) describes why end-user research is good, how business tensions tug at the user experience, and it presents a philosophy that will create balanced, usable, and profitable products.

It also contains a short chapter on a technique that will teach you in 15 minutes everything you need to know to start doing user research tomorrow. Really.

The second section (Chapters 5 through 16) is a cookbook that describes in depth a dozen ways for you to understand people's needs, desires, and abilities. Each technique chapter is self-contained, presenting everything you need to know about when to do research, how to do it, and how to understand the results.

The third section (Chapters 17 and 18) describes how to take your results and use them to change how your company works. It gives you ideas about how to sell your company on how user-centered design can make your company run better and more profitably.

What's Not in This Book?

This book is, first and foremost, about how to define problems. All the techniques are geared toward getting a better understanding of people and their problems. It's not about how to solve those problems. Sure, sometimes a good problem definition makes the solution obvious, but that's not the primary goal of this text.

I strongly believe that there are no hard and fast rules about what is right and what is wrong when designing experiences. Every product has a different set of constraints that defines what is "right" for it. A videogame for preschoolers has a different set of constraints than a stock portfolio management application. Attempting to apply the same rules to both of them is absurd. That is why there are no guides for how to solve the problems that these techniques help you to define. There are no "top 10" lists, there are no "laws," and there are no heuristics. Many excellent books have good ideas about how to solve interaction problems and astute compilations of solutions that are right much of the time, but this book isn't one of them.

Acknowledgments

I would first like to thank my heroes in the HCI community who have done so much to create this field and whose work inspired me to enter it: Stuart Card, Thomas Moran, Allen Newell, Herbert Simon, Jakob Nielsen, and Don Norman.

Dave Kieras and Jay Elkerton made me learn GOMS in college, and although I resented it then, I kind of get it now. Kind of.

Most of what I learned about this topic I learned by working at two amazing companies, Presence and HotWired. Presence made me understand that design is a business, and HotWired made me understand that business is design. A special thank you to Tom Soulanille, Mike Ravine, Scott Brylow, and Tod Kurt from Presence. At HotWired, Barbara Kuhr, Thau!, Erik Adigard, Eric Eaton, Jonathan Louie, Doug Bowman, Kevin Lyons, Taylor, and Nadav Savio helped me think about interaction differently, but everyone from HotWired Class of '96 is amazing. Everyone.

Extra double props to Erik Adigard, Kevin Hunsaker, Marshall Platt, and the Webmonkey gang.

My clients' enthusiastic support gave me the opportunity to practice, learn, explore, and tune these methods. Without their sponsorship and input, the material would be much poorer.

Thank you to everyone who gave me advice during the protracted writing process that this book became: David Peters, Victoria Bellotti, Lou Rosenfeld, John Shiple, Jon Katz, Jonathan Gauntlett, Kent Dhalgren, Suzanne Gibbs, Chris Miller, Beth Leber, Phil Barrett and Meriel Yates at Flow Interactive, Christina Wodtke, Kim Ladin, Ken Small, Josh Grossnickel, Jen Robbins, and Avery Cohen.

My technical editors gave great advice, only some of which I followed. Blame me for not always listening to Carolyn Snyder, Jared Braiterman, Chris Nodder, and Chauncey Wilson.

Many thanks to Lynda Weinman for her wonderful foreword contribution.

Richard Koman started this whole process when he asked me whether I wanted to write a completely different book and then listening when I said "No, I don't want to write that book, but here's one I do want to write." Lorrie LeJeune kept me going with wisdom, a sense of humor, and the amazing ability to identify cow breeds over the phone. Lucie Moses read a draft that was for to early for prime time and gave me great feedback. Joslyn Leve was my second set of eyes, reading the whole thing and moving it along while keeping a straight face. Diane Cerra and everyone at Morgan Kaufmann rescued it from my perpetual procrastination with a hard deadline and a warm smile.

My business partners at Adaptive Path, Lane Becker, Janice Fraser, Jesse James Garrett, Peter Merholz, Jeff Veen, and Indi Young were patient and supportive while I disappeared for months at a time instead of nurturing a fledgling company. Jeff and Lane even managed to edit the book in their spare time. I can't imagine a group of people I would more want to work with.

The places where I wrote were a key part of the process. Jonnie Döbele, Hannelore Kober, and Julia Döbele gave me a home in Dagersheim. Susan Argus provided the Black Anguses in Castleton. The cafes of San Francisco's Mission District and Lower Haight were my office, kitchen, and entertainment throughout the whole process (special thanks to Mission Grounds, Café Macondo, and Crepevine).

Several friendships played a great role in how this book was written: Andrea and Scott yanked me out to California and onto the Web in the first place. Moses, Lucie, and Felix gave me advice, food, television, and some drool. Jim distracted me with puppets. bianca gave me love, couches, and grilled cheese. Robin wrote emails. Genevieve called.

Molly Wright Steenson shares with me her life and her 80 boxes of monkey love, which is more than I could ever wish for.

This book is for my parents, who have always believed in me more than I thought prudent.

This book was written entirely using OpenOffice, from the first keystroke to—well, just about to—the last. It only crashed a couple of times. Really.

The music that kept me writing was performed by The Magnetic Fields, The Klezmatics, Photek, Tindersticks, Badmarsh and Shri, Boards of Canada, DJ Food, Nick Cave, and Black Box Recorder.

PART I

Why Research Is Good and How It Fits into Product Development

CHAPTER 1
Typhoon: A Fable

Sometimes it takes a long time for something to be obvious: a shortcut in the neighborhood that you've known all of your life, a connection between two friends, the fact that your parents aren't so bad. It can take a while for the unthinkable to seem clearly natural in retrospect.

So it is with Web sites and user research. For a long time in the short history of Web development, the concept of putting an unfinished product in front of customers was considered an unthinkable luxury or pointless redundancy. The concerns in Web design circles were about branding ("make sure the logo has a blue arc!") or positioning ("we're the amazon.com of bathroom cleaning products!") or being first to market. Investigating and analyzing what users needed was not part of the budget. If a Web site or a product was vaguely usable, then that meant it was useful (and that it would be popular and profitable and whatever other positive outcomes the developers wanted from it). Asking users was irrelevant and likely to damage the brilliance of the design.

Recent history has clearly proved that model wrong. It's not enough to be first to market with a blue circle arc and an online shopping cart. Now it's necessary to have a product that's actually desired by people, that fulfills their needs, and that they can actually use. That means user research. User research is the process of understanding the impact of design on an audience. Surveys, focus groups, and other forms of user research conducted *before* the design phase can make the difference between a Web site (or any designed product) that is useful, usable, and successful, and one that's an unprofitable exercise in frustration for everyone involved.

Nowadays, it seems obvious that a product should be desired by its audience. But that wasn't always the case. Let's step back to the Web world of the mid-1990s, when perfectly smart and reasonable people (including me) couldn't imagine designing a product that users wouldn't like. Here's what happens when you don't think about the user.

The Short History of Typhoon

In the heady days of 1996, PointCast was king. A service that ingeniously transformed the mundane screen saver into a unique advertising-driven news and stock service, it was the wunderkind on the block. It attracted tens of thousands of users and landed its creators on the covers of all the industry magazines. Information coming to people, rather than people having to ask for it, was a brand-new concept and quickly acquired a buzzword summarizing it. It was *push technology,* and it was the future. Soon, everybody was on the push bandwagon, building a push service.

Let me tell you a fable about one company that was on the bandwagon. It's based on a true story, but the details have been changed in the interest of storytelling (and to protect the innocent, of course). Let's call the company Bengali. Bengali had several high-profile successes with online news and information services, and now was confident, ready, and eager to take on a new challenge. They wanted to create something entirely revolutionary—to challenge everyone's assumptions about media and create the next television, radio, or printing press. They decided that their dreams of creating a new medium through the Internet had its greatest chance for success in push.

It was going to be called Typhoon, and it would put PointCast to shame. Bengali went into skunkworks mode, developing Typhoon completely in-house, using the most talented individuals and releasing it only when it was completely ready.

PointCast Killer development takes a lot of work. The developers worked on the project in secret for a year, speaking about it to no one outside the company (and few inside). Starting with "How will the society of the future interact with its media?" the development team created a vision of the medium of the future. They questioned all of their assumptions about media. Each answer led to more questions, and each question required envisioning another facet of the future.

The software and the vision grew and mutated together. The final product was intricate, complex, and patched together in places, but after a year Bengali was ready to release it.

When it was ready to launch, it was shown to top company management. Although undeniably impressed with the magnitude of the achievement, the executives felt some apprehension. Some wondered who the audience was going to be. Others asked the team how people would use it. Although the team had answers for everything (over the year, they had developed a very thorough model of the program and how it was to be used), they admitted that they had to qualify most of their answers because the software had not been put in front of many end users. They were experienced developers, and they had done some in-house evaluation, so they figured that—if not right on—their design was pretty close to what their users would want. But, to placate the executives and check where the rough spots were, the developers decided to do some user research before launching it.

A dozen people were picked and invited for one-on-one user tests. They came in, one at a time, over the course of several days. The plan was to have them sit down, give some initial thoughts about the product, and then let them try a couple of different tasks with it.

The tests were a disaster. This is a portion of a verbatim transcript from one session.

USABILITY TEST SESSION TRANSCRIPT

If this is just graphics that are supposed to look that way it's kind of confusing because you think that maybe it's supposed to do something ... I don't know.

All of these words down here are barely legible.

If this is supposed to say something that I'm supposed to understand, I guess it's very hard to figure what that stuff is.

(Continued)

None of these headlines are making any sense to me.

I don't know what to make of these.

I know if I click on them they'll do something but ...

It's not inspiring me to click on any of them so far.

Also, there's no status bar so you're not really sure when a page is finished being loaded.

I don't know if these numbers have anything to do with that or not ...
I don't know.

I hope that that's a story that I'm going to follow the link to.

This must be [downloading over] a 28.8 [modem] I'm assuming.

It seems a little slow.

This doesn't seem like what I was looking for.

I'm really curious about what these numbers are down here.

They may be nothing.

I just want to know what they're about.

OK, I don't really want to follow that ...

I'm waiting for some sort of text to tell me what this is going to be about.

Since there's nothing, I don't know what's it's about.

I'm not even sure if the page is finished loading.

OK, there it is ...

When I hold that down I would hope that it would stay there but it keeps going away.

Even without seeing what the user is talking about, the frustration and confusion are clear. When the test participants tried to use it, either they used it differently from how the developers intended or, when they used it as intended, it didn't behave as they expected. From a usability standpoint, it was largely unusable.

As bad as this situation was, one point was even worse: none of the participants knew what Typhoon was. It became clear that people would never begin trying to work with it because they had no idea what it was for. Usability was beside the point because the product was incomprehensible.

The developers scrambled to fix the problems, to make Typhoon clearer, and to help people use it, but there were no clear directions for them to go in. The product launch was coming up fast, and they were able to fix some of the most obvious problems. Many problems remained, however, and their confidence shaken, they nervously suspected that many more problems existed.

When Typhoon launched, it was met with confusion. Neither the press nor its initial users knew what to do with it. It got significantly less traffic than Bengali had projected and, despite an aggressive advertising campaign, the number of users kept dwindling.

As the development team worked on the next revision of Typhoon, the direction in which to take it became less clear. Fundamental questions kept popping up. There was constant debate about scope, audience, purpose, and functionality. What had seemed certain suddenly seemed precarious. The executives were quickly losing confidence in the team's ability to fix Typhoon. The debates continued. Their fixes failed to keep visitors from abandoning the product, and after a couple of months, the project leader was replaced with someone who had a more traditional software background. The new project leader tried to revamp Typhoon into a more ordinary news service, but the new specs made Typhoon look just like the company's other products, which ran contrary to the very premise of the service. Requests for additional staff to implement deeper changes were denied. Opinions about how to attract visitors began to multiply and diverge. The team felt betrayed; they felt that their creativity had been wasted and that their good ideas had been being thrown out by management.

Four months after the project launched, the last of the original members abandoned it for other projects within the company. Two months after that, it was quietly closed down and written off as a complete loss. Today, only the T-shirts remain.

Sadly, this is a true story. The details have been changed, but the core of the situation is true. It happened to me. I watched Typhoon's creation, was the person who ran those tests, and watched it disintegrate. Years later, some of the people involved still have feelings of bitterness that so much effort, so many ideas, and so much innovation was abandoned.

It was abandoned for good reason. It was a bad product. What made it bad was not the quality of the code (which was very tight) or the core innovations (which were real and legitimate). What made it bad was that it was a good product with no understanding of its audience. And a good product that doesn't satisfy the needs, fulfill the desires, or respect the abilities of its audience is not a good product, no matter how good the code or the visual design.

This book is about knowing your audience and using that knowledge to create great software. It will help you avoid situations like Typhoon while still retaining the creativity that leads to innovative, exciting, unique, profitable products. User experience research is a collection of tools designed to allow you to find the boundaries of people's needs and abilities, and its core, the philosophy espoused here, is not about creating solutions but defining problems. The ultimate goal is not merely to make people happy; it's to make successful products by making people happy. When you know what problems people have, you are much less likely to create solutions that address the wrong problem, or worse, no problem at all.

CHAPTER 2

Do a Usability Test *Now!*

Basic user research is easy, fast, and highly effective. Some form of user experience research can be done with any product. The question is whether you want to do it yourself. And there's only one way to find that out. Try it. In this chapter, you will learn how to do a fast and easy user research technique, a usability test done with your friends and family. After 15 minutes of reading and a couple of hours of listening, you will have a much better understanding of your customers and which parts of your product are difficult to use.

Note If you don't have a working product or a semifunctional prototype, then it's a bit too early for you to take best advantage of this technique. You should use one of the research techniques that can be done with nothing but an idea, such as contextual inquiry or focus groups. These are discussed in Chapters 8 and 9 of the book, respectively.

A Micro-Usability Test

The *usability test* will tell you whether your audience can use what you've made. It helps identify problems people have with your site and reveals difficult interfaces and confusing language. Normally, usability tests are done as part of a larger research series and involve preparation and analysis. That's what Chapters 5 through 16 of this book are about. However, in the interest of presenting something that's quick and that provides good bang for the buck, here is the *friends and family usability test*. It's designed to let you get almost immediate feedback on your product, with minimal overhead. If you're reading this chapter in the morning, you could be talking to people by the end of the workday and rethinking some of your product's functionality by tomorrow. But give yourself a day or two to prepare if this is your first time conducting user research.

There are four major steps in the process of conducting a usability test.

1.   Define the audience and their goals.
2.   Create tasks that address those goals.
3.   Get the right people.
4.   Watch them try to perform the tasks.

1. Define the Audience and Their Goals

"An evaluation always proceeds from 'why does this thing exist?"
—Dave Hendry, Assistant Professor, University of Washington
Information School, personal communication

You are making a product for some reason. You have decided that some people in the world can make their lives better with your idea. Maybe it helps them buy something cheaper. Maybe it's to get them information they wouldn't have otherwise. Maybe it helps them connect with other people. Maybe it entertains them.

Regardless, you are making something that you feel provides value for a specific group of people. For them to get that value, there's something they have to do. Usually, it's several things. For a site selling something, it can be "Find the widget, buy it, and subscribe to the newsletter." For a matchmaking site, it can be "Find someone, write her a note, send it, and read her response."

So the first thing you should do in a usability test is to figure out whom the site is for. What describes the people who you expect will use it most often? What differentiates them from everyone else? Is it their age, their interests, their problems? It's probably all of the above, and more.

For example, say that you want to examine the usability of the browsing and purchasing user experience of an online cutlery store. You can quickly create an audience definition for the site's audience. The target audience is people who

want to buy cutlery

But this isn't very specific. My grandmother regularly buys plastic forks for family picnics, but she's not going to be doing it through a Web site. So the definition should be a little more inclusive. The target user audience is people who

- want to buy high-end cutlery
- are value conscious
- want a broad selection
- are computer savvy and ecommerce friendly
- are not professional cutlery buyers

Next, figure out what the key product features are. Write down what your product is about. Why are people going to use it? Why is it valuable to its users? If you were at a loud party and had 30 seconds to describe your site to someone who had never heard of it, what you would tell them? Write it down.

forkopolis.com enables people all over North America to buy cutlery from one of the largest ranges available, featuring all the major luxury brands and the best designers. It allows for easy location of specific styles and pieces so that buyers can quickly and cheaply replace a single damaged teaspoon or buy a whole restaurant's worth of silverware.

2. Create Tasks That Address Those Goals

Now write down the five most important functions of the site. What should people be able to do above all else? In a sales site, they should obviously be able to purchase things. But they should also be able to find them, whether or not they know exactly what they're trying to buy. Furthermore, they should probably be able to find what's on sale and what's an especially good value. Make a list, describing each function with a sentence or two.

1. Find specific items by style.
2. Buy by single item.
3. Buy by whole setting.

(Continued)

> 4. Find special offers.
> 5. Find information on returning merchandise.

In a couple of sentences describe a situation where someone would perform that function, written from his or her perspective. Call this a *task*. If "Find specific items by style" is one of the functions, a task for it would be

> You decided that you want to buy a set of Louis XIV forks from forkopolis.com. Starting from the homepage of forkopolis, find a set of Louis XIV forks.

Finally, order the tasks from the easiest to the hardest. Starting with an easy task makes people comfortable with the product and the process.

3. Get the Right People

Now, find some people who fit the profile you created in step 1. When doing a quick exercise like this, you can get a decent idea of the kinds of problems and misunderstandings that occur with real users by bringing in five or six people who are similar to the people you expect will be interested in your product. The fastest way to get such people is through the people you already know. If you're in a large company, this could be co-workers from departments that have nothing to do with your product. If you're in a small company, this can be your friends and family and your co-workers' friends and families. It can be people from the office down the hall. It can be people off the street. As long as they're somewhat like the people you expect to visit your site, it can be anybody who is unfamiliar with the product and unbiased to like or dislike it (so a doting grandmother and the CEO of your biggest competitor are probably excluded). Unless your product is designed for developers, avoid people who make Web sites for a living: they know too much.

Contact these people, telling them that you'd like to have them help you evaluate the effectiveness of a product you're working on. Don't tell them any more about it than the short description you wrote at the top of the task list. Tell them that no preparation is needed, that they should just come in. Schedule them a day or two in advance for half-hour individual interviews, leaving 15 minutes in between each interview.

4. Watch Them Try to Perform the Tasks

First, write a script that you and your invited evaluators will follow. Put your short site description at the top of the page. This will be all that the evaluators will be told about your product. Don't tell them anything else. In the real world, a short description and a link is often all that someone will know. On separate pages, write down your tasks, one per page. Don't include any information that users wouldn't have if they had just started using the service.

Now get a computer and a quiet room where you and the evaluators can talk about the product without being distracted. Small, out-of-the-way conference rooms often work well. Make sure that there is nothing related to the product around, so as not to distract the evaluators or provide information that could be confusing. Thus, no notes, no company propaganda posters, no whiteboard leftovers, and no tradeshow mouse pads.

Set up the computer for the tasks. Set up the browser in the most generic configuration possible, removing custom toolbars, custom colors, display options, and extraneous bookmarks. Bookmark the start pages people are going to need for each of the scenarios you've written.

When each evaluator arrives, prepare him or her for what's going to happen. Make the evaluators feel comfortable. Introduce the process by saying the following:

- They've been invited to help you understand which parts of the product work for them and which are confusing.
- Even though it's called a test, they're not the ones being tested, but evaluating how well the product works, so there's *nothing* they can do wrong. Emphasize that it's not their fault if they can't get something to work and that they won't hurt anyone's feelings if they say something bad about the product.
- It's really important that they speak all of their thoughts aloud. Suggest that they give a "play-by-play" narration of what they're doing and why they're doing it.

- You'll stay in the same room and quietly listen to them while taking notes, but they should ignore you, focusing on the tasks and their play-by-play descriptions.

(You'll probably want to write specific wording for each of these points ahead of time into the script you started with the product description.)

Once the participants are comfortable and you've given them the initial instructions, read the product description and the sheets with the task descriptions. Tell them to do the tasks in the best way they can, but if they can't figure one out in a couple of minutes, they should feel free to move on to the next task. Reinforce that they should be speaking aloud the whole time.

Then, let them talk. Sit back and watch, quietly taking notes. If they get stuck, don't tell them where to click or what to look at. No matter what, don't tell them how to do something. If they seem to be particularly frustrated, tell them that it's not their fault if something seems impossible, and they should move on to the next task.

Once all the tasks have been completed, or the half hour is over, it's time to stop. Ask the evaluators to tell you their general impression and whether they would use the site "in real life." Then give them a present for their time (a gift certificate to a local restaurant or a bookstore, a coupon for lunch at the company cafeteria, a tank of gas—whatever seems appropriate for your audience), thank them, and send them on their way.

Finally, reset the computer for the next evaluator, clearing the cache and history and setting it to a blank page.

What Did You Learn?

As soon as the usability test is over, ask yourself the following questions:

- What worked well?
- Did the users consistently misunderstand anything? If so, what?
- Were there any mistakes consistently made? If so, what?
- Did they do the things that you had expected them to do? If not, what did they do?
- Did they do things in the order in which you had expected? If not, what order did they do them in?

- What did they find interesting?
- What did you expect them to find interesting that they did not find interesting?
- Did they know what the site is for? Did they miss any big ideas?
- How many of the tasks were they able to do? Which ones did they have the most trouble with?
- When did they look frustrated? What were they doing?
- Did the site meet their expectations? If not, where did it fail them?
- Do you know what their expectations were?
- Were they ever confused? What were they doing when they were confused?

At this point, you should have some ideas of where your product has problems. You've probably seen several things come up again and again. Maybe people don't understand the name you've given to a certain function. Maybe they don't see a critical piece. Maybe they aren't interested in what's being offered. Maybe they love it and it fulfills everything they want. All these things are good to know since they tell you where you are having problems and, equally important, where you're not.

Warning Friends and family usability testing is fast, easy, and convenient, but it's a quick and dirty technique. Your friends and family may give you a general idea of the problems with your product, but (more often than not) they're not representatives of your actual user audience. Whenever possible, use actual representatives of your audience.

What to Do Next

Having done your first usability test, you probably have an idea of what the technique is good for and how it's useful for you. If you read the rest of the first section of this book (through Chapter 4), you should be able to put together a research plan for your product, incorporating discount usability testing (which the friends and family usability test is an example of) and a number of other techniques. The in-depth techniques described in the second part of the book (Chapters 7 through 13) will tell you how to go far beyond this basic test to understand every facet of your users' experience in your product's development. The final part (Chapters 14 through 19) will help you present your findings in such a way that convinces your development team to make the changes that will make your product really work for your audience and to keep directing it toward users' needs well into the future.

CHAPTER 3
Balancing Needs through Iterative Development

In a perfect, egalitarian, happy-dappy world, product development processes would only be about making the user happy. Perfectly user centered, they would focus on creating the ideas users experience at any cost. All software (and hardware and VCRs and cars and pretty much anything with a human interface) would be standardized, optimized, consistent, and transparent. Everything would be focused on helping the users perform their task.

But the world is far from ideal. Finding a single perfect way of doing any task is unlikely. Even ideal user solutions do not always make ideal products. Moreover, products are generally not created solely for the benefit of their users: they are created by companies whose goal is to make money. Making money and satisfying people's needs are two very different goals; they can be made to work together, but they will always remain distinctly different goals.

Furthermore, modern software—especially Web sites—exists in a unique competitive environment. Not only does it have to satisfy the users and the makers, but it often has to address an additional set of stakeholders: advertising partners. Ads don't just add a new element to the user experience, but create a whole new business relationship that permeates the development process. Where before the two primary features driving software design were the quality of the user experience and the profitability of the product, now there's a third element—the effectiveness of the advertising (Figure 3.1). The needs of these three groups of stakeholders are in a constant game of tug-of-war. If any one of them pulls too hard, the other two suffer.

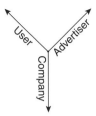

Figure 3.1 Tensions affecting product priorities.

This book focuses on understanding the user experience and will not dwell too much on either advertising effectiveness or corporate profitability; nevertheless, it is critical to keep this tug-of-war in mind when doing development and to consider the environment in which user experience is developed.

In Chapter 4, the focus is on just the user experience, and later in this chapter I present a method of resolving these tensions, but first it's useful to look at what makes a product a success when examined from the perspective of each group.

Success for End Users Is . . .

A product's end-user experience is the cornerstone to its success. A good user experience doesn't guarantee success, but a bad one is nearly always a quick route to failure. However, experience quality is not binary—total malfunction is rare—but, surprisingly, mediocrity in user experience can actually be worse than complete failure. When something doesn't work at all, at least it's obvious where the problem lies, but something with intermittent problems—a shopping cart with a high dropout rate or a search engine that only 40% of the people can find things with—can make a product underperform even if the rest is perfectly designed. A mediocre user experience can go unnoticed and be the most serious problem in the whole business venture.

Note Don Norman has some beautiful examples of unusable products in his book, *The Design of Everyday Things.* His examples illustrate that although we may not always know what makes a product usable, we can really tell when it's not.

What makes a good experience varies from person to person, product to product, and task to task, but a good general definition is to define something as "usable" if it's *functional, efficient,* and *desirable* to its intended audience.

. . . Functionality

A product—or a portion of a product—is functional if it does something considered useful by the people who are supposed to be using it. Each product has a set of things its users are expecting it to do, and to be considered usable it needs to be able to do them. This is a simple idea, but it is remarkable how often it is forgotten. For example, a high-end subwoofer came with its own amplifier and its own remote control, but—in the interest of minimizing controls on what was ostensibly a speaker—the manufacturer made some functions available only on the remote control. One of these was the control to switch between equalizer modes ("Theater," "Concert Hall," "Radio," etc.). Unfortunately, if the remote were lost, the amplifier would stay in the equalizer mode it was last in forever. So if the subwoofer was set on "Radio" and the remote was lost or broken, the owner would then have to listen to all music amplified as if it were a tinny talk show, with booming vocals and almost no treble. This defeated the basic purpose of having an expensive subwoofer in the first place: to make music sound good.

A more common phenomenon is the deep concealment of key features by the complexity or incomprehensibility of the interface. The classic example is the process of programming VCRs before the advent of on-screen programming: the functionality was so difficult to understand that it may as well not have been included in the product at all.

. . . Efficiency

People—on the whole—value efficiency, and how quickly and easily users can operate a product attest to how efficient that interface is. A product's interface may enable a task to be accomplished in a single step, or it may require many steps. The steps may be prominent or hidden. Maybe it requires its users to keep track of many things along the way. In the traditional perspective, these factors boil down to speed, how quickly someone can perform a task in a given situation with the smallest number of errors.

. . . Desirability

Although long recognized by usability specialists and industrial designers (and certainly marketers), this is the least tangible aspect of a good user experience. It's hard to capture what creates the surprise and satisfaction that comes from using something that works well, but it's definitely part of the best product designs. It's something distinctly different from the packaging of the product (the esthetics) or its marketing, but it's an emotional response that's related to those.

Usability and Design

Ultimately, usability is good design. That's not to say that all good design is usable since there are things that are well designed from one facet (identity, technology, value, etc.) that are not usable. For example, a lot of expensive designer furniture is beautiful and instantly identifiable, but often you can't put many books on the bookshelves or sit comfortably in the chairs. Similarly, the Unix operating system is incredibly elegant and powerful, but requires years of practice and memorization before any but the most basic functions are usable. Coke's OK Cola had brilliant packaging but tasted terrible. On the other hand, Yahoo! became popular by focusing so much on the end-user experience that their visual identity lacked any readily identifiable characteristics. In the end, despite all marketing efforts, products that are hard to use are likely not to get used much. People using an unusable product will either be unable to do what they need to do, unable to do it quickly enough, or unhappy as they do it.

There are, of course, exceptions to this: occasionally, a product will be unique, and people will excuse any usability problems because of its functionality (content management systems are a good example of this: they can be incredibly hard to use, but taming huge amounts of content is nearly impossible without them). However, those situations are few and far between. In almost all other cases, the usability of a product is critical to its success.

Success for Advertisers Is . . .

It would be naïve to deny that ads—and, therefore, advertisers—are part of nearly all of our experiences. Until the Web, however, they were a minor part of our experience with software. Word processors in the 1980s didn't have commercials. Spreadsheets weren't co-sponsored. Killing a monster in Zork didn't get you frequent flier points on United. However, on the Web, ads are everywhere, even inside other ads (just count how many co-branding deals, ads, and product placement markers there are in Figure 3.2, a typical advertising-driven Web site).

Now even non-Web products like Intuit's Quickbooks have marketing messages in their interfaces. There are now sponsored links, co-branded advertorial content, interstitial ads, pop-unders, traffic-sharing deals, affiliate programs, affinity incentives, and a host of other kinds of revenue-earning devices. There are pages with 20 different content areas that are essentially ads. Even most subscription services have some revenue that's based on a relationship with a second company.

All these things are parts of the user experience, but they're really there for the advertiser. The user is supposed to see them, act on them, remember them. And, in the end, advertisers are primarily

Figure 3.2 Advertising units on ESPN.com in 2002.

interested in the effectiveness of their advertising for their chosen market. They may be willing to wait and let an advertisement's popularity grow, or they may be interested in a good end-user experience insofar as it can positively affect their ad sales, but ultimately they want to know how much revenue a given ad deal is driving. On the Web, they measure results by *traffic* or by *awareness.*

. . . Traffic

On the Web, there are three primary measures of advertising performance: *impressions, click-throughs,* and *sell-throughs.*

Impressions measure how many times the advertisement is inserted into a Web page that is subsequently downloaded. Thus, it's a measurement of how many times an ad can hypothetically be seen.

Note A traditional Web advertisement is, in one way or another, a link to another site; the advertisers' fundamental goals are frequently in direct opposition to those of the user or company. Simply put, at some level, the advertiser wants the user to leave your company's Web site and go to theirs. And when evaluating the balance in a user experience, this is often the most difficult relationship to resolve.

In other kinds of advertising or partnership relationships such as affiliate programs or traffic-sharing deals, this fundamental split isn't as profound or obvious, but it's still a major underlying influence in the relationship between the parties.

Unfortunately, just putting an advertisement on a Web page does not guarantee that someone sees it, just as putting up a billboard does not guarantee that everyone who drives by reads it. So the online advertising industry developed a second measure, the *click-through.* This is a measure of how many people click on a given advertisement, how much active interest they display in a given ad. The goal of advertising is, of course, more than just interest, so even click-through is still an imperfect measure.

The most direct measurement of advertising effectiveness is the *sell-through,* which is specific to advertisements where something is for sale. It is a measure of how many people actually bought a given product based on a given advertisement. However, even this measurement has problems: people may be inspired by an ad long after they've left the site with the ad.

. . . Awareness

Advertising effectiveness is the subject of a large branch of research, but three common metrics that appear in Web site research are *brand awareness, brand affinity,* and *product sales.*

Brand awareness measures how many people are aware of the product. *Brand affinity* measures how much they like it and, more generally, what associations they have with it. *Product sales* is the bottom line: how many people bought whatever it was that was advertised during the time it was advertised, or soon thereafter.

These three metrics are not necessarily dependent, and can sometimes work against one another. For example, when Oldsmobile launched their "This is not your father's Oldsmobile" campaign, it was initially quite successful, leading to great brand awareness. People remembered it and brand affinity was high: many people in the advertisement's target market reconsidered the image of the car company and saw it as younger and more adventurous than they had previously. Unfortunately, the impact on the bottom line was disappointing because when people went to the showrooms to see the actual cars, they discovered that it *was* their father's Oldsmobile, so product sales did not reflect the success of the ad campaign. Why? Because the car did not produce a user experience that matched the one that was advertised for it.

In the end, even the best of the traditional marketing measurement systems—Starch scores for print advertising and the Nielsens for television—can produce only approximations of an advertisement's effectiveness in raising awareness and sales. Web metrics are easier to come by (log files abound), but determining the success of an ad campaign is often still an art determined by the gut of the media buyer.

Note Standards for Internet advertising can be found on the Internet Advertising Board's Web site at *www.iab.net*.

Success for the Company Is . . .

With few exceptions, companies don't invest in product development to lose money or to remain anonymous. Two primary ways that companies measure the success of a product is through *profit* or how well it promotes the company as a whole.

. . . Profit

Though forgotten for a while in the heat of the dotcom era, the fundamental purpose when creating a product, whether it's a Web site or a fork, is to make money. Maybe it won't make money immediately, or it won't make a lot of money, but few things are designed to lose money. With the exception of the products of nonprofit organizations, making money is the primary reason companies do anything (in the case of nonprofits, it's also a top reason—it's just not intended to be the biggest one).

. . . Promotion

To some extent, everything is an advertisement for itself, but other than in fashion or in extreme circumstances—I once rented a car that was plastered on all sides with ads for Hertz—corporate self-promotion in a user experience is generally pretty subtle. Except on the Web. On the Web, with its giant, fast, competitive market full of similar products, it's a lot more important that a site actively serve as an advertisement for itself. There are several general things that a site needs to do well to market itself: it needs to be *different, recognizable, memorable,* and it needs to *communicate its function.* Designing purely for these things is likely to create a product that seems all surface glitter lacking substance, but ignoring this role in development is equally dangerous.

Without going into an ode to the beauty of being different, individuality is important for products. It's important to *differentiate* a product from all its competitors. In search engines, for example, there was a time when there were few differences between the largest search services. Infoseek and Excite, for example, had nearly identical interfaces and services, as did Yahoo! and Lycos (Figures 3.3 and 3.4). While doing competitive research for HotBot, we saw that in users' minds these interfaces merged, became identical and interchangeable. As such, none communicated that there was any reason to go to it versus the other or that there was any inherent value over the other. Thus people didn't necessarily care which one they used and never bothered to learn why one was better than the other.

For a product to consciously find something that makes it different from its competitors, it needs to distinguish itself by features, layout, color, editorial tone, or something else important (even usability!). CNET had a broad and general editorial mission that would not allow them to vary their editorial tone or content, so they concentrated on visual design for their identity. They were so successful that they managed to be identified with a certain shade of yellow for a long time. Netscape Netcenter similarly owned teal, while Yahoo! tried to create identity by being "generic gray" and placing round buttons on top. Other sites used different tactics. HotWired had a new animated front door every day. ICQ had more text on their front door than some sites have on their whole site. Amazon could deliver virtually any book overnight. All these things—even when they interfered with functionality—made these sites easy to remember and recognize.

In cognitive psychology and advertising, there exists the concept of *recognition,* which goes beyond just being memorable. It means being uniquely identifiable, and the faster, the better. And

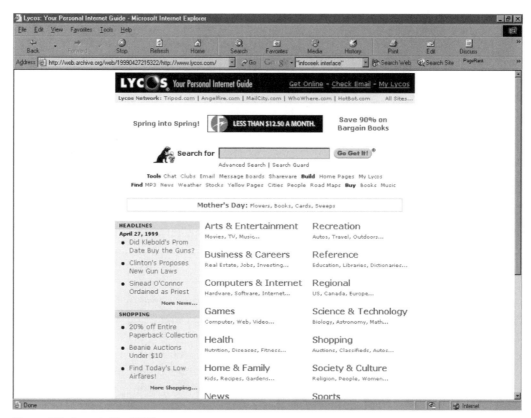

Figure 3.3. Lycos in May 1999.

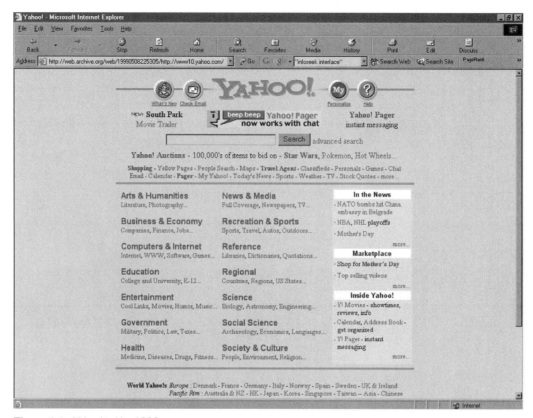

Figure 3.4. Yahoo! in May 1999.

though recognition is largely visual, it also involves the name of the site, the site's URL, its logo, its attitude. It can encompass all the aspects that make a site stand out from its competitors and from all other sites. Erik Adigard, one of the principals of the cutting-edge Web design firm M.A.D. said that an interface should be recognizable if it's the size of a postage stamp and on a page with 100 other interfaces.

Finally, there's *tone,* the "spirit" of the site. The things that communicate tone differ from application to application and from market to market, but they exist for every product type and for every type of user. *The New York Times* Web site doesn't look *exactly* like a newspaper (it's not as big, it doesn't have ink smudges, the head-

Figure 3.5 Google's interface, circa 2001.

lines are placed differently, there are ads in the corners), but it communicates enough "newspaperness" through its layout and type-face that it's almost instantly recognizable as such (though maybe not to a 13-year-old skateboarder who hasn't spent a lot of time with newspapers—this is why skateboarding news sites look much more like skateboarding magazines than newspapers). Google looks like a search engine (Figure 3.5). Why? Because it has a big type-in box in the middle of the page, and the word *search* is prominently shown.

Self-promotion does little to the immediate measurable bottom-line profitability of the product and the company, but it is still a key element in what makes a successful product.

A System of Balance: Iterative Development

If the desire to focus on one of these sets of success criteria overwhelms the others, the long-term success of the product can suffer. For example, watching a couple of trailers before a movie is fun, but it's unlikely that watching 120 minutes of trailers would be a particularly popular way to spend Friday evening. Like a person who can talk only about how great he or she is may be memorable, but doubtfully popular, a design that places the uniqueness of its identity over usability and advertising effectiveness is likely to be unsuccessful in the long run (though it may win some design awards). And as street curbs are rarely memorable, any product that is solely focused on usability risks appearing generic and uninviting when compared to one that balances usability with good advertising effectiveness and a strong identity.

To make matters more complicated, the balance between these elements changes as the product matures. Uniqueness and functionality may be most important in the early part of a product's life, when people are first finding out about it. At that point, trying to squeeze the last drop of advertising revenue from a product will likely result in an interface that alienates first-time users, and associates images of crass commercialism with the brand (generally, an unwanted association). Later, however, when the brand has become established and the user population has learned what the product is for and how to use it, the quantity and prominence of advertising can be increased.

When listed out, the complexity of interaction between these elements can be daunting. Compared to the quick and easy usability test in the last chapter, it can seem like suddenly going from making ice cubes to trying to catch all the snowflakes in a blizzard. What's needed is a systematic way of integrating the process of finding the problems and creating solutions, focusing on individual elements without losing sight of the whole. That's where *iterative development* comes in.

Iterative development is based on the idea of continual refinement through trial and error. Rather than trying to create a perfect vision from the beginning, iterative development homes in on the target, refining its focus and perfecting the product until it has reached its goal. Each cycle consists of the same basic steps, and each cycle infuses the process with richer information. Solutions are created, examined, and re-created until the business and user needs are met in a consistent, regular, and predictable way.

How Iterative Development *Doesn't* Work

Before planned iterative development grew in popularity, the popular development styles (which still exist in a frightening number of companies) were *corporate edict* and the *waterfall method*.

Corporate edict is when someone, or some group, decides what's going to be done and then the rest of the company builds it, no questions asked. The method suffers from a lack of omniscience on the part of the people issuing the proclamations. If the chief architect (or whoever is issuing the edict) doesn't know everything about the business climate, the users, the needs of the business partners, and the capabilities of the technology, the product is likely to miss its mark, sometimes spectacularly.

A real-life example: the CEO of a popular digital greeting card company had a favorite card that he liked to send to his friends. After a complete redesign of the site, he had a hard time finding the card. Thinking that this would be a problem for many of the system's users, he insisted that the development team create a search engine for the service. After several months of development, they developed a full-featured search engine for the site, which allowed the CEO to find his favorite card quickly and in a number of different ways. Unfortunately, when they launched the search engine, it hardly got any use. After some research, it turned out that the very concept of looking for one specific card was alien to many people. They were happy with a general category of similar cards, and had little interest in sending—or finding—the same card over and over. Restructuring the information architecture closer to people's expectations resulted in a much larger increase in the use and satisfaction (and ad revenue) of the site than did the search engine, and it required fewer resources and much less time. Creating the feature by edict, the company missed a crucial piece of information, misunderstood their core strength, and lost several months of developer time in the process.

The waterfall method (Figure 3.6), although less arbitrary, isn't much better. Working as an assembly line, its practitioners begin by creating an extensive requirements document that specifies every detail of the final product. Maybe the requirements are based on the target audience's real needs and capabilities, but there's a good chance they are a collection of the document authors' gut-level guesses and closed-door debate. What if those assumptions are wrong? Or what if the company's needs change? Even with built-in feedback, the rigid waterfall method allows little backtracking, just as a waterfall rarely allows water to flow up. When backtracking becomes necessary—as it almost always does—the rigidity of the model almost guarantees that it'll be expensive.

Both of these methods share an Achilles' heel: they lack built-in sanity-checking steps that would modify their assumptions to match the reality of the environment. They are dependent on the assumptions being correct from the start and on the initial set of data being complete. If the initial ideas are even a bit off, then the end product is at risk of providing the wrong solution to the wrong people at the wrong time.

The Iterative Spiral

Iterative development methods have existed for years in large-scale software and manufacturing sectors. They carry many names: rapid application development, rational unified process, total quality management, joint application development, and the evolutionary life cycle, to name a few. Although the specific details of these methods

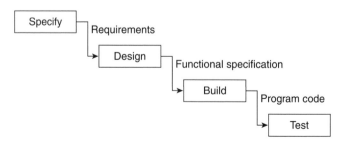

Figure 3.6 The waterfall method.

vary quite a bit, they share the underlying idea of progressive refinement through cyclical data-driven development, and although they
may describe the iteration with five or more steps, the core ideas behind them can be summarized in three basic stages (Figure 3.7).

1. *Examination.* This step attempts to define the problems and
   whom they affect. Questions are raised, needs are analyzed,
   information is collected, research is conducted, and potential
   solutions are evaluated. Strengths and weaknesses are enumer-
   ated and prioritized. Customers' needs and their capabilities
   are studied, and existing products or prototypes are evaluated.
   For example, maybe the company extranet is bringing in new
   customers, but the support mailbox is always full of messages
   from people who can't seem to find what they're looking for.
   Maybe there's a usability issue in the interface, but it could
   also be that a fundamental service is missing or that the user
   population isn't the one that had been expected.
2. *Definition.* Solutions are specified. Maybe the extranet's support
   mail is pointing to a fundamental feature that's missing from the
   product. At this stage, changes in the product are mapped out
   with ever greater detail as additional information about the real
   needs and capabilities of the target audience are uncovered.

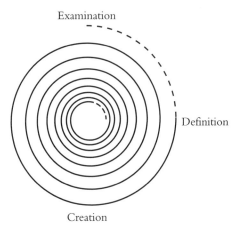

Figure 3.7 Iterative development: the final product is at the center, and the development orbits it, adjusting as it goes along.

3. *Creation.* Solution plans are carried out. Since it's the most expensive and time-consuming phase (taking as much as half of the development time), if the work done in the creation stage is not backed by data collected during the examination phase and by careful planning in the definition phase, much of it could be wasted.

Note Although I wasn't aware of it when I first came up with these diagrams and principles, these ideas are indebted to Barry Boehm's "Spiral Development" method, which he introduced in the May 1988 issue of *Computer* magazine.

So far, this resembles the waterfall method, but what makes iterative development different from that assembly line is that *creation* is immediately followed by another cycle, beginning with *examination.* Each cycle—and there may be many cycles between initial examination and launch—isn't expected to produce a complete product, but add to the quality of understanding and to flesh out the feature set. Thus, the project is adjusted with every iteration, making the process thorough and responsive to new information and to changes in the business environment. This, in theory, minimizes unnecessary development while making products that are more in tune with what people need.

Benefits of Iterative Development

Flexibility

All the constraints on a project are never known at the beginning. No matter what the process, as development goes along, more is discovered about the needs of the audience and the company, and limitations in the technology are uncovered. Since edict and waterfall processes are dependent on initial conditions, they're brittle and susceptible to being undermined by later information.

For example, for those few months in 1997 when push technology was the greatest thing since "sporks," a number of companies developed whole products and business models around the idea. They didn't do a lot of research to see what their users needed or liked, they just assumed that since PointCast was popular, their product would be, too.

Iterative methods can put flexibility where it's most needed, leaving flexibility at the beginning of the project and then locking in only the things that are known to be reasonable solutions. Dave Hendry, Assistant Professor, University of Washington Information School, refers to this process as going from "low fidelity and high provisionality to the opposite." Initially, the product is rough, but there are lots of things that can be changed, and there are still many fundamental questions that need to be answered. As the process continues, the questions get answered, the details get filled in, the prototypes start looking more like the completed product, and the flexibility of the process goes down. Good applications of iterative development gradually reduce flexibility and collect appropriate information to make sure that decisions are binding only when they're right.

Adaptability

Every design is a trade-off. Or, more accurately, the design and production of any complicated product involves making a lot of trade-offs. Big, fast cars can't be as fuel efficient as smaller, less powerful ones. If this book had larger type, it would have to have more pages. Every part of every product is the result of a trade-off that was made at some point in that product's creation. Nearly every trade-off changes the fundamental character of the product. Some choices move the product in a direction where it will be more usable by a certain group of people, some choices move it in a direction that will bring in more money, some choices will make it more desirable. The ideal choice moves it in all three directions at once.

Knowing how to make the right trade-offs is difficult. Like a new organism evolving on an island, an idea isolated in a company is exposed only to certain environmental conditions. It only has to face a certain number of predators, deal with a certain kind of climate, adapt to certain kinds of diseases. The only way to know whether an idea will survive outside its sheltered world is to expose it to the environment in which it will ultimately have to live. However, rather than the shock of the waterfall method—where the final product is pushed out into the big bad world and left to fend for itself—iterative development attempts to understand the environment and predict how the idea needs to adapt in order to flourish before it is released into the wild.

Shared Vision

In addition to creating good products, the iterative development philosophy can focus the whole company on continually improving the user's experience and company profitability. The focus is no

Note Throughout this book, I use the term *development team*. By this, I mean the group of people who are responsible for creating and maintaining a product. Depending on company structure, this group could include representatives from many different disciplines. Some development teams are actually *product teams,* responsible for all aspects of the product. Such groups could include visual designers, business strategists, market researchers, quality assurance engineers, and so on. From my perspective, these are all development teams, even if the majority of the staff don't write code or design screen layouts.

longer on creating a series of single, one-off products; it's about evolving a set of tools and techniques to respond to the needs of your clients and your company, no matter what those needs are or how they change.

Iteration can easily apply to marketing the product, designing its identity, developing its business objectives, or creating a support system for it. For greatest effect, everyone who has responsibility for the product—engineering, marketing, information architecture, design, business development, customer support—should be part of a single iterative development process. Everyone needs to iterate through the process along with the core development team, sharing information and improving the product with every turn. For example, after the initial market has been determined, marketing can be researching the size and composition of market segments in conjunction with the development teams' research into the nature of the work and the audience's work habits. These two sets of information can be combined to produce a set of desired features, which can be used by business development to look for potential partners to provide or enhance those features, or for large clients who would be especially interested in those features.

Not only can the whole company develop the product identity together, but using the same research methods reduces the need to alter plans after the product launch by taking into account the changing needs of all facets of the organization. In treating the product as a system of solutions developed over time, rather than as a single release, the business uses its resources strategically, planning for the long term while reacting to short-term developments.

Iterative Development Problems

Despite its benefits, iterative development isn't perfect. It creates a lot of uncertainty throughout the process, which can be frustrating to a development team that wants to be able to delve deeply into feature development. It requires discipline and dedicated project management because it can be a complex process that requires every iteration to focus on a subset of the product, when other glaring problems may be screaming for attention. It can require backtracking to review earlier assumptions, which may extend development time. Mostly though, the biggest difficulty in implementing iterative development is creating a company culture—from the CEO to marketing to customer service—that understands the process and integrates it into the way the company works.

Iterative Development and User Research

Iterative development is especially appropriate for Web-based products since prototypes can be made and evaluated quickly. Sculpturally, it's like working with plaster, clay, or wax before committing to stone or bronze. Changes can be put into effect rapidly, and release cycles can be arbitrarily tight. In the interest of rapid response, one search engine goes through a full iteration every week.

Unlike traditional software products, the immediate user experience presented by a Web site is critical. Usability has always been important, but in traditional software, the threat of instant abandonment didn't hang over every moment someone used the product. Moreover, since the user (or the company) had paid for the software and was planning to use it for extended periods of time, there was an incentive to make it work, so even a broken interface would be tolerated until a replacement was found. Such stability and loyalty are luxuries few Web sites enjoy. For the rest, the user experience needs to be right from the start.

User experience research need not be a part of iterative development. Iterative development can happen without any user research (for example, extreme programming is a highly iterative development process, but includes no explicit research component), and user experience research techniques can be used as part of any software development method. But the two work especially well together, where the results of one research project can answer questions asked by the ones before it and guide those that come after.

User research provides a consistent, rapid, controlled, and thorough method of examining the users' perspective. It appears at every rotation through the development spiral, providing a way of answering questions as they come up. Early on, background information about the users is gathered, the work they do is studied, and their problems described. Later on, features are prioritized in the order that people desire or need them. By the time that specifics

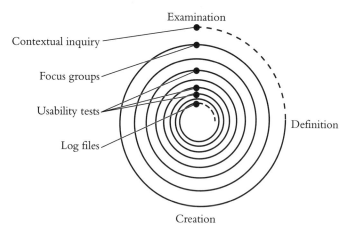

Figure 3.8 A sample research program.

are being nailed down, it's known which group of people want the product, what the product is supposed to do for them, and what is important for them to know and remember about it. When the details are designed and tested, it's known that the only thing that needs to be focused on is presentation rather than people's needs or product functionality because those have already been thoroughly researched. Graphically depicted, user research cuts through the development spiral, with different techniques appropriate at different times in a product's development. Figure 3.8 is a sample user research program, depicted as part of an iterative development spiral (the specific techniques will be discussed later in the book).

Example: A Scheduling Service

Here is a simplified and idealized example of how an iterative development process could work, based on a hypothetical product. In most cases, things never go this smoothly, but it's useful to see how things could be.

Suppose your company wanted to make a Web-based appointment scheduling product because some easily adaptable backend technology had been developed.

Cycle 1

Examination

Your initial assumption is that the target audience will be people who are really busy and who travel a lot, so they need a sophisticated scheduling package that's easily accessible. Revenue will come from ads sold on the service and a subscription service for advanced features.

In your first round of research, you visit a number of busy people and observe them as they manage their schedules (a form of *contextual inquiry,* as described in Chapter 8). You discover that busy people are fairly comfortable with existing technologies (daytimers, Palm Pilots, etc.) for scheduling their work lives, and they're generally unwilling to change to a new technology unless it's much more useful than what they currently use. They would rather not be the early adopters of a new technology unless they knew it was worthwhile and would be adopted by their colleagues. They seem apprehensive about the reliability of the service, and the Internet as a whole, saying that a down connection on a busy day could be disastrous.

Put bluntly, this means that your target market isn't interested in your product unless it blows away what's there already. This limits its appeal to a segment of the market that will be unlikely to bring in enough revenue to offset development costs. One option is to look for a larger market for the product (maybe students), but let's say you decide to follow the original market but at a different tack. Several people you spoke with expressed interest in scheduling solutions for their personal life rather than their work life (which seems to be already covered). Your results reveal that for this audience

- Their personal schedules are almost as complicated as their work schedules.
- They need to share their personal schedules with friends and family.
- They can't use their office software because it isn't available outside the firewall, and their family and friends aren't likely to have access to it.
- All existing scheduling software is seen to be entirely focused on business scheduling tasks.

Definition

Realizing this, you decide to stay with your target audience of busy execs, but you modify your idea to better fit their lifestyles. You change the focus of the functionality to personal shared schedules, rewriting the product description with goals that all focus on helping people share schedules in a way that's *significantly* better than their current methods. The description defines in detail the problems that the software needs to solve and explicitly lists problems that are outside its purpose (or *scope,* using the project management term). Simultaneously, you redirect the marketing and identity efforts to concentrate on the personal nature of the service.

Creation

Using the new problem definition, you rewrite the product description to reflect the new purpose for the scheduling application and the new knowledge you have of the audience's needs. The bulk of this phase is spent creating a detailed listing of the features that the product provides and the benefits it offers. You vet this list with the engineering team, making sure that the features proposed are within the capabilities of the software. In addition, you create a tentative research plan, outlining the questions that need to be answered, the markets that need to be investigated, and the areas that need to be focused on in the next round of research.

Cycle 2

Examination

Taking the product description to several *focus groups* (described in Chapter 9) of busy executives, you discover that although they like the idea of Web-based shared schedules a lot, they're worried about security. In addition, they consider the most important part of such a system to be rapid information entry and easy sharing. One person says that he should be able to do everything he needs with a shared schedule in five minutes a day. Other features that get mentioned include the ability to separate the schedules of friends and colleagues from those of his family and to get the schedules of special events (such as sports) automatically.

Definition

This shows that although the core idea is solid, several key functional requirements need to be addressed for the system to be successful. You add security, entry speed, and schedule organization to the software goals and pass them on to the group working on marketing the product.

Creation

Taking these ideas into account, you redefine the solution as a scheduling system with "layers" that people can overlay onto their regular schedule. Some of the layers can come from family schedules, others can come from shared business schedules, and still others can be promotional content for TV and sports, which not only would capitalize on the personal nature of the schedules but would add a potential revenue stream. You modify the system description to include this functionality and to address the concerns voiced in the focus groups.

Cycle 3

Examination

You are worried about the "five minutes per day" requirement. Informal *usability testing* (Chapter 10) shows that it's hard to do *all* daily scheduling stuff in five minutes a day, but if that's the perception that most people want, it's important to be able to meet it. You decide to do more research to see how long people *really* spend on personal schedules and if there are common trends in schedule management. Watching (using contextual inquiry methods) a half dozen people maintain their schedules, you uncover that they spend an average of 20 minutes a day—not 5—dealing with their personal schedule and that their biggest scheduling headaches are not knowing the whole family's schedule and not getting confirmations from invited participants to upcoming events. Further, you learn that they check their schedules anywhere from 3 to 10 times a day on average, which gives you some parameters for how many ad impressions they're likely to generate. Through several users' comments you also uncover that there may be two other potential markets for the product: teenagers and doctors. Teenagers have complicated schedules that involve many people (most of whom have Web access), and doctors' offices spend a lot of time scheduling, confirming schedules, and reminding people of appointments.

You also field a *survey* (Chapter 11) of your primary target audience to discover their exact technological capabilities and desires, as well as what associated products and media they use. You discover that they often have several fast, late-model computers at home that are shared by the family, but only one family member is ever on the Internet at a time. You decide that this means there needs to be an easy way for all the family members to use the service without stepping on each others' schedules (and to maintain privacy).

Definition and Creation

As in the two previous rounds, you refine your product goals. You add goals that focus on sharing schedules, family scheduling issues, and confirmation. Finally, you create the general outlines of a system that fulfills all these goals and then write a detailed description of it.

Cycle 4

Examination

Your survey also showed that the households you're interested in have at least one cell phone per person and use them a lot, that they're interested in sports, and that they watch a lot of television. So you decide to run another round of focus groups to investigate whether people are interested in portable phone interfaces for the service and whether they want to get schedule "overlays" for sports team and television schedules (both potential targets for lucrative advertising markets).

The focus groups tell you that schedule sharing and confirmation are the most highly desired by the target audience, whereas the family scheduling and special events features are considered desirable and cool, but not as important. Cell phone interfaces are considered interesting, but the majority of people who have Web-enabled phones have never used the Web features and are somewhat worried that it will be awkward and confusing. You discover that teenagers think that a shared personal scheduler is a great idea, especially if they can schedule instant messaging reminders and chats with it and if they can get to it with their cell phones. Doctors—an audience suggested by the last round of research and desired by the business development and advertising staff because of their buying power—don't seem to be interested in the scheduler. Although useful in theory, they figure that not enough of their patients will use the system to warrant training their staff.

Definition

Using the new information, you define two fundamentally different audiences: busy executives (your original audience) and highly social teenagers. These two groups have wildly divergent needs in terms of how the product needs to be presented, even if the underlying scheduling functionality is shared between them. Although realizing that you may not have the resources to pursue both groups, you split the product in two, defining the audience needs and product goals for each group.

Creation

You create new descriptions of the product for each of the new audiences. Although the teenagers' needs are not as well studied as those of businesspeople, you feel that you know enough about the groups' problems and their solutions to begin expressing the solution descriptions in paper prototype form. You create paper prototypes for both the Web- and telephone-based interfaces based on the description. At the same time, you direct the marketing group to focus the upcoming campaign on the sharing and invitation capabilities when presenting it to the primary markets, and the easy-to-use telephone interface and TV schedule overlays when talking to the teenage market.

Cycles 5, 6, and 7

Now, having determined the target audiences for your product, the features they need, the features they want, the priority they want them in, and roughly, how to present it to them, you build it. You

Note This is a highly simplified and rather idealized version of a production cycle. Its main focus is to show how user research interacts with product development, but it's not an exhaustive description of a development cycle that may have lasted six months. At the same time that what's described here is happening, so are all the usual project management tasks. Resources are scheduled, budgets are created, software is written and tested, and so on. Research forms part of the process, but it is not necessarily the most time-consuming or even the main driving component. This description highlights how studying a product's users at all times reveals new markets, needs, desires, and capabilities, constantly making it a better and greater part of people's lives.

run it through multiple rounds of usability testing, and you test the marketing with focus groups. With each round, you uncover more about how to align the scheduler with the identity of your other products while making it more understandable and efficient, and presenting the sponsored content so that it's noticed but not considered intrusive.

In addition, you create a management system so that your staff and your sponsors can add and manage content, testing it with them at the same time as you're testing it with the consumers.

When you're done with cycle 7, you release the product.

Cycle 8

You immediately begin a survey of the user base, the first in a series of regular surveys to observe how your user base is changing and what direction it's changing in. This will let you target sponsorship and capitalize on the special needs of new groups of users as they appear.

You also begin a program of extensive *log file* and *customer feedback analysis* (Chapter 13) to help you understand whether people are using the system as you had expected and what kinds of problems they're having.

In addition, you continue the program of field research to see what other related needs people have. One of the common scheduling tasks is bill payment, and you begin thinking of your product as not only a scheduler, but a family bill-paying service, and maybe in the future, a complete suite of family management tools.

CHAPTER 4
The User Experience

From the users' perspective, their experience is continuous. Your Web site, their browser, their computer, their immediate environment, and their life all interact and feed back on one another. What they understand affects not just what they can accomplish, but what attracts them to the product, and what attracts them to a product affects how willing they are to understand it. If a site is visually attractive, they may be more motivated to expend extra effort to understand and use it. If they feel it's easy to use, maybe they'll be motivated to use it more often.

Thus defining "the user experience" is difficult since it can extend to nearly everything in someone's interaction with a product, from the text on a search button, to the color scheme, to the associations it evokes, to the tone of the language used to describe it, to the customer support. Understanding the relationship between these elements requires a different kind of research than merely timing how quickly a task is accomplished or testing to see how memorable the logo is.

However, trying to look at the whole user experience at once can be vertigo-inducing, and dividing it into manageable chunks is necessary to begin understanding it. For Web sites (and other information management products), there are three general categories of work when creating a user experience.

- *Information architecture* is the process of creating an underlying organization system for information the product is trying to convey.

- *Interaction design* is the way that structure is presented to its users.
- *Identity design* amplifies the product's personality and attraction.

This chapter will describe these facets by focusing on the research needs, tools, and titles of the people engaged in doing these things.

Information Architecture

The most abstract level on which people experience a Web site is the *information architecture*. All information that's created by people has some underlying structure, and there is always some organizational idea that defines how all the information in a given work fits together. Often that structure is quite explicit, as in the case of the phone book, the Library of Congress, or the Yahoo! hierarchy. In these cases, there's little question about how information is arranged.

Sometimes, however, the creator's unifying idea is less easy to see; it's implicit. When an architecture is implicit, it's hidden behind an analogy to another organizational structure, a metaphor that maps one kind of information to another. The person trying to navigate it has to navigate the "real" information structure using the metaphor. An implicit architecture sometimes makes things clearer, and sometimes it confuses things further. The desktop metaphor of the Macintosh and Windows clarifies and organizes a lot of concepts about files and their manipulation, whereas the geography metaphor of Yahoo!'s Geocities Web hosting service has little connection to the content found there. With the Macintosh, visually moving file icons from one "folder" to another requires less labor and information about the system than, say, file manipulations in DOS, which require typing and an understanding of the layout of the whole file system. In Geocities, however, the geography metaphor is both dependent on cultural queues ("Silicon Valley" communicates little about the information a section named that contains) and breaks down if taken literally. Santa Clara and Mountain View are both cities in the real Silicon Valley—if Geocities had sections called that in their Silicon Valley, what would they communicate about the kind of content that's in those sections? Very little. Yahoo!, in fact, recognized this and abandoned the geographical metaphor long ago in favor of a more explicit organizational structure; now there's no Silicon Valley; instead, there's Computers & Internet.

Whether it's explicit or implicit, there's always some structure to the information, but often the people making the structure may not even realize that they're building an information architecture. Their way of organizing may be so deeply buried in their knowledge of a certain subject or understanding of a certain task that they can't imagine any other way to think about it. For example, a corporate information site organized using the company's org chart is using an architecture that may seem reasonable and explicit to the creator of the site, but from the users' perspective may be unrelated to how they need to see the company. A user looking for support information in such a site may not care that the technical support staff can be found in the operations unit of the North American subsidiary of a Taiwanese company; he has a question about a product he bought and—from his perspective—all this other information is completely unrelated to either asking or answering his question.

Information Architects

It's the information architect's job to make the implicit architecture explicit so that it matches what the users need, expect, and understand. The architect makes it possible for the users to navigate through the information and comprehend what they see. The ultimate goal is for the audience to be able to predict what's going to happen around the next corner, even if they've never been there, and be able to get from point A to point B without getting lost.

When the underlying model isn't obvious, people create one. Humans are always looking for patterns in data, things that can be used to simplify our interaction with the world, make it more understandable. Even when we don't know what to call it or we can't articulate it, we still create an image or a pattern or a story to understand the information space we're in. People always think they've found a pattern in the stock market or a roulette wheel when the vast majority of the time no pattern exists. Thus, although there may not be a specific information architect position in a development team, there is always someone who is creating a pattern in the information. Someone is playing the role of information architect though he or she may not know it yet.

Information Needs of Information Architects

Information architecture frequently happens (or should happen) at the beginning of the development process, and the kinds of research that inform it are fundamental. Specifically, it's information about who the audience is, how they think about the task, what words they use, and whether the existing information architecture makes sense to them.

Knowing exactly who is going to be using the product is often a critical part of creating an information architecture. Different groups of people have different contexts with which to understand information that's being presented to them and different assumptions about how to use that information. The more finely a target audience is described, the more accurately the information architect can make the Web site work as they think. The fundamental way to measure any community is through its *demographics,* which describe their physical and employment characteristics. Typical demographic characteristics include age, education level, income, job title, and so forth.

For Web sites, it's also important to create a *Web use* profile that summarizes a community's Web experience. Typical Web use characteristics include how long someone has been using the Web, how much time he or she spends using it, and what kinds of things he or she uses it for.

Appropriate *terminology* is one of the most important elements in a successful interaction. Most interfaces are largely made out of words, and words can be ambiguous and easily misunderstood, so their comprehension is especially critical. Examining the words that people use to describe a task, and how they organize those words, is one of the keys to creating a product that meets their expectations and needs.

The audience's *mental model* makes up a third major piece that's used in creating an information architecture. A mental model is how people currently understand the topic, what kind of picture they've built for themselves of how a given task is done or organized, the names and relationship of terms they use. For example, even though food in supermarkets is mostly organized by either food group or storage requirements (all the things that are bottled go together, all the things that need to be cold go together, etc.), research conducted by Indi Young shows that people rarely think of their food in those terms when shopping. People often make up their shopping lists based on meals that they're planning or by which foods go with which other foods. Their mental model is therefore based on meals,

Note Many of these needs overlap with interaction and identity designers, and much of the research described in the next section is equally useful to them. In the interest of presenting the techniques in roughly the order they appear in de-velopment, I'm intro-ducing several things as information architecture concerns when they're really concerns that under-lie the whole product, no matter which aspect is being examined or designed.

Note A complete list of the factors that make up demographic and Web use profiles is available in the Appendix and discussed further in Chapter 11 on surveys.

not on how something looks or how it's stored. Since a Web site doesn't have to work like a supermarket, it can be organized in a way that's closer to how people plan their meals rather than by food storage constraints.

Mental model research can be done both before a service is created—to see how people perform a certain task in order to emulate it with a software interface—and after an interface has been designed—to see how well users' ideas match the designers'.

Useful Tools and Techniques

For information architecture, the most useful tools are the ones that give insight into both *who* the target audience is and *how* they think about information: how they organize it, how they prioritize it, what they call things.

- For a brand-new service, a *profile* of potential users provides an idea of what kinds of people will use the service, how they will use it, and what they will use it for. Profiles are described in Chapter 7.
- For an existing service, a *survey* reveals who is already using the service. Surveys are covered in Chapter 11.
- Once the target audience has been established, *contextual inquiry* and *task analysis* are the basic tools for creating the mental model. Contextual inquiry sheds light on the kinds of situations in which a typical user uses your product (or doesn't, but should). Task analysis then determines exactly how users think about what they're trying to do, what assumptions they make, what kinds of words they use to describe the tasks, and how the tasks interact with other things they're trying to do. These techniques are covered in Chapter 8.
- *Card sorting,* a process by which people group ideas into categories that make sense to them, helps reveal how people organize topics, and what they call groups of ideas. Card sorting is also covered in Chapter 8.
- Analyzing *diaries* kept by users helps reveal how mental models change with time. They provide insight into how users' expectations and understanding change as they become more experienced with the tool. Diaries are discussed in Chapter 12.

The knowledge provided by these tools can be used to determine a good information architecture and to provide context for other fundamental questions about the product. Knowing which features are most attractive can, for example, be immediately used in the marketing of the product. Likewise, studying a site's mental model can uncover unmet needs in the target audience, suggesting additional features for the product in mind, and—occasionally—whole other products. For example, a mental model of how people use search engines showed that people expected to be able to use them to search the latest news. However, this was outside the focus of what the search engine was supposed to do, but it still seemed like a valuable idea, so it was spun off as a wholly separate product.

Interaction Design

Traditionally, all the knobs, buttons, and displays that were used to operate a machine (whether real or simulated in software) were thought of as "the user interface." Indeed, that's true in a traditional universe of machines and static information; however, in the world of dynamic information, there is not a single interface. On the Web, every page is a different interface. The interface can be thought of as *everything* that goes into the user's immediate experience: what the user sees, hears, reads, and manipulates. The interface experience isn't just functionality, but readability, navigation, and (the black sheep of the family) advertising. In short, it encompasses all facets of someone's interaction.

Interaction Designers

Interaction designers control the immediate user experience. They determine how to navigate around the information architecture, arrange that users see what they need to see, and make certain that the right data are always presented in the clearest way, with the appropriate emphasis. Interaction design is different from information architecture in the same way that the design and placement of road signs is different from the process of laying out roads—information architects determine the best path through the terrain, whereas interaction designers place the signs and draw the maps.

Information Needs of Interaction Designers

Interaction design requires more specific, more narrowly focused information than that collected for information architecture. After the mental model and the target markets have been determined, the focus shifts to the specifics of interaction. Depending on the stage in the development process, the designer may need to know general information either about whether his or her designs are on the right track or about whether people can actually do what they're supposed to be able to do.

- *Task flows* are strings of actions that are necessary for something interesting to happen. Researching task flows include knowing in what order people look at the elements, what their expectations for the next step are, what kind of feedback they need, and whether the results are what they had anticipated.
- The *predictability* and *consistency* of interfaces is critical. Research determines how much predictability is enough for people to feel comfortable with the task flows and how much consistency is necessary for different task flows to feel familiar.
- The relationship between the features on a site and the *emphasis* of specific interface elements is likewise crucial; for example, whether a large illustration on the right of the screen takes attention away from core functionality on the left, or whether the repetition of a feature in different parts of the interface affects how often people use it.
- Different *audiences*. First-time users need different features and use them differently than experienced users. Teenagers understand terminology differently than 40-year-olds. If a product serves various target markets, it's important to know what those markets want and what they can use.

Useful Tools

Task analysis is the most useful tool for finding out what interaction sequences should be. It's also good for establishing the terminology and, to some extent, the emphasis of features.

Focus groups are by far the easiest way of determining people's priorities. They can gauge what the target market finds most valuable about a service, and they help determine the relationships people already make about the interactions of certain features (though they are not useful for figuring out how people actually behave or whether a system is usable). Focus groups are described in Chapter 9.

Task-based *usability testing* is often the most useful tool for getting information that is immediately applicable to interaction design. Although it's not the best tool for discovering what people want and how they want it, it's the best one for finding out whether they understand what's been created. Usability testing is also one of the most flexible of the techniques. It can be done at nearly every point of the development process and provides valuable insight throughout. Chapter 10 describes how to conduct and analyze a usability test.

Log analysis gives immediate hard numbers of where people go and how often. When the analysis includes clicktracks, it also says how they get there. Chapter 13 describes log analysis issues and techniques.

Identity Design

Note Identity is a big part of the product's *brand* but is not the whole of the brand. Brands are incredibly powerful parts of the user experience and can color users' expectations to the point that all other factors virtually vanish. Unfortunately, there is much confusion, debate, and punditry surrounding what makes up and affects the product's brand. However, despite its importance, brand building and research is—to my honest relief—outside the scope of this book.

A product's identity communicates its values and permeates both its information architecture and its interaction design, but is separate from them. It is the style, the feeling, the vibe of a Web site. It's what makes it memorable and what makes it unique. In some cases, it rivals the importance of the product's functionality (though, as proved by many marketing campaigns that failed to overcome bad functionality, it's rarely more important). The identity is the combination of what a site does, how it looks, what associations it evokes, its editorial voice, and how it emphasizes certain features over others.

- Some elements that play a role in determining a site's identity include the way that text copy on a site is written. This conveys a lot about the site's values. Is it funny? Is it technical? Is it condescending? These factors make up the *editorial voice* of the site.
- Consistent *visual themes* can create an element of recognition for a site or for a group of sites. For example, nearly all of CNET properties have a yellow background with green highlights and the round red logo somewhere. This combination is recognized by most people once they've used one of CNET's

sites for a while. They can even make the connection if they end up on a CNET site they've never seen. It's also possible to maintain an identity through more basic visual consistency.

- The *features* a site emphasizes also tell its clients where it's coming from. Two sites may have both shopping cart features and a bulletin board, but the impression people will have of the site that puts the bulletin board front and center will be totally different from the one that puts the shopping cart as its main focus.
- The Nike site is obviously related to an existing identity and brand by its *association with an existing brand.* The signals of online brand association are the same as those that defined the brand offline: the logos, the colors, the slogans, the vibe, and so on.

Identity Designers

The identity designer's job is to communicate an identity for the site that's distinctive from its competition and consistent with the company's other products. Though the identity designer's job is closely related to the marketing of the site, there's one key difference: the identity designer aims to make an enjoyable and unique experience *on the site* and to make it memorable when people are not using it, not to convince them to try it for the first time.

Information Needs of Identity Designers

The information needs of the identity designer are similar to those of the marketing research department. There are some key differences, however, since designers are more concerned with the immediate experience of the product rather than the perception of its brand or its prevalence in the market. Thus, identity designers need information about people's immediate emotional responses and how well they remember the product later. Assuming that a target audience for the product is defined, here's what they'll need to know about it.

- The *competitive strengths* of the product relative to others in its class. This tells the identity designer what features to emphasize since these are the things that the product does better than its competitors.

- The direction of the users' *attention*. This includes what people see when they look at the interface, what they ignore, and what they consider to be the important parts of the interaction.
- Who the *current users* are. This includes how they compare with the demographic and Web use makeup of the target market and what they like, dislike, and remember about it.
- What kinds of *references and associations* they prefer and understand. For example, people over 50 tend not to like bright colors as much as teenagers.

Useful Tools

The goal of identity design is to create a satisfying, memorable user experience, both immediately and in the long run. Thus, the tools are similar to market research tools, and the results can be both shared with marketers and (sometimes) obtained from them.

- *Focus groups* are one of the fastest ways to find out which things are most attractive about a product. They provide information about both where people's attention goes and what their preferences are.
- *Surveys* can determine the demographic and Web use makeup of the existing audience. It's difficult to determine potential audiences with them, but they're quite good at figuring out who is using a product, and if they're using any competing or complementary products. This information can then be used with *interviews* to determine why users choose the products that they're using.
- *Competitive analysis* can be used to create a list of features that competitive products have, which can then be used for research to find out which of those features are most valuable. Competitive research is covered in Chapter 14.

The User Experience Researcher

The user experience researcher has the broadest job of all. Every aspect of the user experience places different demands and constraints on those who are trying to create a good product. They all have different needs, different vocabularies, different constraints, and are often operating on different schedules. But they share similar and interrelated needs for information, often without realizing it. The job of the user experience researcher is to provide insight into the product's users, their perspectives, and their abilities to the right people at the right time. The researcher is in the unique position to draw all this information—and all these information needs—together and have it make sense, making the entire development process more streamlined and effective.

Bringing all those people together and combining each of the facets of the development process into a single coherent development culture is the subject of the next chapter. It will cover how to integrate research at key points while including users as an inherent, inseparable part of the team that creates a product.

PART II

User Experience
Research Techniques

CHAPTER 5

The Research Plan

Note These instructions present a somewhat idealized situation that starts with a blank slate as far as user experience product goals are concerned. This isn't the case for many projects, which may work with preexisting goals and processes. It's easier to enumerate goals in such projects, but it may be more difficult to create a unified vision of how research should be integrated with existing processes. Deborah J. Mayhew's *The Usability Engineering Lifecycle* and Hugh Beyer and Karen Holzblatt's *Contextual Design* describe a completely iterative development environment that thoroughly integrates experience research.

Never research in a vacuum. Every piece of user research is part of an ongoing research program, even if that program is informal. Making it formal provides a number of advantages: it provides a set of goals and a schedule that stretches limited user research resources; it delivers results when they're needed most; and it avoids unnecessary, redundant, or hurried research. You should start working on a research plan as soon as you've decided to do any research at all, even if it's only a tiny usability test or some client visits. A well-structured research plan is also a communication tool that lets others in your company work with your schedule. It educates your colleagues about the benefits of user research and provides a forum for them to ask questions about their users and an expectation of the kind of knowledge the process can produce. But even if you don't show it to anyone, it will still prove invaluable in helping you figure out what to research when.

A research plan consists of three major parts: why you're doing the research (the *goals*), when you're going to be doing it (the *schedule*), and how much it's going to cost (the *budget*). These are in turn broken up into practical chunks such as report formats and timetables.

Goals

Before you begin writing a research plan, you need to know two things: why you're doing the research and how your results will be

57

implemented. Together, you use these two things to figure out which questions should be asked in order to have the most impact on the product.

The first involves determining corporate priorities and setting research goals that can meet them. The second involves an understanding of the development process so that the research can make the greatest impact on the final product.

Every product interacts with every department in your company, and every department has a different method of measuring its success. For development, success could be measured as meeting the schedule or the number of bugs per thousand lines of code. For marketing, it could be the number of positive reviews and increased site traffic. For identity design, it could be the ease with which the product is integrated into the corporate brand. For customer support, it could be a low number of questions they have to field. For sales, it's how much revenue it brings in. Each of these represents a different perspective on the final product, and each demands something different from the user experience.

Research can go on in any direction. To get the most benefit from it, it needs to be focused on the most important features of the product. But a product's "features" include much more than just the screen layout. Its most important features are those that affect the business goals of the company. Thus, the first step is to make a list of issues of how the product's user experience affects the goals of the company. Each issue represents a goal for the research program; it focuses the research plan and helps uncover how the product can be improved for the greatest benefit to the company. Collected and organized from the perspective of the company, these issues will not (and *should not*) be solely focused on the user's ability to efficiently use the product. There may be goals for advertising effectiveness, customer support load, brand recognition, and so forth.

In other words, since the user experience affects every facet of the product, every facet needs to be considered. The process consists of the following three steps:

1. Collecting issues and presenting them as goals
2. Prioritizing the goals
3. Rewriting the goals as questions to be answered

1. Collect Issues and Present Them As Goals

Ideally, before any project is begun, everyone in the company knows why it's being created, what it will do for its customers, and how it will help the business. It will have clear, specific, and measurable goals, which everyone knows.

Unfortunately, life is never ideal. Thus, the process of determining the important issues can be a research project in itself.

Begin by identifying the stakeholders. Every department will own some piece of every product, but some will own more than others (or will care more). The product manager—who is probably the most important person to talk to, anyway—can help start the list since he or she will know which groups and individuals have the biggest stake in the project. These will almost certainly consist of engineering, design, marketing, and advertising sales, but it can include any other department that has a stake, or say, in the product's success. There could also be a significant managerial presence in a product that's a major moneymaker (or loser) or if it's brand-new.

SAMPLE SPORT-i.COM STAKEHOLDER LIST

Alison, VP of Product Development

Erik, Interaction Design

Michel, Marketing

Sun, Frontend Development

Janet, Sales

Ed, Customer Support

Leif, QA

Joan, Identity Design

Maya, Rob, frequent users

If there isn't a single person who's responsible for the product in a given department, find the person who dealt with it most recently. Odds are that this person regularly deals with it or can tell you who does. Once you have your list of stakeholders, find out what they consider to be the most important issues. You can do this either by getting all the stakeholders together and spending an afternoon setting companywide priorities for the product or by speaking to each person independently (often a necessity with executives and other busy people). The key questions each person (or department) should answer are as follows:

1. In terms of what you do on a day-to-day basis, what are the goals of the product?
2. Are there ways that it's not meeting those goals? If so, what are they?
3. Are there questions you want to have answered about it? If so, what are they?

Once you've talked to all the departmental representatives, make a list of the goals and issues.

Note What if stakeholders have conflicting goals? An advertising sales manager may want to increase revenue by introducing additional ad units at the same time that the vice president of content wants to add more news stories to the front door. Since there's a limited amount of real estate on the interface, these goals may appear to be at odds with each other. At this stage, it's too early to attempt to resolve them, but investigating the relationship between them may be an important near-term goal for the project.

USER EXPERIENCE GOALS AND QUESTIONS FOR SPORT-i.COM

Who	Goals and Questions
Alison, VP Product Development	Better conversion of viewers to shoppers
	More stickiness: people coming back more often
Erik, Interaction Design	To help people use the search engine better and more often
	Why are so many people starting and then abandoning the shopping cart?
Michel, Marketing	For people to know that we'll give them the latest information about their favorite local sports throughout the year, no matter where they live
Sun, Frontend Development	Is the dynamic map useful enough to wait for the Java applet to load?
Janet, Sales	Increase revenue by 30% by fiscal year-end
Ed, Customer Support	Reduce support calls about expired promotions
	Shift more support from the phone to email

After you've talked to everyone in-house, you should talk to a couple of users for their perspective. That may seem like a catch-22: why research the user's needs before you even have a plan to research their needs? Because getting their voice into the research plan gets the research focused on them early and sets a precedent that can prove important in selling your research efforts within the company. See Chapter 6 for some hints on how to find users to talk to. Add this information to the list.

Who	Goals and Questions
Maya, Rob, frequent users	Would like Sport-e.com to remember what brands they prefer for each sport they're interested in
	Want to know what the best values are based on the performance of the items

As part of this process, you should try to collect the other user experience knowledge that may be floating around the company, answering research questions without doing any original research. This can include surveys done by marketing, customer support feedback summaries, interviews by the development group, and unused reports from usability consultants. The user experience researcher can play the role of information collector and integrator, and, becoming the repository of all user-related information, spread information about the value of user experience research and build stakeholder trust in the process. More information sources are described in Chapter 15.

2. Prioritize the Goals

Based on your interviews, you will have some idea of the corporate priorities with respect to the goals you've defined. Some things may be important because they're seen as preventing people from using a key feature of the product. Others may be important because they differentiate the product from its competitors. Still others might be less important because they may create a big drain on resources or are currently a hot topic of debate within the company.

To get an idea of the order in which to tackle the research, you should prioritize the questions. If the prioritization is unclear, you can try the following exercise (which uses the same technique as in Chapter 10, where it applies to choosing specific features):

A PRIORITIZATION EXERCISE

Make a column next to your list of questions and label it "Importance." Go down the list and rate each item on a scale of 1 to 5, where 5 means the feature affected is a "must have," critical to the success of the product, and 1 means it's a "nice to have," but not essential.

Next, make a second column and label it "Severity." This will reflect how bad the problem is. Write a number on a 1 to 5 scale here, too. Five represents bad problems (generally ones that are directly affecting the bottom line right now), and 1 refers to problems that are annoyances or information that would be good to know.

Now multiply the two entries in the two columns, and write the result next to them in a third column called "Priority." This combines and amplifies the two factors in deciding which problems should be investigated when. Ordering the list by the third column gives you a starting order in which to investigate the product's user experience.

Goal	Importance	Severity	Priority
To help people use the search engine better and more often	3	4	12
Increase revenue by 30% by fiscal year-end	4	5	20
Better conversion of viewers to shoppers	5	3	15

You should now have a prioritized list of what the company as a whole considers to be important user experience questions. There shouldn't be more than half a dozen or so "big" questions and a dozen or so smaller, more specific ones. These, taken together and coupled with a schedule, a budget, and some more fleshed-out goals, will be the heart of your research plan.

3. Rewrite the Goals as Questions To Be Answered

With the product goals in hand, start rewriting the goals raised during your interviews as user-specific questions or information to be gathered. Broaden narrow questions into general topics to get at the root causes of the problems. If there's a concern voiced about a specific feature, for example, you may need to broaden the focus to include the underlying reasons for that feature's existence.

The questions should be simple so that they give the most bang for the buck. Every problem presents a host of questions and issues, many of which are complicated and interrelated. But this is "easy pickin's time." Pick one or two questions for each goal that, when answered, will address the goal. When you later research and revise the plan, you'll be able to tease out the more subtle questions and important interactions.

GOALS FOR SPORT-i.COM REWRITTEN AS RESEARCH QUESTIONS

Issues	Research Questions
Better conversion of viewers to shoppers	Why don't some visitors become shoppers?
More stickiness: people coming back more often	What are the reasons why people come back? What determines how often they return?
	What is the demographic makeup of the user population and how they use the Web?
Help people use the search engine better and more often	How do people navigate the site, especially when they're looking for something specific?
Why are so many people starting and then abandoning the shopping cart?	How do people expect the shopping cart to function? Where is it failing them?
For people to know that we'll give them the latest information about their favorite local sports throughout the year, no matter where they live	What services do people value? What services are they aware of?
	What on-screen information do they pay attention to (and are they paying attention to the feature promo sections)?
Is the dynamic map useful enough to wait for the Java applet to load?	How do people navigate the site, especially when it comes to lateral movement (as facilitated by the dynamic map)?

Continued

Issues	Research Questions
Would like Sport-e.com to remember what brands they prefer for each sport they're interested in	How important is customization? Which things are most useful to customize?
Want to know what the best values are based on the performance of the items	How do people shop with Sport-e.com? Is it based on sport, brand, tools, price, or something else?

Expand General Questions with Specific Ones

In the final step, flesh the larger, more abstract questions into specific ones that can be answered by research.

General Question	Specific Questions
Why are so many people abandoning the shopping cart?	What is the ratio of people who abandon the shopping cart to those who complete a transaction?
	On what pages do people abandon it?
	What pages do people open a shopping cart from most frequently?
	Do people understand the instructions on the cart pages?
	Do they know they're abandoning the cart?
	Do they know what a shopping cart is?
	Under what circumstances do they open the cart?
	How do they use the cart?
	How do they shop on the site?

Of course not all these questions can be answered in a single research project or by a single technique, but having a big list of questions from which to draw can help you when you're putting together your research schedule. Moreover, the process of making the list often helps define the boundaries for the larger issues, reveals relationships between the larger issues, and sometimes reveals new questions and assumptions.

Tips

- Never go into user research to prove a point, and never create goals that seek to justify a position or reinforce a perspective. The process should aim to uncover what people really want and how they really are, not whether an opinion (whether yours or a stakeholder's) is correct.
- Learn the product thoroughly. Research goals can be framed more precisely if you can understand how the software currently works. Do what you can to become a user: read the documentation, take a training course, and talk with tech support.
- Be prepared to deal with fundamental questions about the product. If a question comes up during research—even if it's "should we be in this business at all?"—then there should be a way to deal with it and create research that will answer it (or at least escalate it to a senior stakeholder who can address it).

Note The mantra for determining which questions to ask is simple. *Test what's testable.* Don't ask questions whose answers won't be actionable or test things that you can't change. For example, it's generally of little use to inquire about the identity design of a product before the feature set has been determined since the feature set will greatly shape the product's identity. Likewise, it's fairly useless to be researching feature desirability after you've already committed to an interaction design since the design assumes that people want what it's showing them.

Schedules

Once you have the questions you want to answer, you're close, but it's not your research plan yet. Before it can be a research plan, it needs a schedule, and before it can have a schedule, you need to integrate it with the existing development system.

If you're lucky, the development process is well defined, with good schedules and specific deliverables. If you're not, then your research plan may *become* the development schedule (if you can convince the development team that it's worth their while to let it do so).

Often talking to the person immediately in charge of the product is the fastest way to determine the actual development process. This could be a project manager, a senior production person, or the marketing manager. Show him or her your list of prioritized questions, and rearrange the priorities to take advantage of the development schedule, moving research that's going to affect near-term development efforts up in the list. Concentrate on the big issues, but feel free to include secondary issues as techniques and schedules allow.

See Chapter 18 for more ways of integrating user experience research into your corporate culture.

The output of every research project not only provides information on how to improve the product, but it feeds into the next research project. Surveys describe the current audience so that you know whom to recruit. Contextual inquiry outlines what their problems are. Focus groups tell you which problems people feel strongest about, and so on. Every piece of information that research provides helps you know who your users are or what they want. You use that information, in turn, to focus subsequent research.

Thus the order in which you schedule the projects, although constrained by immediate priorities and the development schedule, should still be organized so that one project informs and reinforces subsequent projects. In practice, this means that procedures that gather general information fall before those that collect information about specific preferences and behaviors.

Starting Research in the Beginning

For an existing product in an early phase of redesign, the following order makes sense (see Chapter 4 for other thoughts about integrating research into development processes):

Early Design and Requirement Gathering

- *Internal discovery* to identify the business requirements and constraints. (Internal discovery is described more in Chapter 18.)
- A *survey* to determine demographic segmentation and Web use of the existing user base. (Surveys are described in Chapter 11.)
- *Log file analysis* of their current behavior if such logs exist. (Log analysis is described in Chapter 13.)
- *Profiling* of the ideal users, based on knowledge of the existing users or users of competitive products. (Profiles are described in Chapter 7.)
- *Usability testing* of the existing product to uncover current interaction problems. (Usability testing is described in Chapter 10.)

- *Contextual inquiry* to uncover problems users have (both with the product and with the task it's supposed to aid), and *task analysis* to specify how they solve them right now. (Both of these techniques are described in Chapter 8.)
- Two to three rounds of *focus groups* to determine whether people feel the proposed solutions will actually help them and which features are of highest value. And *competitive focus groups* to determine what users of the competition's products find most valuable and where those products fail them.

Realistically, only a couple of these techniques are generally possible to do given release schedules, but this would be an ideal list to prepare for a major overhaul of the product, assuming there were four to six months of time devoted to this stage in the process.

Development and Design

- Four to five back-to-back *usability tests* of prototypes that implement the solutions and test their efficacy. And *competitive usability tests* to determine strong and weak points in the competitors' products.

After Release

- *Surveys* and *log file analysis* to compare changes in the product to past behavior.
- *Diaries* to track long-term behavior changes.
- *Contextual inquiry* to study how people are actually using it.

Starting in the Middle

A user research plan often may have to begin in the middle of a development cycle. Decisions have already been made about who the users are, what their problems are, and what solutions to use. These cannot be revised—at least until the next development cycle. In such cases, the research plan should begin with procedures that will give immediate benefit to the product before release and plan for more fundamental research to take place during the next development cycle. The following order may make sense for such a project:

Design and Development

- Rapid iterated *usability testing* and *competitive usability testing* until release. (Competitive research techniques are described in Chapter 14.)

After Release

- *Log file analysis* before and after release in order to know how customers' behavior changed.
- A *survey* to determine the makeup of the user population.

Requirement Gathering

- *Contextual inquiry* with the existing population to determine outstanding issues for the next release.

After this, the plan can continue as the first plan.

Organize Research Questions into Projects

Let's go back to the example. In the list of research questions, it appears that there are some quantitative questions about people's current behavior (the ratio of abandonees to those who complete a transaction, the page where the abandonment happens, etc.), and there are questions about their motivation and understanding of the site. The first set of questions can be answered through log analysis, and the second set can largely be accomplished through usability testing. There's one question, "How do they shop on the site?" that's probably too abstract to be easily answered through usability testing. It's one of those fundamental questions that will probably need to be researched over an extended period of time and with several different techniques. It can begin with a round of contextual inquiry.

CHOOSING AMONG THE TECHNIQUES

Picking the right techniques and grouping them can be difficult. The more experience you have with the methods, the better you will know which techniques best address which questions. If you don't have any experience with any of these techniques, start with the descriptions in this book, and pick one that seems right. Try it out. If it doesn't help you answer your question, note what kinds of information it was able to gather well and try a different technique.

Here is a table of the techniques with some trade-offs. It provides a basic overview of the techniques, but it's certainly not comprehensive.

Name	Stage in Development	Duration	Cycle Time
Profiles Chapter 7	Beginning of development process	Two to five days' work over two weeks	Once per major design, or when new user markets are defined
	Description: Developers turn audience descriptions into fictional characters in order to understand how audience needs relate.		
	Benefits: Low-cost method that creates good communication tools for the product team. Focuses on needs of specific audiences rather than "The User."		
	Pitfalls: Based primarily on team's understanding of users, not external research.		
Contextual Inquiry and Task Analysis Chapter 8	Initial problem definition	Two to four weeks, not including recruiting	Once per major set of features
	Description: Observe people as they solve problems to create a mental model that defines users' current understanding and behavior.		
	Benefits: Creates a comprehensive understanding of the problem that's being addressed.		
	Pitfalls: Labor intensive.		
Focus Groups Chapter 9	Early development feature definition	Two to four weeks, not including recruiting	Once per major set specification, then after every feature cluster

(Continued)

Name	Stage in Development	Duration	Cycle Time
	Description: Structured group interviews of 6-12 target audience representatives.		
	Benefits: Uncovers people's priorities and desires, collects anecdotes, and investigates group reactions to ideas.		
	Pitfalls: Subject to group-think among participants; desires can be easily misinterpreted as needs.		
Usability Testing Chapter 10	Throughout design and development	One to two weeks, not including recruiting	Frequently
	Description: Structured one-on-one interviews with users as they try specific tasks with product prototypes.		
	Benefits: Low-cost technique that uncovers interaction problems.		
	Pitfalls: Doesn't address underlying needs, just abilities to perform actions.		
Surveys Chapter 11	Beginning of development, after launch and before redesign	Two to six weeks	Once before major redesign, regularly thereafter
	Description: Randomly selected representatives of the audience are asked to fill out questionnaires; quantitative summaries of the responses are then tabulated.		
	Benefits: Quantitatively describes the audience, segments them into subpopulations, investigates their perceptions and priorities.		
	Pitfalls: Doesn't address the reasons why people have the perceptions they hold or what their actual needs are. Subject to selection bias.		
Ongoing Research Chapter 12	Throughout life of product	Ongoing	Regularly after release
	Description: Long-term studies of users; done through diaries and advisory boards.		
	Benefits: Investigates how users' views and use patterns change with time and experience.		
	Pitfalls: Labor intensive. Requires long-term participation.		

Name	Stage in Development	Duration	Cycle Time
Usage Logs and Customer Support Chapter 13	Beginning of development, after launch and before redesign	Varies	Regularly after release
	Description: Quantitatively analyze Web server log files and customer support comments.		
	Benefits: Doesn't require additional data gathering. Reveals actual behavior and perceived problems.		
	Pitfalls: Doesn't provide any information about reasons for behavior or problems.		

Based on what you know about the company priorities, group the questions into clusters by technique, and make a rough schedule. Log analysis can be started immediately, whereas the usability testing will take several weeks to prepare and recruit. The contextual inquiry can start at just about any time, but since, in this hypothetical situation, there are not enough resources to do a complete study immediately, a small round is begun immediately with the assumption that more can be done later.

What	When	Questions
Log analysis	Immediately	What is the ratio of people who abandon the shopping cart to those who complete a transaction?
		On what page do people abandon it?
		What pages do people open a shopping cart from most frequently?
Usability testing	Immediately (recruit now, test in two to four weeks)	Do people understand the instructions on the cart pages?
		Do they know they're opening the cart?
		When they abandon it, do they realize that they're abandoning it?

(Continued)

What	When	Questions
		Under what circumstances do they open the cart?
		How do they use the cart?
Contextual inquiry	Immediately (recruit now, interview people in one to two weeks) and ongoing	How do they shop on the site? How do they shop for these things outside the site? Do they know what a shopping cart is?

Continue through your issue list in order of priority, expanding all the items this way. As you're expanding them, look for similarities in the questions and places that research can be combined to simultaneously address a number of issues. In addition, look for places where competitive analysis can produce an interesting perspective.

You can also start with the list of techniques and use that to generate further questions and research ideas. So, for example, you could start by saying, "What can we learn with contextual inquiry? Will that address any of the research goals?" and work your way through the other techniques.

A single entry from the final list could look something like this.

What	Usability testing
When	Plan immediately, test in two to four weeks
Questions	*Shopping cart questions*
	Do people understand the instructions on the cart pages?
	Do they know they're opening the cart?
	When they abandon it, do they realize that they're abandoning it?
	Under what circumstances do they open the cart?
	How do they use the cart?
	How long does it take to make a purchase?

> *Navigation questions*
>
> How do people find specific items? (What tools do they use? How do they use them?)
>
> How do people move from one major section to another? (What tools? How do they use them?)
>
> *Promo section questions*
>
> What order do people look at the items on the front door?
>
> Do people understand the information in the promo section?

Consider this as a single unit for the purposes of scheduling. It's something that can be put into a scheduling or project management program. The specifics of what is tested may change when the test plan is being put together, but this will get you something that can be scheduled and a good idea of what is being tested and when.

Asking Questions across Multiple Projects

Because of the fast pace of most Web development schedules, the plan should concentrate on the short term, but it should not short-change the long term. It's always tempting to focus on the goals for the next release and leave fundamental questions about a product and its users to long-term projects. But deeper answers are precisely what can make or break a product over the long run. These questions should not be put off because they're general or difficult to answer. In fact, they should be investigated as soon as possible since the earlier they produce results, the quicker that planning, design, and implementation of core product changes can be made.

However, just focusing on deep questions when there's a release coming up is rarely a wise plan, either from the perspective of the product or the role of the researcher in the company. Thus, the research plan should be structured as a set of parallel projects, with long-term goals cutting across several projects. Each project addresses whatever short-term questions need to be answered, but also asks a couple of key questions to nudge knowledge about the fundamental questions at each time, too.

This can be represented as a grid, with each fundamental question in a column, while research projects label the rows. Thus it's possible to keep track of which projects are asking questions about which fundamental goals they're addressing. This keeps long-term goals from being neglected by the research process. The following table shows one such representation, with the dark shaded cells representing which project gathers information investigating which goal (with project 4 an in-depth investigation of issues studied in projects 2 and 3).

	Search Engine Results	Comprehensibility of Navigation	Shopping Cart Abandonment
Usability testing 1			
Focus group 1			
Log analysis			
Usability testing 1			
Etc.			

Note The research plan should be updated frequently: in between every round of research, with every major update of the software, and, in general, with every addition to the knowledge of the user experience and whenever company priorities change. It would not be unusual for there to be updates every week or two. Versioning every update helps keep track of all the changes.

Of course, not all projects are going to provide data for every goal, but keeping this structure in mind will allow you to keep the long-term needs in perspective while still getting the short-term work done.

The Format of the Plan

Until this point, I have intentionally avoided presenting a specific structure or look that the research plan should have since that will vary based on your needs and resources. It should be flexible and adapted to your environment. If you use project management or scheduling software, a lot of the plan can be represented in it. If you plan to show it to management on a regular basis, it can be in a more formal written form that can be folded into the product development plan. If your company culture prefers to organize with Post-its, it can be a wall of Post-its. Whatever. It should fit a style that is useful and comfortable for you, but that can be shared and integrated with the larger product plan. The plan is a document that you are going to use to communicate the structure of your research and to sell the value of your work to your product team and your company as a whole.

There are some things every research plan should do.

- *Set expectations.* The people conducting the research and the recipients of the results should know what research is being done, how it's being done, and what results they can expect. Don't overload expectations for any single round of testing. A round of testing will not validate or condemn the entire project, and it should not be expected to. A research plan should also communicate that it is a flexible and ever-changing document. This can be done through version numbers or even expiration dates ("This research plan is valid until 12/2/2003").
- *Set schedules and responsibilities.* Who is going to do what when? How does the research schedule integrate into the larger development process? This should be specific in the short term, but it can be more general in the long term, except for research that's directly tied to the larger schedule.
- *Specify goals.* Every research project and the research plan as a whole should have specific goals associated with them. The goals collected at the beginning of the process drive the specifics of the research. It should be clear what they are.
- *Specify outputs.* There should be outputs for every research project based on the needs of the stakeholders, specifying the information that's going to be presented. Ideally, the actual deliverables (report, presentation, etc.) should be described.

Budgets

The budget will be based on the cost of resources available to you, but it'll probably come in three big chunks:

- People's time (including your time and the research team's time)
- Recruiting and incentive costs
- Equipment costs

In my experience, useful times for calculating the duration of a qualitative user research project such as a usability test (including project management time and typical inefficiencies) are roughly as follows:

Task	Time
Preparation for a single research project (for just about anything other than repeated research)	Ten hours
Recruiting and scheduling	Two to three hours per person recruited
Conducting research	
• Contextual inquiry/task analysis	Five hours per person
• Focus groups	Three hours per group
• Usability tests	Three hours per participant
Analyzing results	
• Contextual inquiry/task analysis	Five hours per person
• Focus groups	Four hours per group
• Usability tests	Two hours per person
Preparing a report for email delivery	Twelve hours
Preparing one-hour presentation based on report	Six hours

Quantitative research, such as surveys and log analysis, will vary greatly in effort based on the complexity of the task and the tools and expertise available. What a good statistician can do in a couple of hours can take days for someone with less training.

Incentive costs are described in detail in Chapter 6, but (as of spring 2003 in San Francisco) they tend to fall around $100 per person per 90-minute session for most research.

Likewise, equipment costs will vary based on how ambitious your research is in terms of documentation and how demanding it is in terms of space. It's possible to spend $5000 a day renting a usability lab for a series of highly documented usability tests, or it can be free if you conduct a focus group in a conference room with a borrowed video camera and the tape of last year's holiday party.

Research Plan for Company X

This is an excerpt of a research plan prepared with Indi Young, a user experience research consultant, for presentation to the development team of a consumer product comparison Web site. It presents an extensive research program designed to get a broad understanding of problems and users prior to a major redesign. Since it's designed for presentation, it includes more process explanation than an internal document and fewer details than would be used for internal delivery (which would include tables like all the ones described earlier), but it gives a good outline of how such a research plan can look when fully expanded.

Summary

This research plan outlines the needs and goals of company X in order to conduct rapid user research on company X's and the competitors' products, and presents a schedule designed to meet this goal. It includes plans for five rounds of usability testing, four focus groups, and the beginning of an ongoing contextual inquiry process. A schedule of all research through the week of July 8 is included, and an estimated budget is proposed.

This research plan is valid between 5/22/2003 and 6/26/2003, at which point an updated plan will be submitted.

Research Issues

Based on conversations with representatives of design, information architecture, product development, marketing, and customer service, we have identified five large-scale issues that our research will attempt to shed light on.

- *While many people use the core product comparison service, less than 1% (based on analysis of tracking cookies) ever purchase anything from the online shop.*
- *While the top levels of the content tree get a fair amount of use, the deeper levels, especially the product-specific sections, do not.*
- *The competitors' design is a lot less polished and much more chaotic, yet they get twice as much traffic with a similar amount of advertising.*

- *Other than knowing that they're comparing one product against another, there's little information about the circumstances under which people use the service.*
- *People often complain about being unable to find a specific product entry again after they've found it once.*

Research Structure

The research will be broken into two parallel segments: interaction research and a profile of the existing user population.

Immediate User Research

In order to provide actionable results in time for the next release, we will immediately begin a testing process to evaluate the existing site interfaces. This will determine which elements of the design work best, which are most usable, and which features are most compelling, while finding out what doesn't work and shedding light on how users prioritize the feature set as a whole. There will be some competitive analysis included to uncover the strengths and weaknesses of the user experiences provided by competitors' products.

The techniques used will include four rounds of usability testing *and, potentially, some* focus group *research.*

> *Usability testing: We will conduct four sets of one-on-one structured, task-oriented interviews with five to eight users apiece from company X's primary target audience, for a total of 20 to 32 interviews. The interviews will last about an hour apiece and will focus on how well people understand the elements of the interface, their expectations for structure and functionality, and how they perform key tasks. Videotapes of the interviews will then be analyzed for feature use trends and feature preference. There will be one round per week from 6/5 until 6/26. For each round, a report summarizing findings will be prepared within two to four business days of the completed research and presented to appropriate parties within company X. Each round will use the most recent prototype and will concentrate on the most pressing user experience issues at the time as determined by company stakeholders and previous research.*
>
> *A fifth set of tests will be of the same format with the same tasks, but will be conducted with the services provided by company Y and company Z.*

Focus groups: If no additional usability testing is needed before launch, we will conduct a series of three focus groups with six to eight users apiece from two key segments of the user base, member researchers and shoppers (as defined in the market segmentation studies obtained from marketing). These groups will concentrate on uncovering what the users consider to be the most valuable parts of the service and where the service performs below their needs and expectations.

In addition, a competitive focus group will be conducted featuring users familiar with company Y's product discussing that company's product.

Existing User Profiling

In addition, we will begin a program to create a profile of the existing user base and to better understand how they comparison shop. This will (we hope) uncover opportunities for the service to expand into and provide a closer fit to people's lives, further encouraging its use.

The technique used will be contextual inquiry *with one to two people.*

Contextual inquiry: We will visit the homes or offices of three to five people representing a couple of the primary target audiences. We will schedule the visits for times when they expect to be comparison shopping for a specific item, and then we will observe and document (with video recording and handwritten notes) how they go about this task. We will create a model of the process they use to comparison shop based on analyzing the video and notes, enumerating what tools and techniques they use, what problems they face, and how they solve them.

Schedule

The following schedule lays out the planned research. Most work is done in parallel between several different tests in order to get the most research in the available time. The usability tests all involve about the same amount of preparation and recruiting, which can happen simultaneously for one test as the next test is being conducted and analyzed.

Focus groups involve a fair amount of preparation, but since the groups themselves are relatively short (two hours apiece), they can all be conducted in the same week (although the schedule allows for a week's slippage for the last of the regular focus groups). There's also a competitive focus group, which has its own deliverable.

The contextual inquiry project is not slated to be completed in this time period because it was determined that although understanding the use of the product in context is very important, understanding immediate usability needs is a higher priority. Thus, there are no deliverables listed for it on the schedule, but preparation for it is displayed.

RESEARCH DATES

(preparation weeks are shaded the light color; test and analysis weeks are shaded the dark color)

	5/20	6/05	6/12	6/19	6/26	7/03	7/10	7/17	7/24	7/31	8/07
Usability test 1	light	light	dark								
Usability test 2		light	light	dark							
Usability test 3			light	light	dark						
Usability test 4				light	light	dark					
Competitive usability test					light	light	dark				
Focus group 1							light	light	dark		
Focus group 2								light	light	dark	
Focus group 3									light	light	dark
Competitive focus group										light	dark
Contextual inquiry									light	light	light

Budget

These are the projected budgets, broken out by total estimated time and total estimated costs. These are approximate figures based on experience, and they will be adjusted in future research plans to reflect actual amounts as the research progresses.

Five Usability Tests

Preparation	10 hours
Recruiting and scheduling (assuming 40 participants—32 regular and 8 competitive)	80 hours
Conducting tests	120 hours
Analyzing tests	80 hours
Writing report and presenting results	15 hours
Integrating with development (meetings, presentations, etc.)	10 hours
Total time	*315 hours*
Recruiting incentive (25–40 people)	$2500–$4000
Supplies (food, videotape, etc.)	$500
Total cost (not counting salary)	*$3000–4500*

Focus Groups

Preparation	10 hours
Recruiting and scheduling	40 hours
Conducting and analyzing groups	20 hours
Writing report and presenting results	15 hours
Integrating with development	5 hours
Total time	*90 hours*
Recruiting incentive	$2400
Supplies (food, videotape, etc.)	$400
Total cost	*$2800*

Deliverables

The results of each usability test will be sent in email as they are completed. Each email will include an outline of the procedures, a profile of the people involved, a summary of all trends observed in their behavior (as they apply to the initial research goals), problems they encountered, and a series of supporting quotations. A presentation of the results of each test will be scheduled for every-one affected. The presentation will allow the analyst to answer questions about the results and give further explanations of the proceedings of the test.

The results of all the regular focus groups will be collected into a single report, which will be sent by email as soon as it is complete. In addition to outlining the procedures used and providing a summary of the trends as they apply to the research goals, it will analyze any differences observed between various market segments. There will be a separate report from the final focus group that will compare the values and reactions of users of company Y's services to those observed with company X's.

Maintenance

It's important to revise the research plan every time new knowledge comes in. Everything is subject to change as your team and the company's understanding of the user's experience grows. The research goals, especially, should be reevaluated, refined, and rewritten to take every piece of additional knowledge into account.

Since every piece of research you do is likely to affect your understanding of a number of different research goals, all knowledge about the user experience should be consolidated whenever possible. A good way to do this is to create a minisite for your intranet that contains all the reports and goals and that links each goal to the information that applies to it, and to enter all problems into the development group's bug-tracking software.

Eventually, you should have a set of interlinked documents that, together, make up a more-or-less complete picture of your user population.

CHAPTER 6

Universal Tools: Recruiting and Interviewing

No matter what the research, there are two things you're always going to be doing: looking for people who will give you the best feedback and asking them questions. These two elements, *recruiting* and *interviewing,* make up the backbone of every successful research project, and although some of this information is covered in other chapters, they deserve a chapter of their own.

Recruiting

Even if everything else is perfect, if you get the wrong people to talk about your product, your research can be worse than useless since it gives you confidence in results that don't represent the views and behaviors of your real users. Every product has a target audience, from toasters to missile guidance systems. You need to understand the experience of the people who are actually going to want to use, understand, and buy your product. Anyone else's experience will be of marginal use, or even deceptive. So if you're making a missile guidance system and you invite the North American Toaster Enthusiasts to discuss how it should be improved, you're going to get little feedback that will help you make a product for the Army (and you'll probably end up with a missile that has a 30-second pop-up timer).

The process of finding, inviting, and scheduling the right people for your research is called *recruiting,* and it consists of three basic steps: determining the target audience, finding representative members of that audience, and convincing them to participate in your research.

Although the details of who is recruited vary from project to project, the process generally takes about two weeks with roughly the schedule shown in Table 6.1.

Warning It is useful to have someone recruiting full-time, rather than trying to do it in between other work. Recruiting is almost a full-time job in itself, and it always turns out to be more work than anticipated. To reduce costs, a temp or an intern can recruit full-time if given some training.

Timing	Activity
t − 3 weeks to t − 2 weeks	Determine target audience(s).
t − 2 weeks	Recruit initial pool or prescreen initial group from a database of qualified participants if one is available.
t − 2 weeks to t − 1 week	Screen for final candidates.
t − 2 weeks to t − 1 week	Send invitations to primary qualified candidates.
t − 1 week	Send invitations to secondary qualified candidates.
t − 3 days	Create schedule for all candidates and contact list for alternatives.
t + 1 day	Follow up with participants and researchers.

t = testing day (or days)

Budget at least two hours per participant for recruiting and scheduling—more if you've never recruited that kind of participant before.

Pick Your Audience

Before you begin doing any kind of user experience research, you should have a solid idea of who is going to be using your product. If you don't have a complete audience profile and a thought-out purpose for the product, the project is in danger of veering off into a direction that no one wants or needs.

An audience profile should have been done before the recruiting process begins, but it needs to be refined for recruiting. Start with demographic, Web use, and technological profiles of the audience, and narrow from there. As described in Chapters 4 and 11, a *demographic* profile is one that describes a person's physical and employment characteristics; a *Web use* profile describes someone's Web experience; and a *technological* profile describes their experience with computer technology in general. You want a subset of people who have qualities that make them good research participants. For example, you probably don't care if your regular users have visited competitors' sites, but if you're recruiting for a competitive analysis focus group, then you need to get people with experience using competitors' products. If you want to usability-test a new version of your site, you may want to recruit groups of people who have experience with the old interface. Or you could do the opposite and pick people who have never seen the product to see how they react to it "fresh." These are considerations that don't normally play a large role in determining the target audience for the product as a whole, but they can be important for determining what makes a good user research audience.

Before beginning the recruiting process, you need to flesh out what an ideal research audience is for the specific piece of research you're going out to do. Start by making the demographic and Web use profiles of the product's target audience explicit. If you're making a product that helps people schedule events, your primary audience may be young professionals who throw a lot of parties and have some Internet experience.

EVENT SCHEDULING PROFILE

Demographics

Ages: 25–35

Gender: male or female

College educated

Income: $60K+

Typical reasons for including groups in a target market for the product's marketing—such as the amount of disposable income they have or if they make up the largest proportion of the population—may have nothing to do with providing good feedback to your research. Ask yourself about what makes the research audience different from the target market as a whole. What kind of people will give the best feedback for your research goals?

Which market segments are most affected by the research?
Is there a single group or multiple groups?
Which factors most affect this research?
What are desirable characteristics? What are undesirable?

Explore the answers to these questions, and modify your profile accordingly. Remove factors that are not going to affect how people use or view the product, and add information. Focus on isolating the factors that will make them an ideal *research* audience.

EVENT SCHEDULING RESEARCH PROFILE

Demographics

Ages: 25–35

Gender: male or female

College educated

Web Use

Must have a personal computer at home or work

Must use the Internet

Must have one or more years of Internet experience

Must use the Internet three to five hours a week for personal tasks (shopping, researching, etc.)

Should have some experience with Web productivity applications (calendars, email, portfolio management, etc.)

Behavior
Should regularly hold social events involving at least three other people and have held a social event recently
Social events must involve explicitly inviting people

Be careful not to overdetermine your target audiences. If you find yourself trying to define multiple conditions to the point where you're not sure you can find people that meet them, or if some of the restrictions are mutually exclusive, consider breaking the research into several groups. Thus, if you're making a Web site for truck drivers and you need the perspectives of both long-haul and short-haul drivers, rather than mixing the two groups into one piece of research or finding drivers with experience in both fields, consider running the same research with two groups.

Find Your Audience

Once you have the research profile, you need to go out and look for those people. There are two steps to this: finding *some* people and finding the *right* people.

Note The decision about whether to work with a commercial recruiting firm or do it yourself largely depends on available resources. Recruiting is a time-consuming process, especially for relatively rare groups or for people with complex schedules. However, basic recruiting can be a fairly straightforward process if organized well and given sufficient time.

Commercial recruiters have databases with thousands of people from all walks of life. For them, the task of finding people is fairly straightforward: they search through their databases for basic demographic matches, and then they screen those people for the Web use, technological, and behavior criteria that you've determined. If you're going to use a commercial service, then your next task is to create an appropriate script for the recruiter to filter the general population for the criteria specific to your research. This is called a *screener*. However, if you are doing the recruiting yourself, you need to build your own database.

Your Personal Database

Building your own database is not difficult, but it is time consuming. If you want to recruit for research that's going to happen in the next month, it's probably better to go through a professional service. Once your database is built, however, it's a valuable resource that you can use for years and for all different kinds of research.

The more people you have in your database, the better, but only if they are likely to use, understand, and appreciate your product. Getting a database full of the wrong people is more hassle than it's worth.

Recruiting by email is the most efficient method, although it's possible to use all kinds of methods to fill your database. First, set up a special email account for your recruiting effort. It's important to collect all recruiting-related information in a single place, and a dedicated email account accomplishes this quickly.

Start with Friends and Family

For your first round, send out a note to everyone in the company or put a notice in the company newsletter. Invite your co-workers' friends, roommates, significant others, and family to help the company by participating in your research (in exchange for an honorarium, of course). Ask for people who have no direct connection with the product you're testing. Tell them to send email to the special address you've set up.

Reply to the email with a message containing an explanation of the process and a questionnaire that asks for their basic demographic and Web use information. The questionnaire shouldn't take more than five minutes to fill out and should be as specific as possible so that the responses can be more easily compared. Include questions that will give you insight into people's behavior relative to the kinds of products you expect to do research with, but don't ask questions that are so specific that people's answers are likely to change quickly. Thus, a question about the classes of products the respondent regularly buys is more useful in the long run than a question about the last product bought.

> Thank you for expressing interest in helping _____ make the best products we can. We are continually striving to create services and products that are innovative, compelling, useful, and usable. As part of this effort, we're implementing a system by which select members of the general public evaluate our products while they are still in their formative

stages to determine where those products succeed in their design and where they need to be revised.

That's where you come in!

However, before we can set you loose on our newest and greatest ideas, we need some information to help us determine which people are best suited for which products. Thus, this questionnaire. Please fill it out and return it to the address below as soon as you can. As soon as we can, we will contact you to schedule a day and time for the evaluation. This could be from several months from now to this week, depending on which products are ready.

Email completed questionnaires to mikek@adaptivepath.com

Questions

Instructions: for multiple-choice answers, please place an X in the brackets next to the most appropriate choice, like this: [X].

How many hours do you use the Web every week for work?
[ ] None
[ ] Less than 5
[ ] 5 to 10
[ ] 10 to 20
[ ] 20 to 40
[ ] 40+

How many leisure hours do you spend on the Web per week?
[ ] None
[ ] Less than 5
[ ] 5 to 10
[ ] 10 to 20
[ ] 20 to 40
[ ] 40+

What kind of information do you most frequently look at?

What is your primary source of news and information?

(Continued)

What computer platform are you most familiar with?
[ ] Apple Macintosh
[ ] Microsoft Windows
[ ] Linux/Unix
[ ] Other: (please specify)

What software are you most familiar with?

Are you available to come into our downtown San Francisco offices to participate in these evaluations?

Personal Information
Name:

Please check [X] how you'd prefer we contact you.
[ ] Email address:
[ ] Phone number:
[ ] Fax number:

Thank you!

—Mike Kuniavsky, mikek@adaptivepath.com
Adaptive Path

Once the responses start rolling in, you need to collect them into a database. Since the database is not likely to be large by database standards, the software doesn't need to be particularly heavyweight. Microsoft Access or FileMaker Pro are good general-purpose database programs, but even a spreadsheet will work as long as it allows you to do full-text searches on all the fields (though spreadsheet-based databases start getting awkward after 100 or 200 entries, so starting with dedicated database software makes for easier maintenance in the long run). Allocate plenty of time—at least several hours a day if you're in a large company—for data entry in the first couple of days after the request goes out. If the list is large and you expect many responses, consider automating some of the data entry with a Web form. Often, just having consistent output, as provided by a script that emails what's typed into a form, is all that's necessary to make the data entry task significantly more efficient.

Note You should try to get 10 times as many people in your first round of recruiting as you expect to invite to your first round of research.

Expand Your Horizon

Once you've recruited your first group of friends and family and you've done your first round of research, you're going to need to continue to build your database. For a research program of two to five research projects per month, you need to have a database of about 500 people. If you're planning on doing regular research, building your database should become part of your regular "infrastructure maintenance" ritual, always going on at a low level.

Having recruited a basic, friendly group of people, you should have all the tools to continue recruiting ever larger groups. Finding those groups, however, can be a challenge. There are no foolproof methods. For some audiences, it's fairly easy to find people who are willing to participate in your research, for example, "people who buy groceries." Others, such as "Fortune 500 CEOs," are incredibly hard. Here are some techniques that have worked in the past.

- *Community email mailing lists and online bulletin boards.* Some communities have their own email mailing lists. Whether it's people who live in a certain area or people who use a certain product or people who are in the same industry, there are a lot of mailing lists in the world. Lists that cover a specific city or area are probably the most useful since you don't end up sending mail to people who can't possibly go to your research. Make sure that you know the community's rules and you have the organizers' permission before sending mail. Never *spam* (send unsolicited email). Spam doesn't work, and people get really angry when they get it. Personalize the invitation to the group, making it clear why you're sending the message and what the benefits of participation are.
- *Neighbors.* Your corporate neighbors are a great research resource. They may be familiar with your company, and it's easy for them to come into your offices during a lunch break. Send a note to your neighbors' office managers and ask them to post an invitation in a public place.

- *Your users.* If your site already collects information about its users (either through sales or through marketing research), you can invite people from that list. Filter the list for people in your geographic area, and send messages to those who have agreed to accept mail from your company. Again, never spam, and clearly explain why they were chosen and the nature of the research.

- *New employees.* Although they may not be unbiased, they won't have the intimate knowledge of in-house people and projects, and they'll be motivated and available. One company I know of invites every new employee, whether the receptionist or a vice president, to participate in a research project as soon as he or she starts work. However, be sensitive to the ethical and legal implications in making employees do work that could be considered to be an evaluation of their abilities; the invitation should make it clear that such research is not a job requirement and that results of such evaluations will not be used to judge job performance.

- *Past research participants.* People who match your recruiting criteria are likely to know other people like themselves. If you're planning to do multiple rounds of research with the same target audience, tell the people you've recruited to tell their friends about your research and how they can join the participant pool (you can even make up handouts for them to take home from tests that explain the research and how others can participate).

- *Ads.* You can take out ads on your site and on other sites. Make sure that the ads are clear about the location-specific nature of your recruiting effort and that they specify that an incentive will be paid. And make them attractive (they're ads, after all, and they need to compete with all the other ads). An animated banner can, for example, read "San Francisco resident? Want 60 bucks? Click here!"

- *Traditional methods.* Since you need people who can come into your office, you can also use traditional advertising methods. Classified ads in local newspapers can work, though an ad in the Help Wanted section might get confused for a job offer. If you're in an urban area, there may be leaflet distribution services that can put your invitation on every corkboard in town (college campuses are an especially good source of such bulletin boards and are a great way to recruit college students if they're part of your audience). If you're ambitious, you can even take out a billboard (though if you do, please send me a note since I've never heard of anyone who's actually done that, and I'd like to know how well it works).

If you're at a loss for how to target a certain group of people, first find one person that matches your research participant profile. Then sit down with him or her and brainstorm about other ways that similar people can be reached. Talk about places he or she goes—online and offline—and habits and interests. Suggest some of the methods in the preceding list and ask how to tailor them specifically to his or her lifestyle.

However, don't get to the point where everyone you're recruiting has identical qualities or has been recruited in the same way. Every attribute in a profile has a range of values that could satisfy it, and recruiting should strive to get a diversity of people within the range. For example, when participant ages are defined to be between 25 and 35, it would be better if the recruits ranged throughout the whole range rather than all being 35.

Additional Recruiting Tips

- Rather than including lengthy explanations in email, you can make a Web page that explains the research program and then send email that points people to it. This can be the same page that collects their demo or Web info, but it can be a purely informative page, too. The page should explain the purpose of the recruiting, the incentive, the occasional nature of the research (so people don't think it's a job), and how they can get more information. Add frequently asked questions to it as the recruiting process matures.
- Clearly state the location of the research and the geographic area from which you'd like to recruit in all invitations. You can't predict who will read a request, and it's generally of little use to have people offer to participate from halfway around the world (or even 100 miles away) unless you're willing to pay them for their transportation costs.

- Keep track of when and how people found out about your program. This will tell you which techniques work best and, moreover, how your recruiting methods may affect the perceptions of the participants. People who have purchased something from your company will know more about your product and have stronger opinions than people recruited through your neighbors, who will in turn have stronger opinions than people who saw an ad in a newspaper.
- Update every person's entry every six to eight months to know whether his or her information has changed and whether he or she is still interested. Note the last time the entry was updated in the database and regularly send email to people whose last update is more than six months old, asking them to confirm that the information in your database is still current.
- Try to keep the number of repeat recruits down. In most cases, it's generally acceptable to recruit someone who hasn't participated in any kind of usability or marketing research in six months. In some cases, however, this requirement will have to be waived—for example, when time is short or the person has a rare profile or he or she is in a popular market that gets recruited a lot (IT managers are few, and the targets of much market research, for example).
- When someone gives you especially good feedback, make sure to note it in the database (you can have a check box for "great response"). If you ever need a couple of people on short notice, you can just pull people who you know are articulate and insightful.
- If time allows, run a small recruiting test. Recruit one or two people and run them through the research. If they provide good feedback and they're in the right audience, proceed with recruiting everyone else the same way.

Prescreening

Once you have a database of potential participants, you need to start finding the right people and inviting them to participate. Two or three weeks before the research is supposed to happen, prefilter the database for the people who are close to the group you intend to invite. Use your database searching tools to filter for the general demographic Web use segments that you're interested in. Try to get people that represent the breadth of your target audience while staying within its parameters. Use as much of the information you've collected as you can to whittle down the list to the most promising subjects. For example, if you're going to be testing a chat room component of your service, you may want to look for people who have listed sites with strong community components as some of their favorite sites.

Take the initial list of people you've selected from the database and separate it into *primary* and *secondary* lists, noting the most promising ones. You will use this list later to prioritize whom you schedule and when.

Once you have the list, send everyone on it a screener.

The Screener

The screener is probably the most important part of the recruiting process. It's a script that filters out the people who will give you good responses from the ones who merely match the demographic segment. The screener is read by the recruiter over the phone or sent in an email.

Getting the screener right can get you people who are likely to be interested in the product and can speak about their experiences intelligently and eloquently. Getting the screener wrong means getting people who are, at best, only marginally interested in what you have to offer and, at worst, uninterested and inarticulate.

Screeners vary from project to project and from recruiter to recruiter, but there are some general rules that apply to most.

1. *Stick to 20 questions.* There's a reason that game exists. It's possible to find out almost anything about someone in 20 questions. Most target audiences can be defined in 10 to 15 questions, and if the people are prescreened through your database, you can get away with fewer than 5.
2. *Make it short.* It should be possible to get through a whole screener in five to ten minutes.
3. *Be clear and specific.* The person responding to the question should know exactly what kinds of answers are expected.

4. *Never use jargon.* Use simple, straightforward, unambiguous language.

5. *Ask for exact dates, quantities, and times.* This eliminates the problem of one person's "occasionally" being another's "all the time."

6. *Every question should have a purpose.* Each question should help determine whether this person is in the audience or not. Don't ask questions that are incidental or "nice to know" since answers to them will not be useful in recruiting and take everyone's time. Nice-to-know questions can be asked at the beginning of the test.

7. *Order questions from general to specific,* especially in telephone screening. The earlier a question is in the screener, the more people it should eliminate from the pool of potential participants. This saves both the recruiter and the participant time since earlier questions weed out later questions that would be irrelevant otherwise. For example, if a person's age is a major factor in defining the target audience while the amount of Internet experience he or she has is fairly flexible, put the age question before the Internet experience question.

8. *Questions should not lead.* There should be no value judgments or answers implicit in the questions. "Are you bothered by the excessive lag times on the Web?" implies that the person perceives lag times and that he or she should be bothered by them. Instead, phrase questions in a more general (but not more ambiguous) way, and then look for specific responses. "Are there things on the Web that regularly bother you? If so, what?" could get at the same kinds of issues as the first question, without its bias.

9. *Clearly state the format of the research.* State what the research is for, when it's going to happen, how long it's going to take, how much the incentive is, and whether the participants should do anything ahead of time (and whether they should do nothing ahead of time).

10. *Build in flexibility.* Let the recruiter know the acceptable parameters for answering each question, so that you don't needlessly dismiss people who can provide valuable feedback.

Sample Phone Screener

This is a telephone screener for a site that offers an online calendar. The target audience is mostly existing users, but the screener has been expanded to include a couple of potential users and a power user (to get a taste for several different kinds of user experiences).

This screener consists of three sections: an introduction for the recruiter that specifies the ideal target audience, an introduction for the participants, and the main set of questions and selection criteria. It is a relatively complex screener that would probably be too involved for a first user test.

Warning Although it's often tempting to try to recruit for several target audiences, it's critical that their descriptions be very close together and that the bulk of the recruits come from a single audience. Otherwise, you risk fragmenting your data to the point that there is insufficient information to be able to identify patterns. One technique to avoid this is to prioritize your audiences and recruit enough people (usually four to six) for the primary audience before you begin recruiting for secondary audiences.

Target Audience

6–9 people total: 4–6 current users, 1 power user, 1–2 nonusers (but likely potential users)

Current eCalendar Users

People who use eCalendar on a regular basis and have used it recently

Men or women
Any age, but prefer 35–50
Personal income $60K+
Have Internet access at home or work
Use the Web five or more hours a week
Have one or more years of Internet experience
Have created at least five eCalendar events in the last month
Have used eCalendar for at least two months

eCalendar Power User

Someone who uses eCalendar frequently and regularly uses the advanced features

Men or women, but prefer men
Any age, but prefer 40+
Creates at least 20 eCalendar events per month
Has used reminders and calendar overlays
[rest of profile the same as current users]

(Continued)

Potential Users

    Have never used eCalendar, but may be aware of it

    Have at least five scheduled appointments per week

    [rest of profile the same as current users]

Note that some of the criteria are specific, such as the amount of time on the Web and the number of events entered into the calendar, whereas others (such as the gender and age) have ranges.

Logistics

Available on January 20 or 21 between 8 AM and 6 PM

Can come into the downtown SF office

Are not immediately affiliated with eCalendar or its competitors (but can be aware of it)

Have not participated in any usability or marketing research in the last six months

Current User Screener

Hello, my name is _____ from _____. We are seeking a few people who are interested in participating in a paid evaluation of a product that you may find useful. This is not a sales call, and no sales or solicitation efforts will be made at any time.

The evaluation will consist of a one-on-one interview on January 20 or 21 in downtown San Francisco. It will be during working hours and will last about one hour. If you participate, you will receive a cash stipend of $60. The interview will be strictly for research, and all of your comments will be confidential. If you are interested in participating, I need to ask you a few questions to see if you've had the kind of experiences we're looking for.

The introduction simultaneously sets people's expectations and serves as the first round of questioning since people will immediately say if they're unavailable on the given date or if they're unwilling to participate. It's also careful to describe the general nature of the research without going into specifics that may skew people's responses.

Note Alternatively, you can use a more generic introduction ("We are conducting a study, and I would like to ask you a few questions"), but you run the risk of going through the whole process just to find that the person is not available on a given day or is uninterested in participating in this type of research.

Question	Answers	Instructions
1. Do you or any member of your household work in any of the following businesses or industries?	Market research Advertising or media sales Public relations Usability or quality assurance Web design or development	IF YES TO ANY, TERMINATE

Eliminate people who work in industries that can present a conflict of interest. People who are in advertising, usability, Web design, and market research should almost always be eliminated since they're too aware of the kinds of issues that research is aiming to uncover and are unlikely to give an unbiased perspective (even if they want to).

"Terminate" is an instruction to the recruiter that tells him or her to stop the recruiting process and wrap up the interview. There is some termination text provided at the end of the screener.

Question	Answers	Instructions
2. We're looking for people of various ages. Which of the following categories includes your age?	Less than 30 30 to 34 35 to 39 40 to 45 46 to 50 More than 50	TERMINATE ASK Question 3 TERMINATE
3. We're also looking for people of various income levels. Roughly speaking, what's your personal yearly income?		IF LESS THAN $60K, TERMINATE; OTHERWISE, ASK Question 4
4. Do you have a personal computer at home or work?	Yes No	ASK Question 5 TERMINATE

(Continued)

Question	Answers	Instructions
5. Do you have Internet access at home or work?	Yes No	ASK Question 6 TERMINATE
6. When did you start using the Internet?		IF LESS THAN 1 YEAR TERMINATE; OTHERWISE, ASK Question 7
7. On average, how many hours a week do you estimate you use the Web?		IF LESS THAN 5, TERMINATE; OTHERWISE, ASK Question 8

Although many of these questions will have already been filtered for if these names were pulled out of a database, it's still useful to make sure that the information is accurate, so it's a good idea to verify the information again. Additionally, the age and income questions may be considered to be invasive by some people. In many cases, that information doesn't affect people's behavior and the questions can be eliminated; in cases where the information is of secondary importance, it's possible to move the questions to the end.

Question	Answers	Instructions
8. How many scheduled meetings or events do you have to keep track of per week?		IF LESS THAN 5, TERMINATE; OTHERWISE, ASK Question 9
9. Have you kept track of any scheduled meetings with an online service in the last month?	Yes No	ASK Question 10 TERMINATE
10. How many?		IF LESS THAN 5, TERMINATE; IF MORE THAN 20, ASK Question 11; OTHERWISE, ASK Question 13
11. Which online calendar service or services did you use?		IF eCalendar IS MENTIONED, ASK Question 12; OTHERWISE, TERMINATE

Question	Answers	Instructions
12. How long have you used eCalendar?		IF 2 MONTHS OR MORE, ASK Question 13; OTHERWISE, TERMINATE
13. Which of the following eCalendar features have you used in the past?	Reminders The address book Calendar overlays The buddy list	IF overlays AND reminders, CONSIDER FOR POWER USER SCHEDULING; ASK Question 14
14. Are you currently working on any projects with eCalendar.com or another company that makes online calendars?	Yes No	TERMINATE ASK Question 15
15. Have you ever participated in a market research interview or discussion group?	Yes No	ASK Question 16 SCHEDULE
16. When was the last time?		IF LESS THAN 6 MONTHS, TERMINATE; OTHERWISE, ASK Question 17

Note When you are short on time or when you can interview only a couple of people, it's sometimes useful to filter for people you've interviewed before rather than filtering them out. People who are known to give good, honest, articulate feedback provide a shortcut to useful information. In such situations, it's important to inform the analyst about the participant's background since it'll probably affect the way he or she interprets the results.

When people have participated in user research recently, they're more likely to give unconsciously biased responses since they'll be familiar with the format of the research and may try to anticipate the "appropriate" answers. Since you're almost always looking for unguarded, unbiased responses, it's generally a good idea to eliminate these people from the research unless you have no other choice. Moreover, some people see the incentive payments as a good way to supplement their income and may try to get into any kind of marketing or usability research project. Inviting such people should be avoided entirely since they're unlikely to provide natural or truthful responses.

Question	Answers	Instructions
17. In a couple of sentences, describe what your favorite Web sites have been lately and why you like them.		[NOTE DOWN] TERMINATE IF INARTICULATE; OTHERWISE SCHEDULE.

Open-ended questions like this serve two purposes. They give the recruiter an idea of how articulate a potential participant is, and they can collect information that's not easily formatted as a multiple-choice question. Save them for the end, and don't put more than one in any given screener since they're time consuming and don't filter many people out. (That said, some recruiters prefer to ask the open-ended question at the beginning since it's less intimidating and can catch terminally inarticulate participants early in the process.)

Note If you're using the more generic introduction, you can also replace the termination statement with something less specific, such as "That's all the questions I have. Thank you very much for participating in our study."

Question	Answers	Instructions
TERMINATE		That's all the questions I have. Thank you very much for participating. Although we're not scheduling people who fit your profile right now, we may call you again for a different research project.

NOTE: Potential user screener is identical, minus questions 12,13, and 14.

That's it for the questions. Would you be willing to come into our downtown San Francisco offices for a one-hour paid interview on January 20 or 21? You will be reimbursed $60 for your time, and your help will be greatly appreciated by a development team that's currently making a product you may be interested in.

Email Screeners

Email screeners are similar to telephone screeners in terms of the kinds of questions that are asked, except that email screeners are designed to be answered by the participant. This makes them closer to a survey questionnaire in formation. They need to clearly specify the full range of answers that are expected, and they need to be explicit in their descriptions. They should also have fewer and simpler questions. This makes it easier on the participants since they don't feel compelled to write long descriptions and are more willing to respond (since answering 20 questions with sentences is too daunting and time consuming for most people). A question such as

> How many scheduled meetings or events do you have to keep track of per week?

would be written in an email as

> Roughly how many scheduled meetings or events do you have to keep track of in a typical week? (please check one)
> [ ] None
> [ ] 1 to 5
> [ ] 6 to 10
> [ ] 11 to 15
> [ ] 16 to 20
> [ ] More than 20

Once written and formatted in such a way that it'll look good in any email program, a screener can be emailed to the invitation list (don't forget to set the "Reply to:" address to be your catchall research email!). Avoid HTML email because many email programs can't display HTML correctly. In addition, if you have a system that can quickly create online surveys, you can just put up a Web page with all the questions in a quickly accessible fill-in form (but give people the option to respond via email in case they don't have Web access or have problems with the online form).

Scheduling

Once you have your list of potential participants, you need to create a schedule. First, define a *scheduling window.* What are the appropriate times for the researchers? Are there times that are inappropriate for your target audience? (Physicians and network administrators, for example, are almost impossible to schedule during weekday working hours.) Are there key observers who need to be there at certain times? Company meetings? Holidays?

With the scheduling windows in hand, start scheduling. There are lots of ways to schedule people, and you should feel free to use whatever procedure is right for you. The following sequence was used successfully at Wired Digital and is similar to the procedures used by other recruiters:

- Write the invitation.
- Invite primary candidates.
- Receive responses and schedule primary candidates.
- Invite secondary candidates.
- Receive responses and schedule secondary candidates.
- Confirm primary candidates.
- Confirm secondary candidates.
- Send thank-you notes to unscheduled candidates.
- Make email and telephone confirmation calls to all participants the day before their scheduled time.
- Create and distribute a schedule of all participants.
- Create and put up signs guiding participants to the testing facility.

For events with fixed schedules, such as focus groups or when critical observers have limited schedules, invitations are straightforward.

For more flexible situations, schedules should be constructed around the participant's preferences. It's often as effective to ask candidates for a list of times when they're available as it is to dictate times when they should show up. Allowing participants to drive the scheduling also shows them, up front, that their input is valuable. Asking them to provide a primary time and a couple of backup times eliminates most conflicts.

The Invitation

The invitation, whether delivered by phone or email, should reiterate what the research is about, why participation is important, how much the participant will be paid, where the research will take place, and when they should show up (or, in the case of site visits, when they can expect the visitors to arrive).

It's time again for another Wired Interface Testing Group usability study, and you've been selected from our database to receive this invitation to attend. The next series will be held on WEDNESDAY, DECEMBER 8, 2003, and THURSDAY, DECEMBER 9, 2003. If you would like to participate, you MUST RESPOND TO THIS SCREENER BY THIS FRIDAY, DECEMBER 3, 2003.

SESSION DETAILS:
-DATES: WED, 12/8 and THURS, 12/9
-LENGTH: One hour
-LOCATION: Wired Digital offices, San Francisco

An honorarium of $60.00 will be paid to you by check within two weeks of your test session, and you will be required to sign a nondisclosure agreement prior to beginning the study.

Please respond to the following statements or questions by FRIDAY, DECEMBER 3, 2003:

*If you CANNOT participate in this series, that's no problem. But to help us keep our records up to date, please check one of the following statements:

[ ] I can't make it this time, but keep me in the WITG database for future tests.
[ ] I won't be able to partipate in the WITG program any longer. Please remove my name and address from the database.

*If you CAN participate in this session, please answer the questions below.

For each of the sites below, please indicate how many times you visit it in an average week. Put 0 if you've visited it before, but don't go there

(Continued)

often; 1 for once a week; 2 for twice a week; and so on. Leave it blank if you've never been there:

_____ New York Times On The Web

_____ Wired News

_____ CNN

_____ Yahoo

_____ ZDNet

_____ Slashdot

_____ Salon

_____ Other: _____ (please list)

Now please indicate your FIRST and SECOND preference for an appointment by choosing a day and time between the hours of 11:00 AM and 6:00 PM ONLY:

1. App't Day and Time—FIRST PREFERENCE
   [ ] Wed, 12/8/03 at _____ (11:00 AM - 6:00 PM ONLY)
   [ ] Thur, 12/9/03 at _____
   [ ] Either day at _____

2. App't Day and Time—SECOND PREFERENCE
   [ ] Wed, 12/8/03 at _____ (11:00 AM - 6:00 PM ONLY)
   [ ] Thur, 12/9/03 at _____
   [ ] Either day at _____

OK, that's it for now. As soon as we've received everyone's answers and had a chance to coordinate a schedule, we'll get back to you with an update of our test schedule. Thanks very much for your participation!

—Mike and Kevin

Confirmation and Reconfirmation

Since the scheduling process can involve a lot of dates and times flying around, at Wired we found it useful to request a final confirmation that the times we scheduled were the times to which the participants thought they were agreeing. This consists of a short, clear, message that says something like this.

Dear Terri,

Thank you for responding to our invitation to next week's usability study. We'd like to set up your appointment for the following day and time:

Day: Monday, Nov 15, 2003
Time: 5:00 PM

*VERY IMPORTANT—YOU MUST CONFIRM YOUR APPOINTMENT: in order to confirm this appointment time, please either REPLY TO THIS EMAIL or CALL 415-235-3468!! If you don't respond, we will assume you are not coming, and we'll have to schedule another participant in your time slot.

All confirmations should also contain a line to the effect of "Because we have tight schedules, it's critical that you show up exactly at the time you're scheduled or a few minutes early," as well as specific transportation and parking instructions.

OUR ADDRESS

We're located at 582 Market Street at Montgomery, Suite 602, in the Hobart Building. There is a BART and Muni station right in front of the building, and all the trains stop there. The number 2, 7, 9, and 14 buses run at street level. If you're driving, the closest parking is an underground pay lot at Mission at Second that is best approached from Mission Street going east.

OTHER GOOD STUFF TO KNOW

This session should last about one hour, and you'll receive an honorarium in the amount of $60.00 by check within two weeks following your

(Continued)

> participation. The schedule we have set up for this test is very tight, so if you think you're going to be running late, PLEASE CALL (415) 235-3468 TO INFORM US. If at all possible, plan to arrive 10 minutes before your scheduled appointment time, and you'll really be a star!
>
> Thanks again and we'll see you next week!
>
> —Mike and Kevin

In addition, we found it helpful to standardize the format of all correspondence with a one- to two-sentence summary of the message at the beginning; a standard layout for all messages; and a contact person's name, email address, and phone number at the end. Encourage the participants to contact that person as soon as they know they won't be able to make an appointment or if they have any questions. Keeping the text tight, but with humor and personality, helps make the process feel less clinical, and people are more likely to read it.

Finally, the single most effective way of preventing no-shows is a combination email and telephone reminder the day before the scheduled appointment. It reminds people, subtly reinforces the importance of their input, and gives you time to schedule an alternate in case they can't make it.

Choosing an Incentive

An incentive is something that encourages and rewards people for their help. As such, it needs to do two things: it needs to convince someone that they should share their time and experience, and it needs to communicate their value to your company. Never shortchange people on an incentive.

Although the chance to give input into a favorite product is a strong motivator (and should always be emphasized), for most people the best incentive is cash. Everyone knows what to do with it, and it's immediately useful. The basic cash incentive formula in the San Francisco Bay Area in 2003 is $0.75 for every minute spent doing general consumer research and $1 per minute for one-on-one interviews and for professionals' time. So a one-hour interview should carry a $60 incentive, and a two-hour focus group can pay each participant between $70 and $120 (depending on the complexity of the profile). Similar amounts apply in Boston and Chicago.

Extra incentive should be paid to people with unique perspectives or who are willing to come in at awkward hours. How much extra will be based on the conditions. If you need someone to come in tomorrow, an additional $20 to $40 to the basic incentive may be appropriate. A busy manager may not be willing to break up his or her day for less than $200. It's often useful to budget for a range and then let the recruiter up the incentive to get good candidates.

For certain people, no amount of money will be enough to encourage them to participate. For these people, you need to come up with alternative incentives. Executives may value meeting other executives in the same industry, so presenting the research as an opportunity to hobnob with peers may be attractive to them. Charity donations are sometimes valued, as are gift certificates to luxury restaurants or theater tickets. A luxury cruise line site had retired millionaires who liked to travel as its customers. It recruited them by giving them all-expenses paid flights to New York. It cost the site several thousand dollars per participant, but they were able to get their exact target audience from all over the country. Merely offering the same amount in cash would not have showed the understanding and respect for the participants' priorities to convince them to participate.

Sometimes people are willing to participate for less than you're offering, or even for free, but it's not a good idea to take advantage of such audiences. For one thing, groups of people who are available to do research for cheap are a self-selecting bunch: either they have a lot of time on their hands or they're really eager to talk to you or they need the money. The people who fit any of those criteria are unlikely to be representative of your target audience.

Pitfalls

The Wrong People

Sometimes you recruit the wrong group. Maybe you misworded a key screener question, and everyone answered it opposite to what you had intended. Maybe you forgot a key element when determining the target audience. Maybe the recruiter always picked the minimal criteria when you only wanted a couple of people with that description. Regardless, sometimes you will mistakenly invite the wrong people. Every researcher has stories about coming into a room and realizing that it's a roomful of people who shouldn't be there at all.

Preparation, a good screener, a carefully chosen target audience, and asking some key questions at the beginning of the research will minimize this situation, but it still happens. If you find yourself in such a situation, there are two things you can do: cancel the session and re-recruit, or try to get as much information out of the group, hoping that some of their feedback will be usable. Sometimes having the wrong group can be enlightening since the comparison of answers with a group of the right people can lead to a better understanding of the whole population (maybe your target audience isn't so unique after all?). However, when time is short and accurate results are critical, cancellation is a perfectly acceptable option, with the efforts channeled toward getting a group of the right people.

Before you decide to re-recruit (or you start blaming the recruiter), you have to determine why the recruiting failed. In some cases, it will be really obvious—you wanted newbies, but not people who have never seen a computer—but sometimes it may not be clear why a certain group didn't fit your vision of an ideal audience. Identify the elements that resulted in the wrong group being brought in: is it because of their age? Is it because of their experience? It could be that you have not specified a key element ("factory workers" versus "factory workers who work on the shop floor," for example). Or maybe your expectation of how people behave may not match how your target audience thinks. In some cases, there may be *no* way to recruit the right group because it simply doesn't exist.

Warning Always pay people who show up what was promised, even if you made a mistake in recruiting them. They had no idea they were the wrong audience and showed up in good faith. Likewise, if the recruiter scheduled the wrong people and the problem lies with your screener, the recruiter should also be paid in full.

No-Shows

It seems to be human nature that about a quarter of any invited group won't show up, for one reason or another. You can compensate for this by scheduling extra people and removing unexcused no-shows from the database.

If you would like to guarantee that you don't get any no-shows, you can double-schedule every time slot. This makes for twice the recruiting and scheduling work and twice the incentive expense (since you have to pay everyone who shows up, whether or not you need them to participate in research), so it's rarely worth the trouble, but it's useful in certain situations such as when a senior stakeholder is scheduled to observe the research. You can also use the extra people for other kinds of research if you have the resources and a secondary research project. You could have a usability test as a primary research project and a questionnaire or card-sorting task as a secondary project since these don't need as much interaction with a researcher as the usability test. You could even have members of the development team who aren't observing the usability test interview the participants (provided that the team members who do this have some user research experience).

Likewise, you can schedule a "floater" for a block of time, say, three hours, to hang out in case someone doesn't show up. However, qualified people who have two to three hours in the middle of their day are difficult to find, so this isn't as attractive an option as it may seem at first. Floaters should be paid the proportional amount of incentive for the amount of time they spend waiting (two to three times what someone scheduled for a single slot would get), and they, too, can participate in secondary research if they're not needed as substitutes.

If the schedule and facility rental budget permits, you can also create "makeup" slots a day or two after the initial batch of research. People who can't make their initially scheduled time may be amenable to rescheduling during one of the additional slots.

"Snow Days"

Carolyn Snyder, a user experience consultant and principal of Snyder Consulting, suggests that in areas with snowfall that there be alternative days decided ahead of time in case the roads are bad. If there's a possibility of inclement weather, she suggests picking a school near the testing facility and telling people to check the school closure report. If that school is closed, odds are that roads are impassable, so people automatically know they're rescheduled for the alternative day.

Make sure you note down who did not show up. Unless the people contacted you or the recruiter ahead of time to warn of their absence, do not pay them and remove them from the database, or tell the recruiter to do likewise.

Bias

The methods you use to recruit can create a bias in the kinds of people you find. If you recruit 20-somethings with $30K incomes from a discussion list on day trading, you're likely to get people with different perspectives than if you get people with the same demographic makeup from a mailing list about labor relations. Those differences may not matter if you're going to be talking about music, but they probably will if you talk about politics.

Nearly all recruitment techniques bias the population. A truly random sample is impossible, so there's no getting away from some amount of bias. The question to answer is whether the bias matters for this project. Often it does not, but when you recruit, you should mind the potential for bias and how it can affect the research. Include a field in the database for how each person was recruited, and evaluate the sources that come up often for their potential to skew the results. So, for example, if half of your participants come from the same source, you may want to consider whether that recruitment method is affecting your results.

Anonymity

Your company's image and its reputation can also bias the attitudes of people coming to test with you. A famous name can be intimidating, but an unknown company or product can seem more trivial than it really is. Preconceptions may alter the way people behave and affect the results of research.

If you don't want people to know your company's name as they are recruited and scheduled, it may be useful to maintain an alternative identity. Don't deceive people, but working through an alternative email address (even one from a free service) and describing the company and research without giving any specifics can be useful. In general, people don't mind if you tell them that you'd rather not reveal the name of the company or its products.

Teenagers' Schedules

Teenagers are hard to recruit even though they're one of the most sought-after demographics. They're difficult to find, difficult to engage, they are often difficult to contact, they need parental consent to participate, they have complicated schedules, and there are state and federal laws that restrict their employment. To verify that their schedules haven't changed, you should get as much contact information as you can (portable telephone numbers, pager numbers, parents' numbers) and contact them the day before the research, but prepare for last-minute changes and overbook more than for adult groups.

Building and Space Preparation

Although not technically a recruiting pitfall, a common problem with scheduling participants is that the company isn't prepared to greet them. If they're arriving at an office, everyone they meet should be expecting them. The doorman should know where to send them, the receptionist should know they're coming. There should be clear signs pointing them in the right direction.

Working with a Professional Recruiter

A professional recruiter can take a lot of the headache out of doing the recruiting. Pros have access to a large number of people in a broad range of markets and can schedule them in short order. They can be a great asset if you are short on time, if you don't want to maintain your own database, or if you aren't sure how to recruit a certain audience.

However, working with professionals is more involved than just picking up a phone and saying that you need people that match this-and-such a profile. Recruiters do not know your business or your research requirements. Careful preparation and collaboration on the part of the research team is necessary for the recruiter to be able to get the people you need when you need them.

Where to Find a Recruiter

Since recruiters serve the market research industry, they are often associated with companies that offer a broad range of market research services, from providing special conference rooms to focus group moderation to designing and running whole research projects. If you're in a major metropolitan area, finding one should not be hard. You can generally look up "marketing research" in the phone book and find half a dozen. You can also contact the American Marketing Association *(www.ama.org)*, the Marketing Research Association *(www.mra-net.org)*, or the European Society for Opinion and Market Research *(www.esomar.nl)*, and they can point you toward other resources.

When choosing a recruiting firm, do some research. As with any service, ask for quotes from several different firms and request references to their last couple of user experience research clients. If you're recruiting for usability testing, ask them whether they do recruiting for "one-on-one interviews" (or, ideally, for usability testing) and if they recruit for offsite facilities. Follow up on the references they provide, and ask about the accuracy of the recruiting, how receptive the recruiter was to changes, how many people were recruited, and how specific the recruiting criteria were. Ask the recruiting firm whether they have ever done usability recruiting for Web sites or software. Most big firms have done some, but many have only dabbled in it and are not yet experienced in interpreting people's responses for Web usability research.

You're not likely to find out how they get their user lists and how big their databases are since that's the heart of their recruiting business, but if you can, it's useful information for comparison.

Since recruiting may only be part of their business, full-featured marketing research companies may be reluctant to just recruit, and may insist on renting out their research spaces (which can be expensive) or providing other services. In such cases, you may want to consider their services, but if you're only interested in recruiting, then it's important to find a place that's willing to specialize in it.

For small, fast user research projects, the best bet is to find an independent recruiter who specializes in recruiting and scheduling. These types of companies are rarer than the general market research services, but they exist in most metropolitan areas. If you can't find one, ask some colleagues or check with one of the usability or human factors associations such as the Usability Professionals Association or Human Computer Interaction SIG of the Association of Computing Machinery (ACM SIG-CHI).

What Recruiters Can Provide

Every professional recruiter should handle all the aspects of finding the right people, scheduling them, answering their questions, and reminding them of their appointments. In addition, an experienced recruiter can also help you focus your research by narrowing your target audience to just to the people you're interested in. If you are not sure about how to specify the right market for your research, ask your recruiter to help you put together a profile.

Some recruiters will write a screener for you, and in practice, they'll often modify your screener to better fit their style and policies. You should participate in the process by requesting a copy before the recruiting begins to ensure that appropriate emphasis is placed on the elements that are of prime importance to you.

In addition to providing you with the profiles of the scheduled participants, many recruiters are willing to take notes about the responses of people who do not get scheduled. Although this tally does not qualify as a survey, it can be interesting information since it can reveal unexpected patterns in your target audience.

Many recruiters will do incentive payment administration, too, cutting checks or providing cash as appropriate. In addition, larger recruiting companies can recruit in various geographic markets for you.

What Recruiters Need from You

The most important thing to provide a recruiter is a complete audience description. They will be happy to recruit just about any description you give them, but since they don't know your business, they can't filter based on unstated assumptions you have about your audience. If your description isn't sufficiently specific, you're likely to get people you don't want. If you say that you're looking for people with less than a year of Internet experience without saying that you want them to have at least some Internet familiarity, the recruiter may get you a bunch of people who have never seen a browser. Be as specific as possible. If you're looking for white-collar workers, define what you mean by "white-collar workers."

Include a list of whom to exclude. What are industries that present a potential conflict of interest? How much past participation in research is too much? What companies make competing products to yours?

Provide enough time (at least a full week) and avoid changing the parameters of the recruiting after it has begun. Changes are a hassle for the recruiter, and they're likely to pass the cost of that hassle on to you. If you cancel, be prepared to pay at least part of the incentive fee (all of it if you cancel on the same day) and all the recruiting costs.

Tell the recruiter where to get qualified candidates. If you already have a list of customers, such as people who have signed up for a newsletter, and you can filter it for your geographic area, offer the recruiter the list (though be aware that list members will likely know your product and have positive preconceptions about it, otherwise they wouldn't have signed up for the newsletter). If you don't know where to find candidates, you should give the recruiter as much information as you can about where to look for the target audience and how prevalent you expect them to be in the population as a whole. If you have no idea, then you're essentially asking the recruiter to do a telephone survey, which can take a long time and be quite expensive.

Provide direction for how to handle marginal candidates. Clearly note which qualities are flexible and how flexible they are. ("We prefer 25- to 35-year-olds, but will accept people between 20 and 40 if they match all the other criteria well.")

Describe the research to the recruiter. This will help the recruiter understand how to answer questions and may give him or her additional ideas for how to structure the target market description. Is it a series of groups? Is it a series of one-on-one interviews? Will it be done at a special facility? Will it be at the participant's house? Will it be focused on their attitudes, their experiences, or how well they can use a prototype? Tell the recruiter how much of this information is appropriate to tell the participants.

Finally, explain any terminology that's necessary so that the recruiter can interpret people's responses appropriately. If you're looking for IT managers who regularly buy "hot-swappable, fault-tolerant, low RF, Mil-spec, narrow-gage U-racks," you should probably tell the recruiter something about what all those words mean. The recruiter may not need to use these words in conversation, but knowing what they mean will help the recruiter understand the questions he or she is asking.

What They Cost

As I'm writing this, in 2002 in San Francisco, recruiting typically costs between $60 and $200 per participant scheduled, with $100 as the typical rate. Consumers fall on the lower end of the scale and professionals on the upper end. For common groups with few restrictions, such as grocery shoppers who have used the Web at least once, it may be even cheaper. For other groups, such as human resource vice presidents who run organizations with enterprise-wide knowledge management systems, the cost may be significantly higher.

Other services, such as screener writing or response tabulation, can be rolled into the whole cost or charged on an hourly basis, with hourly rates of between $50 and $100 an hour.

When There Are Recruiting Problems

Don't accept bad recruiting. If it's clear that the priorities and questions in the screener were not strictly followed, ask for your money back or for some better recruiting. First, however, make sure that your audience description did not allow the recruiter to interpret it in a way you hadn't intended. Most recruiters, although not elated by the prospect, will re-recruit participants who didn't fall into the target description.

Further, as a final courtesy to the recruiter, tell him or her when a participant was particularly good or bad. This will help the recruiter in future recruiting efforts.

Interviewing

Most of the research described in this book boils down to one technique: the interview. Observation is critical, but to really know the user's experience, you have to ask him or her about it, and that's an interview. The usability interview—the other tool that's a basic part of nearly all user experience research—differs from the kind of interview an investigative journalist or a prospective employer would hold. It's more formal, more standardized, and as a kind of *nondirected interview*, tries to completely remove the perspective of the person asking the questions from the interview.

The Interview Structure

Nearly every user experience interview, whether it's a one-person lunchtime chat or a ten-person focus group, has a similar underlying structure. It's an hourglass shape that begins with the most general information and then moves to more and more specific questions before stepping back for a bigger perspective and concluding with a summary and wrap-up. Here is one way of dividing a standard interview process into six phases.

1. *Introduction.* All participants introduce themselves. In groups, it's important to know that the other people in the group are somewhat like you in order to feel comfortable, so a group introduction emphasizes the similarities between all the participants, including the interviewer. In contrast, an individual interview introduction establishes the role of the interviewer as a neutral, but sympathetic, entity.

2. *Warm-up.* The process of answering questions or engaging in a discussion needs everyone to be in an appropriate frame of mind. The warm-up in any interview is designed to get people to step away from their regular lives and focus on thinking about the product and the work of answering questions.

3. *General issues.* The initial product-specific round of questions concentrates on the issues that surround the product and how people use it. The focus is on attitudes, expectation, assumptions, and experiences. Asking these kinds of questions early prevents the assumptions of the product development team from skewing people's perceptions. Often, the product isn't even named during this phase.

4. *Deep focus.* The product, or product idea, is introduced, and people concentrate on the details of what it does, how it does it, whether they can use it, and what their immediate experience of it is. For usability testing, this phase makes up the bulk of the interview, but for contextual inquiry, where the point is to uncover problems, it may never enter the discussion.

Warning Do a dry run with every new interview script. Run through it with a colleague or a sample participant, complete with all recording devices and prototypes, and then revise it appropriately.

5. *Retrospective.* This phase allows people to evaluate the product or idea in a broader light. The discussion is comparable to the "General issues" phase, but the discussion is focused on how the ideas introduced in the "Deep focus" phase affect the issues discussed earlier.

6. *Wrap-up.* This is generally the shortest phase of the interview. It formally completes the interview so that the participants aren't left hanging when the last question is asked, and it brings the discussion back to the most general administrative topics.

Nondirected Interviewing

A famous scientist once asked the following question on a survey:

Does your employer or his representative resort to trickery in order to defraud you of a part of your earnings?★

This is a leading question. Before you read on, think about what makes this a leading question. What in it implies a "right" answer? What is the actual information the author is trying to elicit? What would have to be different for the question not to be a leading question?

The scientist who wrote it was Karl Marx, and he clearly had an answer that he was expecting, and it wasn't "no."

Leading questions are the bane of all social research since they inject the prejudices of the person asking a question into a situation that should be completely about the perspective of the person answering it. But avoiding directed questioning is easier said than done. It requires a constant vigilance on the part of the person asking the questions and a deeply held belief in the need to know people's thoughts *unconditionally*.

Nondirected interviewing is the process of conducting interviews that do not lead or bias the answers. It's the process of getting at the user's thoughts, feelings, and experiences without filtering those thoughts through the preconceptions of the interviewer.

The Neutral Interviewer

As the person writing and asking the questions in a nondirected interview, your job is to step outside everything you know and feel about your product. Forget all the hard work and creativity. Put away all hopes for success and all fears of failure. Ignore everything you've ever heard or thought about it. See it in a completely neutral light, as if it's not yours at all. It's merely a thing you're asking questions about, a thing that you care nothing about.

This seems harsh, but it's necessary in order to be able to understand the feedback people give you, both positive and negative,

---

★[T.B. Bottomore and Maximilien Rubel, eds., Karl Marx: Selected Writings in Sociology and Social Philosophy (New York: McGraw-Hill, 1956), p. 208; as cited in Earl Babbie, Survey Research Methods (Belmont, California: Wadsworth, 1990), p. 37]

and relate that to the process of making the product into what *they* want and need, not what you think they want and need. Otherwise, you'll always be seeing either the silver lining or the cloud, when you need to be seeing both.

Zen aside, asking questions so as to not bias the respondent's answer involves a lot of self-imposed distance and a rigorously critical examination of your assumptions. This can be especially difficult when the product under examination is one you are intimately familiar with or one you have a lot of interest in. At first, it's going to feel like you're expending a lot of energy not to ask the obvious questions or that your questions are coming out stilted. With some experience, it becomes clearer which questions lead people and how to phrase questions so that you get the most natural responses. Eventually—when you've achieved nondirected question enlightenment—your questions will sound natural, analysis will be easier, and the unbiased answers you get will give you greater confidence in your results.

Composing Nondirected Questions

Most important, every question should be focused on the person answering it. It should focus on *experience,* not extrapolation. Our understanding of our own behavior rarely corresponds to how we really behave. When we try to put ourselves into others' shoes, we idealize and simplify. That's useful in trying to understand people's ideals, but it's rarely useful in understanding their behavior. A question such as "Is this a useful feature?" can be easily misinterpreted as "In the universe of all things, do you think that someone somewhere could find some use for this feature?" Even if most people take it at face value, the potential of misunderstanding makes all replies questionable. "Is this feature valuable to the work you do right now?" clarifies the perspective.

Similarly, questions should concentrate on *immediate experience.* People's current behavior better predicts their future behavior than do their predictions. If you ask people "Is this interesting to you?" they may imagine that at some point they could find it interesting and say yes. But the things that are interesting in theory are quite different from the things that people will remember and return to. If they find something compelling right now, they're likely to continue to find it compelling. Thus, the responses to "If it were available right now, would you use it? Why?" will be more useful.

Questions should be *nonjudgmental*. The person answering the question should not think that you're expecting a specific answer or that any answer is wrong. You can (and should) state this explicitly, but it works better if the question reinforces that view. "Don't you think that this would be better if it was also available on PDAs?" implies that the person asking the question thinks that it would be a good idea and that they will disapprove if they hear otherwise. "If this feature were available tomorrow on PDAs, would you use it?" doesn't imply that there's an expected answer (though it suffers from being a binary question, as described later). An even better approach would be to ask, "Is there any other way you'd like to use a feature like this?" and then prompt to discuss PDAs after they've stated their initial thoughts.

Questions should be *focused on a single topic*. A question that has an "and" or an "or" linking two ideas leads to ambiguity since it's often unclear which part of the question is being answered. "How would this product be useful to you in school or at work?" is actually two questions. An answer to it may insufficiently differentiate between them.

Keep questions *open-ended*. If given a limited choice, people will choose one of the options, even if their view lies outside those options or if more than one is acceptable. They'll adjust their definitions of the options and pick the one that's closest to how they feel. But that's not how they really feel. You should always provide an out from a close-ended question, unless you're absolutely sure that the options cover all the possibilities. That's rarely the case since you're most often looking for the shades of meaning. "Which feature from the following list is most important to you?" assumes that there *are* features that are important, and it assumes that there is one that's more important than any other. A better way would be to say "Rate from 1 to 5 how important each of the following features is to you, where 1 is least important and 5 is most important. Put 0 if a feature is completely unimportant. Write down any features we may have missed" or, ignoring the feature naming scheme entirely, "Does the product do anything that's particularly useful to you? If so, what is it? What makes it useful?"

Avoid *binary questions*. They're an especially insidious form of close-ended questions. Binary questions are of the form "yes/no" or "true/false" or "this/that," and they force people to make a black-and-white choice when their attitude may not lie near either extreme. "Is this a good product?" misses a lot of the subtlety in people's attitudes. Although it may be nice to get a quick sample of people's off-the-cuff opinions, it's much more valuable to know what they find good and bad about the idea, rather than just whether they think the whole thing is good or bad. "What, if anything, do you like about this product?"

Running a Nondirected Interview

A nondirected interview is conducted just as you would any other interview, except that you have to listen more closely to the meaning of your words and the words of the person you're talking to for signs of bias. There are a number of things you can do to increase the quality of the responses.

Define terms. Words are ambiguous and easily misused. "That thing" can refer to a button, a feature, or the whole site. Personal definitions of words can be different from either the dictionary definition or the development team's definition. Someone may speak of a simple function as a "module," whereas the development team may call complex clusters of functions "modules." When using a technical term, make sure that you clearly define it first. Whenever possible, use the respondent's definition of a word (even if it's not how you use it), but make sure that you understand what that definition is first (which may mean asking the respondent to define it). This is especially important in group interactions, where everyone can come in with different definitions.

Don't force opinions. There are times when we just don't have an opinion about something. We may have never thought about a given question in qualitative terms, or we may not have enough information about it in order to form an opinion. When asked for an opinion, most people will form one, but it's not going to be carefully considered or deeply held. When asking a question that requires an opinion, it's good to make sure that the people answering are likely to have an opinion already. "Would this be better if it were done automatically?" may not make any sense to someone who has no experience with "this."

Restate answers. One of the best techniques to cut through problems with questions is to bounce the respondent's answer back at him or her using different words. It clarifies a lot of the subtlety of terminology and verifies that you've understood the answer and that the respondent understood the question. Immediately after someone has finished a thought, you can say something like "So I hear you saying that . . ." and state it as you just understood it, but using different words. However, avoid substituting the "correct" terminology for the words that the person has used. Investigate his or her understanding of the terminology first. So if someone refers to the "order summary," but it's really the "confirmation page," ask the person to elaborate what he or she expects to find on an "order summary" before using the term confirmation page in restating the point.

Follow up with examples, but always wait for an undirected answer first. Sometimes people understand a question, but may not know how to start answering it. If you are precise with your wording, it shouldn't be an issue. Occasionally, though, you may want to ask a question that's intentionally broad, to see how people understand a concept or what their most general thoughts are. Prepare an example (or two) for the questions you feel may need examples. After the participants have given their initial answers, you can refocus their thoughts with an example. Say you're running a focus group that's brainstorming new features. If they're defining features too narrowly and seem to have reached an impasse, you can say, "Now what if it were to email you whenever items you liked were on sale?" and see if the participants can come up with other ideas along the same lines. Don't give more than a couple of examples since that tends to frame people's perceptions too strongly.

Use artifacts to keep people focused on the present and to trigger ideas. Artifacts are the material products of people's work: the notes, the papers, the tools, and so on. Bring participants back to their immediate environment by asking questions that have to do with the physical objects (or the software objects) that they deal with on a regular basis. When someone is talking about "shopping carts" in the abstract, ask about "this shopping cart." When you're in the field and they're talking about how a certain procedure is done, ask them to show it to you with the actual objects. The idealized situation people imagine and discuss in the abstract is often different from the practical situation in which they live, and the objects they use help remind them of the grungy details that are missing from the ideal.

Be aware of your own expectations. Watch for situations that surprise you or when you find yourself predicting the interviewees' next statement. Despite the exhortations at the beginning of this section, it's impossible to be a blank slate when coming into an interview situation. There are going to be things you assume or expect from the interaction, and these are going to affect how you run the interview. If you're aware of these assumptions, it makes avoiding them easier.

Never say the participant is wrong. Even if someone's understanding of how a product works or what it's for is completely different from what was intended, never tell the person that his or her perspective is wrong. Study the person's perspective and try to understand where it comes from and why he or she has it. It may well be that the person's understanding doesn't match others' or yours, but it's never wrong.

Listen carefully to the questions that are asked of you. Questions reveal a lot about how people understand a product or a situation, and they're important to understanding people's experience and expectations. Probe why people are asking the question. If someone asks, "Is that how it's supposed to work?" for example, answer with a question that reveals more of the person's mental model: "Is that how you think it works?" or "Is that how you expected it to work?"

Keep questions simple, both in language and in intent. Use questions to uncover assumptions and perceptions, not prove points or justify actions. A good question does the minimum necessary to elicit a perspective or view, and no more. Analysis of the answers will provide the meaning that can prove and justify. Questions should focus on getting the clearest raw information.

Always review your tapes. It's easy to miss a key statement or a subtle distinction when relying on your memory and notes. Always spend some time with your tapes—whether audio or video—verifying that your views of the discussion accurately represent what happened and how future research can be conducted better.

Note Observers can be present during interviews. Having an observer present makes the interview less intimate, but observers can be useful as note takers or just as a second set of eyes. The extent of their participation should be determined by the moderator, but there generally shouldn't be more than one in-room observer, and he or she should always be introduced. I've found that it works well to create special times when observers are allowed to ask questions.

Common Problems

- Close-ended questions that should be open-ended. "Which of these three logos do you like the most?" is not particularly useful if they don't like any of them. "Is there anything you like about any of these logos?" will tell you what underlying characteristics people find compelling, if any. That will allow you to tailor the logo to those characteristics rather than to an arbitrary choice.

- Questions with complex answers posed as binary questions. "Is the Daily Update an important feature to you?" ignores all the reasons it would or would not be. Maybe they don't plan on checking the site every day, but a weekly update would be great. Maybe there's no need for an update at all. "Is there anything about the Daily Update that you find interesting?" will tell you which parts of it are interesting.

- Loaded words or words with multiple meanings. Be precise in the words that you use. "When you're trying to find something in a site and you get hopelessly lost, what do you do?" "Hopelessly" is imprecise. It can be interpreted by one person as meaning "pretty lost" and by another as "lost without any possibility of ever finding anything." Rewriting the question as "What do you do if, in course of looking for something on a site, you realize that you don't know how to get back to an earlier point?"

- Asking people to predict the future. As mentioned earlier, when people try to project their actions into the future, they often oversimplify and idealize to the extent that their predictions have little to do with what they actually do. People are much better at explaining the reasons for their actions as they're doing them than they are at predicting their actions ahead of time. If you're interested in how someone will behave in a given situation, put him or her into that situation (or a suitable simulation).

- Invocation of authority or peer pressure. For example, "Most people say that it's pretty easy to find information with this tool. Was that your experience, too?" or "Our designers have a lot of experience making navigation tools, and they came up with this one. How well did it work for you?" These questions can almost always be simplified to the actual question being asked: "Describe your experience using this tool."

- Assuming you know the answer. I've found myself half-listening to a response to a question, assuming that it's going to be a variant on what I've already heard, only to do a double take when someone answers in a way that I'm totally unprepared for. Sometimes people even use many of the same words as what you're expecting, but a critical negation or spin may reverse or fundamentally change the meaning of what they're saying. Listen carefully to every word.

- Assuming that they can answer the question. Not everyone knows what they know and what they don't know. If you ask someone whether something is the best in its class, you're assuming that he or she is familiar enough with all the products in the class and that he or she can make a balanced, knowledgeable evaluation of all the products.

Problems don't just arise in the formulation of questions. The interpretation of answers also depends on the way questions are asked. There are a couple of behaviors to watch out for when asking questions, so that you can catch them and follow up quickly, making later analysis less ambiguous.

- People won't always say what they believe. Sometimes they'll say yes to avoid conflict when they mean no. Watch for the clues about what they really mean. These can take the form of hesitant answers or answers that are inconsistent with previous statements. There can be even more subtle cues, such as someone shaking his or her head no while saying yes or suddenly losing articulation. Attempt to catch such situations as they're happening and ask the person to clarify. Often, just giving the person the floor gives him or her the confidence to say what he or she really means.

- People will sometimes answer a different question from the one you asked. In a situation where someone is thinking hard about a topic—maybe because he or she is in the middle of a task or trying to remember a situation—he or she may easily mishear the specifics of your question. Sometimes participants have their own agenda and really want to discuss things you're not asking about. Listen carefully for what they're really saying and whether it's directly related to what you're asking. If it's clearly off track, interrupt, and ask the question again, using slightly different wording and emphasis. Don't be afraid to be persistent.

When to Break the Rules

Clearly, following all these rules and suggestions will make for a pretty dry conversation, and that may be worse than the bias it eliminates. People should feel comfortable talking to you and answering questions honestly. You should feel comfortable talking to them.

So take all these rules as suggestions when constructing your questions and try to follow through as much as possible. However, feel free to improvise and humanize your interviews by providing examples or letting the participant "off the hook" if a question seems too difficult to answer as it was posed. An interview can be both nondirected and comfortable. Ultimately, the best interview is the one that provides the information you need when you need it. What it takes to do that will be different in every interview. These rules and guidelines will help you get the best information you can, but only you will know how to implement them appropriately.

Videotaping Interviews

Every single interview and interaction should be videotaped, if at all possible. Many people consider video documentation a fancy form of audio recording. Sometimes that's true, but it can reveal crucial moments in any interaction that just can't be captured on audio. A crucial shrug while someone is saying yes, but they really mean no, can be the crux in understanding the person's perspective correctly. A momentary pause of a mouse over one button before clicking on another can reveal the core confusion in a feature. Plus, it frees the moderator from having to simultaneously take notes and think about moderating.

Videotaping is quite inexpensive and, if introduced and placed carefully, quickly disappears into the background for most people, so it's a relatively unobtrusive technique. The video camera can be introduced in the beginning of the interview, placed on a tripod in an inconspicuous location, and the interview can continue normally. The tape then becomes a permanent record that can be mined for critical nuances and exact quotations (both verbal and physical).

Photography uses less equipment and allows you to collect a close-up record of specific items and arrangements in an interview, but it creates a disruptive process where the researcher stops the flow of conversation in order to take a picture. However, in some situations—such as on-location contextual inquiry interviews in security-conscious organizations—it's the only way to document. In those cases, it should be coupled with an audio recording of the interview.

CHAPTER 7
User Profiles

"Who's going to use your product?"
"Everyone!"
"And what will they do with it?"
"Everything!"

As technology and bandwidth allowed for real-time voice communication over the Internet, a bunch of companies entered the market to promote and develop it. Many decided to aim big; otherwise, the reasoning went, why aim at all? When asked about who would use their product, an executive at one of these companies replied, "Everyone who uses a telephone!"

Although at the time that was a great ambition to have, and a good story to tell investors, the group of people who would have been likely to use an Internet telephone in 1998 was a lot smaller than "everyone who uses a telephone." By defining the audience so broadly, they were, in effect, not defining it at all. Of course, they could have claimed to be happy if they captured a small fraction of the large market, but that reasoning would have been equally flawed. Aiming for a small share of a large market would have created an impossible task for the company. To capture even a small piece of a big market, they would have needed to understand the dynamics of the *whole* market. There are a lot of telephone users in the world. To understand the market they had so flippantly defined, the Internet telephone companies would need to know the needs, abilities, and desires of a large chunk of the world's population—in a 1.0 product.

The company in question eventually realized that they would have to focus their efforts. After trying to make a completely generic product and failing, they settled on a more focused audience definition, but only after spending a long time working on features that most of their (few) users didn't care for and that didn't make sense when taken together with the rest of the product.

This is where user profiles would have been valuable. When you create *user profiles* (or *personas,* as Alan Cooper, founder of Cooper Interaction Design, a major innovator and proponent of the technique, calls it), you create one or more fictitious users and try to model them and their lives. From general characteristics, you model specific individuals who would buy and use your stuff. Each final profile is a tool that helps you define and compare your ideal with reality. Role playing with user profiles can reveal functionality and needs that would be difficult to uncover otherwise, while adding a dose of reality to product feature brainstorming sessions ("Keeping the 'nifty factor' down," as Christina Wodtke, senior interaction designer at Yahoo!, puts it). User profiles allow you to focus on specific images of users that everyone on the team can reference and use as sounding boards for development ideas. They're also much simpler to work with than "everyone."

The bulk of this book is about understanding who your users are, what they can do, and what they want. That information is going to guide your product in the long run, but even before you start collecting hard data, you should begin focusing on the user and his or her experience. In *user profiling,* you model your users based on your intuition, your judgment, and the information you have at hand. This quickly gives you insight into what makes a good user experience and can keep your product out of the "everything for everyone" trap. Profiles provide a conceptual envelope to work in and benchmarks against which to focus the rest of your research. When you follow up with surveys, contextual inquiry, or user tests, you have a model with which to compare your results.

Except for the fact that they're fictional, your user profiles are people whom you will get to know, to spend time with, to like. They are more than just a face put on a list of demographic data; they are entities whom you work with to make a better product.

When to Do It

Start thinking about your user profiles before you start developing your product. The concept of your audience should emerge simultaneously with the concept of your product. After all, you're making something for someone, so who's that someone?

Products are maximally flexible before you start the nitty-gritty work of product development. Before you've committed yourself to a development path, you can adjust what the product does and whom it's for. These early decisions determine the direction for the whole process and commit a lot of energy and resources. Early mistakes can haunt you for a long time. It's doubtful that you want costly features or groups of users who require exorbitant amounts of support for little return. A set of carefully constructed user profiles can help you understand why you're making what you're making and why people are going to buy it.

Creating a set of user profiles (Table 7.1) should always be the first step of a research plan. It can be done in a couple of days and requires only a whiteboard, Post-it notes, and the development team's participation. It also has the side effect of helping build a new team and giving them a common foundation from which to communicate.

Timing	Activity
$t - 2$ weeks	Organize space and invite participants (generally in-house stakeholders). Begin preliminary research.
$t - 1$ week	Complete participant scheduling. Continue preliminary research.
$t - 2$ days	Complete preliminary research and summarize. Confirm participants.
$t - 1$ day	Prepare space; verify schedule.
t	Profile exercise (1-2 days, usually).
$t + 1$ day	Begin compilation of profile.
$t + 3$ days	Complete compilation of profile. Present profile to whole development team. Distribute documentation.

How to Do It

Creating a user profile is a collective activity. It does not come from the mind of one person or one group. It has to be decided on, fleshed out, and agreed on (by consensus or compromise) with the whole development team. Key members from each facet of the development of the product need to participate because everyone is going to bring different information to the profile and a different perspective.

The two groups who need to be part of the profile-making process are the people who know the characteristics of the users and the people who need to know those characteristics.

EXAMPLE GROUPS THAT NEED TO PARTICIPATE IN PROFILING

Knows User Characteristics	Needs to Know User Characteristics
Marketing research	Engineering
Support	Identity design
Sales	Interaction design
Business development	Information architecture

Each person will bring a unique perspective on whom they want as their user. Information architects may discuss how they expect people to organize their information. Marketing and sales may be concerned with the things the users read and the reasons they gravitate to this product versus some other one. Interaction design and information architecture may be concerned about the specific things people are trying to get done and the ways they interact with others. Everyone will shine a light on a different side of the user. When all these are seen together, the profile will have a richness that will reveal restrictions and opportunities that are difficult to determine otherwise.

Five to eight people should be invited to be part of the profiling process. More than that, and meetings tend to get unwieldy; fewer, and the profiles produced may not be useful to the whole team.

"This Is Not Quackery"

If this is the first time that this type of exercise is being done in your company or with this team, it's likely that you'll have to overcome some people's apprehension. It's easy for someone who has never participated in a profiling exercise to write it off as marketing gibberish or a fluffy team-building exercise (and we all know how much we like those). To overcome this, it needs to be presented as a legitimate, although fun, part of the development process.

The important things to communicate are that this is a way to get everyone talking about the same thing and that it's an effective way to understand the constraints and desires of your audience. By creating a customer model with a name, it creates an efficient shorthand. Rather than describing a feature for "infrequent large-scale Fortune 1000 purchasers who use SAP," you can say "it's for Leonard" and marketing, engineering, and design will all know the qualities of the audience and how they will use the feature. "Leonard" represents a shared understanding of a class of user experience issues that are important to the success of the product.

The rest of the benefits of the procedure—the ability to understand subtle interaction problems, the coupling of people's desires with a model of their understanding, the team building—are side effects of this communication benefit.

Preliminary Research

Before you get everyone together, you should do some research. Having some direct knowledge of your audience before you start creating an audience profile can jump-start the profile building and resolve issues in its development.

Begin with Internal Research

The first place you should start is right around you. Someone in your company has an idea of who your target audience is. If it's not you, then maybe someone in business development. If not biz dev, maybe the product design crew. If not the product folks, maybe the CEO. If not the CEO, maybe the CEO's hairdresser. *Someone,* somewhere, has an idea of who your audience is. (If no one does, then you have bigger problems than user experience research can solve.) Maybe all of them have ideas.

Start by asking local experts—the people who have contact with the audience—to describe it for you. If your product has an established client base, talk to the people who work directly with its users—salespeople, support staff, market researchers, technical sales consultants, trainers, and the like. They have had direct experience with who the audience really is. These groups often have detailed demographic profiles and market research that can give you big-picture breakdowns of your audience. Support staff sometimes have "Top 40" lists of user questions and problems.

Say you're creating a small-business banking service for an established bank. The marketing group, which has been selling the bank's services to small companies for many years, will certainly have an idea of who they're selling to and what their values and needs are. If there's a phone number just for small-business clients, then the people who answer the calls will have had special training and have valuable personal experiences with these customers.

Warning Customers are not always users! The people who spec, research, and buy a product may be people who never use it. In large information technology organizations, a manager may decide to buy a product that gets deployed companywide, yet he or she never uses it. Parents often buy educational software they never touch. Find out from your local experts who is responsible for choosing the products versus who ends up using them.

Interview these local experts about their personal experiences with users and customers. You may want to recruit some development team members to help conduct the interviews, maybe assigning one interview to each participant. The interviews shouldn't last more than an hour or so. Collect the experts' understanding of the audience's characteristics. What kind of people are the users? What do they do for a living? How often do they use the product? Is there common behavior? Is there something that makes them particularly happy? What are common problems? Ask for anecdotes that illustrate typical client situations and particularly interesting atypical situations.

For the banking project, you may want to get the names of several managers who have experience with small-business customers and call them or visit them.

You may see conflicting profiles emerging: sales may be selling to a group of people entirely different from those who contact support; market research may have constructed a profile different from the one business development is using. This is typical and fine. Capture all the profiles, regardless of whether they're conflicting. Don't attempt to resolve them before the profiling process (and don't get into fights about which one is more "right").

Talk to Users

Having gotten some idea of who the users are (or should be), interview people who are roughly like the users. It's great if you have access to people who are actual users of the product (maybe the bank branch managers have some clients whose contact information they can share), but friends and relatives who are close to the audience are fine subjects, too. Talk to three to ten people. Ask them to talk about how they currently do the things that the product is supposed to assist them with, ask them to describe the problems they've had and the positive experiences. Keep a list of good quotations, problems, and anecdotes.

Before the day when you create the profiles, try to extract common threads from the information you have collected. What do the people have in common? Are there problems that seem to crop up frequently? Are there perceptions that seem to be popular? Note conflicts in the various descriptions since differences in the way that people approach a problem are as important as similarities.

Summarize and present your findings before the meeting or at its start.

List the Attributes

Profile building should be done all at once, preferably in one day. That way, the participants can immerse themselves in the information and create coherent models. Two consecutive days can work, but more than that, and the process starts to break up as time dilutes people's memory and enthusiasm. By making it all happen in one (sometimes long) push, the profiles come out as vivid images.

The first step is to make a list of audience attributes. Give all the people in the room a stack of Post-it notes and have them write down things they know or suspect about the audience. These can be as far ranging as the participants want. For example, one person's list for the small-business banking site could be as follows:

40-something
Store manager
Female
Stubborn
Computer literate
Doesn't have a lot of time during the day
Surfs in the evening
Manages two stores
Gets a shipment once a week per store
Has 30 employees
Has kids
Doesn't own the stores, but acts as though she does
Etc.

Have all participants keep going until they've exhausted the attributes they can readily think of (maybe for half an hour). They should finish with (typically) 50 notes apiece, although it's all right if they have more.

Tell the participants that when they're listing attributes, they should use not only the knowledge they gained from the preliminary research, but also, equally important, their gut feelings. People often have a much richer internal model than they're willing to share in normal circumstances because they're not completely confident about it. They should be encouraged to share their suspicions, hunches, and hopes, and be comforted that any one isn't more "right" than any other. There won't be definitive information about all these attributes, so some educated guesses will always have to be made. It's best that these ideas come out early, and as long as they're flagged as guesses and the profiles are revised with new information as it appears, this is fine. Further, since there are specific problems that the group will be trying to solve, it's fine to develop certain aspects of the profile (such as goals or specific tasks) more than others.

The list of attributes isn't a checklist or an exhaustive list of attributes, but it can serve as seeds when thinking about how to describe your users. Each one has a number of questions that can be asked to flesh out the profile.

Demographic

Demographic descriptions are likely to be found in marketing research reports and business development documents. They divide the audience with traditional measurable values such as age, title, industry, income, and zip code. Since we're looking to address people's experiences beyond what is merely measurable through census data (where many of the core demographic constraints come from), this information is only a beginning. There's a relatively complete set of demographic questions in the Appendix, but here are some of the key ones.

- *Age.* How old are your users? If they're representing a company, how old is the company?
- *Gender.* How does your user population divide by gender? Does their gender matter in terms of how they use the product?

- *Income and purchasing power.* If you're selling something for people's personal use, what is your users' household income? What economic constraints do they face as individuals? If for business use, what is their purchasing power? What are the constraints on their industry?
- *Location.* Are your users urban, suburban, rural? Do they come from certain regions, a certain country, or are they spread out all over the world?
- *Cultural.* What's their primary language? Does their culture affect the way they would buy or use your product?
- *Title.* What job titles do they hold?
- *Company size.* If your product is for people who are working in a company, how big is the company? How much money does it make? Does it have large or small margins?

Don't overdo it on the demographics. Although it's important to have an idea of the demographic makeup of the audience, don't obsess about getting every last specific about the users' income or their geographic location (unless it's important to the product, of course).

Technological

Your users' hardware and their skill with it are key constraints on the way they're going to use your product. boo.com, an ecommerce clothing store, was a spectacular failure for a number of reasons, but the most immediate and severe was that their first site—the site that they had spent many millions promoting—was unusable to a large portion of their population. It required higher bandwidth and more computing power than their customers had. Many of their potential customers never even saw the shop because they couldn't get to it.

- *Computer.* What kind of computer does your typical user have? How long has he or she had it?
- *Monitor.* What kind of monitor do your users use? Do they have the latest giant high-resolution display or a low-resolution hand-me-down?
- *Net connection.* How fast is their connection to the Internet?
- *Experience.* How have they been using their hardware? What kinds of things do they use it for? How comfortable are they

using computers, in general? What experiences have shaped your users' attitudes toward computers and the Internet?

- *Browser brand and version.* What browser do they use? Which version? The browser platform determines a lot of someone's experience since different browsers present (sometimes drastically) different environments.
- *Operating system.* Similarly, the operating system in which the browser is running creates constraints on how people perceive the information.

Web Use

How people have been using the Web is important in terms of the context in which they're going to use the product and their expectations for it.

- *Experience.* How long have they been using it? How often do they use it? How often do they use it for personal versus work tasks?
- *Typical tasks.* What do they do on the Web? How often?

Environment

The environment in which people use your product can affect the way that they perceive it. Placing a bid on a ton of steel from the factory floor is different from placing it from an office cubicle or a living room. The complexity of your description will depend on the nature of your product, but you should always have some model of the context in which people are going to be using it.

- *Use location.* Is the service going to be used from home? From an office? If so, what kind of office? If they're using it from home, are they going to be constantly interrupted by kids and pets? Do they share a computer?
- *Use time.* Are they going to be using the product during work or during their off hours? Will they be using it first thing in the morning, when they've just returned from the opera, or after the day's last milking?

- *Tool context.* What other tools are they going to use at the same time as they're using your software? How important are the tools? How does your product fit in with them?
- *Competition.* What products or services are competing for your users' attention? What is the nature of the competition? What benefit do competing products offer?

Lifestyle/Psychographic

Besides the way they use your product, people have interests, ideas, and values. They may not directly affect the immediate use of your product, but these attributes are still important when thinking about how your users experience the product. When creating a profile, consider the lives of your users outside the immediate sphere of use, and define who they are as *people,* not just as customers or clients.

- *Values and attitudes.* What are your customers' values? What is important in their lives? Thrift? Speed? Ease? Fun? Comfort? What has their experience been with services like yours?
- *Media.* How do they learn about new products, services, and ideas? What magazines do they read? Why do they read them? What TV programs do they watch? What Web sites do they go to most often?
- *Activities.* What kinds of things do they do besides using your site? What other sites do they like? What else do your users do in their lives? What do they do for entertainment?

Roles

People play different roles in life, and they interact with other people playing roles. A public defender and a district attorney may do fierce battle in the courtroom, but play racquetball together on the weekends. The roles people play in their lives are often more important than their titles or their listed responsibilities. One materials exchange site, for example, was geared toward plastics manufacturers. Initially, it was thought that the target audience was sales and sourcing managers. However, audience research showed that the managers did little day-to-day managing of the procurement and

Note Roles are especially important where target markets and *user markets* diverge. Target markets consist of people who make purchasing decisions. User markets consist of people who have to live with those choices. Ideally, the two sets overlap or communicate, but that doesn't always happen. If you define separate profiles for the two groups and specify the relationships between them, it can clarify the needs of the user experience.

had (as a group) weak computer skills. Their job descriptions and what they really did were different. The people who did most of the materials exchange were their assistants.

- *Titles.* What are the groups involved? What are they called?
- *Responsibilities.* What are job responsibilities of each group? What do they get rewarded for (both formally and informally)? How?
- *Training.* What training have they received at work? How often do they get retrained or trained on new features?
- *Power.* What is their responsibility for the product? Do they choose it, or are they assigned to it? Do they pay for it, or does someone else sign the checks? What happens if something goes wrong?
- *Relationships.* Whom do they work with? Whom do they consult with when making a choice? Whom will they be working with after using your product? What will those people need?
- *Interactions.* How do they interact with others? Will those relationships change in the future? What is the nature of the interactions? Informational? Regulatory? Commercial?

Goals

There's a reason people use your product. They're trying to accomplish something in a way that's easier, faster, cheaper, or more fun than the way they're doing it right now. Which of those is it? Specifying the end results (both short term and long term) can help explain people's behavior and their attitudes.

- *Short term.* What problems are your users trying to solve? Which of their business needs does this address? How are these needs going to change with time?
- *Long term.* What effects does using this service repeatedly have on the business as a whole?
- *Motivation.* Why are they using your product? What is driving them? Are these goals personal? Professional? What's the relationship of the goals to the user's job or life? Are they using your product voluntarily, or does their employer or school require them to use it?

- *Outcome.* What does the successful completion of each goal mean? How is success defined? Is there an ultimate goal? What is it?
- *Pain.* What is keeping them from solving their problems with their current tools? How severe is the pain? Are there multiple points of pain? Are they mild irritations or severe show-stopping problems?

Needs

There are two different kinds of needs: those that relate directly to the task at hand and those that are incidental and nonfunctional, but still important. The first set is an expression of goals—a completed goal is a satisfied need—but the second set doesn't have a direct relationship to the functionality of the product; it is more ephemeral, emotional. Some users may need to feel reassured. Others may need to feel they're in control. Still others may need to feel they got a bargain. None of these needs relates directly to the functionality of the product, but they're still important since they can include the secret ingredient that changes a functional product into a great user experience.

- *Functional.* What has to happen for the problem to be solved, for the goal to be reached? What are the factors that differentiate something that works tolerably from something that works perfectly?
- *Emotional.* What do they need to enjoy using the product? Are there needs that the user isn't aware of? What's more important: that the users aren't annoyed or that they're ecstatic? What are their fears?
- *Reasons.* Why are they using your stuff? What are their reasons for sticking with your site? What triggers their use of it? What reasons does the competition offer?

Desires

Desires are not the same thing as needs. Desires are what people *think* they need rather than what they actually need. From the perspective of the user, it may be difficult to tell the two apart, but a distinction should be drawn when creating a profile. Desires, when fulfilled, may not make the product any more effective or efficient, but they may make the user experience more satisfying, so they need to be taken into account.

- *Stated desires.* What do your users say they want?
- *Unstated desires.* What do they *really* want?

Knowledge

As they say in *noir* detective stories, "What did she know and when did she know it?" The back story tells you how people got to your Web site and why they ended up there. There are plenty of things she could have been doing on that sultry August afternoon when she walked into your office, er, clicked to your site. So what is the context in which you find "her" on your doorstep?

- *Domain knowledge.* How much does your audience know about what they're trying to do? Are they experts trying to find a more efficient tool or newbies who need to be taught about what's going on?
- *Product knowledge.* How much do your customers know about your product or service? How much do they know about their own needs? About the options available to them?
- *Competitive awareness.* How aware are they about the various brands competing with yours? How much do they care?

Usage Trends

The patterns in which people use a product determine much about what they want and expect from it.

- *Frequency.* Will they use your service just once, or will it be a regular part of their job cycle?
- *Considerations.* Will they do a lot of research before settling on a service the first time they use it? Will they do this research every time, or will they just do it once?
- *Loyalty.* How loyal are they to their chosen product? Do they just choose the cheapest or most convenient one, or do they stick with one for a while?

Tasks

Ultimately, people are using your product to do *something*. What? Tasks are actions that users do to move themselves closer to their goals. For the purposes of the user profile, tasks should be seen from the user's perspective. They should be considered at the granularity at which the user thinks. Users rarely think of database row locking (as a software engineer would); they think of transferring money to their checking account or making a hotel reservation. The profile should contain a list of the most important tasks that the user is going to want to do with the system (whether or not the current technical implementation can do these tasks).

- *Reason*. Why do they want to do this?
- *Duration*. How long do they do it for?
- *Order*. Which tasks come after which other ones? Where does the user think the sequence matters? Where does it not matter? How are tasks linked?
- *Criticality*. How important are the tasks? Are they rare, but extremely important, tasks? For example, data recovery should not happen frequently, but it's very important when it does.
- *Method*. How do they want to accomplish the task?
- *Model*. Is there some way they're doing this already? What tools are they using, and how are they using them?

As you're creating tasks, you may notice clusters that are completely independent for otherwise identical profiles. For example, almost all tasks done by people selling homes and people buying homes are completely different although they're related topically, and the people doing the buying and selling are pretty similar. This is an important difference to recognize. The two clusters do more than just define two different profiles; they define two different *products*.

Cluster the Attributes

Once you've gathered the giant list of attributes, it's time to cluster them into profiles. This is done in a similar way to the Beyer and Holzblatt *affinity diagrams* used in contextual inquiry, but somewhat simpler.

1. Start by picking someone and asking him to put his attribute Post-its into several clusters he feels may make useful user profiles. For an online banking site, he may want one cluster with "40-something," "male," "vice president," "Internet newbie," and "responsible for corporate budget," as well as another cluster with "40-something," "female," "store manager," "does books every night." Although everyone started out with an image of his or her audience, this will likely produce multiple profiles.

2. Ask another participant to put her notes that relate to the clusters around them one at a time. It doesn't matter how the notes relate, just as long as the participant feels that they do relate. If necessary, have people copy their notes so that attributes can exist in more than one profile.

3. If a participant has notes that don't fit one of the existing clusters, put those up as new clusters.

4. After each person has put his or her attributes up, discuss them with the group. Do they make sense where they are? Why are they there? Move notes around until you have clusters that everyone agrees on.

5. Repeat with everyone in the group.

This may take several hours since there may be a lot of attributes and because the discussion can uncover assumptions about what users want and what they're going to be doing.

There may be clusters that define prominent user markets and smaller clusters that define potential markets or secondary user profiles. The clusters may be similar to the target market segments that business development or marketing has created but with greater precision in terms of the audiences' relationship to your product.

Once the attributes are put up on the board, stop and discuss the trends that you see in the clusters. Are there obvious trends? Do they fit the user types that the participants had expected? Where are the surprises?

If there are many different clusters, winnow the number of profile clusters down. Keep the number of major clusters between three and eight. More than eight clusters will probably be unwieldy; fewer than three will not provide enough diversity for the profiles to be useful.

Warning Be wary of bias creeping into the profile when participants with an agenda or disproportionate status (say, a senior vice president in a group that comprises primarily junior staff) emphasize a particular view of users. If there are clear contradictions in the profiles, attempt to talk through them, stress that user markets are not the same as target markets, and that unless there's hard data, it's mostly conjecture.

Warning There is a misconception that each site has one user type. That's not true. There is no single profile that describes The User. Some user markets may be more important than others, but none of them will represent all of your users. Generalizing about The User or discussing users as if they were a homogeneous group is crude oversimplification and should be avoided.

The process is flexible. Once you've seen how the attributes cluster "naturally," feel free to combine or modify clusters such that your main user markets are represented. Viable profiles of user markets are more important than slavishly following the rules.

At this point, the clusters you've defined—and subsequently the profiles you base on them—should be fairly different from each other. Although it's fine if several of your profiles have some common attributes, you should not have profiles that are similar in all major ways. The ultimate goal is to create a set of profiles that will not just show the breadth of potential users, but that will exercise the most important product functions. It may be true that most people will use most of the same features, but it's also important to create profiles that will need to use the less common features. This may involve stretching or overloading a "natural" attribute cluster with attributes that you feel are important for *someone* to have. For example, if it's critical that you examine how people can use an online banking system from multiple machines, you could add "actively uses the Web from home and work" to a cluster where it seems plausible.

Likewise, if there are large audiences who are not represented and yet you know are part of the user market, you should continue discussion with the group until you feel that you've identified your main user groups. Again, keep in mind that these are not sales markets, but user markets, and these audiences may not necessarily match the audiences that sales and marketing have in mind when selling the products.

The Guerilla Method

A less labor-intensive way of creating user profiles from lists of attributes is to shorten or eliminate the Post-it clustering and focus on fewer profiles. Try to come up with *three* good profiles through discussions based on the lists of attributes rather than having everyone write down everything. This method requires the participation of a good group moderator since it'll be important that everyone in the discussion has a chance to contribute his or her perspective. The group should start by coming up with a couple of major profiles, fleshing them out until they seem relatively complete. Other profiles are added using attributes that haven't been used until everyone feels that all the important user groups have been described.

Create People Around the Clusters

Until this point, the process is similar to defining a target market, but here it starts to diverge. A target market defines a market for a good or a service that's large enough to be valuable and homogeneous enough that the differences between individuals are negligible. It does this by abstracting out the details between certain individuals. User profiling, on the other hand, *introduces* personal details to create a realistic portrait of a user to focus on specific user needs rather than market tendencies.

This means making stuff up.

Now is the time to make the clusters come alive by creating enough "narrative glue" between attributes so they all make sense together as a description of an individual. You may want to assign each profile to someone in the group; he or she can flesh it out and bring it back to the group for refinement. The added details should not be major defining factors (those have all been determined already), just embellishments that create a rounded character.

In many cases, adding details is as straightforward as creating a specific "fact" that falls within an attribute range you've defined. So, for example,

> 40-something
> Female
> Children
> Suburban
> Store manager

becomes

> Doris Washington
> 45 years old
> Married to Steve
> Lives in Livonia, Michigan
> Has two kids: Greg, 17, and Andy, 13
> Manages three 7-11 convenience stores in Troy, Michigan

Add enough details that people seem real and believable, but try not to introduce features that are going to distract from the basic issues. If it doesn't matter whether Doris lives in Livonia, Michigan, or in Willamette, Illinois, don't make a big deal of her residence, just pick one. Don't create idiosyncrasies. Strong features tend to distract from the important attributes. So if the base audience is made up of typical teenagers, don't suddenly make your profile a 45-year-old professional ice climber and jazz trumpeter.

Now flesh out the rest of the attributes. You've decided that Doris works for someone else, is "confident in her knowledge" of her domain, and has "direct (though not ultimate) responsibility" for her business. Now you may want to write a little story about it, working those features into a more extensive profile.

> The stores are all owned by Sammy, whom she's been working for since she was in her late 20s. Over the years, she's gone from working as a clerk to being Sammy's most trusted employee, to the point that they both agree that she knows how the stores run better than he does.

You may want to add some specific banking information.

> She works out of the office in back of one of the stores. Every evening, she drives to the other two stores, checks the stock rooms, and picks up the day's receipts and register tapes. After dropping all three deposit bags off at Comerica (while they're still open), she goes back to do the books. Often, she ends up staying late, doing the books well past dinnertime.

This can then be mixed with specifics about her computer and software use.

> Although their family has a newish PC at home—and she uses it to surf
> the Web when Andy's not chatting—she's been using the same machine
> at work for at least five years. It hasn't been upgraded because books
> take enough of her time that she doesn't want to risk getting behind
> while the new system is being configured.

Complete the profile by creating a story tying all the attributes
together, highlighting the problems and anxieties Doris faces on a
regular basis. Think of it as wearing someone else's life, trying to
put all the elements together so that they make sense, so that they
tell a coherent story about how a real person, a real character, could
live. Flesh out the rest of the attribute clusters. You can break up the
discussion group into teams and have each team spend an hour
coming up with a story for each profile, presenting them to the
whole group afterward.

After doing this, you end up with five profiles (for the purposes
of this example).

> Doris, manager of three 7-11 stores
> Sammy, owner of the 7-11s that Doris manages
> Clarence, antique and crafts store owner
> Keith and Jeff, building contractors, co-owners of KJ Build
> Jennifer, freelance writer

When you're done, discuss all the profiles. Are they believable?
Do they seem like the kinds of people who would be using the
service?

Prioritize

Not all profiles are equally important, so the group should prioritize
them. The prioritization may be dictated by business needs, in
which case the priorities will be similar to the target market order.
It can also be dictated by the needs of design. An audience may be
important for the success of the product, but what it needs is sub-

sidiary to the needs of another group. By focusing on the needs of the more challenging group, you're satisfying both their needs and the needs of the more fiscally prominent users. Porsche's auto design philosophy, for example, is to surpass the expectations of luxury performance car geeks. Since most of us aren't luxury performance car geeks, this ensures that most of us will be *really* impressed and satisfied if we buy a Porsche, and the geeks, whose opinions are important for Porsche's image, keep recommending the cars.

For the banking example, this means that the needs of someone like Doris, who has three busy stores to run, will probably subsume the needs of Clarence, who has only one. Clarence may have other niche needs, but his general needs will be served by most of the same functionality that will work for Doris. It may be that there are more Clarences out there than Dorises, so Clarence may be the target market for sales and marketing, but by serving Doris's needs you satisfy them both.

From a development perspective, prioritizing also creates a coherent way of deciding between competing solutions. When you have two ways of resolving a problem, always choosing the one that favors your primary profile ensures continuity and consistency.

Tell Stories

Note If you spent your college evenings acting or playing role-playing games, now may be your big opportunity to put that knowledge to use in the working world. Dust off those improv and Dungeons and Dragons skills and show your co-workers how it's *done!* (You may want to leave your Beckett collection and your 20-sided dice at home.)

Once you have your profiles, it's time to create scenarios with them. *Scenarios* are stories that describe how a person behaves or thinks about a task or a situation. They contain the narrative of what the person does along with his or her motivations, expectations, and attitudes. Scenarios are created by role playing with the profiles that you've created, by putting on the shoes of the people you've created, and looking at their problems and your solutions through their eyes.

To some extent, this is what the user profiling exercise has been leading up to. User profiling works on the model of the story. We are wired to think and communicate through stories and to understand the world as interpersonal relationships tied together in a narrative. Models make it easier to understand the subtleties of your product and to see relationships and issues with it. A table of statistics or an abstract market description would not reveal relationships nearly as well as a story.

Start by retelling some of the stories you may have written down in your preliminary research from the perspective of each user profile. These steps can be done as a group, by individuals, or in pairs. How would Doris handle a situation that you know has actually happened? What would she do? How would she think about it? How would Jeff, the building contractor, handle it?

Next, try to create the ideal scenario for each of your profiles. If this were Heaven, how would everything work for them? In what situations would the software anticipate their wishes? How would it help them make decisions? What would be the perfect situation?

> At 5 PM Doris goes home. She talks to the kids, has dinner with Steve, and then sits down to do the books at 7 PM. She's confident that the deposit bags have been safely picked up. She signs on to the site to check the day's register totals. Dragging the day's totals into her spreadsheet, she can see how each of the stores is doing and can run a total for the week's performance, comparing it to the same time last year. At 7:20, she's done.

Introduce constraints one at a time and see how the story changes. Say that Doris can't get the day's totals input automatically into the site. What will she do? What would happen if she couldn't download it into her spreadsheet? When will she stop using the product because it's too cumbersome or too complicated? Role-play with the profile to determine which values drive Doris's decision making, what is most important to her.

Now think about the problems you have listed for Doris and the other profiles. What are the values and constraints that affect the way the characters look at those problems? What are the profiles going to do when faced with task X or problem Y? Understanding and communicating how different people approach situations will help you create solutions that work for all of them.

Using Profiles

The process of creating profiles can be useful by itself. It creates a set of documents that communicate a shared understanding of users, their perspectives, and their problems. However, to get the full benefit from the process, the profiles need to remain in use. They should be documented, shared, updated, and used in everyday product development.

Document

Teaching the whole team about the profiles and how to use them is the best way to ensure that the work remains useful in the long run. Not all the people using a profile will have been part of the group that developed it, and even those who were will need reminders.

The documentation you create should be a distillation of what you have created. Even though you may have developed large, involved character studies as part of the profiling process, the final product should be short, easily readable, and focused on the specific needs of the project.

Since a user profile is a concise communication tool, you should first determine the audience for your profiles so that you can present the profiles appropriately. Different groups will have different needs: identity design deals with branding, engineering with technical constraints, business development with partnerships and competitors, and interaction design with the functionality and organization of features. The document you create should reflect the needs and concerns of its audience.

Everybody on the team will need to know about what people are trying to accomplish, the problems they have, their desires, important behaviors, and the roles they play. A basic profile will contain the following elements:

- The name of the profile
- A demographic description
- The profiled person's goals
- His or her needs
- His or her abilities
- His or her perspective on the task and the product

In addition, other groups will have specific needs because of the way they use profiles (Table 7.2).

Audience	Information Needs
Identity design	Models of the users' associations and emotional responses to the brand
Business development	Potential complementary and competitive products and services
Interaction design	Usage goals, specific tasks, usage patterns
Information architecture	Familiar task domains and known naming schemes
Engineering	Primarily Web use and technological capabilities, but also usage goals, specific tasks, and usage patterns

Warning Never use pictures or names of people you know when creating a profile. Or, for that matter, never base a profile on someone you know. It's distracting and restrictive when it's time to extend or change the profile ("But Charlie doesn't own a car!").

A portrait is the final element. An image that represents a real person adds a human touch to the profile and makes it seem more "real" than a textual description. Also, the process of finding just the right picture can crystallize many of the decisions that you've made. Some product teams keep a picture of their primary user profiles in a frame near their work area, where a picture of "Our President" would have hung 100 years ago. Many create posters with the picture and key attributes of the user (designing them as Old West–style "Wanted" posters). Others give them their own cube, where everything that relates to a profile (and consequently to the project) is displayed. This reinforces that there are real people who depend on you every day. Moreover, picking a picture is fun and can be a good way to wrap up a long brainstorming session.

Find a source of stock photos (your design department may have some CDs or you can get one from a royalty-free Web stock photo site such as PhotoDisc). They contain pictures of many different people who no one on your team knows. Walk through them together until you find one that says "Doris!" and then make that the face of Doris.

Share

The most challenging part of sharing user profiles is communicating them in a succinct yet useful way. The best dissemination method will depend on the size and makeup of the development team. Smaller teams can be part of the profile specification process itself or can work with someone who was. Larger teams will need to have more formal documentation methods.

An introduction meeting, however, is a useful step for teams of any size. The creation process should be described to the whole team and the profiles introduced. Describing how this specific set of profiles was created and walking through the key characteristics of each profile will ground the profiles and reinforce their function as useful abstractions.

Summarize the profiles in an easily usable form. San Francisco-based design firm Hot Studio creates a one-page "digest" version of their profiles, which is laminated (according to Cooper's suggestion) and given to everyone on the development team. That way everyone will always have the profiles available. The lamination makes them more durable, easier to find in a stack of papers, and less likely to get thrown out by accident.

Although you can share a lot of information, there is always going to be more information than everyone can remember. A profile wrangler (or profile keeper) position can be useful for centralizing the information. The wrangler is present during the profile creation process and is responsible for keeping profiles updated. He or she also serves as a resource for interpreting profiles to the development team ("What would Jeff think about a Palm Pilot download option?").

Note This chapter concentrates on the creation of user profiles; it does not deal with the specifics of integrating them into your development process. For an excellent treatment of how profiling dovetails with software design and business development, see Alan Cooper's *The Inmates Are Running the Asylum.*

Develop with Profiles

It's easy to go through the process of developing a set of profiles and then never use them again. In order for the profiles to remain useful, they need to be actively used. Most immediately, they can serve as bases for recruiting screeners (though they're too specific to use entirely: you generally want more variety than a roomful of Dorises). More important, you should encourage the development staff to talk using profiles during meetings and to think about how features work for the various profiles.

One of the easiest ways to get people thinking in terms of profiles is to use the profile names in your documentation and specs. For example, when describing a new feature, discuss how it would help Jeff or Sammy and how you think they would approach it.

Use profiles to evaluate your competitors. Go to a competitor's site and try to determine which profile they're creating for. Try to identify how your profiles would use the site. Whom would the sites be attractive to? Why? Where do they succeed? Where do they fail?

Of course, not all aspects of your profiles will be useful or used. Sometimes you may spend a lot of time developing a certain profile or a set of scenarios only to discover that some minor facet is much more useful than the whole thing. This is normal and typical. Don't regret the other work you did; just leave it as background information.

Regularly Update

Profiles should be sanity checked and updated on a regular basis.

For example, at first you decide that Doris is a 45-year-old mother of two. But when you run a survey, you discover that there aren't many 40-something women in your user base who fit the rest of Doris's profile. It mostly consists of 50-somethings who have grown children or no children at all. Since Doris's age and the number of children she has are not critical to the product, you can just change her profile. Now she's 55 and has grown kids. Conversely, if you discover that there are almost no businesses like hers in the bank's existing customers, you may want to shift emphasis and concentrate on a more representative profile.

As you're doing other research, compare people who match the general description of your profiles. If you find that many people don't match your idea, adjust the profile to reflect the actual user base.

If you have time, you may also want to sanity-check your profiles with some interviews. Recruit people who match your user markets and interview them, concentrating on your previous assumptions about their behavior and values. How well do they fit your idea of what that market is like? If there are big discrepancies, adjust the profile (but before you make large adjustments, interview

Example   155

a few more people from that market to verify that the differences are consistent and substantial).

You may also want to consider how the user experience will change with time. What happens to Doris after she's used the service regularly for six months? What happens after a year? What happens if, one day, she finds that the site has been redesigned? The original group can meet on a regular basis (every six months or so) to consider how new information has altered your understanding of profiles and how your profiles' goals, reactions, and needs have changed with time.

Example

Here is a short page summary of Jeff, a potential, online, small commercial banking service customer.

Jeff Monroe

Building contractor, co-owner of KJ Build with Keith Grimaldi.

Personal Description

35 years old

Has been a carpenter for most of his adult life, primarily working for small construction companies like the one he now runs.

Works 50–70 hours a week building single-family homes in Ann Arbor and Dexter, Michigan.

Has owned KJ Build with Keith for five years.

Portrait

Jeff Monroe

Technological

Jeff has a three-year-old Dell computer that he shares with his wife, Janet. They have an account through MichNet, a local ISP. He uses the computer to exchange email with friends, check up on the Redwings, and occasionally check out some of the carpentry and homebuilding sites.

Last year, he bought some tools from sears.com, mostly as an experiment.

He bought MYOB, the small-business accounting software and installed it a couple of years ago, but he never managed to make the transition to using it from having a pile of papers and a calculator on his desk.

Roles

KJ employs a part-time accountant, and Jeff and Keith share the financial responsibilities, but Jeff does most of the day-to-day books.

In the future, Keith and he would like to expand KJ Build to include several permanent employees and be able to build two houses at once, each supervising a job site.

Tasks

Both Jeff and KJ Build have accounts with Great Lakes Bankcorp, and Jeff uses Great Lakes' Web service to check on his personal account and pay bills.

Typical tasks that he does include the following:

> *Paying salaries to contractors*
> *Paying for materials*
> *Collecting income from clients, often in installments*
> *At tax time, collecting all of his invoices and expenditures to give to the accountant*
> *Keeping track of deductible expenses*
> *Paying various small-business fees (license, bond, etc.)*
> *Paying business taxes (for both Ann Arbor and Dexter, Michigan)*

He often uses credit cards for short-term revolving credit.

Example **157**

Current Problems

Money comes in "feast or famine" waves to KJ, occasionally causing cash flow problems as materials and hourly subcontractors have to be paid before KJ receives the final contract payment.

Sometimes Jeff has to let the bills pile up because he's too busy working on the houses, and this further complicates the payment process.

All of the paperwork needs to be organized for tax time.

When a client is late with a payment, some credit card and utility bills don't get paid.

Desires

Would like to be able to pay his materials and subcontractor bills more easily and keep track of which contracts are outstanding.

Wants to reduce the amount of paper (and numbers) he needs to keep track of.

Would like to be able to share financial information more easily with Keith.

Would like to better predict upcoming cash shortfalls.

Values

Jeff prefers to work with small family-run businesses like his rather than giant conglomerates.

In the end, profiles are still just convenient abstractions of factors that need to be taken into account when developing a product. But personifying a set of ideas and values is an old technique for communicating complex sets of ideas by tapping into people's natural ability to remember things in the form of stories. It goes all the way back to the morals taught by Aesop and histories passed on over the campfire. By creating a cast of characters and engaging them in a representative set of stories, you create not only an effective tool for communicating an understanding of the audience, but one that helps you reach that understanding in the first place.

CHAPTER 8

Contextual Inquiry, Task Analysis, Card Sorting

Although a Web site is many things—entertainment, advertising, information—every Web site is also a tool. It's a tool to help people do something that, otherwise, would be difficult, time consuming, expensive, or inefficient. Even if the efficiency it introduces is merely a shortcut to something funny or interesting, it's still serving as a kind of tool. It's something that makes their lives a little easier. It solves some problem.

Tools solve problems, and to build the right tool, you need to know what the problem is. There are a number of ways to do that. You can guess, using your knowledge of the target audience and what they're trying to do. This is fast, but it's fraught with danger: if you're not a member of the target audience (which, as a developer, you rarely are), your understanding of the nature and severity of your users' problems will not be the same as theirs. You could decide that someone needs a bigger hammer, when in fact, he or she needs smaller nails.

Another method is to ask representatives of the target audience what their problems are, but this too can lead you in the wrong direction. People tend to idealize their needs and desires, and their statements often don't correspond to their actual needs and behavior. Many sites have been perplexed about why no one uses their personalization functionality after everyone in a survey said they wanted it. The reason is simple: ideally, people would love to have everything tuned perfectly to their preferences and needs, but the actual tuning process is much harder than they first imagine. So although they would love a service that's personalized as they imagine it, when faced with the task of having to make it that way themselves, they'd rather use the plain vanilla service.

Moreover, the obvious problem isn't always the real problem. The person who wants a new hammer and smaller nails? Maybe she really just needs a cheap birdhouse, so she's making one. Once she's done, maybe she'll never need the hammer and nails again. The best way to find out what people's real problems and needs are, and how they really do things, is to discover them for yourself. The techniques in this chapter are designed to reveal how your target audience lives, how they think, and what problems they run into.

These procedures are best done before specific solutions have been created, which is generally at the beginning of a development process. Ideally, they're done even before any technologies have been developed or ideas for solutions have been suggested. Then, all the development effort can go into solving the target audience's problems rather than trying to adjust existing technology to fit their needs. In practice, that rarely happens, but it's still good to do this research as early as possible.

Contextual Inquiry

The definitive book on *contextual inquiry*—and one that this chapter is deeply indebted to—is Hugh Beyer and Karen Holtzblatt's *Contextual Design: Defining Customer-Centered Systems.* They define this procedure as follows:

> *Contextual inquiry is a field data-gathering technique that studies a few carefully selected individuals in depth to arrive at a fuller understanding of the work practice across all customers. Through inquiry and interpretation, it reveals commonalties across a system's customer base.*

In other words, contextual inquiry is a technique that helps you understand the *real* environment people live in and work in, and it reveals their needs within that environment. It uncovers what people really do and how they define what is actually valuable to them. It can reveal unexpected competition (is it just other Web sites, or are you competing with some real-world phenomenon?) and people's real values.

As a technique based in anthropology and ethnography, the basic method of research involves visiting people and observing them as they go about their work. In watching them carefully and studying the tools they use, it's possible to understand what problems people face and how your product can fit into their lives.

When Contextual Inquiry Is Appropriate

Ideally, as stated previously, every development cycle would start with a contextual inquiry process—not technologies, or solutions, or problem statements, or development teams. The researchers would pick a target audience and research them to uncover their needs. Maybe the biggest cause of their problems lies in the exchange and transportation of their data, but maybe it's not that at all. Maybe the users' biggest problem is that people spill a lot of coffee on their printouts. In an abstract development cycle, either problem would be acceptable to uncover and tackle. The first would lead to some kind of software solution. The second, to cupholders and laminated paper.

Since the focus of this book is information related, we will ignore the cupholder solution because there *are* practical limits to the problems that software designers can tackle, but it's useful to remember that the problems people encounter and their ultimate goals will not just be informational. The consideration of users' experiences should not be limited to their actions with the product. Their goals will have something to do with their lives, and that could be anything. Thus, from the users' perspective, a Web site that's about skateboarding tricks is not about sharing or sorting skateboarding trick information—that's a secondary purpose; it's about getting out on a skateboard and doing new tricks. The information and the site are tools that make finding trick instructions more efficient, but the real goal lies with the skateboard, not the Web site.

Most projects begin with an idea about what problems must be solved and also a rough idea about how to solve them. Contextual inquiry clarifies and focuses these ideas by discovering the exact situations in which these problems occur, what these problems entail, and how people solve them. Thus, it's best done before the process of creating solutions has begun, which is most often the very beginning of the development cycle.

It can also be done in between development cycles or as part of a redesign. In those situations, it can tell you how people are using the product, when they're using it, and what they're using it for. This serves as a check of your initial assumptions and as a method of discovering areas into which the product can naturally expand (Table 8.1).

Timing	Activity
$t - 2$ weeks	Organize and schedule participants.
t	Begin interviews. Begin analysis scheduling process for development team.
$t + 1$ week	Complete interviews. Review videotapes and take notes. Complete analysis scheduling.
$t + 2$ weeks	Prepare space for group analysis. Verify participant schedule.
$t + 2$ weeks	Analyze affinity diagram (one day).
$t + 2$ weeks + 1 day	Begin results analysis. Write report and present to stakeholders.

The Contextual Inquiry Process

Since you'll be going out of your office and into the workplaces and homes of your customers, it's especially important to be thoroughly prepared. You won't have the option to go back and get something you've forgotten, and you'll be the one making the first impression about your company (not the cool new leather waiting room furniture).

Target Audience

Choosing an appropriate target audience is described in detail in Chapter 6 of this book, but the short version is that you should pick people like the people you think will want to use your product. Maybe they use the product already. Maybe they use a competitor's product. Regardless, they should have the same profile as the target audience that will eventually use what you have to offer.

You should specify this target audience in as much detail as you can, concentrating on their behavior.

* What is their demographic makeup?
* What is their Web use profile?
* What tasks do they regularly do?
* What tools do they regularly use?
* Are there tools they must occasionally use to solve specific problems?
* How do they use them?

Concentrate on the most important customers. Your product may appeal to a varied group of people, but there are only going to be a couple of key target markets. In fact, there may be only one. Focus all of your research there until you feel that you know what there is to know about their behavior, and then move on to secondary markets.

Recruiting

Once you have your profile, you need to find people that match it. A complete description of recruiting is in Chapter 6, but here are some things to consider when recruiting for contextual inquiry.

First, decide how many people you want to visit. The number will depend on how much time you have allocated to the research and the resources available. Beyer and Holtzblatt suggest observing 15 to 20 people, but that can be prohibitive because of the amount of interview and analysis time it requires. Five to eight people should give you a pretty good idea of how a big chunk of the target audience does their work (or entertains themselves, or shops, or whatever the focus of your product happens to be) and should be enough for a first round of inquiry. If you find that you have not met the goals of the research or you don't feel comfortable with the results at the end of the first round, schedule a second round.

Scheduling

Once you've found your group of candidates, you need to schedule them. Contextual inquiry sessions can last from a couple of hours to a full workday, depending on the length of the tasks and how much ancillary information you'll be collecting. The most important criterion in scheduling is that the people need to be doing the kinds of activity you're going to study while you're observing them. It may be necessary to negotiate with them so you show up when they're planning to do the relevant tasks or to ask them to wait until you arrive.

Interviews can last from an hour to three or four. Schedule one or two interviews per day, along with some time to review your observations. If you have multiple observers, you can schedule several interviews at once (this makes some logistics easier, but requires extra equipment).

Since the research is going to be onsite, give the participants some idea of what to expect. Tell them the general goals of the research, how long it will take, what equipment is going to be used, and what kinds of things you're going to be looking at. You don't have to be specific (and, in fact, leaving some specifics out can produce a more spontaneous response), but they should have a good idea of what's involved before you show up. Tell them not to prepare for your arrival at all, that it's important that you see how they work, warts and all.

When studying people in office environments, it's often necessary to get releases and to sign nondisclosure agreements. Sometimes it's possible to do stealth research under the promise of anonymity, but video equipment is pretty visible, and it's hard to ignore a stranger hanging out all morning watching a certain cube and taking notes. If there's any doubt, ask the people you've scheduled to tell everyone who needs to know about your arrival and to get you all the forms you need to have as early as possible.

The incentive payment should reflect the length of the observation and should be between $100 and $200 for most research.

However, companies may have policies restricting such payments to their employees, which should be determined ahead of time (this is especially true when the company being studied is the same company commissioning the research—as is often the case for intranet or in-house software projects). If cash payment is not allowed, then a small gift may be appropriate (though not for government agencies or regulated industries). Follow-up interviews should be treated likewise unless you agree with the participants ahead of time on a single lump sum (in which case, it should reflect the total amount of time spent).

Learn the Domain

In order to be able to understand what people are doing and to properly analyze your data, you need to be familiar with what they do. This means familiarizing yourself with the terminology, the tools, and the techniques that they are likely to be using in their work. You don't have to know all the details of their job, but you should be somewhat familiar with the domain.

If you know nothing about a task, before you begin your research, you can have someone familiar with it walk you through a session. If you have the time, you can also use the "sportscaster method," having one expert explain what another one is doing, as in a play-by-play commentary. They don't have to go into complicated technical explanations, just enough to familiarize you with the job.

If possible, try the task yourself. If it's something that is done with software, ask to borrow a copy (or a training manual) and use it for a couple of hours. If it's something that's done physically and you can try it without risk, ask to try it (this works for things like making pizza and data entry, but it's not as successful for things like nuclear chemistry). If the environment you're studying is a technical one, ask a member of technical support or quality assurance to walk you through some typical tasks to see how they, as expert in-house users, do them.

In general, the more you know about the tasks your target audience does, the better you'll be able to interpret their behavior when you observe it.

Warning Be careful not to let your scenarios bias your observations. Use them as a framework to structure your interview, not to create expectations of how people do or don't behave in general.

Develop Scenarios

As part of your preparation, you should be explicit about your expectations. Attempt to write down how and when you expect the people you're observing to do certain things that are important to your product, and what attitudes you expect they will have toward certain elements. You can do this with other members of the development team, asking them to profile the specific actions you expect people to take in the same way that you profiled your audience's general behavior in Chapter 7. This will give you a platform against which you can compare their observed behavior.

When you're in the interview, keep these scenarios in mind while watching people. Keep an open mind about what you're seeing, and use the situations where observed behavior doesn't match your expectations as triggers for deeper investigation.

Practical Stuff

In addition to all the contextual inquiry–related preparation, there are a number of things you should do just because you're leaving the comfort of your office:

• Make a list of everything you're going to bring—every pencil, videotape, and notebook. Start the list a week before you're going to do your first interview. Then, whenever you realize there's something else you should bring, add it to the list. A day before the interview, make sure you have everything on the list (I put a check next to every item I have) and get everything you don't. On interview day, cross off everything as it's loaded into your backpack or car.

• If you're going to get releases (either to allow you to observe or for the participants to participate), make sure you have twice as many as you expect to need.

• Bring everything you need for the incentive payment. This could be a disbursement form from accounting, a check, or an envelope with cash. Blank receipt forms are useful, too (though some accounting departments will accept a participant release as proof of receipt of payment).

• Know how to operate your equipment. Set up a test site that will simulate the user's work environment ahead of time. A day or two before, set up everything as you're going to use it

Note Sometimes real-life situations unfold very differently from how you may have expected. You may be expecting to find one kind of situation—say, a typical day using the typical tools—and you find something completely different, a crisis where the main system is down or they're scrambling to meet an unexpected deadline. In such situations, pay attention to how the unexpected situation is resolved and compare that to the situation you had expected and that which others experience. If the situation is totally atypical—it happens only every five years or the people you're interviewing have been pulled into a job that doesn't relate to a task you're studying—try to get them to describe their normal routine, maybe in contrast to what they're doing at the moment. If the situation seems like it's too far off from what you're trying to accomplish, reschedule the interview for a time where their experience may be more relevant to your research goals.

onsite, complete with all cords plugged in, all tripods extended, all cameras running, and all laptops booted. Then break it down and set it back up again. Get a set of good headphones to check the quality of the audio. Good audio quality is the most important part of the video-recording process.

- Have more than enough supplies. Bring an extension cord, two extra videotapes, two extra pads of paper, and a couple of extra pens. You never know when a tape will jam or an interview ends up being so exciting that you go through two notepads. If you plan on using a laptop to take notes, make sure that you bring either extra batteries or an AC adapter (one will suffice).

- Make plans for meal breaks. Closely watching someone for several hours can be draining, and you don't want to run around an office frantically looking for a drinking fountain while worried that you're missing a key moment. Bring bottled water and plan to eat in between sessions, or have lunch with your participants, which can be a good opportunity to get background on their jobs in a less formal setting.

Conducting the Inquiry

One of the keys to getting good feedback in a contextual inquiry situation is establishing rapport with the participant. Since you want to watch him or her working as "naturally" as possible, it's important to set out expectations about each other's roles. Beyer and Holtzblatt define several kinds of relationships you can strive for.

- The *master/apprentice* model introduces you as the apprentice and the person who you'll be watching as the master. You learn his or her craft by watching. Occasionally, the apprentice can ask a question or the master can explain a key point, but the master's primary role is to do his or her job, narrating what he or she is doing while doing it (without having to think about it or explain why). This keeps the "master craftsman" focused on details, avoiding the generalizations that may gloss over key details that are crucial to a successful design.

- *Partnership* is an extension of the master/apprentice model where the interviewer partners with the participant in trying to extract the details of his or her work. The participant is made aware of the elements of his or her work that are normally invisible, and the partner discusses the fundamental assumptions behind the work, trying to bring problems and ways of working to the surface. The participant is occasionally invited to step back and comment about a certain action or statement and think about the reasons for his or her behavior. Although this can potentially alter the participant's behavior, it can also provide critical information at key points.

Beyer and Holtzblatt also point out several relationships to avoid.

- The *interviewer/interviewee.* Normally, an interviewee is prompted by an interviewer's questions into revealing information. Interviewees won't reveal details unless specifically asked. That's not the situation you want in a contextual inquiry situation. You want the participant's work and thoughts to drive the interview. When you find yourself acting as a journalist, prompting the participant before he or she says something, refocus the interview on the work.
- The *expert/novice.* Although you may be the expert in creating software for helping them, the participants are experts in their own domain. As Beyer and Holtzblatt suggest, "Set the customer's expectation correctly at the beginning by explaining that you are there to hear about and see their work because only they know their work practice. You aren't there to help them with problems or answer questions." They suggest that it should be clear that the goal is not to solve the problems then and there, but to know what the problems are and how they solve them on their own. If you are asked to behave as an expert, use nondirected interviewing techniques and turn the question around, "How would you expect it to print?"
- Don't be a *guest.* Your comfort should not be the focus of attention. You are there to understand how they do their work, not to bask in the light of their hospitality. Be sensitive to the protocol of the situation. If good manners dictate acting as a guest for the first few minutes of your visit, then do so to make the participants comfortable, but quickly encourage them to get on with their work and move into a more partnership-based dialogue.

• Another role to avoid is *big brother.* You are not there to evaluate or critique the performance of the people you are observing, and that should be clear. If they feel that way, then they're not likely to behave in typical ways. Moreover, if participation in your research is at the request of their managers, it can seem that this is a sneaky way to check up on them. Emphasize that you are not in a position to evaluate their performance. If possible, once you've gotten permission from management to do so, contact and schedule people yourself rather than having it come as a demand from above.

Inquiry Structure

The structure of the inquiry is similar to the structure of most interviews, except that the majority of it is driven by the interviewee's work rather than the interviewer's questions. The structure follows the general interview structure described in Chapter 6: introduction, warm-up, general issues, deep focus, retrospective, wrap-up.

The *introduction* and *warm-up* should be times for the participant and the interviewer to get comfortable with each other and to set up expectations for how the observation will proceed. This is the time to get all the nondisclosure forms signed, describe the project in broad detail, and set up the equipment. Check that the image and sound recording is good, and then don't fuss with the equipment again until the interview is over since it'll just distract people from their work. Describe the master/apprentice model and emphasize your role as an observer and learner. Remind the participant to narrate what he or she is doing and not to go for deep explanations.

Once you're in position, you may want to ask some *general questions* to gain an understanding of who the person is, what his or her job is, and what tasks he or she is going to be doing. Ask the participant to provide a description of a typical day: what kinds of things does he or she do regularly? What are occasional tasks? Where does today's task fit into a typical day? Don't delve too deeply into the reasons for what he or she does; concentrate on actions and the sequence.

This will begin the *main observation period.* This phase should comprise at least two-thirds of the interview. Most of the time should be spent observing what the participants are doing, what

Warning Sometimes management *may* want you to report on specific employees and their performance without telling them ahead of time that you'll be doing so. In such situations, explain the ethical problems with doing so—that it violates the confidentiality that your interview subject has placed with you—and that it may violate labor laws.

Note I'm using the word *action* to refer to a single operation during a task. In most cases, it's something that takes a couple of seconds and can be described with a single, simple idea. Actions are then grouped into *tasks,* which are things that satisfy a high-level goal. Task granularity can range all over the board. A task can involve something as straightforward as filling out a form or something as complex as picking out a car.

Warning Maintaining authenticity is a crucial part of observation. If you sense that the person you're watching is not doing a task in the way that they would do it if you were not watching, ask him or her about it. Ask whether how he or she is doing it is how it should be done, or how it is done. If the former, ask him or her to show you the latter even if it's "really messy."

tools they are using, and how they are using them. Begin by asking them to give a running description of what they're doing, as to an apprentice—just enough to tell the apprentice what's going on, but not enough to interrupt the flow of the work—and then tell them to start working. As an apprentice, you may occasionally ask for explanations, clarifications, or walk-throughs of actions, but don't let it drive the discussion. I find that taking occasional notes while spending most of my energy concentrating on their words and actions works well, but it requires me to watch the videotape to get juicy quotations and capture the subtlety of the interaction. Others recommend taking lots of notes onsite and using the videotape as backup. Regardless, you should have a clear method to highlight follow-up questions. I write them in a separate place from the rest of my notes.

When either the task is done or time is up, the main interview period is over. An immediate *follow-up interview* with in-depth questions can clarify a lot. Certain situations may not have been appropriate to interrupt (if you're observing a surgeon or a stock trader, that may apply to the whole observation period), whereas others may have brought up questions that would have interrupted the task flow. As much as possible, ask these while the participant's memory is still fresh. To jog people's memories, you can even rewind the videotape and show them the sequence you'd like them to describe in the viewfinder (but only do this if you can find it quickly since your time is better spent asking questions than playing with the camera). To quote Victoria Bellotti, senior scientist at Xerox PARC, "You'll never understand what's really going on until you've talked to people about what they are doing. The [follow-up] interview . . . gives you the rationale to make sense of things that might otherwise seem odd or insignificant." If there are too many questions for the time allotted, or if they're too involved, schedule another meeting to clarify them (and schedule it quickly, generally within one or two days of the initial interview since people's memories fade quickly).

Note Provide privacy when people need it. Tell the people you're observing to let you know if a phone call or meeting is private—or if information being discussed is secret—and that you'll stop observing until they tell you it's OK to start again. Pick a place to go in such a situation (maybe a nearby conference room or the cafeteria) and have them come and get you when they're finished.

Wrap-up the interview by asking the participant about the contextual inquiry experience from his or her perspective. Was there anything about it that made him or her anxious? Is there anything the participant would like to do differently? Are there things that you, as the apprentice, could do differently?

Beyer and Holtzblatt summarize the spirit of the interviewing process as follows:

> Running a good interview is less about following specific rules than it is about being a certain kind of person for the duration of the interview. The apprentice model is a good starting point for how to behave. The four principles of Contextual Inquiry modify the behavior to better get design data: *context,* go where the work is and watch it happen; *partnership,* talk about the work while it happens; *interpretation,* find the meaning behind the customer's words and actions; and *focus,* challenge your entering assumptions.

So what you want most is to come in unbiased and, with open eyes and ears, learn as much as you can about how the work is done while trying to find out why it is so.

What to Collect

There are four kinds of information you should pay attention to when observing people at work. Each of these elements can be improvised or formal, shared or used alone, specific or flexible.

- The *tools* they use. This can be a formal tool, such as a specialized piece of software, or it can be an informal tool, such as a scribbled note. Note whether the tools are being used as they're designed, or if they're being repurposed. How do the tools interact? What are the brands? Are the Post-its on the bezel of the monitor or on the outside flap of the Palm Pilot?
- The *sequences* in which actions occur. The order of actions is important in terms of understanding how the participant is thinking about the task. Is there a set order that's dictated by the tools or by office culture? When does the order matter? Are there things that are done in parallel? Is it done continuously, or simultaneously with another task? How do interruptions affect the sequence?
- Their *methods* of organization. People cluster some information for convenience and some out of necessity. The clustering may be shared between people, or it may be unique to the individual being observed. How does the target audience organize the

information elements they use? By importance? If so, how is importance defined? By convenience? Is the order flexible?

- What *kinds of interactions* they have. What are the important parties in the transfer of knowledge? Are they people? Are they processes? What kinds of information are shared (what are the inputs and outputs)? What is the nature of the interaction (informational, technical, social, etc.)?

The influences of all four of these things will, of course, be intertwined, and sometimes it may be hard to unravel the threads. The participant may be choosing a sequence for working on data, or the organization of the data may force a certain sequence. Note the situations where behaviors may involve many constraints. These are the situations you can clarify with a carefully placed question or during the follow-up interview.

Artifacts

Artifacts are—for the purposes of contextual inquiry—the nondigital tools people use to help them accomplish the tasks they're trying to do. Documenting and collecting people's artifacts can be extremely enlightening. For example, if you're interested in how people schedule, it may be appropriate to photograph their calendars to see what kinds of annotations they make, or to videotape them using the office whiteboard that serves as the group calendar. If you're interested in how they shop for food, you may want to collect their shopping lists and videotape them at the supermarket picking out items. It's doubtful that you'd want to collect a surgeon's instruments after an operation, but you may want a record of how they're arranged. Having a digital camera with a large storage capacity can really help artifact collection and digital pictures of artifacts, and how people use them can make great illustrations in reports and presentations.

Always make sure to get permission when you copy or collect artifacts.

Here is a snippet of the notes from an observation of a health insurance broker using an existing online system to create an RFP (request for proposal):

Looks at paper [needs summary] form for coverage desired. Circles coverage section with pen.

Goes to Plan Search screen.

Opens "New Search" window.

"I know I want a 90/70 with a 5/10 drug, but I'm going to get all of the 90/70 plans no matter what."

Types in plan details without looking back at form.

Looks at search results page.

Points at top plan: "Aetna has a 90/70 that covers chiro, so I'm looking at their plan as a benchmark, which is enough to give me an idea of what to expect from the RFP."

Clicks on Aetna plan for full details.

Prints out plan details on printer in hall (about three cubes away) using browser Print button. Retrieves printout and places it on top of needs summary form.

Would like to get details on similar recent quotes.

Goes back to search results. Scrolls through results and clicks on Blue Shield plan.

Video Recording

I recommend videotaping every contextual inquiry (in fact, every interview you have, period) since it provides an inexpensive record that allows for more nuanced analysis than any other method. Some key events happen only once. Notes take the interviewer/moderator/observer's attention away from the participants and may not be able to capture all the details that make the event important. Two-person teams can be intimidating, and require two skilled people to be present for all interviews. Audio recording doesn't record body language or facial expressions, which can add vital information to what people really think and feel. Only video can approach the full experience of being there. At worst, it's no worse than audio; at best, it's much better.

However, recording good interviews on video takes some practice, especially when working in the field. The twin dragons that can keep you from a good recording are *insufficient light* and *noisy sound*.

(Continued)

- *Light.* Most video cameras aren't as sensitive as human eyes, so a room that looks perfectly fine to the human eye can be too dark for a run-of-the-mill video camera. When there's not enough light, you don't capture the details of the environment. Fortunately, recent generations of consumer cameras have enough low-light sensitivity to be useful in all but the dimmest environments. If you anticipate having to tape in a dark environment, try to find a camera that can work in 2 lux or less. This will give you enough sensitivity that even things in partial shadow can be videotaped. Be aware of different light levels and the way your camera compensates for them. A bright computer monitor in a dim room can cause the camera to make the rest of the image too dark. A picture window onto a sunny day can cause everything inside a room to appear in shadow. Many cameras can compensate for these situations but need to be set appropriately.
- *Sound.* The hum of a computer fan. The hiss of an air conditioner. Laughing from the cafeteria next door. It's amazing what ends up recorded instead of what you wanted. Good sound is probably the most technically important part of the whole recording process. Getting it can be tricky. Most video cameras have omnidirectional microphones that pick up a broad arc of sound in front (and sometimes behind) the camera. This is great for taping the family at Disney World, but not so great when you're trying to isolate a participant's voice from the background noise. Get a camera with a good built-in microphone, an external microphone jack, and a headphone jack. Get a decent set of headphones, plug them into the headphone jack, and walk around with the camera, listening to how it picks up sound. Then, when you're onsite, adjust the camera with the headphones to minimize how much external noise it picks up. You may have to do this at the cost of getting a good image, or you may have to get an external directional microphone and mount it separately. If worse comes to worst, you can use an external lapel microphone on a long cord. Keep the headphones attached to the camera throughout the interview and discreetly check the audio quality every once in a while.

Even the best equipment is sometimes insufficient or superfluous. Some situations are impossible or awkward to videotape. In others, you can't get permission. In those cases, audio recordings can often be used, but they carry only part of the information and tend to be more labor intensive to analyze. Use audio recording when you can, but be prepared to fall back on paper and pen.

How to Analyze Contextual Inquiry Data

The output from Contextual Inquiry is not a neat hierarchy; rather, it is narratives of successes and breakdowns, examples of use that entail context, and messy use artifacts.
—Dave Hendry, Assistant Professor, University of Washington Information School, personal email

How data should be interpreted should differ based on the task under examination. Contextual inquiry helps you understand how people solve problems, how they create meaning, and what their unfulfilled needs are. It does this largely through six methods.

- Understanding the *mental models* people build. People don't like black boxes. They don't like the unknown. They want to understand how something works in order to be able to predict what it will do. When the operation of a process or tool isn't apparent, people create their own model for it. This model helps them explain the results they see and frames their expectations of how it will behave in the future. This model may have nothing to do with the actual functionality of the tool, but if it matches their experience, then it's the one they're going to use. Knowing the model being used allows you to capitalize on that understanding and meet people's expectations.
- Understanding the *tools* they use. Since you're building a tool that's supposed to replace the tools people use now, it's important to know what those tools are and how they're used. Rather than leisurely browsing a catalog as you would expect them to do, they may just check the specials page and let an online comparison engine find the cheapest price. They may keep addresses in a Palm Pilot, a carefully organized address book, or they may just have a pocketful of scribbled-on scraps of paper. Maybe your competition isn't Outlook or the Day-timer, but napkins!
- Understanding the *terminology* they use to describe what they do. Words reveal a lot about people's models and thought processes. When shopping for food, people may talk in terms of meals, calories, or food groups. They may use one ("bread") to represent another ("carbohydrates") or misuse technical terminology (using "drivetrain" to talk about a car's suspension, for example). Paying attention to the words people use and the way they use them can reveal a lot about their thought patterns.
- Understanding their *methods*. The flow of work is important to understanding what people's needs are and where existing tools are failing them. Unraveling the approach people take to solving a task reveals a lot about the strengths and weaknesses

of the tools they use. If someone composes a message in a word processor and then cuts and pastes it into an email program, that says something about how he or she perceives the strengths of each product. If he or she is scribbling URLs on a pad while looking through a search engine, it says something about the weaknesses of the search engine and the browser and something about the strength of paper.

- Understanding their *goals*. Every action has a reason. Understanding why people perform certain actions reveals an underlying structure to their work that they may not be aware of themselves. Although a goal may seem straightforward ("I need to find and print a TV listing for tonight"), the reasons behind it may reveal a lot about the system people are using ("I want to watch *The Simpsons* at eastern time so that I can go bowling when it's on normally, but I don't know which satellite it's going to be on and there's no way to search the on-screen guide like you can search the Web site").

- Understanding their *values*. People's value systems are part of their mental model. We're often driven by our social and cultural contexts as much as by our rational decisions. What is the context for the use of these tools? Are they chosen solely because of their functionality, or do other factors apply? Is the brand important? (If so, why? What qualities do they associate with it? Are they aware of other brands that do the same thing?) Do they work in the context of others who use the same tools? If so, why does the group do things the way it does?

There are several ways to do a full analysis of the data you collect. Beyer and Holtzblatt recommend what they call the *affinity diagram* method (which is loosely patterned on the technique of the same name pioneered by Jiro Kawakita and known in the industrial quality management world as a *KJ diagram*). This method creates a hierarchy of all the observations, clustering them into trends. A paraphrased version of their method is as follows (see Chapter 9 of *Contextual Design* for a complete description of their method):

1. Watch the observation videotapes to create 50–100 notes from each 2-hour interview (longer interviews will produce more notes, though probably not in proportion to the length

of the interview). Notes are singular observations about tools, sequences, interactions, mental models—anything. Number the notes and identify the user whose behavior inspired it (they recommend using numbers rather than names: U1, U2, U3, etc.). Randomize them.

2. Get a group of people together in a room with a blank wall, a large window, or a big whiteboard. Beyer and Holtzblatt recommend 1 person per 100 notes. Preferably, these are members of the development team. By making the development team do the analysis, a group understanding of the customer's needs is formed, consensus is built, and everyone is up to speed at the same time. Have them block out the whole day for the work. The whole affinity analysis should be done in a single day.

3. Divide the group into pairs of analysts. Give each pair an equal number of notes (ideally, each pair should have 100–200 notes).

4. Write a note on a yellow Post-it (yes, *yellow;* Beyer and Holtzblatt are very specific about Post-it colors) and put it on the wall/window/board.

5. Tell the groups to put notes that relate to that note around it one at a time. It doesn't matter how the notes relate, just as long as the group feels they relate.

6. If no more notes relate to a given note cluster, put a blue note next to the group. Write a label on the blue note, summarizing and naming the cluster. They recommend avoiding technical terminology in the labels and using simple phrasing to state "the work issue that holds all the individual notes together."

7. Repeat the process with the other notes, labeling groups in blue as they occur.

8. Try to keep the number of yellow notes per blue group between two and four. One note cannot be a group, and often groups of more than four notes can be broken into smaller clusters. However, there's no upper bound on how many notes may be in a group if there's no obvious way to break it up.

9. As the groups accumulate, they recommend using pink notes to label groups of blue notes, and green notes to label groups of pink notes.

Eventually, you run out of yellow notes, and the group of analysts reaches a consensus about which notes belong in which group and how to label the blue, pink, and green notes (Figure 8.1). At that point, you have a hierarchical diagram that shows, to quote Beyer and Holtzblatt, "every issue in the work and everything about it the team has learned so far, all tied to real instances."

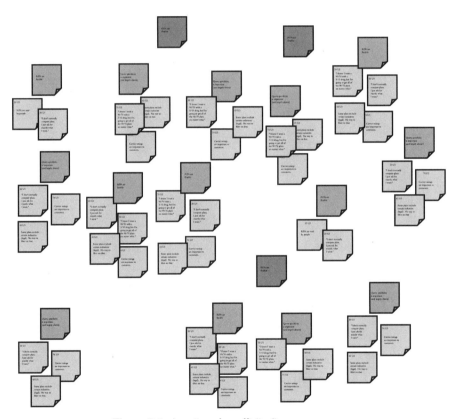

Figure 8.1 A portion of an affinity diagram.

The insurance broker observation might produce an affinity diagram with the following fragments:

RFPs are tools that collect most of the information

RFPs are flexible

RFPs are read by people. (note 35, U2)

"I don't normally compare plans. I just ask for exactly what I want." (note 20, U1)

. . .

Plan comparisons provide critical information

Query specificity is important (and largely absent)

"I know I want a 90/70 with a 5/10 drug, but I'm going to get all the 90/70 plans no matter what." (note 55, U2)

Some plans exclude certain industries (legal). No way to filter on that. (note 43, U3)

Carrier ratings are important to customers. (note 74, U3)

Query output requires a lot of filtering

"Most of my time is fishing for information." (note 26, U1)

In addition to the affinity diagram method, it's also possible to do a more traditional kind of analysis based on an expert reading of the data. The observers can all meet and discuss their observations and hypothesize about how those observations are linked and what they mean. Although not as rigorous, this process can cut through voluminous data (which the Post-it process often produces) and create workable models that adequately describe people's behavior and attitudes. It's also a process that can be done by a lone researcher if the development team is unavailable. However, the affinity diagram process is recommended, when possible, because of the benefits it provides in communicating people's needs to the development team and getting maximum use out of the collected data.

Building Models

In many situations, this will be enough to begin building models of where the unmet needs are and how solutions can be made to fit with people's existing work practices. Beyer and Holtzblatt define five models that can be extracted from the information in the affinity diagram: flow models, sequence models, artifact models, physical models, and cultural models.

- *Flow models* are representations of "the communication between people to get work done." They show what information, knowledge, and artifacts get passed among the members of the development team. Their elements can be formal or informal, written or verbal. They seek to capture the interaction, strategy, roles, and informal structures within the communication that happens in a product's life cycle.
- *Sequence models* represent "the steps by which work is done, the triggers that kick off a set of steps, and the intents that are being accomplished." They show the order that things are done, what causes ("triggers") certain steps, the purpose ("intent") of each step, and how they depend on each other. They are sufficiently detailed to allow the team to understand, step by step, how a task is accomplished.
- *Artifact models* represent how people use real-world tools to accomplish their goals. Starting with a simple photograph, drawing, or photocopy of the object, artifact models "extend the information on the artifact to show structure, strategy, and intent." They provide insight into the tools people use, how

they use them, what problems they have, and most important, why they're necessary.

- *Physical models* represent the actual physical environment that users do their work in. They provide an understanding of the layout of the workspace, the artifacts in the workspace, what controls people have (and don't have) over their environment, and how they use their environments to get work done.

- *Cultural models* represent an understanding of the users' values and how they see themselves. It places the product in the context of the users' lives and the real-world environment in which they live. It includes both the formal organization of their experience—their other responsibilities, the competitive climate—and the informal—the emotions associated with the work, the work environment, the users' esthetic values and style, and so on.

Producing Results

In many cases, the "Aha!" moments come either during the actual observation or in the affinity diagram creation phase. The aha! may be sufficient to turn the conceptualization of a product around and provide enough information so that product-specific (as opposed to problem-specific) research such as focus groups and paper prototyping can begin.

It's never good to jump to conclusions, but even if time is scarce, the results of the research should be consolidated into a document that sets out your understanding of the audience and compares it to the assumptions and scenarios you had at the beginning. Consisting of your thoughts about your users' mental models, tools, terminology, and goals, this document can serve as a "statement of understanding" that drives other research and feeds into the research goals as a whole. Return to it after every additional piece of user information is obtained, and attempt to understand the new information in light of the statement. If the new information is contradictory or confusing, it may be time to repeat the research with a new group of people.

If you have more time and resources to look at the information you've collected, do so. The data can provide a rich and subtle understanding of the mental models and task flows people use in

Note Frequency does not equate to importance. Just because something happens often doesn't mean that it's more important to the design of a system than something that happens rarely. For example, most people observed may keep paper notes of a certain transaction, and they may do it several times a day. Although this is a prevalent problem, it may not be as important as the half hour they spend browsing through new documents because the search engine isn't up to date. The paper notes may get used often and are clearly compensating for a deficiency in the product, but maybe they represent a solution that's tolerable for the users. This makes them a less important issue than the search system, which is a problem for which they have no good solution at all.

doing their work. Beyer and Holtzblatt spend a good deal of their book discussing just how to do this.

Task Analysis

The primary purpose of task analysis is to compare the demands of the system on the operator with the capabilities of the operator, and if necessary, to alter those demands, thereby reducing error and achieving successful performance.
—B. Kirwan and L.K. Ainsworth in *A Guide to Task Analysis*

There are a number of techniques that fall under the definition of task analysis. They range from structured, standardized questionnaires to unstructured interviews with usability experts. For this book, I use the definition that I believe to be the most common, that task analysis is a structured method of hierarchically analyzing a single task in order to understand the interaction of its components.

This means that it's quite closely associated with contextual inquiry, and in fact, the data for it can be collected during a contextual inquiry process. It differs from that procedure in its degree of focus. While contextual inquiry attempts to understand the entire context that surrounds and informs a task, task analysis focuses on the task itself. What is the exact order of things? What are the tools involved? Where is there flexibility in the process? What kinds of information do people need and use at various parts of the task?

When Task Analysis Is Appropriate

Task analysis is best used when you already know what problem you're trying to solve and you want to know how people are solving it right now. This generally falls in the examination phase of a spiral development process or the requirements-gathering phase of a waterfall process. It requires that you know what the task is and, roughly, who your audience is. Although it *can* be done when there's already a solution of some sort under consideration, it should ideally be done before effort has been invested in features and technologies since it's likely to induce a lot of revision in the fundamental assumptions of how solutions should be implemented.

So if you've already decided that you're going to be selling supermarket-style groceries online, but you haven't yet built the ordering system, now would be a good time to find out how a grocery shopper picks out groceries. Again, you'll be looking for many of the same things as contextual inquiry: tools, sequences, organizations, interactions. But whereas that process investigates the decision-making process people go through in determining what they're going to eat, how they're going to get it, where they're going to get it, and so forth, task analysis will concentrate solely on the task of buying groceries in a supermarket.

In addition, although it can reveal places for interaction with advertising or promotion, the goal-oriented nature of the analysis makes the process better at uncovering opportunities for improving usability rather than promotion or advertising (Table 8.2). That said, there's still much untapped potential in the technique that can produce interesting results when applied to the domain of the entire user experience rather than just their immediate pragmatic goals.

Timing	Activity
$t - 2$ weeks	Organize and schedule participants.
t	Begin interviews.
$t + 1$ week	Complete interviews. Review videotapes and take notes.
$t + 2$ weeks	Begin results analysis.
$t + 4$ weeks	Complete results analysis. Present to development team. Distribute documentation.

How to Do Task Analysis

The form of task analysis described here is a somewhat relaxed combination of the two methods described as *decomposition methods* and *hierarchical task analysis (HTA)* in Kirwan and Ainsworth's *A Guide to Task Analysis.*

Preparation

The preparation for task analysis is almost identical to that of contextual inquiry. You need to pick a target audience, recruit them, and schedule them. You need to plan for the interview by learning the domain and to develop scenarios about how you feel the task will commence. Finally, you need to be organized in the way that you conduct the interview so that you have enough supplies, the right equipment, and the knowledge to use it.

Gathering the Information

The work published in Kirwan and Ainsworth's book was done before the advent of the Web, and it concentrates on installed software and the issues surrounding it. So although they discuss starting with published information and experts as sources for uncovering the actions that make up a task flow, you won't often find such sources for most Web-related work. Moreover, what's important is not how people are supposed to do their work, but how they actually do it. In Kirwan and Ainsworth's task domain, nuclear power and nuclear chemistry, safety requires that people follow the stated rules much more rigorously than for just about any other field. In modern software environments, direct observation is again the basis for data collection.

The interview format is much the same as contextual inquiry: the interviewer acts as an apprentice to the person performing the task, watching as the participant does the task and explains key elements. The apprentice watches and attempts to understand the nuances of the task, eliciting occasional explanations of motivations and options.

Where it differs from contextual inquiry is in terms of focus. Everything should be geared toward understanding how the participant performs the task at hand.

- What do they see as the options at any given point?
- What are the tools available?
- How do they choose one over the other?
- Where do they change their minds?
- How variable is the process?

- Where do they make mistakes? What are common mistakes?
- What causes the mistakes, and how are they corrected?
- What are the inputs to the process? The outputs?
- What is the frequency and importance of the tasks they perform?
- What are the risks of failure?

The kinds of information gathered should be similarly structured and focused as contextual inquiry, but with extra emphasis on sequence information and the exact tools used.

Here's a snippet of the notes from a session observing an interior designer picking out a couch (for an online furniture-buying tool).

"I get out my catalogs. I go to [manufacturer A] first, unless it's for a waiting room, then I go to [manufacturer B]. I have a big shelf of catalogs. Recently, I've been getting on the Internet, but I get better results on the catalogs. Hard to find things. Each Web site is so different, it takes time to find your way through the Web site."

Gets four catalogs: A, B, C, D. Gets the [B] catalog. Looks in index for "couch," flips to couch section.

"I usually find a couple of options and weigh cost, availability, delivery, if there's something similar I've seen. You can't tell color from pictures, and they're often slow about getting fabric swatches. I talk to sales reps on the phone and try to get as complete a picture as I can. Some of the companies we don't do so much business with will come in and also try to sell me other stuff."

Marks several sofas with small notepads, in preparation to call the manufacturer about fabric/color availability.

"I know I can get this one pretty fast since I've gotten a couple before, but I'm not sure if they can offer it in the fabric we want. I'll make a note to ask about it. Sometimes they can make it out of a different fabric even if they don't officially offer it in that, but it depends."

(Continued)

"I total it all up. This is what we need, and this is what it will cost, and this is how long it'll take to get it made, assuming they have the fabric in stock. I'll fill out purchase requisitions, going through the catalog and picking out the options I want. I put together a description for the client. Project explanation, list of things to buy, schedules, and so on. I may not have time to explain it all to the client, so I have to make sure the write-up is clear enough."

"Different vendors offer different warranties. I don't shop for warranties, though, I shop for matches and manufacturing time. Cost is important, too, but once the client has signed off on a budget, that limits your options right there."

Prepares to call vendor.

How to Analyze Results

Task decomposition and *hierarchical task analysis* are complementary techniques. One describes the inputs, outputs, and triggers for the actions in a task while the other arranges the actions into a coherent flow. The order in which these two techniques are used depends on the primary needs. If you're mostly interested in how the components of a task fit together (for example, if you're looking for where a tool can optimize a task's speed), then start with HTA and flesh out key details with decomposition. If you're interested in making a tool that fits with existing practice, then start with decomposition and put the pieces back together in a hierarchical form.

Break the Task Apart (Task Decomposition)

Task decomposition is the process of breaking the task into its component actions. This is easier said than done. If someone is operating a control panel with a bunch of buttons and dials, then every time he or she presses a button or reads a dial, it's an action. But when that same person is shopping for a new car, the decomposition is more difficult since the steps taken—the choices, the capitulations, the comparisons—aren't nearly as obvious. In such situations, encourage the participant to speak all of his or her thoughts aloud and prompt him or her for explanations of specific actions.

Keep the end goal in mind since this will help you pick out the most relevant aspects of each action. If you have a specific tool or solution in mind, you can emphasize one or the other in your decomposition. Sometimes you can work backward from the solution you have in mind to the problem people are facing to see if one matches the other.

Describe each action. Kirwan and Ainsworth list several dozen categories that have been used to describe various facets of an action. Some common ones include

- *Purpose.* Why is this action here? How does it move the task toward its goal?
- *Cues.* What tells the person that it's time to perform this action?
- *Objects.* What does the action operate on?
- *Method.* What is the action?
- *Options.* What other actions are available at this point? How did this action get chosen?

While you're describing the actions, do some error projection. Ask what would happen if the action weren't done or if there were an error. If there are enough actions with interesting error conditions, you can even make errors a separate category you use to describe each action.

For each action, provide answers in as many of these categories as you can. Often the process of describing an action will create questions and inspire new interpretation, so it can be useful to walk through the decomposition a couple of times to make sure that it's consistent and thorough.

Here is a snippet of the furniture-buying decomposition.

Prepare for decomposition by determining the categories that are likely going to be useful ahead of time and then creating forms that you fill out as you observe. That way, you know what information you have about each action and what else you need. In situations where there are a lot of actions in every task or they come quickly, this can be a pretty daunting method of working. In such situations, it may be better to observe the task closely and decompose it into its components later.

Action Name	Purpose	Cues	Objects	Method	Options
List requirements	Clarify choice categories		Word template: size (h,w), color, budget, style notes	Talk to client	
Get available catalogs	List available options		Catalogs, requirements list	Compare options in catalogs with requirements	
Set order for catalog perusal	Start with best-known/best-chance manufacturers	Knowledge of vendor's options	Catalogs, requirements list	Flip through catalogs, comparing options with requirements	Go to A first, unless it's a waiting room, then B
Mark items in catalog	Get primary candidates		Catalogs, requirements list	Visual inspection and comparison to list	
Mark items that need follow-up	Separate items for further investigation	When it's not clear whether all options are available for a specific item	Catalogs, marked items	Visual inspection and comparison to list	
Investigate marked items	Complete list of available options based on requirements	List of items for further investigation	Catalogs, list of items needing follow-up	Call reps	
Total options	Make final list for client	All follow-up is completed	Completed options template, budget template, requirements list	Fill out budget template with options and costs	

Guerilla Task Decomposition

In many situations, it's not practical to do this level of task decomposition because of resource or time constraints. In such situations, you can use a more informal version of this process. Use the basic ideas of task decomposition, but instead of going all the way to the atomic task and filling out all the facets, concentrate on larger ideas and use only the facets that you think are most important. If after several interviews, you feel that you can write down the basic tasks, do so on Post-its, create some preliminary organization, and flow with them. Then, as you interview more people, you can adjust these to fit your new information. This is not as thorough of a process, but it can be a lot faster.

Put It Back Together (Hierarchical Task Analysis)

HTA consists of taking the individual actions that make up a task, putting them in a hierarchy, and creating rules for how to move through the hierarchy. The final product is a flowchart that details the sequence that leads up to every action, the choices that are made, and the consequences of actions.

HTA doesn't have to be done following task decomposition. It's possible to do hierarchical task analysis by just sitting down after having interviewed and observed users doing a task. The procedure is a top-down analysis method, which is essentially a formalization of the process that interaction developer, information architects, and technical writers go through when they stand up at a whiteboard and try to understand how something is done.

1. Start with a goal. This can be the person's ultimate goal ("Furnish the house"), but abstract end goals often require analysis that's too involved for straightforward task analysis. You may want to start with something more direct ("Get list of available couches") and work down from there.
2. Determine the subgoals for that goal. Subgoals are all the things that have to happen before the main goal can be met. For example, if your goal is to get a list of available couches, you may need to get a list of couches from the catalogs and a list of couches that are not listed (or unavailable) from furniture company representatives. You should rarely have more than three or four subgoals for every goal. If you do, you may

want to create a couple of intermediate goals that will sub-sume several of the intermediate tasks.

3. Determine how those actions have to be arranged and create a plan for how they flow together. This includes determining which ones have to follow which others, which are optional, which can be swapped out for each other, and so forth. When goals don't have a natural flow, pick one that seems to work and adjust it later if it turns out to be awkward.

4. Repeat the decomposition with each goal and subgoal until you are down to individual actions.

The end result is a diagram in the familiar "boxes and arrows" style, where a single goal has been turned into a goal tree, with all the subcomponents of every goal beneath it and linked to it, creating a procedure for accomplishing that goal (Figure 8.2).

When you've formally decomposed a task, the procedure is nearly identical, except rather than making up the list of goals and relationships on the fly, you use the ones that you've extracted from your interviews. The procedure to do this is a bottom-up method similar to the way an affinity diagram is created in contextual inquiry.

1. Start by ordering and clustering actions into groups that are all associated with the same result. Actions that occur in parallel are optional or are alternatives for each other and should be labeled as such.

2. Label the clusters with the results. These are the subgoals.

3. Order and cluster the subgoals in terms of what ends they achieve.

4. Label these clusters. These are the goals.

5. Repeat until all the actions have been clustered and all the clusters have been ordered and labeled.

6. Create a diagram by organizing the subgoal clusters underneath the goal clusters and linking these with arrows that show how goals are related to their subgoals.

This procedure produces diagrams identical to Figure 8.2.

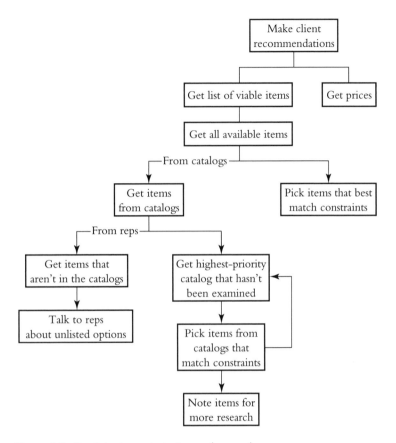

Figure 8.2 Couch-buying analysis diagram (segment).

Checking for Diagram Validity

Once you have your diagram, you can check it for validity and completeness using a technique mutated from the *function analysis system technique* (FAST, also described in Kirwan and Ainsworth).

- The boxes in the chain *above* a given box in the hierarchy answer the question *"Why do I _____?"* where _____ is what's written in the box. So using the example, when asking "Why do I talk to reps about unlisted options?" the diagram answers "Because you need to know what items are available that aren't in the catalog so that you can make a complete list of all available items to make a list of viable options for the client recommendation."

(Continued)

- Boxes *below* a given box answer the question *"How do I _____?"* So asking the question "How do I get items from a catalog?" is answered by "Find the highest-priority catalog that hasn't been examined and pick items from it while noting down which ones require more research."
- Items with arrows only go in one direction (generally "how"). If you can answer both of the above questions for every box, your diagram is complete.

When you've completed a task analysis diagram, walk through it with a few people who know the task to make sure that it matches their experience and that the sequences, tasks, and goals are familiar to them from their experience.

Granted, this particular method can be time consuming and may be unable to capture the subtlety of certain tasks, but it forces deep consideration of the task that can reveal the true nature of underlying processes and can disentangle complex interactions. It's much easier to create a product that works the way that people do when you've understood how they behave. Task analysis provides a specific framework for matching people's existing behavior and satisfying their immediate needs. Moreover, it can demonstrate weaknesses and redundancies in the product since it had been described before the analysis was done: there may be tasks people are trying to accomplish that the product was not originally envisioned to assist in, or there may be inefficiencies in the way that people currently perform their tasks that the product can streamline.

The task analysis diagram, if accurate, allows developers to have a consistent road map and a thorough checklist of everything that the product needs to do (the list of goals) and the order in which it needs to be done (the task flow).

Card Sorting

Card sorting is a technique that's used to uncover how people organize information and how they categorize and relate concepts.

When Card Sorting Should Be Done

Card sorting is best done when you know what kind of information needs to be organized, but before an organizational solution has been implemented. It is usually done after the product purpose, the audience, and the features have been established, but before an information architecture or design has been developed, putting it somewhere in the middle of the design process. This differentiates it from contextual inquiry and task analysis, which both come at the beginning of the development process.

In addition, since it's a fast and easy technique, it can be used whenever you change your information structure or want to add elements to an existing structure.

The Card Sorting Process

Preparation

The goal is to get perspective on how your intended audience understands your proposed information space. So unlike other techniques, there aren't any additional constraints on the kinds of people you should invite, other than recruiting people who fit into your target audience. Typically, recruiting between four and ten people from that audience will give you a good perspective on organizing the information.

Schedule people one at a time so that the participants don't feel pressured to compete. You can schedule several people simultaneously if you have facilities where they can sit quietly and if there is someone nearby who can answer questions (though if you have only one person as a monitor, stagger the schedules about every 15 minutes so that the monitor has time to give each participant an introduction to the technique). An hour is more than sufficient for most card sorting studies.

Getting the Cards Together

The core of the card sorting process is, not surprisingly, the cards. On a deck of sturdy identical note cards, write the names of the things that you want to organize (or use a word processor mail merge and print on mailing labels that you then stick to index cards). These can be the names of specific sections, terms you're considering using, concepts behind the various sections of your site, images that you want to use, or even descriptions of individual pages. Use identical cards, except for the text, to minimize distraction.

You can have as few or as many cards as you want, though the size of a standard card deck (52) strikes a good balance between not providing enough cards to make adequate categories and providing so many that it's overwhelming. If you have hundreds of categories that you would like to try this technique on, consider breaking them up into more manageable chunks and doing multiple sets of tests.

The words on the cards should reflect what you're trying to test. If you're trying to uncover how people organize concepts, explain the concepts on the cards with a sentence or two. However, if you're trying to see how people understand a set of titles without necessarily knowing your definitions for them, you can just write the titles on the cards.

The Sort!

After bringing the participant in and going through all the initial formalities, introduce him or her to the concept. Say something along the lines of this.

> This is a stack of cards. Each card has something that you might see on the Web site. I'd like you to organize them into groups that make sense to you. Take as much time as you need. There are no right or wrong groupings. Try to organize all the cards, but not everything needs to belong in a group. You won't have to provide a reason why cards belong in the same group, so if a group feels right, go with it. Focus on what makes sense to you, not what may make sense to anyone else.

Provide a stack of Post-it notes, several pens, and a pile of small binder clips or rubber bands. After they're done grouping, ask them to label the groups if they can, but not every group necessarily needs a label (don't tell them that they'll be labeling ahead of time since that tends to bias people to organize based on labels rather than on what they feel are natural groupings). When they're done, ask them to clip or rubber-band the cards and place the label on the groupings.

Finally, ask them to organize the groupings into larger groups without moving any cards from one group to another, naming the larger groups, if any names come to mind. Then, with larger binder clips or rubber bands, bind the metagroups together and wrap up the session.

Card Sort Analysis

There are two ways to analyze the output from card sorting, a formal way and an informal way.

The Informal Way

When you have the clusters from all the participants, look at them. Copy the clusters to a whiteboard. By eyeballing the trends in the clusters, you can infer how people intuitively understand the relationships between the various elements. For example, if people put "News," "About us," and "What we like" together, it tells you they're interested in putting all the information coming from your perspective into a single place. However, if they group "News" with "Latest Deals" and "Holiday Gift Guide," then maybe they associate all the information that's timely together. The difference between these two can mean the difference between an information architecture that matches its users' expectations and one that forces them to hunt for information.

You can look at the clusters as a whole or follow one card at a time through the participants' groups to see the kinds of groupings it's put into. Don't treat the clusters literally. People's existing organizations may not make a scalable or functional architecture. Instead, look at them for the underlying themes that tie them together. Pay attention to the cards that people didn't categorize or that were categorized differently by everyone. What about the card is giving people trouble? Is it the name? Is it the underlying concept? Is it the relationship to other elements?

When you've gone through all the clusters produced by all the participants and listed all the themes, go through the names they've assigned to the groups. Looking at the labeling and the labels' relationships to the clusters underneath, you should have the basis for creating an architecture that's close to how your user base expects the information to be organized (and even if it's not used by the information architect, the terminology can be useful to marketing when they're explaining the product to potential clients).

The Formal Way

Cluster analysis is a branch of statistics that measures the "distance" between items in a multivariate environment and attempts to find groupings that are close together in the variable space. This is exactly what a whiteboard-based card sorting analysis does, but it's a mathematical way to do it thoroughly and consistently. It allows you to uncover groups of objects that are similar across many dimensions, but may not be obviously alike in any one of those dimensions. Since people have trouble visualizing things in more than three dimensions, and there are often more than three variables that can determine similarity, the technique is used to "see" clusters that would have otherwise gone undiscovered.

The classic example of cluster analysis is from marketing research, and it's the grouping of target markets. People are different in many ways: their age, their income, their race, where they live, their gender, what they buy, and so on. Picking out groups along any one of these axes is relatively straightforward, but picking out clusters along all of them is much more difficult. How do you define a yuppie? Do they all drive Land Rovers? No, some drive BMWs, and some people who drive Land Rovers aren't yuppies. Do they all make $120K per year? No, some may make $30K and live as if they made $120K. Figuring out the clusters in society is hard, but cluster analysis can often extract useful distinctions.

In terms of card sorting, it works in reverse. It's used to find the underlying variables by looking at the clusters people make. Are certain things grouped together more often than other things? Are there hidden relationships between certain cards? These are all things that are hard to see by just looking at the cards.

Unfortunately, the mathematics of cluster analysis is nontrivial and can't be easily done without a computer. Statistical packages such as SAS and Statistica contain modules that can do cluster analysis, but these are expensive and require an understanding of the statistical procedures used in the analysis.

Fortunately, there is a piece of software that is designed specifically to do cluster analysis for card sorting data and is, as of summer 2002, free. IBM's User Involvement Group made EZSort available to the usability research community in 1999, and it's made the process of analyzing card sorting much easier. The program takes as input the groups created by the participants and produces tree graphs that show the relationship between groups of cards, revealing clusters of cards and clusters of clusters. These diagrams make it much easier to separate strong, common affinities from casual similarities and to see larger themes that would have been difficult to see through a haze of cards and groupings.

As of fall 2002, it's available from

http://www-3.ibm.com/ibm/easy/eou_ext.nsf/Publish/410

The process of using it is straightforward: the names of all the cards and participants are entered into the program, then each person's clusters are re-created in the software by dragging the card names into piles; the names for the clusters are associated with these virtual piles, and the software is run. It produces a diagram that represents the relationship between all the items using a tree diagram (Figure 8.3). The more distant one "branch" is from another, the less related they are.

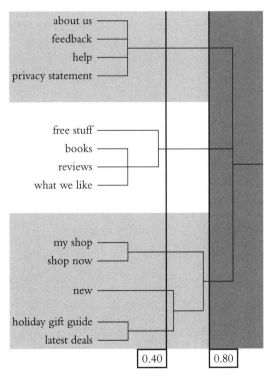

Figure 8.3 EZSort diagram for a typical shopping site.

Note For more information on EZSort, see the documentation or the paper by Jianming Dong, Shirley Martin, and Paul Waldo that can also be found at *http://www-3.ibm. com/ibm/easy/eou_ext.nsf/ Publish/410/$File/EZSort Paper.pdf*

This diagram shows that information about the company strongly clusters (the tree at the very top of the diagram), which likely means that people expect all that information to be in the same place (or at least treated in the same way). Likewise, general product information such as recommendation, reviews, and "free stuff" are all considered similar in some way, with "free stuff" being a bit less similar to the others in the same group. The other elements also form smaller clusters. The two vertical lines represent "threshold" for membership—how close items must be in order to be grouped together—with the number below each one representing the calculated affinity that the line represents.

Card Sorting to Prioritize

Although card sorting is primarily an organization or naming technique, variations of it can also be used for other purposes. Jesse James Garrett, an information architect and one of my business partners in Adaptive Path, and I developed a technique that uses card sorting to understand how people prioritize features.

A group of 12 participants were asked to organize 50 cards that had descriptions of current and potential features for presenting current events on Web sites (this was done when researching how people read news online, as a break during a long one-on-one interview). Each card had a single sentence that described a way that information could be presented or organized on a Web site. The participants were first asked to place the cards into one of four piles describing how *valuable* they felt the feature would be to them, as they used the Web right now. The four piles were titled "Most Valuable," "Somewhat Valuable," "Least Valuable," and "Not Valuable." As participants placed the cards in these piles, they were asked to narrate their thoughts about the topic. This was done to understand why they made certain choices and how they thought about the features.

After the participants completed organizing the cards, they were asked to repeat the exercise, but this time only using the cards that they had put into the "Most Valuable" pile and with a different set of criteria for the placement. The new task was for them to organize the features in terms of how *frequently* they felt they would use each of the features. This was done in order to differentiate between the features that attracted people to a site and those that they felt were the most immediately useful.

To understand where the participants' values lay, each one of the categories was given a numerical rating indicating the strength of preference, from 0 to 5:

0 - Not valuable
1 - Least valuable
2 - Somewhat valuable
3 - Most valuable, rarely used
4 - Most valuable, sometimes used
5 - Most valuable, used often

The participants' choices were then rated, and the *median* value of their ratings was calculated. Since a number of choices had the same median, it was necessary to further organize the list. The *standard deviation* of the choices was calculated and represented the degree of agreement among all the ratings for a given category, with lower deviations representing greater agreement. Both median and standard deviation are defined in Chapter 11. The list was thus ordered first by preference and then by agreement, which gave the development team a much clearer idea of their customers' values and in turn helped them prioritize their own development efforts.

The card sorting process sheds light on people's existing understanding and preference, and it can show subtle relationships that may not be obvious by just examining a list of clusters. It also provides an idea of how concepts relate to each other since what may seem like a strong relationship when casually examined may turn out to be weaker when actually analyzed.

Contextual inquiry, task analysis, and card sorting can take you a long way toward revealing how your target audience understands their environment and what their needs are. As prescriptive techniques, they can focus a project early on, eliminating many wrong turns and reducing the need to ask major, fundamental questions about the product later on, when development should concentrate on honing the product's experience, not its purpose.

CHAPTER 9

Focus Groups

Focus groups are structured group interviews that quickly and inexpensively reveal a target audience's desires, experiences, and priorities. Sometimes vilified by their association with dishonest marketing, they do not deserve the notoriety with which they are often treated. They are neither the panacea for curing bad products nor pseudoscientific voodoo used to justify irrational decision making. When guided by a good moderator, carefully analyzed, and appropriately presented, they are an excellent technique for uncovering what people think about a given topic and, especially, *how* they think about it. They reveal what people perceive to be their needs, which is crucial when determining what should be part of an experience and how it should be presented.

Originally called "focused interviews," focus groups were developed as a social research method in the 1930s, then refined as a method for improving soldiers' lives during World War II and embraced by marketing in the 1950s. As such, they're probably one of the oldest techniques for researching the user experience. A focus group series is a sequence of tightly moderated group discussions among people taken from a thin slice of a product's target audience. The discussions are designed to make people feel comfortable revealing their thoughts and feelings.

In software or Web site development, focus groups are used early in the development cycle, when generating ideas, prioritizing features, and understanding the needs of the target audience are paramount. They can tell you what features people value most highly and why they value them that way. As a competitive research tool, they can uncover what people most value about competitors' products or services and where those products and services fail. Sometimes they even reveal entirely new competitors or applications for the product or service.

By providing a way to hear a lot of firsthand experience in a short time, they can give development teams an early, solid foundation from which to analyze the product and its users' needs. And as a watchable, tangible, jargon-free method, they engage members of the company in product development who would not normally have the opportunity, expertise, or time to participate in the user experience research process.

In short, they provide a unique opportunity to see reality from the perspective of the user quickly, cheaply, and (with careful preparation) easily. Two people working part-time can set up a series of focus groups, run them, and analyze the results in three weeks. Conducting contextual inquiry research with a similar number of participants, however, can take a full-time researcher almost twice as long. A survey, furthermore, would need to sample a much larger number of people—significantly increasing the complexity of the logistics and analysis—while providing less understanding about the motivations and attitudes of the respondents.

That's not to say that focus groups provide the same information as contextual inquiry or surveys. All three techniques uncover different and equally useful information—but focus groups can be an inexpensive route when you need a lot of solid information in a short time.

When Focus Groups Are Appropriate

The purpose of focus groups is not to infer, but to understand, not to generalize but to determine a range, not to make statements about the population but to provide insights about how people perceive a situation.
—Richard A. Krueger, *Focus Groups,* p. 87

Knowing when to use focus groups is one of the keys to using them successfully. Although the technique is straightforward and flexible, it's not applicable to all cases or at all stages in the development of a product.

What Focus Groups Are Good For

Focus groups are good at finding *desires, motivations, values,* and *first-hand experiences;* in other words, they're a tool to get at people's attitudes and perceptions. A focus group is an environment where people (ideally) feel comfortable revealing their thoughts and feelings. This allows them to share their view of the issues and assumptions that lie at the core of an experience and to relate them to real-world situations.

When coupled with contextual inquiry and task analysis, a complete picture of how and why people are behaving *right now* can be built, before a single line of code is written or a single screen layout is sketched on a whiteboard.

As tools for competitive analysis, focus groups come in early in product development, though they can also be done during redesign or update cycles. Understanding fundamental issues and perceptions is generally most needed near the beginning of a product development cycle. That's also when the development team is trying to nail down what problems their product is supposed to solve, how it's supposed to solve them, and why it's valuable for consumers to use their solutions versus all others. Likewise, by bringing users of competitive products in early in the process, it's possible to find out why people value the competition, what they feel are the most critical features, what regularly bothers them, and where they feel the competitors fail. Apart from the obvious marketing angle, this information can immediately drive feature and interaction development, defining a user experience that's closer to what the target audience wants before resources have been committed.

Later in the development cycle, the technique can help identify and prioritize features. Knowing why people value certain features can help determine what gets developed and in what order. Moreover, since focus groups can act as brainstorming sessions, it's possible to achieve a synergy in which participants generate more ideas together than they could have come up with on their own.

One example from my practice was a site for Web novices that concentrated on news and information about developments in the Web world—which companies were doing what, what software was coming out when, and so forth. In conducting a series of focus groups with their target audience, we discovered that most of the people who were new to the Web were also new to computers in

Note Focus groups uncover people's *perceptions* about their needs and their values. This does not mean that they uncover what people *actually* need or what really *is* valuable to them (in some objective sense); it's just what they *think* they need and what they *claim* is valuable. However, relativism (and italics) aside, knowing perceptions of needs is as important as knowing the needs themselves. Ultimately, people are going to judge a product based on what they think it does and how well that matches what they think they need. It doesn't replace accurate functionality or needs assessment, but the closer a product's presentation of its services matches people's perceptions of their needs, the more they're likely to use it.

general. They weren't interested in Web industry developments nearly as much as they were interested in knowing the basics of how their software worked and where to turn for help. Moreover, since the process of getting on the Web was difficult for nearly all of them, they were tired of dealing with it and uninterested in installing or learning new software. They wanted to know what they could do with it and how they could use it to help the rest of their lives. Based on this information, the site decided to de-emphasize its Web news and information and to emphasize the self-help nature of the Web, collecting information about popular software products in one place.

What Focus Groups Are *Not* Good For

First and foremost, focus groups are not a way to get usability information. There's no good way for a group of people to tell you whether they will be able to use a certain interface or a certain feature. They can tell you whether they like the idea of it, but they can't show you whether they can use it in practice.

Second, focus group results are impossible to numerically generalize to a larger population, so they can't replace surveys. Specifically, focus groups create generalized models based on observations by an analyst. These models are assumed to apply to groups similar to the ones interviewed, but because they are not statistically significant samples, there's no guarantee that the proportion of responses in the group matches that of the larger population of users. This is an important distinction between focus groups and surveys. Because surveys are statistically significant (or should be), then the proportions observed in them can be extrapolated to larger populations. With focus groups, there is no such assurance.

Thus, although it's an inadequate technique for investigating the prevalence of a phenomenon in the entire target audience, focus groups can give you a really good idea of *why* the audience behaves how it does. Once the "why" has been determined, it can be verified through statistically significant research, such as a survey. However, identifying trends is often enough to act upon, making specific quantification unnecessary. Just as it can be sufficient to know the block a business is on without knowing the specific address, it's often enough to know that a phenomenon is widespread without knowing its exact magnitude.

Focus groups can create situations that are deceptive both to the participants and to analysts who literally interpret statements made in focus groups rather than extracting their underlying attitudes. This can be seen in the plethora of products (such as many feature films) that are made worse, rather than better, by misinterpreted focus group results. An amusing, if somewhat apocryphal, example of this comes from comic books: in an attempt to give Superman fans what they wanted, a focus group of comics consumers (10- to 12-year-old boys) was asked what kinds of figures they admired. Their replies were interpreted literally, and for a while in the 1960s, Superman did whatever the focus groups decided, leading to a string of surreal stories of the Man of Steel working as a police chief, dressing up as an Indian, or meeting George Washington (and to Jimmy Olsen, a meek supporting character, turning into a giant space turtle). It led to a kind of creative bankruptcy and an impossibly convoluted storyline that had to be eventually scrapped entirely, the comic starting over as if none of those stories had happened.

Finally, focus groups are not useful in situations where it's important to prove a point or to justify a position. The data collection process and analysis is based on multiple levels of human judgment. As such, the results can be called into question when used as a basis for proof, and rightly so. This is an excellent exploratory procedure; it produces deep insight into motivations and thinking processes, but it does not (and cannot) be used to unequivocally prove or disprove anything.

Four Types of Focus Groups

There are four common types of focus groups in software or Web development. The type of group you choose depends on the types of questions you want to answer, which in turn will likely depend on the stage of development the product is in. Don't feel limited by these categories; they're provided only as rough guides.

Exploratory. These groups get at general attitudes on a given topic, helping developers see how the eventual users of the product will understand it, what words they use to talk about it, and what criteria they will use to judge it. For example, a furniture company is interested in what criteria people use to buy furniture and how they buy similar items online. At the beginning of their development process, they run focus groups and find out that, at first, people insist on seeing furniture "in real life" before buying it (thus negating their entire business plan for selling it online). Further discussion reveals that it is only certain classes of products such as couches and beds that are mistrusted without direct experience. With other things (chairs, tables), most people have no problem buying based solely on pictures and descriptions and, in fact, would prefer to do so.

Feature prioritization. These groups focus on what features are most attractive to the group and why. They are held, in general, near the beginning of the development cycle, when it's already clear what the general outlines of the product are going to be. In these types of groups, the assumption is that the participants are interested in a certain kind of product, and the discussion centers on what kinds of things they would like that product to do for them. For example, the participants in a focus group for a homepage creation service were not nearly as interested in community services as they were in tools to help them build and market their own homepage. The "community feeling" that the site was trying to communicate and the tone with which it promoted itself meant little. For them the value in the site lay in the tools and free disk space.

Competitive analysis. Just as it's important to know what people value in the feature set that a product provides, it's important to know what attracts and repels them with respect to competitor's sites. Often held anonymously (with the commissioning client left unmentioned), these focus groups attempt to understand what associations people have with a competitor, what aspects of the competitor's user experience they find valuable, and where it doesn't satisfy their needs and desires. For example, a competitive focus group of online technology news sites revealed that most of the content that wasn't explicitly news was considered superfluous. Most people read only one news site for a few minutes a day. What they valued most were daily updates and links to other sites' content. Opinions, in-depth background stories, and thematic collections of older stories were not seen as valuable.

Trend explanation. When a trend in behavior is spotted, whether it's driven by survey responses, customer service feedback, or log analysis, it's often difficult to determine which of the many potential causes are primary. Focus groups can help explain the behavior by investigating the users' motivations and expectations. These types of focus groups are generally held either as part of a redesign cycle or in response to specific issues. For example, a survey showed that when people used search services, they would use two or three different ones with no particular pattern, but most people used Yahoo! regardless of what or how many other services they used. Focus groups with people who had taken the survey were called, and it was discovered that Yahoo! was consulted first because people felt that it did not contain much, but when it did, its results were of a significantly higher quality than the competitors. Thus, it made sense for them to always check it first, just in case.

How to Conduct Focus Groups

Before you launch into a focus group series, it's important to determine several things.

- A *schedule.* The best results come from situations where there's been enough time to examine the contingencies. A good schedule (Table 9.1) provides sufficient time for everything, especially recruiting and guide writing, and enough flexibility to be able to make a mistake or two.
- The *target audience.* These are the people you're going to invite to the test. Specifically, you need to know the subset of the target audience that is likely to give you the best feedback.
- The *scope* of your research. Focus group series can have a few groups of a handful of people or as many as a dozen groups with ten or more participants apiece. The number of groups and people will depend on the complexity of your questions, the depth to which you want to explore the answers, and the certainty with which you want to know these answers.
- The *topics* that you want to research. Not all groups feel equally comfortable talking about all subjects, and not all

subjects lend themselves to group discussion. Choosing topics carefully and thoughtfully writing a discussion guide helps you get the most information out of the group process without sacrificing the depth of research or the clarity of the results.

Setting a Schedule

A typical schedule for a focus group series takes about three weeks from beginning to end and should provide sufficient time for recruiting and writing the discussion guide.

Timing	Activity
$t - 2$ weeks	Determine audience and scope; start recruiting immediately
$t - 2$ weeks	Determine broad topics to be investigated; start writing guide
$t - 1$ week	Write first version of discussion guide; discuss exact topic wording with development team; check on recruiting
$t - 3$ days	Write second version of discussion guide with timing; discuss with development team; recruiting should be completed
$t - 2$ days	Complete guide; schedule run-through; set up and check all equipment
$t - 1$ day	Run-through in the morning; check times and adjust guide questions as appropriate; do final recruiting check
t	Conduct groups (usually 1–3 days, depending on scheduling); discuss with observers; collect copies of all notes
$t + 1$ day	Relax; do something else.
$t + 3$ days	Watch all tapes; take notes
$t + 1$ week	Combine notes; write analysis

Picking a Target Audience

It is not the actual differences between participants, but whether they perceive each other to be different, that determines their willingness to discuss a topic together.
—David L. Morgan, *Focus Groups as Qualitative Research,* p. 47

In focus groups, maybe more than in any of the other methods in this book, picking the right audience is crucial. For people to feel comfortable talking about their experiences and their values, they need to know that they are not going to be judged by the others in the group, that they are among peers. Thus, unlike most other kinds of research, focus groups concentrate on homogenous audiences.

Defining what "homogenous" means depends on the context of the research and the group. The participants don't need to be the same in all ways, just in the ways that are important to the research. For example, generational differences can keep a group from completely opening up about their musical tastes.

From your ideal target audience, you should choose a subset or several subsets that are likely to give you the most useful feedback. The right group will vary from situation to situation. First, you need a solid profile of your target audience, complete with a thorough understanding of their demographic, Web use, and technological makeup. For example, if you're just looking to find out what existing users value about your service, you want to pick the people who represent the largest subset of your actual audience. However, if you're looking to find out why there is a lot of turnover in your users, you must be much more specific: you must focus only on the people who are just like your standard population but have used your site once and never again.

Often, it's useful to choose several groups to get an understanding of the breadth of experience and as a way to concentrate on specific groups' experiences. For example, if your system doctors are supposed to use your system, but you see only medical students, then you probably want to talk to both groups. The doctors will tell you why they don't use it, and the medical students will tell you why they do. Maybe you need two separate sites.

Define the group similarly from the perspective of the members of the subgroups. If you feel that certain groups of people would not feel comfortable with each other, then don't put them together. Start with demographic and Web use terms. Income, race, sex, class, age, job, and computer experience all can play a role in how people interact in a group situation and how they react to a given user experience. In order to create a group that can comfortably discuss our topic, we have to take these differences into account. Once the basic outlines are defined, further divide the groups based on behavior: Who does what? What else do they do? Sometimes differences that matter in one group don't in another.

Here are some examples.

- When picking subgroups for a study researching automobile buying experiences, it was pointed out that the men tend to talk a lot more than women in mixed groups when talking about cars. Since the researchers were interested in the opinions of both groups, the choice was made to have separate groups of men and women and a combined group.
- When researching how to expand the customer base of a technology news service, it was decided that apart from matching basic demographics and Web use, it was important that the audience should spend a couple of hours reading news every day.
- A medical services site decided that doctors and doctor-administrators would likely have trouble feeling comfortable with each other because of their roles in the hierarchy of a hospital, even though they would likely be using the same services. Thus, the groups were segregated based on how much time a doctor spent on administrative work.
- A Web site aimed at elderly computer users decided that people living in the San Francisco Bay Area would likely have been exposed to a disproportionate amount of information about the Web when compared to people with otherwise identical profiles who lived elsewhere in the United States. Research was conducted in Washington, D.C., and St. Louis, Missouri.

You should feel free to define the subgroups in whatever way you feel comfortable. However, do not define subgroups based on their opinions or preferences. Prescreening participants for their stated values is likely to introduce unnecessary bias into the groups and defeats the core purpose of the focus groups, which is to determine those values. For example, don't screen for people "who *like* shopping online"; instead, focus on people who shop online and then determine the full range of reasons why these people shop.

Recruiting

Once you've picked a target audience (or audiences), it's time to find them and invite them. Recruiting for focus groups, much like recruiting for other kinds of research, should be done early and should begin as soon as you've picked your audience.

A couple of things distinguish recruiting a *group* of people from the recruiting process described in Chapter 6, which concentrates on finding individuals.

- The exact profile of the participants is very important. With much research, it's possible to have participants who are close, but not exactly ideal target audiences. With focus groups, it's critical that all the people in a given group fall into the audience profile since one person outside it can derail a whole discussion. Owners of small shops, for example, could potentially feel uncomfortable discussing their problems and feelings with an owner of a large store or a franchise. And although good moderation can sometimes overcome such problems, it's best to avoid them in the first place.
- Never recruit people who know each other. When two or more people know each other—sometimes even if they just know who the other person is—it creates an unbalanced dynamic in a group discussion. A raised eyebrow or a sigh says a lot between two people when they know each other, and can disrupt the discussion and inadvertently conceal important information. Thus, when recruiting using the friends and family method, avoid recruiting people who were all referred by the same person, and when using a database, select people who were initially recruited at different times or using different methods.
- Avoid people who know about how focus groups work. The focus group process depends on candid answers and a level of

comfort in the discussion group. Veterans of the process may attempt (often subconsciously) to give the kinds of answers that they feel are expected, or they may try to predict the next topic of discussion. Although not fatal, this can skew the discussion, necessitating extra moderation and analysis efforts. If you have to recruit people with focus group experiences, the experience should be neither frequent nor recent. For these same reasons, you should never include people who work for organizations where they could be exposed to a lot of focus groups, even indirectly. So no marketing companies, no advertising agencies, and so on.

- Screen out people who have significantly more knowledge about any of the topics than the other participants. If there's an "expert" in a group, that person's knowledge can intimidate the other participants, and his or her views can bias the whole group's perspective.

Once you've decided on your target audiences, write a profile of the kind of people you want to recruit.

The following could be a profile for potential users of a home improvement site. It defines a group of people who are actively thinking about home improvement and would be likely to look for information about it online.

A SAMPLE FOCUS GROUP RECRUITING PROFILE

Demographics

Ages 20–55

Income not important if behavior criteria are met, otherwise, $100K+ household.

Gender unimportant, as long as primary decision maker.

Web Use

Have a personal computer at home or work.

Use Internet at home or work.

Have 1+ years of Internet experience.

Use the Internet 5–10 hours per week for personal tasks:

- Shopping for products

- Comparing products or services

- Gathering information about a topic (e.g., Sidewalk, BabyCenter, ImproveNet, CarPoint)

Behavior

Have completed home improvements in the last 9–12 months or intend to perform improvements in the next 3 months.

Total improvement cost at least $20K (estimated if in the future).

Defining Scope

> *Focus groups must be small enough for everyone to have the opportunity to share insights and yet large enough to provide a diversity of perceptions.*
> —Richard A. Krueger, *Focus Groups*, p. 17

You need to decide two things when determining the scope of the focus groups you're going to run: how many groups you're going to have and how many people you're going to have per group.

Never do only one group for the same reasons you shouldn't base conclusions about a class of people on the words of a single person: there may be factors that seem important to the group, but that are not representative of the views of your audience at large. That said, more than four groups is rarely necessary. The first group is, essentially, a dress rehearsal. By the third group you should see confirmation of the views and statements (sometimes verbatim) from the first two groups. The fourth group should be used for confirmation of the trends in the first three. If there is still a lot of new information (especially dissension) coming in during the fourth group, it may be a sign that further groups are necessary or that the makeup of the groups is too broad.

Likewise, although most marketing texts recommend 8–12 people per group, it's generally better to have fewer when examining user experiences and attitudes. The degree of detail that is appropriate for user experience research is often greater than the typical marketing focus group. By reducing the size of the group, it's possible to go into greater depth with each person. Six to eight is a good size, balancing the collection of fine detail with a breadth of perspectives. In cases where you'd like to get a lot of depth from each participant, or if the individual focus groups are short, it may be useful to reduce the number to four. Use fewer than that, and the discussion feels more like an interview and doesn't produce as dynamic a situation as with more people.

Choosing Topics

For an average focus group, you should have three to five main topics to investigate. These should be phrased in terms of the project as a whole. "Understanding the mental model people use when researching insurance" could be a goal for an insurance brokerage site, while a service that recommended home building contractors could be interested in "Knowing at which point people turn to an external service when doing home repair." A high-end online auction site doing a competitive analysis could have "Understanding what repels high-end car sellers from listing their cars on eBay" or "Uncovering what factors will help our product idea to be seen in the same class as Sotheby's" as two of their goals.

Note Not all people are comfortable talking about all topics. Choose questions that your target audience will be comfortable discussing. Different audiences for the same product may react differently to the same topics.

These objectives should be sufficiently focused so that a group could adequately discuss each one in about 10 minutes. They should not be so focused as to be the actual questions you would ask the participants, nor should they be issues that are better answered by other means (such as a survey). "Making a list of our competitors" would generally be too broad and probably better answered by a survey, whereas "Discovering what factors make the user experiences of our competitors more compelling than ours" is probably more appropriate.

Writing a Guide

The discussion guide is a script for the moderator to follow. It creates a consistent framework and a schedule for the focus group series. Groups are asked the same questions in the same order with much the same context, and all the topics are given enough time. This allows a discussion to bring out the subtleties of the participants' views without shortchanging any of the topics.

Before you start writing the whole guide, it's useful to think about the core, the questions. Focus group questions should be

- *Carefully ordered.* Questions put the participants in a certain frame of mind, thinking about certain issues and remembering certain events. A careful sequence of questions takes advantage of that frame of mind to make the flow of the group discussion feel more "natural," which in turn helps the participants to maintain a creative flow of ideas and produce better insights. In general, questions should flow from the most general to the most specific, with each question narrowing the discussion a bit and concentrating on a subset of what was discussed before. There should be planned transitions between topics unless a brand-new topic is introduced and discussion begins from a general question again.
- *Nondirected.* As described in Chapter 6, questions should not imply an answer or a value judgment. They should focus on allowing the participants to fill in their own thoughts and values. For example, asking "Which do you think is a better search service, Google or Lycos?" assumes that the participant feels there *are* advantages of one over the other. Instead, the question should be framed neutrally, "Are there any things you like about using the Google search service? Are there things you like about using Lycos? What are they? Are there any ways in which you can compare them? How do they compare?"
- *Open-ended.* Questions should not constrain the answers to fixed responses. They should encourage people to open up and share experiences. Longer responses tell a greater part of the story and tend to be less ambiguous than shorter responses. Thus, rather than phrasing a question in the form "What's your favorite recipe site?" you could ask "What are you looking for when you search out recipes online?"
- *Focused on specifics.* The questions should encourage the participants to be specific in their answers. Richard A. Krueger, in his book *Focus Groups,* recommends breaking down "why" questions into multiple "what" questions, explicitly asking for the influences that informed the participants' decision and the attributes of their decision. For example, "How did you decide

to go shopping online for forks?" and "What factors went into picking this site?" will provide better insight than asking "Why did you pick this site?"

- *Personal.* People will often attempt to generalize their experiences to the public at large or some hypothetical audience that they are not part of. Since you want to know individual views, values, and experiences, emphasize individual experiences. Questions should be formulated so that they concentrate on people's current behavior and opinions, without presenting the option to project their experiences. Thus, "If you had to redo your kitchen right now, which of these features would you use to find a home contractor?" is preferable to "Which of these features do you think are useful?"
- *Unambiguous.* There should be as few shades of meaning as possible, especially when the participants are introduced to new terminology.

Granted, fulfilling all these criteria with all questions is often difficult (writing questions that are simultaneously specific and open-ended is a particularly tricky challenge), but they should be kept in mind as guidelines that should be followed whenever possible.

Sample Discussion Guide

The guide is broken up into three major sections: the introduction, the main discussion, and the wrap-up.

The guide that follows is from a focus group for an online news site that is (primarily) interested in understanding the criteria its existing users use to pick the news sites that they read.

Warm-up and Intro (10 minutes)

The introduction sets the tone for the discussion, breaks the ice for the participants, and explains the process.

Hi. Welcome.

My name is _____ (first name). I am a researcher working with
_____ (company), who has asked me to help them get some of
your thoughts and opinions about some products and some ideas they
have. I am not associated with the development of any of the products
we'll be talking about today, and I have no emotional attachment to any
of these things, so you can say whatever you want.

We invited you here because you all read a fair amount of news online
and you've spent a lot of time on the Web. What we're going to do today
is talk about some of your experiences so that they can create a service
that is best tailored to experiences of people like you.

Telling people how they were chosen helps them feel comfortable with one another. Informing them of the end goal of the research helps them start focusing their thoughts.

The discussion is going to be a pretty casual conversation, but there will
be a couple of times when I will ask you to concentrate on certain things.

While we're talking, it's important that you be as candid as possible. You
won't hurt anyone's feelings with anything you say, so please say exactly
what you feel.

Furthermore, we want YOUR opinion. No opinion is right or wrong here—
especially about the things we're going to talk about—it's just an opinion,
so even if you disagree with someone in the room we'd like to hear that.

But we'd like you to speak one at a time.

Set out the ground rules for conversation ahead of time and explicitly allow disagreement. This encourages people to feel comfortable voicing their thoughts later.

> Also, since we have a lot of ground to cover today and none of us want to be here for hours, I may have to ask you to wrap up a thought or put it aside so that we can move on.

Again, people don't take being interrupted as personally if the expectation has been set early on.

> Behind that glass wall, as you can imagine, are a couple of people from the company whose idea we'll be talking about and _____ (assistant moderator's first name) who is working with me. Occasionally, _____ may come in here with a note or something we need. Regardless, feel free to ignore them.

Explicitly noting the mirrored wall (assuming there is one in the room) acknowledges the participants' anxiety about it and helps to diffuse that anxiety. Sometimes it's even appropriate to have the participants wave or make faces at the people behind the mirror during the introduction. However, once mentioned, it shouldn't be brought up again.

> As I said, we brought you here to hear what you think, so you won't hurt anyone's feeling by whatever you say. This videotape, in case you're wondering, is here so that _____ and I don't have to sit here feverishly scribbling notes and can concentrate on listening to you. It's purely for research purposes. It may be seen by members of the product development team, but it's not for any kind of publicity or promotion or broadcast.

If the session is videotaped, that should be mentioned.

> Now I'd like to read you what's called a statement of informed consent. It's a standard thing I read to everyone I interview. It sets out your rights as a person who is participating in this kind of research.
>
> As a participant in this research
> - You may stop at any time.
> - You may ask questions at any time.
> - You may leave at any time.
> - There is no deception involved.
> - Your answers are kept confidential.
>
> Here is a form that gives us permission to videotape this discussion and to use the videotape in our research.

It's critical to inform participants of their rights and to get releases that allow you to videotape them. Doing otherwise is both unethical and, in some situations, illegal. Don't be dour when introducing these ideas, however, since it can create an overly formal atmosphere right off. I usually joke that what we're talking about is what we're interested in, and (pointing at the snack dish) that this isn't a secret candy taste test.

> Any questions about any of that? Let's start!
>
> Now I'd like all of us to introduce ourselves. By way of introduction, I'd like you to tell us four things.
>
> - Your first name
> - Which city you live in
> - What TV shows or publications you absolutely can't live without every week
> - Anything that regularly irks you about the Web
>
> (_____ does introduction first, everyone goes around).

The introductory questions introduce everyone and break the ice by sharing something that's fairly personal, such as a favorite TV show or a pet peeve. As such, it's appropriate for these questions to be specific, (somewhat) directed, and unrelated to the topics of inquiry.

General News Reading (20 minutes)
How do you get the news most frequently?

Probe: Are there some other ways you regularly get news?

Which news sites do you regularly read? (make a list on the whiteboard)

Probe: Are there some that you read more than others?

Probe: What attracts you to the sites you read more often? (Ask individuals about specific sites.)

Have you ever switched from one favorite to another? How often (did it just happen once or have you had several favorites)?

Probe: What made you decide to switch?

Probe: How did you pick the site you switched to?

Probes are follow-up questions that dig deeper into a given topic.

Switching gears, what kinds of news are there? (make a list).

Are there any good sites for sports? How about for politics? Technology?

Even though the primary topic is technology news, asking about several different kinds of news keeps the discussion from focusing on technology prematurely.

Are there sites that specialize in any of these (business, entertainment, technology)? Can you name some, even if you don't read them regularly?

Changing gears again, have you ever come across a situation where you think that advertising has affected the news you're reading?

Probe: Can you give an example?

Prioritization Exercise (20 minutes)
Pass out paper with the following exercise:

Rate each of the following things based on how important they are to you. Rate them from 1 to 5, with 1 being least important. Also, if you can think of a site that does that one thing better than any other site, write its name or URL next to the statement. You don't have to put a different site down for every one, and you may not want to put any sites down for some.

- The number of different stories on a given topic
- The number of different topics covered
- How quickly the page downloads
- Who is presenting the news
- How comprehensively each story is covered
- Regular columnists
- The quality of the site's search engine
- The visual appearance of the site
- How quickly stories are covered after they happened
- How easy it is to get around in the site

(going around) Say which ones you picked as the most important.

Probe: What about it makes it so important?

Probe: Is there a site that does it well? Does anyone else have that site written down?

Are there any attributes of news sites that you think are important but that are not on the list?

This exercise is designed to start a discussion about what makes a good news site by focusing on specific features.

Competitor Site Review (20 minutes)
We've been talking about general news reading, but let's talk about a couple of specific news sites for a few minutes.
(turn on projector)

Are any of you familiar with _____ (competitor site)?

Probe (for people who are): Have you ever read it? How often? Under what circumstances do you read it versus other news sources?

Describe _____'s personality.

Does _____ fall into any kind of specialization?

What kinds of stories would you expect to find here?

Probe: Are there situations where you think you would read it versus other sites?

Probe: Are there kinds of technology news that you wouldn't go here for?

Probe: What about columns? Are there any that would entice you to read them on a regular basis?

(go through questions again for another competitor; present competitors in a different order to every group)

Blue Sky and Wrap-up (10 minutes)
We're almost done. I'd like to do a quick brainstorming exercise. I only have one question, but I'd like everyone to think about it for a few seconds and say what comes to mind.

Not thinking in practical terms at all, what would you really like a news service to do that none of them currently offer?

(wait 30 seconds, then go around and discuss, write ideas on board)

All right, that's the last of our questions about news.

I know you're all excited about talking about online news, but we really have to wrap up. If there's something you think of on your way home that you'd really like to tell us, please feel free to send a note to the following email address (write email on board).

I have one final question: is there anything that we could do better, either in terms of scheduling or in terms of running these groups? Should we have different food, a case of beer, whatever?

Once the content for the site had been established, subsequent focus groups can concentrate on the desirability of specific features and how people use news sites in their daily lives.

After you've written the guide, it's important to review it and time it. Members of the product development team, especially the product and project managers, are good guide reviewers. They can point out technical ambiguities, serve as a second perspective, and then prepare the rest of the team for observing the groups.

Guides should always be tested. An easy way to test the guide is to get a couple of people (it doesn't have to be as many people as the actual group) who haven't seen it and walk them through it, paying attention to how they answer the questions and how accurate the timing is. In addition, treat the first group as a dress rehearsal, reviewing the effectiveness of the guide and adjusting it appropriately.

Conducting the Group

The Physical Layout

The groups should be held in a comfortable, large room with good ventilation, good temperature control, and few distractions. Typical setups look like conference rooms or living rooms, depending on whether the participants are supposed to feel they're in a comfortable work area or at home. Actual conference rooms or lounge areas are easily converted to focus group facilities. If the groups are to be held in a conference room with windows to the inside of the office, the windows should be covered or the group should be held as far away from the windows as possible. Outside windows are fine, unless they're on the first floor, in which case they can be too distracting. After the group has started, no one except for the assistant moderator should enter the room (and a sign should be posted on the outside door to this effect). I once observed a focus group that was mistakenly interrupted by a pizza delivery for the observers. After some initial confusion, it became clear that the pizza was for the observers. Although the participants joked about it, it set up an unfortunate dynamic.

Eating is an informal activity that can break the tension in a group that's just forming, so provide food and drink when possible. For late evening groups, people are likely to have eaten dinner, so providing high-energy snacks (such as cookies) can often keep a sleepy group talking. Make sure to provide vegetarian choices and plenty of water. Crunchy food can be quite loud when recorded, so things like celery and potato chips are best avoided. Having plenty of noncarbonated drinks is handy; people drinking carbonated beverages have a tendency to stop themselves from commenting because they're afraid they'll burp in the middle of a sentence.

How to Create a Seating Order

Krueger recommends the following procedure to place people around the table:

- Print *table tents* with the participants' names on them. Table tents are folded sheets of paper that sit upright on the table. Each participant's first name is printed on both sides of the tent, large enough that it can be read from the observation room and on camera (1.5-inch letters printed in black seem to work pretty well).
- Determine who are the quiet and outspoken people by visiting participants in the waiting area and making small talk with the group.
- Figure out a placement for each person (long-winded people next to the moderator, so he or she can break eye contact without disturbing the group dynamic; quiet people across, so the moderator can make eye contact easily and elicit their comments).
- Organize the table tents according to this order.
- Then, when bringing people into the room, drop the table tents seemingly randomly on the table, but actually according to the predesignated order.

The room should have a way for observers to watch the proceedings. This can be a traditional two-way mirrored wall, with a soundproof room behind the mirrors that observers can sit in. The observer's room should have its own entrance, so that observers can come and go without entering the discussion room. If such a room is unavailable, closed-circuit video is an inexpensive and easy solution. A long video cable and a television in a nearby room generally suffice, as long as the observation room is acoustically isolated from the discussion room.

Focus groups should be videotaped, when possible. Unlike an audiotape, it's easy to see who's saying what on video and to see the body language that sometimes betrays a negation of a concept or discomfort with a topic. If the video process is made unobtrusive, it quickly disappears into the background of the conversation.

There needs to be only one camera for a focus group, roughly behind the moderator, and it needs to have great sound. If it has a good wide-angle lens, it's not necessary to have a camera operator, which reduces the cost of the process, as well as the hassle and intimidation of having a person swinging a camera constantly between one side of the table and the other.

Two cardiod microphones are generally sufficient to capture all the participants' comments without a lot of extraneous noise. Cardiod microphones are directional microphones that have a broad area of sound capture in front and a much smaller area facing back. Thus, unlike the omnidirectional microphones that are attached to most video cameras, they can be pointed away from sources of noise such as outside windows and air vents (see Figure 9.1).

For temporary setups, two opposing ones set on the table work well, but they're vulnerable to vibration (so a pencil tapping or a coffee cup being set down or a computer humming will sound

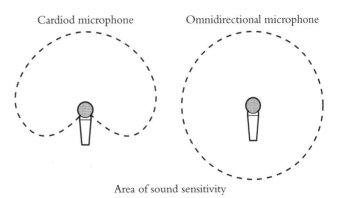

Cardiod microphone   Omnidirectional microphone

Area of sound sensitivity

Figure 9.1 Cardiod versus omnidirectional microphone sensitivity.

much louder to the microphone than they do in the room). Putting some cloth or a mouse pad between the stand and the table can reduce this. For permanent situations, two hanging microphones eliminate most ambient noise from above (such as air conditioners and fluorescent light transformers) while recording conversation well (see Figures 9.2 and 9.3).

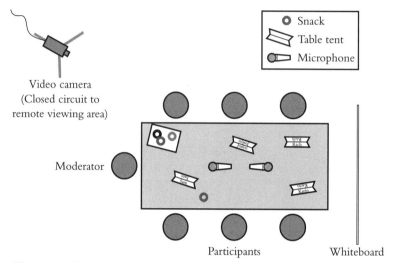

Figure 9.2   Temporary conference room–style focus group layout.

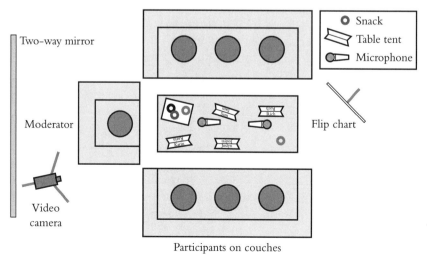

Figure 9.3   Permanent living room–style focus group layout.

The Moderator

Focus group moderation is a skill. The moderator must balance the needs of the participants in the group so that they feel comfortable in the discussion and the needs of the research. To do this without biasing the group takes practice, aptitude, and the right frame of mind.

The basic skills that a moderator must have are a respect for the participants, the ability to listen closely, and the ability to think fast. Often, a moderator must be able to predict where a conversation is headed and either drive it that way or move it in a more desired direction, without the participants realizing that they are being moderated. This can involve many subtle cues in what the moderator says, the tone he or she uses, and even his or her body language.

More specifically, the moderator must be

- Always *in control*. Most of the time the moderator can use body language and verbal emphasis to maintain control, subtly directing the discussion to certain participants and topics. However, if a digression is moving in an unproductive direction for too long, the moderator should not hesitate to exert more overt control and refocus the discussion on the necessary topics. For example, if in the course of discussing a news Web site, the discussion digresses into the current headlines, the moderator should refocus it on the product rather than on the content.
- Always *moving forward*. The moderator should monitor the flow of the conversation and introduce topics at appropriate times, making the transition feel natural rather than controlling the flow by stopping discussion or abruptly changing the topic. That way the discussion doesn't turn into an interview, with the participants answering the questions the moderator poses, one after another.
- *Nonjudgmental*. The moderator acts as mediator, helping the participants express their views without stifling their eagerness to do so. Therefore, the moderator should not express his or her views, but facilitate the views of the group to come out. This sometimes involves suppressing the habits we have learned in maintaining civil conversation. For example, many people nod while someone is talking as encouragement, whether they agree or not. This communicates agreement and an endorsement of the viewpoint being expressed. Since

the moderator is seen as the "official" at the table, the participants may feel that this is official endorsement of a certain position and, as such, may feel uncomfortable voicing a dissenting opinion.

- *Respectful.* The moderator must have the utmost respect for the participants at all times, even if he or she does not agree with them. Every participant in a focus group has a perspective that's useful to the development team, even if it doesn't match with the team's reality. For all participants to feel comfortable speaking their minds, they need to know that the moderator will treat their input with as much validity as everyone else's. This can be accomplished through the use of nonjudgmental statements and strict control of body language, but it's best communicated through the honest belief that everyone needs to be heard.

- *Prepared.* The moderator should know enough about the topics discussed to be able to follow up on participants' statements with specific questions. This does not mean acquiring expertise in the subject matter, but the moderator should have a good working knowledge of the general concepts, the terminology, and the implications of the issues being discussed. The moderator should also have some knowledge of the habits and environment of the people in the group.

In addition, the moderator should have a good sense of timing (knowing when to transition from one participant and one topic to another), a good short-term memory (referring to people's earlier statements and using their own words to describe concepts), and an aptitude for diffusing uncomfortable situations, preferably with humor.

The Assistant Moderator

Although it's certainly possible to conduct a focus group without an assistant moderator, having one helps the process.

The assistant moderator is a key analyst and the connection between the focus group and the outside world. The assistant takes care of the needs of the focus group participants and collects information, leaving the moderator to focus on maintaining a productive discussion.

Note If there is no assistant moderator, the burden of moderating the participants, managing the observers, and analyzing the final results falls on a single person. In such instances, it's useful to create situations where the moderator can leave the participants alone for five to ten minutes and walk back to the observation area to review the discussion with the observers, helping frame the discussion for them.

Before the discussion begins, the assistant should greet the participants when they first come in, bring them into the discussion room, present any initial paperwork (such as nondisclosure participation agreements), and bring them refreshments. As the discussion progresses, the assistant can bring in notes from the observers and take care of requests.

During the discussion, the assistant moderator should take extensive notes on the interesting parts of the discussion (such as key quotations, issues voiced by the participants, and his or her own observations) and manage the observers' discussion (taking notes on that, too). After the group ends, the assistant moderator can use these notes to spur a debriefing with the observers and the moderator.

Moderating the Discussion

Moderating a discussion is the process of balancing the participants' comfort level and keeping the discussion producing useful information for the research. There are few strict rules for how to moderate a discussion since every group and every topic will demand a different approach, and different moderators have different styles that work equally well.

There are, however, several general guidelines that apply to most user experience focus groups and that most moderators seem to follow.

- *Spend some time with the group beforehand.* Talking informally to the participants for five minutes before the group begins can give you a good feeling for the personalities of the participants. You can guess who is going to be quiet, who is going to dominate the discussion, who is going to be obstinate, who is going to lecture, and so on. This helps prepare you for how the group is going to progress. The assistant moderator can also do this and brief the moderator on the personalities just before the group begins.
- *Stick to the guide, but be opportunistic when necessary.* If the discussion turns to a question that's supposed to be asked later, but the participants are comfortable talking about it now, go with it. Ask the questions that were planned for later (unless order is absolutely critical, in which case ask the group to

postpone the discussion), and after the topic is exhausted, move the discussion back on track.

- *Engage everyone in the discussion.* Be wary of people who are losing interest or who don't seem comfortable speaking. Try to figure out what is causing their boredom or discomfort and attempt to alleviate it. Sometimes all it takes is to call the person's name and ask explicitly what his or her thoughts are. When the amount of effort needed to engage someone in a discussion is detrimental to the effectiveness of the discussion as a whole, however, it's best to spend the energy on getting the rest of the group into the conversation instead.

- *Avoid introducing new terminology and concepts.* New words and ideas tend to frame and dominate discussion once introduced. If the group wants to use its own words for a concept or to create its own models for ideas, let it. Don't use industry jargon, even if it sounds as though it should be completely comprehensible, unless it's also the group's jargon. For example, asking "What factors influence your choice of ecommerce portal?" will likely be met with confusion since most people don't characterize the reasons for their choices in terms of "factors," and "ecommerce portal" is likely going to be an alien term.

- *Restrict your body language.* There are lots of body motions that subtly communicate a preference for a particular person's viewpoint or a particular viewpoint, and people are very good at picking up on them, even if they don't do it consciously. Nodding signals to the other participants that the view being expressed is "right." Wincing signals that it's wrong. Consistently leaning toward one participant says that person's comments are more important (even if you're doing it because he or she is speaking quietly). You may want to watch videotapes of yourself moderating to see what your natural body language communicates and then try to reduce the behaviors that communicate a preference.

- *Clarify comments.* When someone says something that's either unclear or contradicts an earlier statement, restate the idea or ask for clarification. Ask for examples of what the person means or definitions of terms he or she is using.

- *Restate ideas.* To make sure that everyone (including the moderator and observers) knows exactly what a participant is trying to say, it's often useful to restate what was just said and see whether it correctly represents the participant's ideas. When heard in different words, the core of the idea is clarified. The technique also reinforces the relationship of the moderator to the group, subtly communicating to the participants that although they're the experts, the moderator is in control.

- *Probe for alternative perspectives.* If someone says something that contradicts earlier statements, or if he or she introduces a new interpretation of what's being discussed, probe the group for agreement or dissent. Let the person finish his or her thought and then ask the rest of the group to volunteer thoughts or experiences, especially different experiences or thoughts on the same topic.

- *Don't dominate the discussion.* Let the group carry on the discussion as much as possible. When one participant makes a comment, give the rest of the group some time (Krueger recommends five seconds) to respond to the comment before asking follow-up questions.

- *Provide time to think.* Not everyone can immediately articulate his or her thoughts or instantly grasp a concept. Explicitly providing opportunities to think or remember before a discussion begins can help participants contribute. Five to ten seconds is all that's generally necessary and can be introduced as the question is asked, "Remember the last time you ordered spare parts? Think for a couple of seconds about what situation led up to that."

- *Use humor when appropriate.* Don't make fun of the topic, of the participants, or of their statements, but feel free to lighten a situation with humor. Don't try to be funny—it seems artificial and sets up the expectation that you're there to entertain—but when something is funny, laugh and don't be afraid of saying something that's funny. Use self-deprecating humor carefully. Humility is valued, but only if it doesn't undermine the subject or the situation.

- *Keep the energy level high.* There will be times when the group is meandering or isn't interested in a particular topic. Maintaining (and inspiring) a high energy level can salvage such a group from boredom and frustration.

- *Give people a break.* Sitting in a room for two hours in intense discussion can be difficult and draining. If a focus group runs for more than 90 minutes, give people a 5-minute break halfway through to collect their thoughts, put change in the meter, go to the restroom, and the like.

Finally, be relaxed. Smile. Really, truly, empathize with people's experiences. Enjoy the opportunity to share in people's lives. Have fun with it.

Asking Questions

The process of asking questions is a subset of moderating, but there are enough elements that strictly relate to questions that I feel it deserves its own section. Several techniques help in asking questions and in clarifying the responses to questions.

- *Prioritize issues.* When coming up with lists of issues, always have participants explicitly prioritize, either through voting on the most important thing on the list (randomize when walking through the list!) or through a spontaneous finger tally for each item (everyone holds up a hand rating the item, the moderator quickly comes up with a rough average of the group's ratings).
- *Write down opinions before discussing them.* When people have written something down, they're much less likely to change their minds and "go with the flow" during discussion. For example, participants who first rate a list of topics on paper have more individual and earnest responses in a subsequent group discussion of the ratings.
- *Use the participants' exact thoughts and words, when possible.* When the group has introduced terminology or defined certain concepts, modify follow-up questions to use those same terms and concepts.
- *Key questions need to be asked verbatim.* For secondary questions, it feels more natural to use the same terminology as the group, but main concepts should be presented in the same way to all groups in order to reduce doubt when analyzing the results.

- *Be ready with examples.* Questions may not always make sense to participants, especially if the concepts are new or the terminology is unfamiliar. Prepare several good examples for questions where you feel that may be the case. First try to get responses without the example, but if people aren't responding well, provide the example. For instance, if the group doesn't know where to start a feature brainstorm, give them an example of what is considered a new feature ("The site emails you whenever items you like go on sale.").

A Feature Buying Exercise

Chauncey Wilson, Director of Bentley College's Design and Usability Testing Center, suggests the following technique for feature prioritization: Give people a "menu" of features on a page with a description of each feature and "price" that's based on an estimate of how much each feature costs to develop, in fictitious dollar amounts ($100 for something that's relatively straightforward to implement, $500 for something that's very involved). Then tell each person to review the feature list and "buy" up to $1000 dollars worth of features, writing them down on a piece of paper. After all participants have made their choices, go around and discuss why people made certain choices.

Common Problems

There are several problems that occur in many focus groups.

- *Group-think.* People are conditioned (or predisposed, depending on whose theories you read) to avoid conflict when in small groups. One of the best ways of avoiding conflict is by rationalizing agreement with the apparent consensus of the group. Thus, people have a tendency to want to agree with the people in the room, even if they don't really agree with the conclusions, because "belonging" is felt to be more important than "being right." Many of the techniques described earlier are designed to minimize group-think, but it still happens. Always be on the lookout for it, and attempt to minimize it by making it clear to the participants that disagreement is not only tolerated, but encouraged, when it's in earnest.
- *Faulty assumptions.* There are situations where the development team and moderator have fundamentally misunderstood

the nature of the user experience, and the whole focus group is based around an incorrect assumption. The best way to avoid this is by interviewing a representative of the target audience beforehand. If the focus group series has already begun and this is discovered, then the guide should be rewritten as soon as possible and, if necessary, new participants scheduled.

- *Latecomers.* Unless the introductions are still going on, don't let people in once the group has begun. Give them their full honorarium and say good-bye. The process of bringing people up to speed is disruptive, and the presence of a "stranger" puts people back on guard, negating the effects of the ice-breaking that happened earlier.

- *Reticent groups.* Sometimes groups of people just don't want to talk. The reasons for this vary from group to group, but sometimes you find yourself in a room full of people who aren't really interested in talking about the topic. Depending on the situation, it may be possible to reintroduce energy into the discussion and still keep with the guide and schedule. Sometimes, though, it's necessary to take drastic measures if the group isn't discussing the topic at all. At this point, the creativity of the moderator comes into play, and he or she has to invent a way to get the participants talking (for example, by turning the session into an open-ended brainstorm or moving on to questions that the group seems to be more interested in).

- *Quiet participants.* The reasons certain people don't talk are varied. They may feel uncomfortable with the subject, or that their opinion is not shared, or that they have nothing to add. They may just be shy. Getting everyone's perspective is critical, so drawing out taciturn participants is important. The easiest way to have people talk is to call on them directly, but when overdone it sets up a "call and response" dynamic to the discussion. Asking the whole group for additional comments, but looking directly at the quiet participant, signals that the comment is directed to him or her, without communicating that this person is being singled out. Finally, nonverbal signals can communicate when someone has a thought even though he or she may not feel comfortable voicing it. The inhalation before speech begins, a lean forward toward the table, eye contact with the moderator, a wince when another participant says something, all of these can be indicators that there's a thought brewing.

- *Overly talkative participants.* Some people just don't know when to shut up. They generally come in one of two breeds: the person who has an interesting idea, but is having trouble articulating it, and the person who has no idea and is hoping that talking will make one appear. The former can be overcome by judicious interruptions and restatements of the participant's position; the latter is somewhat harder. When people are clearly talking without purpose, ask them to wrap up their thought and move on, calling on someone else or asking a different question. If they continue to talk aimlessly, politely remind them that they need to let some of the other people in the room speak.

- *Group dominance* (the "Alpha Jerk" effect). A single dominant or bullying participant can ruin the utility of a focus group. Ideally, the best way to avoid the intimidation caused by such a person is to remove him or her before the group even starts. Such behavior patterns can be obvious when meeting and observing participants in the waiting room. However, once the group is going and it's obvious that there's a person who is vying for the "control" of the group, it's critical to draw attention away from him or her and into the group as a whole and to reinforce the notion of the moderator as the driver of the group. The techniques are basically the same as for a talkative person, but they need to be applied more firmly (and often, more frequently) than for someone who's merely wordy. In addition, physically dominating the discussion space by standing up and walking to a whiteboard helps to regain the floor and control of the discussion.

- *Unqualified participants.* Sometimes people misunderstand what the participation criteria are, or they misrepresent their experience. Weeding these people out early is important since they will likely not be able to contribute to the discussion in a meaningful way, and their presence will tend to make the other participants uncomfortable. Asking the key screening criteria early in the session and gently requesting participants who don't match to leave the room may make the rest of the group much more productive on the whole.

- *Tangents.* Groups will have a tendency to spiral off on tangents. These can be useful discussions of values and ideas, which when important to the topic, should be allowed to run for a while. When they're on points of marginal interest, they should be wrapped up as quickly as possible. After noting that people seem to be interested in a topic—no topic should ever be discouraged flat-out—the moderator should encourage the group to wrap up the discussion or to postpone it.

- *Hostility.* Open hostility in focus groups is rare, but certain people (and certain ideas) can cause it. Vehement disagreement or offensive ideas can lead people to grow hostile. At this point, the moderator should remain impartial and focus the discussion on the ideas rather than the emotions. Thus, a statement full of emotional content should be treated as if it were emotionally neutral. For example, if someone says another person's statement is really dumb, ask what it is that he or she disagrees with rather than dealing with the concept of "dumb."

- *Offensive ideas.* Occasionally, someone will say something that offends the majority of the other participants. When this happens, either it can be used as a trigger to get all participants to share their opinions or it can polarize the group. To guide the discussion in the former direction, rather than letting it degenerate into partisanship or the ostracism of the speaker, ask if anyone else shares that view. Then ask if anyone has a different view and probe how their views are different. It's especially important for the moderator not to side with one view or another—even if you strongly disagree with the stated view—and concentrate on the facts of the statement.

- *Highly emotional topics.* Much like controversial topics and group hostility, emotional topics can get tricky. Again, the best way of dealing with them is by focusing on the ideas behind them, as long as emotional release doesn't become the only topic. This should be taken into account in the guide, and the participants should be given sufficient time to discuss their emotions if emotional responses are expected. If a topic unexpectedly veers in an emotional direction, the emotions of the participants should be respected and discussed, even at the detriment of a couple of questions in the guide. However, the moderator should move away from such a discussion as soon as possible while trying to get enough information about the experiential factors that led to the emotional state.

Managing Observers

You can extrapolate in any direction from one point, but two points determine a line.
—Carolyn Snyder, user experience consultant and principal, Snyder Consulting

As many people from the development team should attend as many focus groups in a series as possible. This gives the team instant information about their ideas, and it provides the analyst access to valuable technical expertise. For the same reasons that there should be more than one group per topic, people should be encouraged to observe at least two groups if they're planning to observe any. It's much easier to know which phenomena are unique to a given group of people and which may be more general phenomena when you've seen several groups discussing a given topic.

Since observers are an active part of the analysis process, it's important that they know how to approach the observation process. There's a right way to observe a focus group and many wrong ways. Make a point of meeting with new observers beforehand and prepare them for observing the focus group. The following instructions help prepare observers and can be presented as part of the initial orientation or as a written list.

FOCUS GROUP OBSERVER INSTRUCTIONS

1. Listen. As tempting as it is to immediately discuss what you're observing, make sure to listen to what people are really saying. Feel free to discuss what you're seeing, but don't forget to listen.

2. Don't jump to conclusions. Use people's statements as guides to how they think about the topic and what their values are, but don't treat the specifics of their statements as gospel. If everyone in a group says they like or hate something, that doesn't mean that the whole world thinks that way, but it is a good indicator that there are enough people who do so that you should pay attention.

3. Focus groups are not statistically representative. If four out of five people say something, that doesn't mean that 80% of the population feels that way. It means that a number of people may feel that way, but it doesn't mean anything in terms of the proportions found in the population as a whole. Nothing. Zilch.

(Continued)

4. Focus group participants are experts. The participants in a focus group know what they want to do and how they currently do it. Listen to their needs and their experience, and treat them as consultants who are telling you what your customers need, not as the consumers of a product or the targets of a sales pitch.

5. Focus groups are not a magic bullet. A couple of good ideas from every group is enough to make that group worthwhile, but not every statement that the group participants make should be followed to the letter.

6. Feel free to pass questions to the moderator, but don't overdo it. Occasional questions to the group are OK, but there should not be more than a couple in a session. Write your question clearly and concisely, and phrase it as if you were talking to the moderator. Then give it to the assistant moderator, who will then take it to the moderator. When appropriate for the flow of conversation, the moderator will introduce the question. However, the moderator may decide never to introduce it, if the timing or topic is inappropriate.

7. People are contradictory. Listen to how people are thinking about the topics and what criteria they use to come to conclusions, not necessarily the specific desires they voice. A person may not realize that two desires are impossible to have simultaneously, or he or she may not care. Two people may think they're agreeing, when they're actually saying the exact opposite.

8. Don't write people off. Sometimes, a participant may say things that indicate that he or she isn't getting it. Never assume that someone has nothing important to say just because they aren't interesting or insightful from the start. Understanding why one participant "doesn't get it" can hold the key to understanding the perspectives of everyone who "does."

9. Save some pizza for the moderator.

Tips

- On rare occasions, it will be necessary to eject someone from the group because he or she is disruptive to the discussion or completely unqualified. The assistant moderator should do the dirty work and ask the person to leave, but only when both the moderator and the assistant agree that continuing the group with the person is impossible. In such a case, a good way of approaching the process is to find a natural break in the group and ask the person to leave. At the beginning, a demographic form or a nondisclosure agreement is a good time to duck out and discuss it with the assistant moderator. Later on, there can be a "5-minute stretch" or a similar pretext for breaking the action. During this time, the assistant moderator should come into the room and politely ask the person to go with him or her. The person should then be thanked for participating, given the promised honorarium, and excused. Everyone will know what happened, but the excitement of seeing someone "get kicked out" will quickly fade.

- Sometimes it's useful to have multiple moderators. If there are a lot of groups, or they're particularly long, or they're done in different languages, it's sometimes useful to use several people as moderators. If multiple people are going to be moderating, it's important that they go through every question and determine how they're going to ask it and what they will probe on.

- Two-way pagers or wireless chat devices (such as the Cybiko handheld) can be used instead of having the assistant moderator running in with notes. The moderator can have the device on the table and occasionally glance at it to see if there are new comments or questions from the observation room, where the assistant moderator (or one of the observers) operates another of the devices. When using a pager, use one that doesn't get a lot of messages so as not to distract the moderator, and turn off sound and vibration to keep new message alarms from interrupting the group.

Hiring Experts

Focus groups are an involved process, and you may choose to hire a company that specializes in organizing them rather than expending the time and energy to do the process in-house. There are several things to consider when hiring a company to run your focus group.

- Does the moderator know the subject? A moderator needs to be able to think on his or her feet about the subject and probe appropriately. Thus, the company should have some experience with either the specific subject or one that's closely related. If he or she does not, then you should prepare to brief the moderator in depth on the subject, the terminology, and the issues associated with the topic.

- Can they recruit the right people? Getting the right people for the focus group is critical to that group's success, thus the recruitment method is important. Ask the company how they get their database and how they will screen people for your focus group. Make sure to review the screener.

- How long is the turnaround time? The analysis method varies from company to company. Depending on the final deliverable, it can be from days to weeks. Make sure to find out what they are planning to do and how long it will take. You may want to forgo a fancy report and slide presentation for a list of findings and a discussion with the moderator and analyst.

As with any contract work, ask for references to the last couple of projects that the company has completed and follow up on them. Do not be shy about asking for satisfaction. If anything is amiss—the recruiting, the moderating, the analysis—call them on it. If necessary, request additional groups be run at their cost.

Focus Group Analysis

"Researchers must continually be careful to avoid the trap of selective perception."
—Richard A. Krueger, *Focus Groups,* p. 130

There are about as many ways of analyzing focus group information as there are analysts. Since the information is, by definition, qualitative and contextual, the focus of the analysis will depend on the purpose of the group. For some research projects, it will be critical to uncover the participants' mental models; for others, their first-hand experience may be what's most valuable. Still others may be completely focused on evaluating the competition.

The two fundamental processes of focus group analysis are collecting data and extracting trends. Although the bulk of data collection usually precedes the bulk of analysis, one does not strictly follow the other. Often, the two intertwine as trends cause a reconsideration of the data and patterns in the data emerge as trends.

Collecting Data

Focus groups produce a lot of information: transcripts, quotations, observer opinions, models, and videotapes. Organizing and prioritizing all this information is the first step in extracting trends from it. This begins with capturing the most ephemeral information, the gut-level trend observations of those who observed the groups. These first-order hypotheses help focus the data collection that happens later.

Capture Initial Hypotheses

The moderator, assistant moderator, and the observers should be debriefed in between every group. Since groups can get confused in people's memory as time passes, getting people's thoughts on each group immediately after it's over reduces the amount of disentanglement of ideas and experiences required later. Everyone's notes should be copied, and their observations should be collected through interviews. An effective way to organize and trigger people's memories is to use the guide. Walking through the guide section by section, ask the moderator and observers to recall their thoughts about it. What was unexpected? What was expected, but didn't happen? What attitudes did people display? What values did they espouse? What interesting statements did they make (and why were they interesting)? What trends did they observe? Which participants provided interesting feedback? What were the problems with the group? These observations often serve as the backbone of later analysis.

After the debriefing, the analyst should write down his or her memory of the events as completely as possible. Afterward, the analyst should organize the observations in the debriefing notes into themes or issues. These can serve as categories in organizing the more formal analysis of the proceedings.

Transcribe and Code

The process of formally analyzing the focus group should begin with *transcription*. The traditional method is to hire a transcription service. The service will provide a document with every word every person said. This can be quite useful for rapidly pulling together a larger number of quotations. Unfortunately, transcription services can be expensive and take a long time, and the transcripts can be unwieldy (it's not unusual for the transcript of a two-hour focus group to be 100 pages long). A simpler method is to watch the videotapes and transcribe just the parts that the analyst considers most important.

Even without formal transcription, carefully review the tapes. Merely remembering a situation can miss subtle behaviors. Words can be misquoted. Observers fall into group-think. Watching the original discussions can clarify ambiguities and reveal shades of meaning that are hidden when working from memory alone. The tapes need not be watched in the order they were made; the ones that you believe will be the most useful should be watched first. If there were a lot of groups in a series (say, five or more) and time is short, you can skip viewing the "dud" groups (though watching fewer than four tapes risks missing some key issues or revealing quotes).

As you're watching the tapes, you should be *coding* the comments. Coding is the process of categorizing responses in order to track trends. The codes should have short, descriptive names, and each should embody a single idea or trend that you're trying to follow. Codes should reflect the topics you're interested in studying. If you'd like to isolate the kinds of experiences people have in specific situations, you could code for different situations or experiences. If you want to understand people's priorities, you could have different codes for expressed preferences. You can start your list of codes with the topics that drove the writing of the discussion guide, adding others that may have come up during the debriefing. For example, if your original goals were "to understand the mental models people use when researching insurance" and "to collect stories of how people's existing insurance failed them" and you observed that people felt intimidated by their insurance company, then your initial set of codes could look like this.

SAMPLE TOP-LEVEL CODES FOR AN INSURANCE FOCUS GROUP

Model: How people understand the insurance claims process and the process by which they choose their insurance, including the parameters they base their choices on and the methods by which they evaluate the parameters.

Bad Story: Episodes where the process of picking insurance or the process of filing an insurance claim has been difficult or frustrating. This can include mistaken expectations, disappointment, or even the insurer's outright failure to deliver on promises. If there are positive stories, these can be coded as "Good Story."

Intimidation: If the participant ever felt intimidated by his or her insurance company, scared by the process, or that the process was not under his or her control.

Note A more formal method of creating a coding structure is described in Chapter 13. There are also a number of software packages that can assist in the process.

Codes can, of course, be divided or combined if the need arises. If you decide that you need to differentiate between situations where people are intimidated by their insurance provider and situations where they're intimidated by the process, it may be appropriate to create several subcategories. Don't get overzealous about it, however. Although some social research studies are known to code hundreds of different kinds of events and utterances, a dozen categories are sufficient for most user experience research.

With code sheet in hand, watch the video. When something that matches one of your codes or seems interesting and relevant comes up, note it down, keeping track of who said it and when during the group it was said. If someone says something that really encapsulates an idea or fits into the coding scheme, transcribe it. The key to transcribing is capturing the meaning of people's words, so although you should aim for exact transcription, don't shy away from paraphrasing, dropping unnecessary words, or adding parenthetical expressions to provide context. However, always make it clear which words are yours and which are the participants'.

When you've transcribed and coded all the tapes you've chosen, go back through the transcriptions and check for accuracy in coding, revising your code system and recoding if necessary.

Warning The analysis of focus group data can be a contentious process. The key to providing good, believable analysis is to create distance between the analyst and the product. Even if you're deeply involved in the product's creation, now is the time to be as objective as possible. Do not let expectations, hopes, or any conclusions you came to while watching or running the groups affect your perception of the participants' statements and behavior. Be ruthless. When you're analyzing the data, pretend that you've never seen these groups before and that you know nothing about either the site or the topic.

Extracting Trends

With the coded list of quotations in hand, it's time to find a deeper meaning in the groups. This section describes a thorough, fairly rigorous approach. Sometimes time or resource pressures make it difficult to do the process to the full extent. In such situations, simplification is perfectly acceptable, although it should be done with care so as not to skew the results so they're no longer useful.

Focus group analysis techniques are similar to the technique used in contextual inquiry research. Observations are clustered and labeled and become the basis for determining the trends in people's behavior and attitudes. Those trends are then fleshed out and hypotheses are made to explain them, using the data to back them up.

Start with your category codes. The codes represent your original intentions and the trends that you observed as you were examining the data. Flesh these out and revise them as necessary to fit your new understanding of the data. So if you've discovered that people aren't really intimidated by insurance companies as much as frustrated by their response in a claim situation, you could rewrite and add a code for situations where people were frustrated (or, if you wanted to concentrate on the claim experience, you could create a new code that labeled all comments about claims).

Next, divide the observations your moderators and observers made, along with your first-cut, gut-level analysis, into trends and hypotheses. Then try to align these trends with the categories you defined earlier, removing overlapping ideas and clarifying the categories. Save the hypotheses for later, when you'll try to explain the trends.

Now rearrange the quotations and observations according to the revised code, organizing everything by what code it falls under (you can organize by moving chunks of text around in a word processor or writing them on Post-its). This gives you the opportunity to see if there are ways to organize previously uncoded observations and to place observations and quotations into multiple categories.

Your clusters should now be showing identifiable trends. Some will be expected and clear. Others will be surprising. There may be situations where you expected to find material to support an idea, but didn't. Try to organize the trends by similarity as much as possible. You can even label groups of trends.

Note If time is tight, coding can be skipped to expedite the process. Then the moderator, assistant moderator, and observers will base analysis on gut-level impressions. Although this captures the most obvious and severe problems, it's susceptible to group-think within the group of evaluators that can lead to unnecessary emphasis on certain topics while less discussed topics are ignored.

The research goals define that trends are important. A focus group series that's concerned with uncovering mental models will be more focused on the language and metaphors people use than a series that's trying to prioritize features, which may be more about the participants' interests and self-perception. Of course, since people's perceptions, values, and experiences are intertwined, there will rarely be a situation where an observation perfectly fits a trend or a trend only affects a single aspect of people's experience. In practice, the borders between trends will be fuzzy, and what exactly defines a trend may be unclear. However, in good research, even if the borders are fuzzy the middle is solid.

Here is a list of some of the things that you may want to extract from your data.

- *Mental models.* Mental models are related to metaphors. They're mental representations of how we understand the way the world works. For example, George Lakhoff and Mark

Johnson describe the "time is money" metaphor in their classic *Metaphors We Live By:* when talking about time, English speakers will often use analogies that equate time with money—time is "made," "wasted," "spent," and so forth. This may be important for the maker of a piece of collaborative software to know since it may make the creation of an information architecture and the naming of interface elements easier. Some people give software a personality and think of it, in some sense, as a helper, friend, or confidant. Of course, mental models have limits. Time can't really be "earned," except in prison, so that models should not be taken too literally. On a more mundane level, certain people may not realize that they can challenge a claim adjuster's estimate. Their mental model doesn't include the concept of arbitration or second opinions.

- *Values.* What do people like or dislike? What are the criteria that they use when they decide whether they like or dislike something? What do they consider important? What process do they use to create their values? How do their values interrelate? People's values determine a lot about the way they experience a product. When someone is excited by the content of a Web site, he or she may be willing to overlook all kinds of interaction problems, to a point. The same content presented another way may bore the person. People's value systems consist of likes, dislikes, beliefs, and the associations they make between these elements and the objects, people, and situations in their lives.

- *Stories.* Stories are a powerful way to understand the intricacies of people's experiences. They provide details about people's assumptions, the sequences in which they do things, how they solve problems (and what problems they have), and their opinions. Stories can illuminate and clarify many uncertainties about product development all at once. The similarities and differences between stories told by different people can reveal what kinds of mental models the target audience shares and what kinds of individual idiosyncrasies the development team can expect.

- *Problems.* Focus group brainstorms can quickly produce extensive lists of problems. Even without formal brainstorming, people's natural tendency to commiserate in a group of peers reveals lots of problems.

- *Competitive analysis.* What do people dislike about competitive products? What do they find important? What *are* the competitive products?

This list is by no means exhaustive. Where one focus group may be interested in the sequence in which people typically do tasks, another may try to uncover what makes a good logo for the company.

Here are some tips for getting the most useful information out of the data.

- Concentrate on the methods by which people come to their decisions. The actual decisions are important, too, but the reasons behind them can be even more revealing.
- Note people's terminology. Products that speak the same language as their users are more easily accepted. Verbatim transcripts can really help with this.
- Watch out for contradictions. How people say they behave or what they say they want may not actually correspond to what they actually do or how they'll actually use a product.
- Watch for situations where people change their mind. Knowing that someone changed his or her mind can reveal a lot about what he or she values.
- Popularity does not necessarily mean importance—what people consider to be important may not be what they talk about—but it *is* a strong indicator and should be noted. Likewise, the lack of popularity does not denote that a phenomenon is unimportant, but if something is only mentioned by a couple of people it should be considered a weak trend at best.

You may also want to do some quantitative analysis on the data. Although the numeric results of focus group data are not, on the whole, representative of your user population, they can be compared to each other. If you run two focus group series with similar groups before and after a redesign, and use the same discussion guide, moderator, and analyst, then comparing the number of certain problems or perceptions may be a valid way to see if people's experience has changed. However, the process needs to be closely controlled, and the results cannot be extrapolated beyond a comparison of the two groups.

In addition, when analyzing any focus group data, potential bias has to be taken into account and made explicit. The recruiting process, the phrasing of the questions, group-think, and the moderator and analyst's personal experiences may all have affected the answers. Even external events may affect people's perspectives (for example, people's views of leisure travel may be different on the day that the news picks up a report about transportation accidents than the day before). Be on the lookout for bias that may have been introduced, and make it clear in the report when it may exist and in what form.

Making Hypotheses

Explaining the causes of trends can be a difficult process. Each phenomenon may have a number of potential causes, and there may be data that support conflicting hypotheses. The analyst must make a judgment call on whether to propose hypotheses for people's behavior and beliefs, or whether to just state the beliefs and let the development team develop their own theories. This is an issue of debate in the industry, and there are no hard and fast rules about when it's appropriate. Often, the trends that are observed in focus groups can point at deep social and psychological issues that are difficult, if not impossible, to explain or justify (for example, "People claim to dislike advertising"). It's often sufficient to know the dimensions of a problem to solve it rather than knowing its exact causes.

Sometimes, however, analyzing the potential causes of problems and comparing their magnitudes to one another can make finding solutions easier. So if people are both intimidated by and angry at their insurance company, knowing why they're intimidated and angry can help determine which is the more important problem to tackle. If root causes are not obvious from the collected data, it may be appropriate to do additional research. Thus, if the exact sequence that someone goes through when he or she is trying to pick an insurance company is not obvious from the focus groups and is important to the product's functionality, a round of field-based task analysis may be appropriate. Likewise, if it's important to know the exact magnitude of people in the target audience who are intimidated by the process of buying insurance, a statistically valid survey can be run.

As with all user experience research, focus groups may produce more questions than answers, but the questions may be better than those asked before the groups were run.

Example

This is a report summarizing the results of a focus group series investigating people's car insurance experiences. The name AutoSafe.com is fictitious.

Executive Summary

Twenty-four people in four groups of six were interviewed about their recent car accident experiences. Although they were often happy with the results of their auto repair process, they did not understand the process well, and wanted guidance about the steps and their options at each step more than specific recommendations. The insurance companies, whom they trusted as protectors and guides, drove the process. Independent third-party information was most useful at the beginning of the process, when people had the largest number of choices to make and the least information about what was ahead. Body shop evaluations and an "accident anatomy" would have proved most useful at this point since body shops were not trusted and the process was unknown.

Their understanding of the process was in several large steps: communication (with family, work, and insurance), insurance (for the beginning of the guiding process), interim transportation, body shop management, and aftermath management (when things were delayed or went wrong). There was also a parallel medical process in the cases where injuries occurred that sometimes involved car insurance.

When presented with the idea for a service that would provide unbiased information in addition to helping people track their car repair, everyone responded positively to it. The highest value was felt to be in a clarification of the process and the unbiased perspective. After hours and email updates were seen as useful features, although people were curious (and somewhat dubious) about how the process would actually work.

Example   249

Procedure

Please see Appendix A at the end of this document for the full discussion guide.

Evaluator Profiles

A chart summarizing participants' demographic, Web use, technological, and car accident profiles was provided with the complete report. This allowed the recipients of the report to better understand the context of specific quotations.

Objectives

1. *Figure out how people understand the repair/insurance process.*
2. *Determine the points of pain in the process.*
3. *Determine where third-party assistance would have helped.*

Process Model

One of the primary goals of this research was to understand how people thought about the postaccident car repair process. This understanding, this mental model, breaks down into two pieces: an emotional component and a procedural component. The emotional component consists of the set of feelings and perceptions that people have about the process. The procedural component is their understanding of how the process is supposed to work and what their role in it is.

In general, the participants' emotions did not seem to run very deeply about the repair aspects of their accident experience. A number of people in each group were happy with their insurance company and their body shop (though not always at the same time). Many were happy with the final outcome. The strongest emotional reactions seemed to fall at the beginning of the experience—because of the uncertainty with the procedure and the foreboding of the expense (and, in some cases, because of the medical issues involved)—and at the end, when anxiety about the completion of the car and the payment of the claim was highest.

Moreover, because of the varied circumstances of people's accidents (some had injury accidents, some had delayed injury, some had cars that were driveable, others didn't, some had good garage experiences, others didn't), the steps in the process and the interaction of the emotional process with the procedural process varied quite a bit in practice.

Therefore, I am attempting to generalize as much as possible based on the responses and to extract both the emotional and procedural components, but place them in context with each other, in order to capture as much of the participants' thoughts as possible. The model has six major components.

- *Background expectations*
- *Postaccident contact*
- *Insurance company logistics*
- *Transportation logistics*
- *Body shop logistics*
- *Aftermath*

Model and observations omitted. Most observations were supported with supporting quotations. For example:

8. *Communication issues were mentioned a number of times, with people feeling as if they didn't know enough about what was happening in the process—especially when it came to the state of their repair.*

   Robert: "You have to do your own follow-up; there doesn't seem to be a follow-up system. You don't know what's happening; you only know the day before you're supposed to pick up your car they'll call you and tell you it'll be another week."
   Manuela: "If you don't do anything, nothing happens. You're initiating everything."

Conclusion

The repair tracking component of the product, though valuable, does not seem to be perceived as being as valuable as the objective recommendation component, so it may be a good point of emphasis when matching people's needs for such a product.

Moreover, because people understand little about the process, and are probably unlikely to do any research to understand it before an accident happens, the most important contribution to their experience may be just the explanation of the process. Thus, matching their existing model, which is weakly formulated at best, may not be as valuable as giving them a model and explaining the steps in it.

Example **251**

Thus, defining and demystifying the process while making it more objective may be more valuable to people than automation.

APPENDIX A: Discussion Guide

This is the discussion guide used in the research.

Warm-up and Intro (10 minutes)

Objective: Introduce process and make participants at ease.
Hi. Welcome.
Mike introduces himself.

- *A market researcher*
- *Not associated with any of the products we'll be talking about today*
- *Have no emotional attachment to any of these things, so you can say whatever you want*
- *Helping a company with a new idea that they have*

What we're going to do today is talk about some of your experiences so that they can create service that is best tailored to experiences of people like you. It's mostly going to be pretty casual conversation, but there will be a couple of times when I focus on certain things.

While we're talking, it's important that you be as candid as possible. You won't hurt anyone's feelings by anything you say, so please say exactly what you feel.

We want your opinion. No opinion is right or wrong—especially about the things we're going to talk about—it's just an opinion, so even if you disagree with someone in the room, we'd like to hear that.

But we'd like you to speak one at a time.

Also, since we have a lot of ground to cover today and none of us want to be here for hours, I may have to ask you to wrap up a thought or put it aside so that we can move on.

Behind that glass wall, as you can imagine, are a couple of people from the company whose idea we'll be talking about, and Mary, who is working with me. Occasionally, Mary may come in here with a note or something we need. Regardless, feel free to ignore them. As I said, we brought you here to hear what you think, so you won't hurt anyone's feelings by whatever you say. This videotape, in case you're wondering, is here so that Mary and

I don't have to sit here feverishly scribbling notes and can concentrate on listening to you. It's purely for research purposes. It may be seen by members of the product development team, but it's not for any kind of publicity or promotion or broadcast.

Informed Consent

Now I'd like to read you what's called an informed consent clause; it's a standard thing I read to everyone I interview. It sets out your rights as a person who is participating in this kind of research.

As a participant in this research

- *You may stop at any time.*
- *You may ask questions at any time.*
- *You may leave at any time.*
- *There is no deception involved.*
- *Your answers are kept confidential.*

Here is a form that gives us permission to videotape this discussion and to use the videotape in our research.

Respondent Introduction

Name

Which city you live in

What TV shows and publications do you make an effort to keep up with?

What are your favorite Web sites? Is there anything that really bothers you about the Web?

(Mike does introduction for himself; everyone goes around).

The Repair Process (10–20 minutes)

Objective: Introduce car accident aftermath topic and make people feel comfortable with it. Try to determine the order they perceive the steps in the repair/claim process (i.e., the mental model they have of what happens between the time their car is hit and it's fixed or totaled).

Example   253

(2 minutes) As you probably guessed from the questions you were asked on the phone, we're going to talk today about car accidents. But don't worry, we're not going to talk about the accidents themselves—I'm sure that was unpleasant enough that it's not worth revisiting. I'd like to talk about what happened after *the accident.*

The first thing I'd like to do is to try to figure out what happens between the time the tow truck arrives and the whole process is over. That way we can see where there were problems and if there's some way in which things can be made better.

(10 minutes) What's the first step of the process? [write down] Does everyone agree? [if not, then start a parallel list]. In a couple of words, describe what goes into that.

What's the next step? [write down]

Let's take a look at the list for a minute. Anyone notice anything missing?

Is there anything that doesn't fit, that doesn't make sense? Would any of you put any of these steps in a different order?

General Impressions (15 minutes)

Objectives: Get top-level points of pain and see if they're consistent for people with few and many accidents.

So all of you are here because you had a car accident ["in the last year"; "a couple of years ago"]. Was this anyone's first car accident?

(3–5 minutes) [If so, ask people who answer] What was the most unpleasant thing about the process for you? [ask one of the other first-timers] Was this the same thing for you?

How about you? [ask one of the people who have had another car accident]

(5 minutes) [ask specific people] On a scale of one to five—where five is something you'd never, ever, ever want to go through again and one is, say, a paper cut—how would you rate how annoyed you were overall? [everyone] Any fives? [if so, ask specific people why]

(3 minutes) Using the list we put together earlier, I'd like to do a quick rating of each of these points. Using a one-to-five scale, put your hand up to indicate how annoying you think each part was; five being really superannoying, and one being not really annoying or mildly annoying. I'll average them in the air. [go through points]

(3 minutes) What about good experiences? Was anyone pleasantly surprised by something? What was it that surprised you? What made it a good experience? Any others?

If time allows:

Any other positive experiences with, say, a mechanic or someone from the insurance company? [describe]

(1 minute) So the rest of you have been in at least one other accident. Has anyone here been in more than two? Three? Four? [keep going]

(2 minutes) [Ask the most experienced] What's been the most consistently annoying thing for you in those times you had to deal with this?

Body Shops (15 minutes)

Objective: Determine points of pain in the repair experience and how people choose their repair shops.

OK, let's change gears here for a second and talk about how your car got fixed.

(5 minutes) Let's rate your body shop experiences. One means it was a good experience, five means it was a bad experience, and three means it was OK, considering the fact that that it's not something that any of us do for entertainment. Just raise your hand with the number. [if someone has a one or two, ask] What was good about it?

(5 minutes) Who had a bad experience? [Ask a couple of people who had fours or fives] What was the worst thing about it? Anyone else have this experience? [pick a person] Was this the worst part, or did you have bigger hassles?

Were there any other hassles that you had to put up with when dealing with the garage?

(5 minutes) Say someone was available to give you advice about body shops or garages. At what point would you have most wanted to be able to ask someone for advice? [ask people specifically] What kind of advice would you have been interested in?

If there's time:

(5 minutes) [Go around] How did you pick where your car was repaired? Would you choose a different place if you had to do this again?

(5 minutes) Let's make a list. What things are important when choosing a body shop?

Example **255**

(3 minutes) [Pick a couple of people] If a friend or a co-worker got into an accident and asked you how to choose a place to get his or her car fixed, what kind of advice would you give him or her?

Insurance (15–20 minutes)

Objective: Determine points of pain in the claim experience and how people choose their insurance companies.

OK, let's change gears again and talk about the insurance part of the experience.

(3 minutes) First thing, did any of you change your insurance after your accident?

Are any of you thinking about changing your insurance? Is it because of the accident? [If so] Why?

(7 minutes) Take a minute to think about the most important thing you learned about car insurance from this experience. Think about all the things that you had to do and everything that went into the process. What were the biggest surprises? The biggest hassles?

[go around and discuss]

(5 minutes) [Ask one person] Say you were giving me advice about picking an insurance company. What kinds of things would you say are important when choosing an insurance company? [Ask second person] Is there anything else I should know? Anyone?

(1 minute) Are there any places I can go for information about various insurance companies and policies? Something that'll compare them for me.

(3 minutes) Say someone was available to give you advice about insurance companies. At what point would you have most wanted to be able to ask someone for advice? [ask people specifically]

If there's time:

(2 minutes) Who here paid their deductible immediately? Who waited two weeks? A month? More?

Anyone put his or her deductible on a credit card?

(5 minutes) Did any of you have any problems with your insurance company as far as your deductible was concerned? What kinds?

(3 minutes) Wrapping up, in one quick sentence, say what you know now about car insurance that you didn't before. [go around quickly]

AutoSafe.com Idea and General Web Stuff (10 minutes)

Objective: Introduce idea of AutoSafe.com and see if people understand and appreciate it; get some feature ideas through a short brainstorm; find out how they prioritize existing feature ideas.

OK, those are all the questions that I have about the problems that you had. I'd like to switch now to ways that we can solve these problems.

(1 minute) Say there was a Web site that helped keep track of your repair and that gave you information about what stage of the repair process you're in. Say this Web site also had links to unbiased information about both other insurance companies and body shops.

(2 minutes) Would you be interested?

(5 minutes) Let's brainstorm for a couple of minutes. Not thinking in terms of practicality at all, what would you like such a service to do for you? [write down ideas, if they get stumped, mention some of the existing ideas and see if that triggers anything]

(5 minutes) OK, how many people would like an unbiased information source that rates insurance companies, something like a Consumer Reports? Now, say you were looking at such a Web site and you noticed that there was an ad on it. Any of you have any issues with having an ad on a Consumer Reports-type of page? What if it were an ad for, say, Ford? What if it were an ad for a car insurance company?

If there's time:

(2 minutes) If this service was described to you as "your one-stop accident shop," do you think that would make sense based on what you know it is?

Now, I'd like to ask a couple of general Web questions.

(3 minutes) Have any of you ever signed up for a service online where you had to enter your name and email address? How about your home address? How about your phone number?

(5 minutes) What kind of personal information do you folks feel uncomfortable giving to a Web site? [write down list] What about in exchange for a service? For instance, if you could have AutoSafe.com take care of all the paperwork for your claim and then just mail it to you at home, would you feel comfortable entering your home address? Is there anything on this list that you would never give to a Web site, no matter what?

Example 257

Wrap-up (5 minutes)

Objective: Conclude focus group and give people contact information for further ideas.

I know you're all excited now and you probably want to talk about this stuff for hours, but unfortunately, that's the last of my questions about cars and insurance. If you're on your way home and something that's really important about all this stuff pops into your head, please contact us and let us know. You can send a note to Mary at [write email] or call her at [write phone number].

I have one final question, and it doesn't relate to insurance or car accidents or Web pages at all: is there anything that we could do better, either in terms of scheduling or in terms of running these groups? Should we have more snacks, a case of beer, whatever?

OK, thank you all very much for coming. It's been really interesting and helpful to hear your thoughts.

CHAPTER 10

Usability Tests

A one-on-one usability test can quickly reveal an immense amount of information about how people use a prototype, whether functional, mock-up, or just paper. Usability testing is probably the fastest and easiest way to tease out showstopping usability problems before a product launches.

Usability tests are structured interviews focused on specific features in an interface prototype. The heart of the interview is a series of tasks that are performed by the interface's *evaluator* (typically, a person who matches the product's ideal audience). Tapes and notes from the interview are later analyzed for the evaluator's successes, misunderstandings, mistakes, and opinions. After a number of these tests have been performed, the observations are compared, and the most common issues are collected into a list of functionality and presentation problems.

Using usability tests, the development team can immediately see whether people understand their designs as they are supposed to understand them. Unfortunately, the technique has acquired the aura of a final check before the project is complete, and usability tests are often scheduled at the end of the development cycle—after the feature set has been locked, the target markets have been determined, and the product is ready for shipping. Although testing can certainly provide insight into the next revision of the product, the full power of the technique remains untapped. They can be better used much earlier, providing feedback throughout the development cycle, both to check the usability of specific features and to investigate new ideas and evaluate hunches.

When to Test

Since usability testing is best at seeing how people perform specific tasks, it should be used to examine the functionality of individual features and the way they're presented to the intended user. It is better used to highlight potential misunderstanding or errors inherent in the way features are implemented rather than to evaluate the entire user experience. During the early to middle parts of a development cycle, usability testing can play a key role in guiding the direction of functionality as features are defined and developed. Once the functionality of a feature is locked in and its interaction with other features has been determined, however, it's often too late to make any fundamental changes. Testing at that point is more an investment in the next version than in the current one.

Moreover, unlike some of the other techniques mentioned throughout this book, usability testing is almost never a one-time event in a development cycle for a product, and should not be seen as such. Every round of testing can focus on a small set of features (usually no more than five), so a series of tests is used to test a whole interface or fine-tune a specific set of features.

The first thing the development team needs to do is decide on the *target audience* and the *feature set to examine.*

This means that a good time to start usability testing is when the development cycle is somewhat under way, but not so late that testing prevents the implementation of extensive changes if it points to their necessity. Occasionally, usability testing reveals problems that require a lot of work to correct, so the team should be prepared to rethink and reimplement (and, ideally, retest) features if need be. In the Web world, this generally takes a couple of weeks, which is why iterative usability testing is often done in two-week intervals.

A solid usability testing program will include iterative usability testing of every major feature, with tests scheduled throughout the development process, reinforcing and deepening knowledge about people's behavior and ensuring that designs become more effective as they develop.

Warning Completely open-ended testing, or "fishing," is rarely valuable. When you go fishing during a round of user research—often prompted by someone saying, "let's test the whole thing"—the results are neither particularly clear nor insightful. Know why you're testing before you begin.

Example of an Iterative Testing Process: Webmonkey 2.0 Global Navigation

Webmonkey is a cutting-edge Web development magazine that uses the technologies and techniques it covers. During a redesign cycle, they decided that they wanted to create something entirely new for the main interface. Since much of the 1.0 interface had been extensively tested and was being carried through to the new design, they wanted to concentrate their testing and development efforts on the new features.

The most ambitious and problematic of the new elements being considered was a DHTML global navigational panel that gave access to the whole site (see Figures 10.1 and 10.2), but didn't permanently use screen real estate. Instead, it would slide on and off

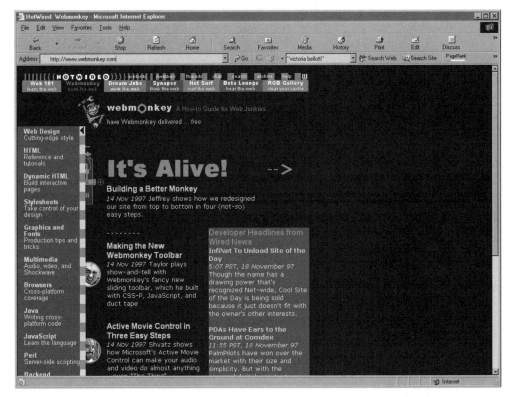

Figure 10.1 The Webmonkey 2.0 Navigation Panel design (open).

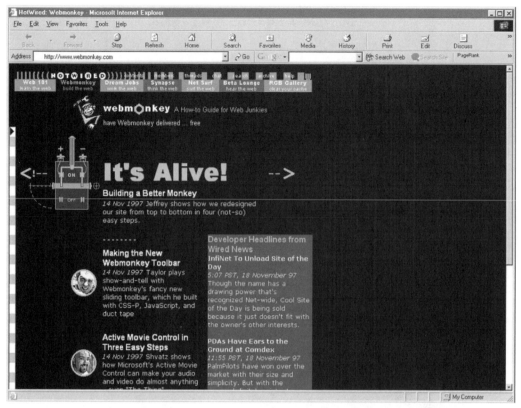

Figure 10.2 The Webmonkey 2.0 Navigation Panel design (closed).

the screen when the user needed it. Webmonkey's previous navigation scheme worked well, but analysis by the team determined that it was not used often enough to justify the amount of space it was taking up. They didn't want to add emphasis to it (it was, after all, secondary to the site's content), so they decided to minimize its use of screen real estate, instead of attempting to increase its use. Their initial design was a traditional vertical navigation bar, identical to that found in the left margin of the 1.0 site, but in its own panel. The panel was hidden most of the time, but would reveal its contents when an arrow at the top of a striped bar on the left side was clicked. The target audience of Web developers would hopefully notice the striped bar and arrow, and click on it out of curiosity.

Webmonkey developed on an iterative development cycle, so Web developers and sophisticated users were invited to a series of tests, with each test phase being followed by a design phase to incorporate the findings of the test. Although the purpose of the test was to examine the participants' entire user experience, the developers paid special attention to the sliding panel. In the first round of testing, none of the six evaluators opened the panel. When asked whether they had seen the bar and the arrow, most said they had, but they took the striped bar to be a graphical element and the arrow to be decoration.

Two weeks later, the visual design had not changed much, but the designers changed the panel from being closed by default to being open when the page first loaded. During testing, the evaluators naturally noticed the panel and understood what it was for, but they consistently had trouble closing it in order to see the content that it obscured. Some tried dragging it like a window; others tried to click inside it. Most had seen the arrow, but they didn't know how it related to the panel and so they never tried clicking it. Further questioning revealed that they didn't realize that the panel was a piece of the window that slid open and closed. Thus, there were two interrelated problems: people didn't know how the panel functioned, and they didn't know that the arrow was a functional element.

A third design attempted to solve the problem by providing an example of the panel's function as the first experience on the page: a short pause after the page loaded, the panel opened and closed by itself. The designers hoped that showing the panel in action would make the panel's function clearer. It did, and in the next round of testing, the evaluators described both its content and its function correctly. However, none were able to open the panel again. The new design still did not solve the problem with the arrow, and most people tried to click and drag in the striped bar to get at the panel. Having observed this behavior, and (after some debate) realizing that they could not technically implement a dragging mechanism for the panel, the designers made the entire colored bar clickable, so that whenever someone clicked anywhere in it, the panel slid out (or back, if it was already open).

In the end, people still didn't know what the arrow was for, but when they clicked in the striped panel to slide it open, it did, which was sufficient to make the feature usable, and none of the people observed using it had any trouble opening or closing the panel thereafter.

How to Do It

Preparation

Although it's similar to the "friends and family" test described in Chapter 2, a full-on usability test takes significantly longer to plan, execute, and analyze (see Table 10.1). You should start preparing for a usability testing cycle at least three weeks before you expect to need the results.

Setting a Schedule

Timing	Activity
$t - 2$ weeks	Determine test audience; start recruiting immediately
$t - 2$ weeks	Determine feature set to be tested
$t - 1$ week	Write first version of script; construct test tasks; discuss with development team; check on recruiting
$t - 3$ days	Write second version of guide; review tasks; discuss with development team; recruiting should be completed
$t - 2$ days	Complete guide; schedule practice test; set up and check all equipment
$t - 1$ day	Do practice test in the morning; adjust guide and tasks as appropriate
t	Test (usually 1–2 days, depending on scheduling)
$t + 1$ day	Discuss with observers; collect copies of all notes
$t + 2$ days	Relax; take a day off and do something else
$t + 3$ days	Watch all tapes; take notes
$t + 1$ week	Combine notes; write analysis
$t + 1$ week	Present to development team; discuss and note directions for further research

Before the process can begin, you need to know whom to recruit and which features to have them evaluate. Both of these things should be decided several weeks before the testing begins.

Recruiting

Recruiting is the most crucial piece to start on early. It needs to be timed right and to be precise, especially if it's outsourced. You need to find the right people and to match their schedules to yours. That takes time and effort. The more time you can devote to the recruiting process, the better (although more than two weeks in advance is generally too early since people often don't know their schedules that far in advance). You also need to choose your screening criteria carefully. The initial impulse is to recruit people who fall into the product's ideal target audience, but that's almost always too broad. You need to home in on the representatives of the target audience who are going to give you the most useful feedback.

Say you're about to put up a site that sells upscale forks online. Your ideal audience consists of people who want to buy forks.

In recruiting for a usability test, that's a pretty broad range of people. Narrowing your focus helps preserve clarity since different groups can exhibit different behaviors based on the same fundamental usability problems. Age, experience, and motivation can create seemingly different user experiences that are caused by the same underlying problem. Choosing the "most representative" group can reduce the amount of research you have to do in the long run and focus your results.

The best people to invite are those who are going to need the service you are providing in the near future or who have used a competing service in the recent past. These people will have the highest level of interest and knowledge in the subject matter, so they can concentrate on how well the interface works rather than on the minutia of the information. People who have no interest in the content can still point out interaction flaws, but they are not nearly as good at pointing out problems with the information architecture or any kind of content-specific features since they have little motivation to concentrate and make it work.

Say your research of the fork market shows that there are two strong subgroups within that broad range: people who are replacing their old silverware and people who are buying wedding presents. The first group, according to your research, is mostly men in their 40s, whereas the second group is split evenly between men and women, mostly in their mid-20s and 30s.

You decide that the people who are buying sets of forks to replace those they already own represent the heart of your user community. They are likely to know about the subject matter and may have done some research already. They're motivated to use the service, which makes them more likely to use it as they would in a regular situation. So you decide to recruit men in their 40s who want to buy replacement forks in the near future or who have recently bought some. In addition, you want to filter out online newbies, and you want to get people with online purchasing experience. Including all these conditions, your final set of recruiting criteria looks as follows:

- Men or women, preferably men
- 25 years old or older, preferably 35–50
- Have Internet access at home or work
- Use the Web five or more hours a week
- Have one or more years of Internet experience
- Have bought at least three things online
- Have bought something online in the last three months
- Are interested in buying silverware online

Note Recruiters will try to follow your criteria to the letter, but if you can tell them which criteria are flexible (and how flexible they are) and which are immutable, it's easier for them. Ultimately, that makes it easier for you, too.

Notice that there is some flexibility in the age and gender criteria. This is to make the recruiter's life a little easier. You may insist that the participants be all male and that they must be between 40 and 50 years old, but if a candidate comes up who matches the rest of the criteria and happens to be 33 and female, you probably don't want to disqualify her immediately. Purchasing experience, on the other hand, requires precise requirements since getting people who aren't going to be puzzled or surprised by the concept of ecommerce is key to making the test successful. Testing an ecommerce system with someone who's never bought anything online tests the *concept* of ecommerce as much as it's testing the specific product. You rarely want that level of detail, so it's best to avoid situations that inspire it in the first place.

For this kind of focused task-based usability testing, you should have at least five participants in each round of testing and recruit somewhere from six to ten people for the five slots. Jakob Nielsen has shown (in *Guerrilla HCI: Using Discount Usability Engineering to Penetrate the Intimidation Barrier,* available from *www.useit.com/papers/guerrilla_hci.html*) that the cost-benefit cutoff for usability testing is about five users per target audience. Larger groups still produce useful results, but the cost of recruiting and the extra effort needed to run the tests and analyze the results leads to rapidly diminishing returns. After eight or nine users, the majority of problems performing a given task will have been seen several times. To offset no-shows, however, it's a good idea to schedule a couple of extra people beyond the basic five. And to make absolutely sure you have enough people, you could double-book every time slot. This doubles your recruiting and incentive costs, but it ensures that there's minimal downtime in testing.

In addition, to check your understanding of your primary audience, you can recruit one or two people from secondary target audiences—in the fork case, for example, a younger buyer or someone who's not as Web savvy—to see whether there's a hint of a radically different perspective in those groups. This won't give you conclusive results, but if you get someone who seems to be reasonable and consistently says something contrary to the main group, it's an indicator that you should probably rethink your recruiting criteria. If the secondary audience is particularly important, it should have its own set of tests, regardless.

Having decided whom to recruit, it's time to write a screener and send it to the recruiter. Screeners and recruiting are described in Chapter 6 of this book. Make sure to discuss the screener with your recruiter and to walk through it with at least two people in-house to get a reality check.

Then pick a couple of test dates and send out invitations to the people who match your criteria. Schedule interviews at times that are convenient to both you and the participant and leave at least half an hour between them. That gives the moderator enough slop time to have people come in late, for the test to run long, and for the moderator to get a glass of water and discuss the test with the observers. With 60-minute interviews, this means that you can do four or five in a single day and sometimes as many as six. With 90-minute

Warning You should strive to conduct a different test for each major user market since—by definition—each user market is likely to use the product differently. User markets are defined in Chapter 7.

In addition, Jared Spool and Will Schroeder point out (in *www.winwriters.com/download/chi01_spool.pdf*) that when you are going to give evaluators broad goals to satisfy, rather than specific tasks to do, you need more people than just five. However, in my opinion, broad goal research is less usability testing than a kind of focused contextual inquiry (Chapter 8) and should be conducted as such.

Warning If you're testing for the first time, schedule fewer people and put extra time in between. Usability testing can be exhausting, especially if you're new to the technique.

interviews, you can do three or four evaluators and maybe five if you push it and skip lunch.

Choosing Features

The second step is to determine which features to test. These, in turn, determine the tasks you create and the order in which you present them. You should choose features with enough lead time so that the test procedure can be fine-tuned. Five features (or feature clusters) can be tested in a given 60- to 90-minute interview. Typical tests range from one to two hours. Two-hour tests are used for initial or broad-based testing, while shorter tests are most useful for in-depth research into specific features or ideas (though it's perfectly acceptable to do a 90-minute broad-based test).

Individual functions should be tested in the context of feature clusters. It's rarely useful to test elements of a set without looking at least a little at the whole set. My rule of thumb is that something is testable when it's one of the things that gets drawn on a whiteboard when making a 30-second sketch of the interface. If you would draw a blob that's labeled "nav bar" in such a situation, then think of testing the nav bar, not just the new link to the homepage.

The best way to start the process is by meeting with the development staff (at least the product manager, the interaction designers, and the information architects) and making a list of the five most important features to test. To start discussing which features to include, look at features that are

- Used often
- New
- Highly publicized
- Considered troublesome, based on feedback from earlier versions
- Potentially dangerous or have bad side effects if used incorrectly
- Considered important by users

A Feature Prioritization Exercise

This exercise is a structured way of coming up with a feature prioritization list. It's useful when the group doesn't have a lot of experience prioritizing features or if it's having trouble.

- Step 1: Have the group make a list of the most important things on the interface that are new or have been drastically changed since the last round of testing. Importance should not just be defined purely in terms of prominence; it can be relative to the corporate bottom line or managerial priority. Thus, if next quarter's profitability has been staked on the success of a new Fork of the Week section, it's important, even if it's a small part of the interface.
- Step 2: Make a column and label it "Importance." Look at each feature and rate it on a scale of 1 to 5, where 5 means it's critical to the success of the product, and 1 means it's not very important.

Next, make a second column and label it "Doubt." Look at each feature and rate how comfortable the team is with the design, labeling the most comfortable items with a 1 and the least comfortable with a 5. This may involve some debate among the group, so you may have to treat it as a focus group of the development staff.

- Step 3: Multiply the two entries in the two columns and write the results next to them. The features with the greatest numbers next to them are the features you should test. Call these out and write a short sentence that summarizes what the group most wants to know about the functionality of the feature.

TOP FIVE FORK CATALOG FEATURES BY PRIORITY

	Importance	Doubt	Total
The purchasing mechanism *Does it work for both single items and whole sets?*	5	5	25
The search engine *Can people use it to find specific items?*	5	5	25
Catalog navigation *Can people navigate through it when they don't know exactly what they want?*	5	4	20
The Fork of the Week page *Do people see it?*	4	4	16
The Wish List *Do people know what it's for and can they use it?*	3	5	15

Once you have your list of the features that most need testing, you're ready to create the tasks that will exercise those features.

In addition, you can include competitive usability testing. Although comparing two interfaces is more time consuming than testing a single interface, it can reveal strengths and weaknesses between products. Performing the same tasks with an existing interface and a new prototype, for example, can reveal whether the new design is more functional (or—the fear of every designer—less functional). Likewise, performing the same tasks, or conducting similar interface tours with two competing products, can reveal relative strengths between the two products. In both situations, however, it's very important not to bias the evaluator toward one interface over the other. Competitive research is covered extensively in Chapter 14.

Creating Tasks

Tasks need to be representative of typical user activities and sufficiently isolated to focus attention on a single feature (or feature cluster) of the product. Good tasks should be

- *Reasonable.* They should be typical of the kinds of things that people will do. Someone is unlikely to want to order 90 different kinds of individual forks, each in a different pattern, and have them shipped to 37 different addresses, so that's not a typical task. Ordering a dozen forks and shipping them to a single address, however, is.
- *Described in terms of end goals.* Every product, every Web site, is a tool. It's not an end to itself. Even when people spend hours using it, they're doing something *with* it. So, much as actors can emote better when given their character's motivation, interface evaluators perform more realistically if they're motivated by a lifelike situation. Phrase your task as something that's related to the evaluator's life. If they're to find some information, tell them why they're trying to find it ("Your company is considering opening an office in Moscow and you'd like to get a feel for the reinsurance business climate there. You decide that the best way to do that is to check today's business headlines for information about reinsurance companies in Russia."). If they're trying to buy something, tell

them why ("Aunt Millie's subcompact car sounds like a jet plane. She needs a new muffler"). If they're trying to create something, give them some context ("Here's a picture of Uncle Fred. You decide that as a practical joke you're going to digitally put a mustache on him and email it to your family").

- *Specific.* For consistency between evaluators and to focus the task on the parts of the product you're interested in testing, the task should have a specific end goal. So rather than saying "Go shop for some forks," say, "You saw a great Louis XIV fork design in a shop window the other day; here's a picture of it. Find that design in this catalog and buy a dozen fish forks." However, it's important to avoid using terms that exist on the interface since that tends to tip off the participant about how to perform the task.
- *Doable.* If your site has forks only, don't ask people to find knives. It's sometimes tempting to see how they use your information structure to find something impossible, but it's deceptive and frustrating and ultimately reveals little about the quality of your design.
- *In a realistic sequence.* Tasks should flow like an actual session with the product. So a shopping site could have a browsing task followed by a search task that's related to a selection task that flows into a purchasing task. This makes the session feel more realistic and can point out interactions between tasks that are useful for information architects in determining the quality of the flow through the product.
- *Domain neutral.* The ideal task is something that everyone who tests the interface knows something about, but no one knows a lot about. When one evaluator knows significantly more than the others about a task, their methods will probably be different than the rest of the group. They'll have a bigger technical vocabulary and a broader range of methods to accomplish the task. Conversely, it's not a good idea to create tasks that are completely alien to some evaluators since they may not know even how to begin. For example, when testing a general search engine, I have people search for pictures of Silkie chickens: everyone knows something about chickens, but unless you're a Bantam hen farmer, you probably won't know much about Silkies. For really important tasks where an

obvious domain–neutral solution doesn't exist, people with specific knowledge can be excluded from the recruiting (for example, asking "Do you know what a Silkie chicken is?" in the recruiting screener can eliminate people who may know too much about chickens).

- *A reasonable length.* Most features are not so complex that to use them takes more than 10 minutes. The duration of a task should be determined by three things: the total length of the interview, its structure, and the complexity of the features you're testing. In a 90-minute task-focused interview, there are 50–70 minutes of task time, so an average task should take about 12 minutes to complete. In a 60-minute interview, there are about 40 minutes of task time, so each task should take no more than 7 minutes. Aim for 5 minutes in shorter interviews and 10 in longer ones. If you find that you have something that needs more time, then it probably needs to be broken down into subfeatures and reprioritized (though be aware of exceptions: some important tasks take a much longer time and cannot be easily broken up, but they still need to be tested).

Estimating Task Time

Carolyn Snyder recommends a method of estimating how long a task will take.

- Ask the development team how long it takes an expert—such as one of them—to perform the task.
- Multiply that number by 3 to 10 to get an estimate of how long it would take someone who had never used the interface to do the same thing. Use lower numbers for simpler tasks such as found on general-audience Web sites, and higher numbers for complex tasks such as found in specialized software or tasks that require data entry.

For every feature on the list, there should be at least one task that exercises it. Usually, it's useful to have two or three alternative tasks for the most important features in case there is time to try more than one or the first task proves to be too difficult or uninformative.

People can also construct their own tasks within reason. At the beginning of a usability test, you can ask the participants to describe a recent situation they may have found themselves in that your product could address. Then, when the times comes for a task, ask them to try to use the product as if they were trying to resolve the situation they described at the beginning of the interview. Another way to make a task feel authentic is to use real money. For example, one ecommerce site gave each of its usability testing participants a $50 account and told them that whatever they bought with that account, they got to keep (in addition to the cash incentive they were paid to participate). This presented a much better incentive for them to find something they actually wanted than they would have had if they just had to find something in the abstract.

Although it's fundamentally a qualitative procedure, you can also add some basic quantitative metrics (sometimes called *performance metrics*) to each task in order to investigate the relative efficiency of different designs or to compare competing products. Some common Web-based quantitative measurements include

- The speed with which someone completes a task
- How many errors they make
- How often they recover from their errors
- How many people complete the task successfully

Because such data collection cannot give you results that are statistically usable or generalizable beyond the testing procedure, such metrics are useful only for order-of-magnitude ideas about how long a task should take. Thus, it's often a good idea to use a relative number scale rather than specific times.

For the fork example, you could have the following set of tasks, as matched to the features listed earlier.

FORK TASKS

Feature	Task
The search engine: can people use it to find specific items?	Louis XIV forks are all the rage, and you've decided that you want to buy a set. How would you get a list of all the Louis XIV fork designs in this catalog?
Catalog navigation: can people navigate through it when they don't know exactly what they want?	You also saw this great fork in a shop window the other day (show a picture). Find a design that's pretty close to it in the catalog.

(Continued)

Feature	Task
The purchasing mechanism: does it work for both single items and whole sets?	Say you really like one of the designs we just looked at (pick one) and you'd like to buy a dozen dinner forks in that pattern. How would you go about doing that?
	Now say it's a month later, you love your forks, but you managed to mangle one of them in the garbage disposal. Starting from the front door to the site, how would you buy a replacement?
The Fork of the Week page: do people see it?	*This one is a bit more difficult. Seeing is not easily taskable, but it's possible to elicit some discussion about it by creating a situation where it may draw attention and noting if it does.* It's a couple of months later, and you're looking for forks again, this time as a present. Where would be the first place you'd look to find interesting forks that are a good value?
	Asking people to draw or describe an interface without looking at it reveals what people found memorable, which generally correlates closely to what they looked at.
	[turn off monitor] Please draw the interface we just looked at, based on what you remember about it.
The Wish List: do people know what it's for?	While you're shopping, you'd like to be able to keep a list of designs you're interested in, maybe later you'll buy one, but for now you'd like to just remember which ones are interesting. How would you do that?
	[If they don't find it on their own, point them to it and ask them whether they know what it means and how they would use it.]

When you've compiled the list, you need to time and check the tasks. Do them yourself and get someone who isn't close to the project to try them. This can be part of the pretest dry run, but it's always a good idea to run through the tasks by themselves if you can.

In addition, you should continually evaluate the quality of the tasks as the testing goes on. Use the same guidelines as you used to create the tasks and see if the tasks actually fulfill them. Between sessions think about the tasks' effectiveness and discuss them with the moderator and observers. And although it's a bad idea to drastically change tasks in the middle, it's OK to make small tweaks that improve the tasks' accuracy in between tests, keeping track of exactly what changed in each session.

Writing a Script

With tasks in hand, it's time to write the script. The script is sometimes called a "protocol," sometimes a "discussion guide," but it's really just a script for the moderator to follow so that the interviews are consistent and everything gets done.

This script is divided into three parts: the introduction and preliminary interview, the tasks, and the wrap-up. The one that follows is a sample from a typical 90-minute ecommerce Web site usability testing session for people who have never used the site under review. About a third of the script is dedicated to understanding the participants' interests and habits. Although those topics are typically part of a contextual inquiry process or a focus group series, it's often useful to include some investigation into them in usability testing. Another third is focused on task performance, where the most important features get exercised. A final third is administration.

Note Usability testing tasks have been traditionally described in terms of small, discrete actions that can be timed (such as "Save a file"). The times for a large number of these tasks are then collected and compared to a predetermined ideal time. Although that's useful for low-level usability tasks with frequent long-term users of dedicated applications, the types of tasks that appear on the Web can be more easily analyzed through the larger-grained tasks described here, since Web sites are often used differently from dedicated software by people with less experience with the product. Moreover, the timing of performance diverts attention from issues of immediate comprehension and satisfaction, which play a more important role in Web site design than they do in application design.

Introduction (5–7 minutes)

The introduction is a way to break the ice and give the evaluators some context. This establishes a comfort level about the process and their role in it.

[Monitor off, Video off, Computer reset]

Hi, welcome, thank you for coming. How are you? (Did you find the place OK? Any questions about the NDA? Etc.)

(Continued)

> I'm _____. I'm helping _____ understand how well
> one of their products works for the people who are its audience. This is
> _____, who will be observing what we're doing today. We've
> brought you here to see what you think of their product: what seems to
> work for you, what doesn't, and so on.
>
> This evaluation should take about an hour.
>
> We're going to be videotaping what happens here today, but the video is
> for analysis only. It's primarily so I don't have to sit here and scribble
> notes and I can concentrate on talking to you. It will be seen by some
> members of the development team, a couple of other people, and me. It's
> strictly for research and not for public broadcast or publicity or promotion
> or laughing at Christmas parties.

When there's video equipment, it's always blatantly obvious and somewhat intimidating. Recognizing it helps relieve a lot of tension about it. Likewise, if there's a two-way mirror, recognizing it—and the fact that there are people behind it—also serves to alleviate most people's anxiety. Once mentioned, it shouldn't be brought up again. It fades quickly into the background, and discussing it again is a distraction.

Also note that the script is written in a conversational style. It's unnecessary to read it verbatim, but it reminds the moderator to keep the tone of the interview casual. In addition, every section has a duration associated with it so that the moderator has an idea of how much emphasis to put on each one.

> Like I said, we'd like you to help us with a product we're developing. It's
> designed for people like you, so we'd really like to know what you think
> about it and what works and doesn't work for you. It's currently in an early
> stage of development, so not everything you're going to see will work right.

No matter what stage the product team is saying the product is in, if it's being usability tested, it's in an early stage. Telling the evaluators it's a work-in-progress helps relax them and gives them more license to make comments about the product as a whole.

> The procedure we're going to do today goes like this: we're going to start out and talk for a few minutes about how you use the Web, what you like, what kinds of problems you run into, that sort of thing. Then I'm going to show you a product that _____ has been working on and have you try out a couple of things with it. Then we'll wrap up, I'll ask you a few more questions about it, and we're done.
>
> Any questions about any of that?

Explicitly laying out the whole procedure helps the evaluators predict what's going to come next and gives them some amount of context to understand the process.

> Now I'd like to read you what's called a statement of informed consent. It's a standard thing I read to everyone I interview. It sets out your rights as a person who is participating in this kind of research.
>
> As a participant in this research
> - You may stop at any time.
> - You may ask questions at any time.
> - You may leave at any time.
> - There is no deception involved.
> - Your answers are kept confidential.
>
> Any questions before we begin?
>
> Let's start!

The informed consent statement tells the evaluators that their input is valuable, that they have some control over the process, and that there is nothing fishy going on.

Preliminary Interview (10–15 minutes)

The preliminary interview is used to establish context for the participant's later comments. It also narrows the focus of the interview into the space of the evaluator's experience by beginning with general questions and then narrowing the conversation to the topics the product is designed for. For people who have never participated in a usability test, it increases their comfort level by asking some "easy" questions that build confidence and give them an idea of the process.

In this case, the preliminary interview also features a fairly extensive investigation into people's backgrounds and habits. It's not unusual to have half as many questions and to have the initial context-setting interview last 5 minutes, rather than 10 to 15.

[Video on]

How much time do you normally spend on the Web in a given week?

How much of that is for work use, and how much of that is for personal use?

Other than email, is there any one thing you do the most online?

Do you ever shop online? What kinds of things have you bought? How often do you buy stuff online?

Do you ever do research online for things that you end up buying in stores? Are there any categories of items that this happens with more often than others? Why?

Is there anything you would never buy online? Why?

When it's applicable, it's useful to ask about people's offline habits before refocusing the discussion to the online sphere. Comparing what they say they do offline and what you observe them doing online provides insight into how people perceive the interface.

Changing gears here a bit, do you ever shop for silverware in general, not just online? How often?

Do you ever do that online? Why?

[If so] Do you have any favorite sites where you shop for silverware online?

[If so] What do you like the most about [site]? Is there anything that regularly bothers you about it?

Evaluation Instructions (3 minutes)

It's important that evaluators don't feel belittled by the product. The goal behind any product is to have it be a subservient tool, but people have been conditioned by badly designed tools and arrogant companies to place the blame on themselves. Although it's difficult to undo a lifetime of software insecurity, the evaluation instructions help get evaluators comfortable with narrating their experience, including positive and negative commentary, in its entirety.

In a minute, I'll ask you to turn on the monitor and we'll take a look at the product, but let me give you some instructions about how to approach it.

The most important thing to remember when you're using it is that you are testing the interface, the interface is not testing you. There is absolutely nothing that you can do wrong. Period. If anything seems broken or wrong or weird or, especially, confusing, it's not your fault. However, we'd like to know about it. So please tell us whenever anything isn't working for you.

Likewise, tell us if you like something. Even if it's a feature, a color, or the way something is laid out, we'd like to hear about it.

Be as candid as possible. If you think something's awful, please say so. Don't be shy; you won't hurt anyone's feelings. Since it's designed for people like you, we really want to know exactly what you think and what works and doesn't work for you.

(Continued)

> Also, while you're using the product I'd like you to say your thoughts aloud. That gives us an idea of what you're thinking when you're doing something. Just narrate what you're doing, sort of as a play-by-play, telling me what you're doing and why you're doing it.

A major component to effective usability tests is to get people to say what they're thinking as they're thinking it. The technique is introduced up front, but it should also be emphasized during the actual interview.

> Does that make sense? Any questions?

> Please turn on the monitor [or "open the top of the portable"]. While it's warming up, you can put the keyboard, monitor, and mouse where they're comfortable for you.

> *First Impressions (5–10 minutes)*

First impressions of a product are incredibly important for Web sites, so testing them explicitly is always a good thing and quick to do. Asking people where they're looking and what they see points out the things in an interface that pop and provides insight into how page loading and rendering affects focus and attention.

The interview begins with the browser up, but set to a blank page. Loading order affects the order people see the elements on the page and tends to affect the emphasis they place on those elements. Knowing the focus of their attention during the loading of the page helps explain why certain elements are seen as more or less important.

> Now that it's warmed up, I'd like you to select "Forks" from the "Favorites" menu.

> [Rapidly] What's the first thing your eyes are drawn to? What's the next thing? What's the first thought that comes into your mind when you see this page?

[after 1–2 minutes] What is this site about?

Are you interested in it?

If this was your first time here, what would you do next? What would you click on? What would you be interested in investigating?

At this point, the script can go in two directions. Either it can be a *task-based interview*—where the user immediately begins working on tasks—or it can be a *hybrid interview* that's half task based and half observational interview.

The task-based interview focuses on a handful of specific tasks or features. The hybrid interview is useful for first-time tests and tests that are early in the development cycle. In hybrid interviews, the evaluator goes through an interface tour, looking at each element of the main part of the interface and quickly commenting on it, before working on tasks.

A task-based interview would look as follows.

Tasks (20–25 minutes)
Now I'd like you to try a couple of things with this interface. Work just as you would normally, narrating your thoughts as you go along.

Here is the list of things I'd like you to do. [hand out list]

The first scenario goes as follows:

TASK 1 DESCRIPTION GOES HERE

[Read the first task, hand out Task 1 description sheet]

The second thing I'd like you to do is

TASK 2 DESCRIPTION GOES HERE

[Read the second task, hand out Task 2 description sheet] etc.

When there is a way to remotely observe participants, it is sometimes useful to ask them to try a couple of the listed tasks on their own, without the moderator in the room. This can yield valuable information about how people solve problems without an available knowledge source. In addition, it's a useful time for the moderator to discuss the test with the observers. When leaving the room, the moderator should reemphasize the need for the evaluator to narrate all of his or her thoughts.

Including a specific list of issues to probe helps ensure that all the important questions are answered. The moderator should feel free to ask the probe questions whenever it is appropriate in the interview.

Probe Questions (investigate whenever appropriate)
- Do the names of navigation elements make sense?
- Do the interface elements function as the evaluator had expected?
- Are there any interface elements that don't make sense?
- What draws the evaluator's attention?
- What are the most important elements in any given feature?
- Are there places where the evaluator would like additional information?
- What are their expectations for the behavior/content of any given element/screen?

A hybrid interview could look as follows. It begins with a quick general task to see how people experience the product before they've had a chance to examine the interface in detail.

First Task (5 minutes)
Now I'd like you to try something with this interface.

Work just as you would normally, narrating your thoughts as you go along.

The first scenario goes as follows:

TASK 1 DESCRIPTION GOES HERE

[read the first task]

Interface Tour (10 minutes)
OK, now I'd like to go through the interface, one element at a time, and talk about what you expect each thing to do.

[Go through
- Most of front door
- A sample catalog page
- A shopping cart page]

[Focus on
- Site navigation elements
- Search elements
- Major feature labels and behaviors
- Ambiguous elements
- Expectations]

Per element probes [ask for each significant element, when appropriate]:
- In a couple of words, what do you think this does?
- What does this [label, title] mean?
- Where do you think this would go?
- Without clicking on it, what kind of page would you expect to find on the other side? What would it contain? How would it look?

Per screen probes [ask on each screen, when appropriate]:
- What's the most important thing on this screen for you?
- Is there any information missing from here that you would need?
- After you've filled it out, what would you do next?
- How would you get to the front door of the site from here? What would you click on?
- How would you get to [some other major section]?

Tasks (10 minutes)
The second thing I'd like you to do is

TASK 2 DESCRIPTION GOES HERE

[read the second task]

(Continued)

The last thing I'd like to try is

TASK 3 DESCRIPTION GOES HERE

[read the third task]

By the time all the tasks have been completed, the heart of the information collection and the interview is over. However, it's useful for the observers and analysts to get a perspective on the high points of the discussion. In addition, a blue-sky discussion of the product can provide good closure for the evaluator and can produce some good ideas (or the time can be used to ask people to draw what they remember of the interface as the moderator leaves the room and asks the observers if they have any final questions for the participant).

Wrap-up and Blue-Sky Brainstorm (10 minutes)
Please turn off the monitor, and we'll wrap up with a couple of questions.

Wrap-up
How would you describe this product in a couple of sentences to someone with a level of computer and Web experience similar to yours?

Is this an interesting service? Is this something that you would use?

Is this something you would recommend? Why/why not?

Can you summarize what we've been talking about by saying three good things and three bad things about the product?

Blue-Sky Brainstorm
OK, now that we've seen some of what this can do, let's talk in blue-sky terms here for a minute. Not thinking in practical terms at all, what kinds of things would you like a system like this to do that this one doesn't? Have you ever said, "I wish that some program would do X for me"? What was it?

> Do you have any final questions? Comments?
>
> Thank you, if you have any other thoughts or ideas on your way home or tomorrow, or even next week, please feel free to send an email to _____. [hand out a card]

Finally, it's useful to get some feedback about the testing and scheduling process.

> And that's all the questions I have about the prototype, but I have one last question:
>
> Do you have any suggestions about how we could run these tests better, either in terms of scheduling or the way we ran it?
>
> Thanks. That's it, we're done.
>
> [Turn video off]

As with every phase of user research, the product stakeholders should have input into the testing script content. The complete script draft should still be vetted by the stakeholders to assure that the priorities and technical presentation are accurate. The first draft should be given to the development team at least a week before testing is to begin. A second version incorporating their comments should be shown to them at least a couple of days beforehand.

Conducting the Interview

There are two goals in conducting user interviews: getting the most natural responses from evaluators and getting the most complete responses. Everything that goes into the environment of a user interview—from the physical space to the way questions are asked—is focused on these two goals.

The Physical Layout

The physical layout should look as little like a lab as possible and as much like the kind of space in which the product is designed to be used. If the product is to be used at work, then it should be tested in an environment that resembles a nice office, preferably with a window. If it's for home use, then it should be tested in an environment like a home office. The illusion doesn't have to be all pervasive; it's possible to achieve the appropriate feeling with just a few carefully chosen props. For the home office, for example, soft indirect lighting and a tablecloth over an office desk instantly makes it less formal.

Often, however, the usability test must be performed in a scheduled conference room or a rented lab, where extensive alteration isn't possible. In those situations, make sure that the space is quiet, uncluttered, and as much as possible, unintimidating.

Every interview should be videotaped, if possible. Ideally, a video scan converter (a device that converts computer video output to standard video) and a video mixer should be used to create a "picture-in-picture" version of the proceedings, with one image showing a picture of the person and the other of their screen (Figure 10.3). The video camera should be positioned such that the evaluator's face and hands can be seen for the initial interview and so that the screen can be seen for the task portion of the interview. The moderator does not have to appear in the shot.

Accurate, clear audio is extremely important, so the video camera should have a good built-in microphone that filters out external noise, or you should invest in a lapel microphone, which the evaluator can clip onto his or her clothing, or a small microphone that can be taped to the monitor. The downside of lapel microphones is that although they capture the evaluator's comments, they don't always catch those of the moderator. An ideal situation is to have two wireless lapel microphones and a small mixer to merge the two sound sources, or a single external microphone that is sensitive enough to capture both sides of the conversation without picking up the external noise that's the bane of built-in camera mics. But that's a lot of equipment.

If a two-way mirrored room is unavailable, closed-circuit video makes for good substitute. This is pretty easy to achieve with a long video cable and a television in an adjacent room (though the room should be sufficiently soundproof that observers can speak freely without being heard in the testing room). So the final layout of a typical round of usability testing can look like Figure 10.4.

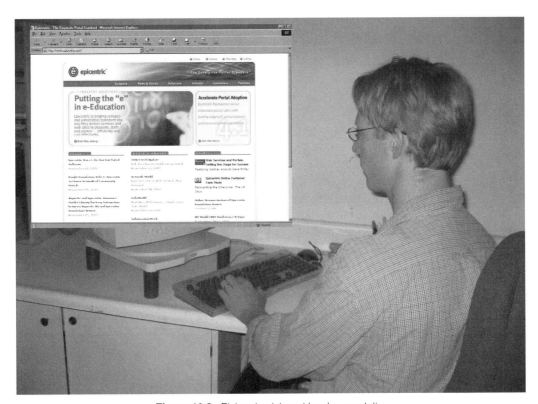

Figure 10.3   Picture-in-picture video documentation.

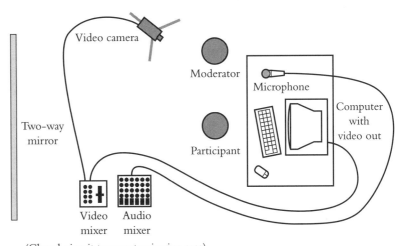

(Closed–circuit to remote viewing area)

Figure 10.4   A typical usability testing configuration.

Moderation

The moderator needs to make the user feel comfortable and elicit useful responses at appropriate times without drastically interrupting the flow of the user's own narration or altering his or her perspective. The *nondirected interviewing* style is described in depth in Chapter 6 and should be used in all user interviews.

Apart from the general interviewing style outlined in Chapter 6, there are several things that moderators should do in all interviews.

- *Probe expectations.* Before participants click on a link, check a box, or perform any action with an interface, they have some idea of what will happen. Even though their idea of what will happen next may not be completely formed, they will always have *some* expectation. After the users have performed an action, their perception is forever altered about that action's effect. The only way to capture their view before it happens is to stop them as they're about to perform an action and ask them for their expectations of its effect. With a hyperlink, for example, asking the evaluators to describe what they think will happen if they click on a link can reveal a lot about their mental model of the functionality of the site. Asking "Is that what you expected?" immediately after an action is also an excellent way of finding out whether the experience matches expectations.

- *Ask "why" a lot.* It's possible to learn a lot about people's attitudes, beliefs, and behaviors by asking simple, direct, unbiased questions at appropriate times. Five-year-olds do this all the time: they just ask "why" over and over again, digging deeper and deeper into a question without ever telegraphing that they think there's a correct answer. For example, when someone says "I just don't do those kinds of things," asking "why" yields better information than just knowing that he or she does or doesn't do something.

- *Suggest solutions, sometimes.* Don't design during an interview, but it is OK to probe if a particular idea (that doesn't exist in the current product) would solve their problem. This is useful as a check on the interviewer's understanding of the problem, and it can be a useful way to sanity-check potential solutions. For example, a number of people in a test said they kept their personal schedule using Microsoft Outlook and their Palm

Pilot. They weren't interested in online schedules since they felt it would involve duplicating effort even though they liked the convenience of a Web-based calendar. When the moderator suggested that their offline schedule could be synchronized with the online, they were universally excited and said that they would be much more likely to use the entire service if that feature were available.

- *Investigate mistakes.* When evaluators make mistakes, wait to see if they've realized that they've made a mistake and then immediately probe their thoughts and expectations. Why did they do something one way? What were they hoping it would do? How did they expect it to work? What happened that made them realize that it didn't work?

- *Probe nonverbal cues.* Sometimes people will react physically to an experience in a way that they wouldn't normally voice. When something is surprising or unexpected or unpleasant, someone may flinch, but not say anything. Likewise, a smile or a lean forward may signify satisfaction or interest. Watch for such actions and follow up, if appropriate. For example, "You frowned when that dialog box came up. Is there anything about it that caused you to do that?"

- *Keep the interview task centered.* People naturally tend to tangent off on certain ideas that come up. As someone is performing a task, they may be reminded of an idea or an experience that they want to explore. Allowing people to explore their experiences is important, but it's also important to stay focused on the product and the task. When someone leans back, takes his or her hands off the keyboard, stops looking at the monitor, and starts speaking in the abstract, it's generally time to introduce a new task or return to the task at hand.

- *Respect the evaluator's ideas.* When people are off topic, let them go for a bit (maybe a minute or so) and see if they can wrap up their thoughts on their own. If they're not wrapping up, steer the conversation back to the task or topic at hand. If that doesn't seem to work, then you can be more explicit: "That's interesting and maybe we'll cover it more later, but let's take a look at the Fork of the Week page."

- *Focus on their personal experience.* People have a tendency to idealize their experience and to extrapolate it to others' needs or to their far future needs. Immediate experience, however, is

Note Throughout this chapter, I have used the words "evaluator" and "participant" to refer to the people who are evaluating the interface, rather than "subject," "tester," "guinea pig," or whatnot. This is intentional. The people who you have recruited to evaluate your interface are your colleagues in this process. They are not being examined, the product is. It's tempting to set the situation up as a psychology experiment, but it's not. It's a directed evaluation of a product, not an inquiry into human nature, and should be treated as such on all levels.

Note Some researchers claim that it's possible to have multiple observers in the same room without compromising the quality of the observations. I haven't found that to be the case, nor have I chosen to have any in-room observers most of the time. It may well be possible to have a bunch of observers in the room and still have the participant perform comfortably and naturally—stage actors do this all the time, after all. However, I try to avoid the complications that this may introduce into the interpretation of people's statements by avoiding the question entirely.

much more telling about people's actual attitudes, needs, and behaviors, and is usually much more useful than their extrapolations. When Peter says, "I think it may be useful to someone," ask him if it's useful to *him*. If Inga says that she understands it, but others may not, tell her that it's important to know about how *she* views it, not how it could be designed for others. If Tom says that something "may be useful someday," ask him if it's something that's useful to him *now*.

Managing Observers

Getting as many members of the development team to observe the tests is one of the fastest ways to relate the findings of the test and win them over.

Make the appropriate staff watch the usability tests in real time, if possible. There's nothing more enlightening to a developer (or even a vice president of product development) than watching their interfaces misused and their assumptions misunderstood and not being able to do anything about it.

The best way to get observers involved is through a two-way mirror or a closed-circuit video feed. Bring in plenty of food (pizza usually works). The team can then lounge in comfort and discuss the tests as they proceed (while not forgetting to watch how the participants are actually behaving). Since they know the product inside and out, they will see behaviors and attitudes that neither the moderator nor the analyst will, which is invaluable as source material for the analyst and for the team's understanding of their customers.

If neither a two-way mirror nor a closed-circuit feed is available, it's possible to have members of the team observe the tests directly. However, there should never be more than one observer per test. It's intimidating enough for the evaluator to be in a lab situation, but to have several people sitting behind them, sometimes scribbling, sometimes whispering, can be too creepy for even the most even-keeled. The observer, if he or she is in the room, should be introduced by name since this acknowledges his or her presence and gives the observer a role in the process other than "the guy sitting silently in the corner watching me."

Observers should be given instructions on acceptable behavior and to set their expectations of the process.

USABILITY TEST OBSERVER INSTRUCTIONS

1. Listen. As tempting as it is to immediately discuss what you're observing, make sure to listen to what people are really saying. Feel free to discuss what you're seeing, but don't forget to listen.

2. Usability tests are not statistically representative. If three out of four people say something, that doesn't mean that 75% of the population feels that way. It does mean that a number of people may feel that way, but it doesn't mean anything numerically.

3. Don't take every word as gospel. These are just the views of a couple of people. If they have good ideas, great, but trust your intuition in judging their importance, unless there's significant evidence otherwise. So if someone says, "I hate the green," that doesn't mean that you change the color (though if everyone says, "I hate the green," then it's something to research further).

4. People are contradictory. Listen to how people are thinking about the topics and what criteria they use to come to conclusions, not necessarily the specific desires they voice. A person may not realize that two desires are impossible to have simultaneously, or he or she may not care. Be prepared to be occasionally bored or confused. People's actions aren't always interesting or insightful.

5. Don't expect revolutions. If you can get one or two good ideas out of each usability test, then it has served its purpose.

6. Watch for what people *don't* do or *don't* notice as much as you watch what they do and notice.

For in-room observers, add the following instructions:

7. Feel free to ask questions when the moderator gives you an explicit opportunity. Ask questions that do not imply a value judgment about the product one way or another. So instead of asking, "Is this the best-of-breed product in its class?" ask "Are there other products that do what this one does? Do you have any opinions about any of them?"

8. Do not mention your direct involvement with the product. It's easier for people to comment about the effectiveness of a product when they don't feel that someone with a lot vested in it is in the same room.

If the observers are members of the development team, encourage them to wait until they've observed all the participants before generalizing and designing solutions. People naturally want to start fixing problems as soon as they're recognized, but the context, magnitude, and prevalence of a problem should be known before energy is expended to fix it. Until the landscape of all the issues is established, solution design is generally not recommended.

Tips and Tricks

- Always do a dry run of the interview a day or two beforehand. Get everything set up as for a real test, complete with all the appropriate hardware and prototypes installed. Then get someone who is roughly the kind of person you're recruiting, but who isn't intimately involved in the development of the product, and conduct a full interview with him or her. Use this time to make sure that the script, the hardware, and the tasks are all working as designed. Go through the whole interview, and buy the evaluator lunch afterward.

- Reset the computer and the lab in between every test. Make sure every user gets the same environment by clearing the browser cache, resetting the history (so all links come up as new and cookies are erased), and restarting the browser so that it's on a blank page (you can set most browsers so that they open to a blank page by default). Clear off any notes or paperwork from the previous person and turn off the monitor.

- If possible, provide both a Macintosh and a PC for your usability test, allowing the evaluator to use whichever one he or she is more comfortable with. You can even include a question about it in the screener and know ahead of time which one the participant typically uses.

- Don't take extensive notes during the test. This allows you to focus on what the user is doing and probe particular behaviors. Also, the participants won't associate their behavior with periods of frantic scribbling, which they often interpret as an indicator that they just did something wrong.

- Take notes immediately after, writing down all interesting behaviors, errors, likes, and dislikes. Discuss the test with any observers for 10–20 minutes immediately after and take notes on their observations, too.

How to Analyze It

Note The moderator and analyst are referred to as separate people here, but in practice the two roles are often performed by the same person.

Although some things are going to be obvious, a formal analysis is necessary to get to underlying causes and to extract the most value from the interviews. Analyzing the output is a three-stage process: collecting observations, organizing observations, and extracting trends from the observations.

Collecting Observations

There are three sets of observations to be collected: the moderator's, the observers', and the analyst's.

Collecting the moderator's and observers' notes is pretty straightforward. Get their notes (or copies), and have them walk you through them, explaining what each one means. In addition, interview them for additional observations that were not in their notes. These are frequently large-scale perspectives on the situation that the person made in the days or hours following the last test.

The analyst's notes are the most important and time-consuming part of the data collection process. The analyst should go through at least four of the videotapes and note down all situations where there were mistakes or confusion or where the evaluators expressed an opinion about the product or its features. He or she should note which features the evaluators had problems with, under what circumstances they encountered those problems, and provide a detailed description of the problem. The majority of the usability problems in the product will likely be found during this phase, as the patterns in people's behavior and expectations emerge.

Quantitative information, although not generalizable to the whole target market at large, is often useful when summarizing and comparing behavior (however, it's fraught with potential problems as people reading reports can latch on to largely meaningless numbers as some kind of absolute truth). To collect quantitative information, first create a measurement range for each question that everyone in the analysis team agrees upon. Don't use a stopwatch, and take exact numbers. The statistical error present in the small sample of people in a usability test swamps out the accuracy of a stopwatch. The most useful metrics are the ones that are the most general. Flow Interactive, Limited *(www.flow-interactive.com),* a U.K.

user experience design and evaluation consulting company, uses the following range to measure how long people take to perform a task:

0—Fail
1—Succeed very slowly in a roundabout way
2—Succeed a little slowly
3—Succeed quickly

Most of the time, this is all the precision you need since an order-of-magnitude measure is all that's necessary to be able to make critical comparisons. Each scale should have three or five steps (don't use two, four, or six since it's hard to find a middle value; don't use more than five because it tends to get confusing) and a separate value for failure.

Make a grid for each participant consisting of the task metrics you're going to collect. As the videotapes are being watched, note the severity in each cell (when appropriate, define severity using the same language and scale that is used by the development team to define how serious code bugs are). For the fork tasks, the following table would reflect one person's performance.

MARLON'S TASK PERFORMANCE

User: *Marlon*	Time to Read	Errors	Time to Complete
Find Louis XIV	1	3	1
Buy replacement	3	1	2
Find similar forks	1	2	0
Key	0—Don't read 1—Read very slowly 2—Read moderately slowly 3—Read quickly	0—Fail because of errors 1—Many errors 2—Some errors 3—Few or no errors	0—Fail 1—Succeed very slowly in a roundabout way 2—Succeed a little slowly 3—Succeed quickly

Then, when compiling the final analysis, create a table for each metric that summarizes the whole user groups' experience. For the completion time metric, the table could look as follows.

TASK PERFORMANCE TIME MEASURES

	Marlon	Eva	Marc	Barb	Jon	Avg.
Find Louis XIV	1	2	1	0	2	1.2
Buy replacement	2	3	2	1	1	1.8
Find similar forks	0	0	1	1	0	0.4

The average numbers, although not meaningful in an absolute context, provide a way to compare tasks to each other and between designs.

Note down feature requests and verbatim quotations from the evaluators, especially ones that encapsulate a particular behavior ("I don't understand what "Forkopolis" means, so I wouldn't click there," for example). Feature requests are often attempts to articulate a problem that the evaluator can't express in any other way. However, they can also be innovative solutions to those same problems, so they should be captured, regardless.

2x Video Decks Are Cool

To make the video review process go faster, I recommend using a video deck (or a digital video player) that can play back video and audio at 1.5 or 2 times natural speed. The speech is still understandable (although silly, since people sound like chipmunks unless the voice is pitch-shifted down, as it is done on Sony's professional-grade video hardware), and it's possible to make your way through a tape much faster.

If time and budget allow, a transcription of the whole session is helpful, but it should be used only as an aid in observing the tapes because it misses the vocal inflection and behavior that can really clarify some situations. For example, a confused pause of five seconds while an evaluator passes his pointer over every single visual element on the screen looking for somewhere to click is insufficiently conveyed by his statement of "Aha! There it is."

Organizing Observations

First, read through all the notes once to get a feeling for the material. Look for repetition and things that may be caused by common underlying problems.

Note Much as with analyzing contextual inquiry information or focus group observations, organizing usability testing information and extracting trends can be done in a group with the development team (and other stakeholders, as appropriate). This allows the group to use its collected knowledge to flesh out the understanding of the problem and to begin working on solutions.

Then put all the observations into a pile (literally, or in a single large document). Opening a separate document in a word processor, go through each observation and group it with other similar observations in the new document. Similarity can be in terms of superficial similarity ("Term not understood"), feature cluster ("Shopping cart problems"), or in terms of underlying cause ("Confusing information architecture"). Group the observations with the most broadly sweeping, underlying causes. Pull quotations out and group them with the causes that they best illustrate.

Extracting Trends

Having grouped all the observations, go through the groups and consolidate them, separating the groups of unrelated topics. Throw away those that only have one or two individual observations. For each group, try to categorize the problem in a single short sentence, with a couple of sentences to fully describe the phenomenon. Explain the underlying cause as much as possible, separating the explanation of the phenomenon from your hypothesis of its cause. Concentrate on describing the problem, its immediate impact on the user experience, and the place where the problem occurred. Be very careful when suggesting solutions. Ultimately, the development team knows more about the technology and the assumptions that went into the product, and the responsibility for isolating underlying causes and finding solutions is theirs. Your recommendations should serve as a guide of where solutions *could be* found, not edicts about what must be done.

Warning It's easy to confuse making user severity measures into priorities for the development of the project. This is generally inappropriate. What's most important to a user's success with the product is not necessarily what's most important to the product's success. The product team should be informed of problem severity from the user perspective and then use that to determine project priorities, but the two aren't the same.

Describe the severity of the problem from the user's perspective, but don't give observations numerical severity grades. If a shorthand for the characterization of observations is desired or requested, categorize the observations in terms of the effects they have on the user experience, rather than giving them an arbitrary severity. Such a scale could be "Prevents an activity," "Causes confusion," "Does not match expectations," "Seen as unnecessary."

Example   297

Once all this is done, you should have a list of observations, hypotheses for what caused the phenomena, and quotations that reinforce and summarize the observations. You're ready to present your results to the team! Effective presentations are covered in Chapter 17.

Example

This is a short report summarizing a test on another Webmonkey prototype for the site's development team. It builds on the previous testing that the site had gone through and focuses on the changes made to the front door and the renaming of various sections in the site.

Executive Summary

Five Web developers were shown the functional prototype for Webmonkey 4.0. In general, they liked it, especially the tutorials and the color scheme, but some of the organization confused them (specifically, the difference between the "Categories" and "Tutorials" sections). The new folderlike navigation metaphor made sense to everyone, and they wished that it was on every page. Everyone saw the "Cool Tools" section, but thought it was an ad and ignored it, and although they liked the "Inspiration" section, they expected it to be more than just animation in the long run.

Finally, a couple of people said that it would be cool to have Webmonkey link to good, useful external content in an unbiased way since it would be useful and would reinforce Webmonkey's street creed.

Executive summaries are very useful when communicating results. The vice president of product development may never read the report, but a couple of paragraphs giving 50,000 of the results of the usability test are likely to be read. When attaching the report in an email, the executive summary should be included in the email, while the rest of the report—including the executive summary—is included as an attachment.

Procedure

Five people who spend a significant amount of time developing Web sites were invited. They were first asked some preliminary questions about their general net usage and where they went for developer information (both on the Web and in general). They were then shown the site prototype and asked to go through it in detail, concentrating on specific details, including the folder-style navigation, and the Cool Tools section. After giving their responses to the front door, they were asked to scroll down through one of the top stories, talking about their experience with the interface and their thoughts on the content. They were then asked to look for some specific content as a way of gauging their understanding of the layout of the site. Finally, they were asked some wrap-up and blue-sky questions, and the test was concluded.

A fast description of the procedure demystifies the process and provides important context for report recipients to be able to understand the results.

Evaluator Profiles

Michael

Michael spends more than 40 hours a week on the Internet, 20 hours of which is spent making Web pages, including design, programming, and production. Of all the development sites, he likes Webmonkey because of its "broad range." He also regularly reads "Flash Zone" because it can give him tutorials that he can't get in print. For CGI work, he follows another site, "CGI Resources" (the "CGI Zone"? The specific site wasn't clear from the interview).

John

John spends 30 hours a week on the Internet, half of which is work related. He spends at least 10 hours a week making Web sites, including design, markup, and code. He uses reference books and Webmonkey for technical Web-related information. He also goes to "SGML University" and has never been to builder.com. Most of the time, he goes to these sites with specific questions. In general, he would like developer sites to be better organized by topic.

Example   299

David

David spends 20–30 hours a week on the Internet, 75% of which is work related, and 5% to 10% is spent doing Web development, most of which is design. His main sources of technical information are Webmonkey and notes from school. He has never seen builder.com and goes to Webmonkey for both technology updates and to answer specific questions.

[remaining profiles omitted]

Evaluator profiles are useful both to help the report reader understand the context in which people's statements were made and as a way to personify the participants to those who were unable to observe the tests. Like the user profiles created in Chapter 7, these profiles help personalize the abstract concept of a product's users and make the results that much more immediate.

Observations

General Observations

1. *People like tutorials above all else. All the evaluators were drawn to the tutorials, sometimes to the exclusion of other content. The tutorials section was often the first one mentioned when the evaluators were asked where they would click on next. It was also the section people preferred to go to for general information even though there was a broader range of content in the "Categories" section.*
2. *Almost everyone said they liked the color scheme. Without being asked about it, most of the evaluators volunteered that they really liked the color scheme on the homepage.*
3. *People generally come to development sites with specific questions in mind, not to see "the latest." When asked whether they go to sites like Webmonkey to catch up on the latest technology or to get answers to specific questions, people generally said that it was to answer specific questions.*

Likewise, when asked how they preferred to navigate through sites like Webmonkey, people said that they preferred searching, rather than browsing, since that brought them closer to the specific information they were looking for.

Features

1. *There was confusion between the content people would find in the "Categories" section and the "Tutorials" section (and, to a lesser extent, between the "Tutorials" section and the "Guides" section). Partially because of the ambiguity of the "Categories" name and partly because of the similar—but not completely identical—labels in the two sections, people were confused about what they would find in each section.*

    📁 **Categories**
    📁 **Tutorials**
    📁 **Guides**
    📁 **Jobs**

    📁 **About Webmonkey**

    Whenever possible, include screenshots.

2. *The "Cool Tools" section was noticed early by nearly everyone, but treated as a big ad and, thus, ignored by most. Until it was pointed out to a number of the evaluators that there was nonadvertising content in "Cool Tools," they did not appear to notice it. Most pointed to the picture and the price as indicators of why it was considered to be advertising content.*

3. *A couple of people saw and liked the idea behind the "First Time Here" link.*

4. *People didn't know to go to "Backend" for CGI topics and were unsure of what kinds of things would be found there. One person mentioned that he'd prefer it be called "Server Stuff" or something similar.*

5. *People didn't notice the reference pop-up on the main page at first, and when they did, they weren't sure about its relationship to the content accessible from the folders in the left-hand margin. However, most everyone found it to be a useful tool with contents that made sense (except for "ISO Entities"). A couple of people suggested that it be put in the left-hand margin along with the folders.*

Example 301

Navigation

1. *Everyone understood the folder metaphor on the front door.*
2. *The inconsistent content and appearance of the left margin navigation was somewhat confusing. A number of people mentioned that they were surprised that the navigation in the left-hand margin changed from the front door to the subsections and the tutorials. Several mentioned that they would have preferred a continuation of the folder metaphor from the front door.*
3. *People generally understood the pathnamelike breadcrumb navigation at the top of the page though not everyone noticed it. The biggest disconnect came when people would jump to a "Tutorial" directly from the top page (thus expecting the path to be something like "home/ tutorial/javascript") and the path read "home/categories/javascript/ tutorial," which did not match their expectation.*

Naming

1. *The "Categories" name wasn't clear. People weren't sure what "Categories" was referring to, and one person didn't even see it as a section to be clicked on.*
2. *"Guides" wasn't clear as a section title. There was confusion in most of the evaluators between the "Guides" section and the tutorials.*
3. *Likewise, "eBiz" wasn't clear. Although not everyone was asked about it, the couple of people who were didn't know what to expect on the other side.*
4. *"Heard on the Street" was ambiguous. Without looking at it when the participants were asked to define what the "Heard on the Street" section was and how it was different from the other content sections, most people said that it was a "most recent" section or that it highlighted some news development.*

Conclusion

The combination of the attraction of the concept of tutorials with the unclear wording of "Categories" caused people to frequently ignore the categories section entirely.

A lot of the confusion comes from the ambiguity of single-word names. "Categories" and "Guides," although they adequately describe the sections after people have already seen them, give people little information about them before they've seen them, since, as words, they're quite general. Thus, the naming of sections (and maybe everything on the site in general) has to be done with the user's context in mind. What may, in retrospect, make perfect sense may be confusing and ambiguous before a definition is produced.

Quotations

Michael

"You know the functionality is out there, you just want to know how to put it together."

"When I started going there, it was a beginning site, it was very good for that, but then it kind of stayed there and I moved on." [re: Builder.com]

"I saw 'Cool Tool Pick,' and I thought that this would say GoLive and this would be Dreamweaver and this would be something else."

"If one of them weren't there, it might be easier [to differentiate between them]." [re: "tutorials" vs. "categories"]

John

"It stands out without being the obnoxious Wired magazine look."

"If I were coming here to find a specific answer on something, I would go to 'Tutorial.'"

"'Categories' is everything and these are just subtopics."

"I would prefer to see the latest tutorial [rather than Inspiration] at the top."

[remaining quotations omitted]

A couple of sentences of evaluators' actual words often better illustrate the points you're trying to convey than a paragraph of explanation. The readers can then see the patterns you're trying to illustrate for them. When placed next to each point, they serve to reinforce each point as it's made. When presented all at once, they communicate the feel of a usability test.

Usability tests are one of the workhorses of user experience research. They can be done quickly and inexpensively, and provide a lot of immediately actionable information. Too often they're used as the only form of user feedback, but when used correctly, they're an invaluable tool.

CHAPTER 11
Surveys

You know whom you want as your ideal target audience, but do you know who your *real* users are? You may know some things about which parts of your site are being used and what kinds of issues people complain about. These things may even point to the fact that your actual audience is the people you want, but how certain are you?

Qualitative techniques such as focus groups, think–aloud usability tests, and contextual inquiry give you insight into why people do the things they do when using your product, but they can't accurately outline the characteristics that differentiate the people using your product from the population in general. Only *quantitative* techniques can predict how many of your users are teenagers or whether they desire the new features you're considering developing. Knowing your audience's makeup can tell you on whom to concentrate your qualitative research and, more important, can give you information about what qualities define your audience.

Who is using your site? Are they the people you had built your site for, or are they completely different from the people you expected? What do they value about your service? Is that what you had anticipated, or are they using your service for something else? Unless you can get the opinions of a large section of your audience, you won't know what makes (or doesn't make) your product popular.

The best tool to find out who your users are and what their opinions are is the *survey*. A survey is a set of questions that creates a structured way of asking a large group of people to describe themselves, their interests, and their preferences. Once the results are counted, statistical tools can be used to examine your audience, revealing broad characteristics and allowing you to extract interesting subgroups of users. When done correctly, surveys can produce a higher degree of certainty in your user profile than any qualitative research method or indirect analysis of user behavior such as log files.

Surveys can answer such questions as

- How old are your users?
- What kind of Internet connection do they have?
- Is your user population homogeneous, or does it consist of a number of distinct groups?
- What do they want? Does the product provide it?
- What do they like about the product? What do they dislike?

However, surveys can easily go wrong. If not designed carefully, they can ask the wrong people the wrong questions, producing results that are inaccurate, inconclusive, or at worst, deceptive. Web-based surveys are especially vulnerable because, lacking any direct contact with respondents themselves, they depend on the perceptions people have of themselves and their ability and willingness to accurately report those perceptions. Without direct contact, they can't tell you what services they really use or whether their descriptions of themselves are accurate. They can only tell you what they think.

When to Conduct Surveys

To survey a group, you need three things: a set of questions, a way to collect responses, and most important, access to the group. This last element can most affect the timing of your survey. If you can't get to your audience, you can't do a survey, and without a stable Web site of your own, gaining access to audiences is difficult. Your competitors certainly won't let you survey their users. Traditional telephone, mail, or in-person surveys are expensive. Email lists are often biased, and email surveys can easily come across as spam. So if you don't have a site to run a survey on, you should be prepared to either wait until your site is up and running or plan for an expensive survey.

Note Although it's possible to use simple surveys to gain a basic understanding of your audience, statistically accurate survey creation is a complex process. This chapter covers only the basic issues. If you intend to field anything more than a simple profile or if important product decisions require accurate numerical results, I recommend finding a professional Web survey company and working with them or reading the following books: *Survey Research Methods* by Earl Babbie and *The Handbook of Online Marketing Research* by Joshua Grossnickle and Oliver Raskin.

If you already have an audience, then timing a survey is determined by what you want to know about that audience. Different surveys require different kinds of timing. A *profile,* for example, can be done at any time, getting a snapshot of your current user community's makeup. A *satisfaction survey* could be run before a major redesign in order to understand where people feel the product is failing them so that the redesign can address the problems. A *value survey* investigating what people find important could be run as a big ad campaign is being designed so that the ad designers know what to focus on when marketing to your audience.

Surveys come in all sizes and structures, and ultimately, timing depends on what kind of survey you want to field and what you want to get out of it.

How to Field a Survey

Before you start designing a survey, you need to know what you're trying to accomplish. Start by writing a sentence or two about why you're doing this survey—your goal. For example, say that you have a mature product, a Web site that's been around for several years, and although revenue has been decent, the rate with which new people have been finding your site has been slowing down. You have an idea of the size of your market, but that's assuming that your market has not changed, that the kinds of people finding your site now are the same as when the site launched. Further, although your site has some unique features, it has several competitors that have similar feature sets. You've been counting on your unique features to drive customers and although the log files show that the features get used, it's difficult to tell whether they're the reason people use your product or whether they're icing on the cake. Completing the sentence "We are going to run a survey," the reasoning could read as follows:

> To understand if our user base has changed since last year, and if so, how; and to understand which features they find most attractive.

Setting the Schedule

Once you've decided on the overall goal for the survey, you need to construct a schedule. Since the preparation of a survey is critical to its success, a typical survey research schedule includes enough time for questions to be written and reviewed, and for the survey to be tested and revised as necessary (Table 11.1). Once a survey has been sent out, no changes can be made to maintain statistical validity, so preparation time is crucial.

Timing	Activity
$t - 3$ weeks	Determine test audience, goals.
$t - 3$ weeks	Start writing questions and preparing collection software.
$t - 2$ weeks	Finish writing questions, review with a few people. Rewrite as necessary. Write report draft.
$t - 1$ week	Finish collection software preparation. Begin building survey site. Pilot test, using both collection and tabulation software. Write report based on pilot test results.
$t - 3$ days	Rewrite questions based on pilot test feedback; review with a couple of people.
$t - 2$ days	Finish preparing site with software and questions. Test site for functionality under multiple conditions.
t	Field the survey (usually 1–14 days, depending on whether there's important daily variation). When done, remove the survey site immediately and shut down data collection.
$t + 1$ day	Begin analysis.
$t + 3$ days	Complete analysis. Begin report.
$t + 1$ week	Complete report. Present to development team, discuss, and note directions for further research.

Writing the Survey

You should start by enumerating the goals of your survey as specifically as possible, based on your primary reason.

- Create a demographic, technological, and Web use profile of our audience.
- Get a prioritized rating of the utility of our main features to the survey audience.
- Get a list of other sites they commonly use.

With this list, you should have enough information to choose the kind of survey you're going to be fielding.

Brainstorm Your Questions

With the survey goals in mind, brainstorm your questions (you can do this by yourself or with a group). Without stopping, write down every question you can think of that you want to answer with the survey. Don't try to phrase them in "survey-ese," just write down what you want to know.

As you're brainstorming, keep in mind that there are two different kinds of survey goals, *descriptive* and *explanatory*.

Descriptive goals aim to profile the audience. They summarize your audience's composition in terms of their personal characteristics, their computer setup, what they want, and how they claim to behave. Although such profiles can be quite extensive and sophisticated, they do not attempt to understand how any of the characteristics affect each other.

Explanatory goals explain people's beliefs and behaviors by uncovering relationships between their answers. For example, a mostly descriptive survey would seek to know which features people use and what their average incomes are, whereas an explanatory survey would try to explain how the size of their income affects the features they prefer. Such goals aim to find inherent relationships between characteristics. The more these relationships can be isolated, the more precise the explanation.

Survey questions themselves come in a variety of flavors. General question categories can be divided into *characteristic* questions that describe who someone is and what his or her physical and software environment is like, *behavior* questions that outline how someone behaves, and *attitudinal* questions that inquire into what people want and believe. Each of these major categories can have lots of subcategories.

Characteristic Categories

- *Demographic.* These are questions about who the respondents are. How old are they? What do they do for a living? How educated are they?
- *Technological.* These questions ask about their computer setup and experience. What operating system do they run? What is their monitor resolution?

Behavioral Categories

- *Web use.* These questions ask people how they use the Web. How long have they been using it? How often do they use it every week? What kinds of things do they use it for? How much computer experience do they have?
- *Usage.* What product features do they (claim to) use? How often do they use them? What are the reasons they come to your site? How long have they been using it? These are behavioral questions.
- *Competitive.* What other sites do they visit? How often? How long have they been using them? What features do they use?

Attitudinal Categories

- *Satisfaction.* Do they like your site? Does it do what they had expected? Are they able to do what they want with it?
- *Preference.* What do they find most compelling? Which features do they tell their friends about? What do they consider unnecessary or distracting?
- *Desire.* What do they want? What features do they feel are lacking?

Now, with your list of questions in mind, ask other members of your development team to come up with a list of their own. You may want to show them your list, but first ask them to do it from scratch so that they're not biased by your ideas. Then, when you've collected everyone's questions, share them and see if any additional questions appear from the mix.

The list could look like this.

How old are you?
How much do you make?
What's your education level?
What operating system do you use?
Have you ever heard of Linux?
Have you ever used Linux?
How often do you use the Automatic Alarm?
Do you ever use Ebay? Yahoo! Auction?
What speed is your connection?
How much time do you spend on the Web?
How long are you willing to wait to get an answer?
Have you ever used Quicken?
How long have you had your current computer?
How long have you been using the Net?
What's the most important thing to you when it comes to a Web site?
What time zone do you live in?
etc.

Write the Questions

> *Ask people only questions that they are likely to know the answers to, ask about things relevant to them, and be clear in what you're asking. The danger is that people* will *give you answers—whether reliable or not.*
> —Earl Babbie, *Survey Research Methods,* p. 133

Now it's time to write the questions. In Chapter 6, there are a number of rules for asking nondirected questions, questions that don't lead the person answering them to think that there's a "right" answer.

Most of the suggestions in that section concentrate on the moderator's immediate behavior and helping staying nonjudgmental, but they apply equally well to survey questions. However, whereas qualitative research questions need to be flexible not to cramp respondents' answers, survey questions need to be more precise and restricted in order to be countable. Unlike most interviews, where the questions should be *open-ended* (in other words, they should not limit the set of responses to a list compiled by the interviewer), most survey questions are *close-ended* by pragmatic necessity. In general, open-ended questions require much more effort from the person answering them and from the analyst. This is desirable in long interview situations with a few people, but much more difficult in a survey situation when there may be potentially thousands of participants. Open-ended questions may be used in surveys—they can provide answers in situations where you have no idea how to write the question in a close-ended way—but they need to be used carefully and sparingly.

The most common type of close-ended survey question is the single-answer *multiple-choice question*. We've all seen this type of question: it has a range of choices for the respondent, only one of which may be picked.

How long have you been using Internet email?
○ Less than a year
○ 1–2 years
○ 2–5 years
○ 5 years or more

Another common type of question is the *checklist*. This question consists of a list of answers, any number of which can be chosen.

What kinds of stories have you read in Wired News in the last week?
(check all that apply)
☐ Telecommunications
☐ New products
☐ Hackers
☐ Fashion
☐ Travel

□ Hardware reviews
□ Software reviews
□ Predictions
□ Sports
□ Industry analysis
□ Political commentary
□ Fine arts
□ Fiction
□ Investment
□ Personality profiles
□ Other
□ I haven't read any Wired News stories in the last week

In order for close-ended questions to be comfortably answerable by the respondents, the answers to them need to be *specific, exhaustive,* and *mutually exclusive.* Specificity reduces the amount of uncertainty when the time comes to analyze the answer. If your audience consists of dance music DJs and you're asking about what kind of music they spin, it may be important to make sure that you don't just ask about "dance music" when the DJs may distinguish between two dozen different subgenres. Exhaustive questions reduce the respondents' frustration, and they reduce errors because people won't be as likely to choose a random answer when they can't find one that represents what they really mean. An exhaustive question features all the possible answers. If you can't make an exhaustive list of answers, the question should not be close-ended. Answers should also be as mutually exclusive as possible to reduce the amount of uncertainty among the choices. If you're asking where people shop and you give them the option to choose between "in my neighborhood" and "nearby," they may not know the differences that you had in mind.

Obviously, close-ended questions limit the kinds of questions you can ask, so rephrase your questions so that they can be asked in a close-ended way, and eliminate the ones that can't be rewritten.

Now, make a grid with four columns. For each question, write the question, the instructions you're going to give to the respondent, the possible answers, and why you're asking the question. The "reasons" column is especially important because you need to make sure that you have a specific justification for each and every question.

Why is it important? What is the information going to be used for? Who wants to know?

SAMPLE SURVEY QUESTION GRID

Question	Instructions	Answers	Reasons
What is your age?	*None.*	Pop-up: Under 13 13–18 19–20 21–24 25–34 35–44 45–54 55 and over	For comparison with last year's survey. Compare with experience.
What is your gender?	*None.*	Pop-up: Male Female	For comparison with last year's survey.
What kinds of stories have you read in Wired News in the last week?	Check all that apply.	Checklist: Telecommunications New products Hackers Fashion Travel Hardware reviews Software reviews Predictions Sports Computer industry analysis Political commentary Fine arts Fiction Investment Personality profiles	A measure of reader information desires. Compare perceived reading habits to actual behavior based on log analysis. Summarize for ad sales.

Question	Instructions	Answers	Reasons
What operating system do you use most frequently to access the Web?	*None.*	Pop-up: Windows XP Windows 2000	Compare with last year's survey.
		Windows 95/98	Compare with log analysis.
		Windows NT	Summarize for design.
		Macintosh	Summarize for editorial.
		Linux	
		Other	
		Don't know	

Note In some cases, people may have little or no appropriate past experience to base their answers on. For example, the process of buying a home (or getting open-heart surgery or enrolling in a university) is relatively infrequent for most people, and their past experience may have little relation to their future behavior. This is the one time when asking a hypothetical question may be better than asking about past behavior since past behavior would unlikely yield any useful information.

You may also want to make a second list of information that can be gathered automatically. Web server log files can collect the time a survey was taken, the operating system of the machine used to take the survey, the kind of browser they were using, what Internet domain the machine was on, and so on. Cookies can keep track of who has visited your site before, who has purchased from you before, what their preferences are, and the like.

When writing questions, *don't make people predict* their behavior. People's past behavior is usually better at predicting their future behavior than their statements are. Unless you're asking about a completely novel concept, keep your questions focused on how people have actually acted in the past, not how they can imagine themselves acting in the future. If you're interested in whether someone would use an online scheduling system, don't ask

Will you use an online scheduling system?

Ask instead

Have you ever used or ever wanted to use an online calendar system such as Yahoo! Calendar or eCalendar?

Avoid negative questions. Negative questions are more difficult to understand and easy to mistake for the positive versions of themselves.

> Which of the following features are you not interested in?

can be easily read as

> Which of the following features are you interested in?

It's much easier to ask

> Which of the following features are you interested in?

and then to infer the ones that are not checked are uninteresting to the respondents.

Don't overload questions. Each question should contain at most one concept that you're investigating. Although multiple concepts may be linked, they should still be divided into separate, clear individual questions. Compound questions are frustrating for the respondent, who only agrees with half of the question, and more complicated for the analyst, who needs to infer the respondent's perspective on both parts of the question.

> Do you find yourself frustrated at the Internet's performance because of bandwidth problems?

can be rewritten as

> Are you frustrated by the Internet's performance?

If so, which of the following aspects of Internet performance frustrate you?
☐ Page length
☐ Download time
☐ Picture size
etc.

Be specific. Avoid words with multiple or fuzzy meanings ("sometimes," "around," "roughly," "any"). When speaking in units other than money, percentages, or other common abbreviations, make sure that the whole name of the unit is written out ("hours" instead of "hrs.," "thousands" instead of "K," etc.). Use exact time periods.

So rather than writing a question about how often someone reads news as

How much time have you spent reading news on the Web recently?
○ Some
○ A lot
○ Every day
etc.

the question can be written as

How much time did you spend reading news and information on the Web in the last week?
○ None
○ 0 to 5 hours
○ 6 to 10 hours
○ 11 to 20 hours
○ More than 20 hours

Never shut people out. Questions should always give people an option that they feel applies to them. This question, for example, assumes a lot of things about the respondents and their attitudes.

> What do you love most about Wired News?

It should be rewritten as

> Which of the following features are important to you in Wired News? (check all that apply)

The latter phrasing avoids most of the problems with the earlier question—especially if it provides an option for "None"—and provides most of the same answers.

Stay consistent. Ask questions the same way every time. This means more than just using similar wording for similar questions. You should also strive to maintain consistency in meaning in the order of answer options and in the way the questions are presented.

Avoid extremes. Extreme situations rarely happen, and most people infrequently find themselves exhibiting extreme behavior, so avoid situations that require or imply the need for extreme behavior.

> Do you check online news *every time* you surf the Web?

This would probably produce almost exclusively negative responses since it's likely that only a few people check news every single time they surf. A better way would be to ask

> How often do you check online news?
> ○ Several times a day
> ○ Once a day
> ○ More than once a week
> ○ Once a week
> ○ Once a month
> ○ Less than once a month
> ○ Never

and compare the responses to how often people say they surf the Web to see the proportion.

Make questions relevant. If people are confronted with a list of questions that don't relate to their experience or their life, they're not likely to finish the survey. For example, a group of computer service technicians will respond differently to questions about the minutia of their computer configuration than will a group of taxi drivers. If the respondent can't answer many of the questions or if they're not interested in the answers, they're not likely to be interested in finishing the survey.

Use Likert scales. Likert scales are a familiar method of presenting multiple-choice answers. They consist of a statement or series of statements followed by a choice of three, five, or seven options (most surveys use three or five) that define a possible range of answers, including a neutral middle option.

Rate the following aspects of news and information Web sites for how interesting they are to you.	Very interesting	Somewhat interesting	Neutral	Somewhat uninteresting	Very uninteresting
The number of different stories on a given topic	O	O	O	O	O
The number of different topics covered	O	O	O	O	O
How quickly the page downloads	O	O	O	O	O
The reputation of the news outlet	O	O	O	O	O
How comprehensively each story is covered	O	O	O	O	O

(Continued)

	Very interesting	Somewhat interesting	Neutral	Somewhat uninteresting	Very uninteresting
A unique editorial perspective	○	○	○	○	○
The quality of the site's search engine	○	○	○	○	○
The visual appearance of the site	○	○	○	○	○
How quickly stories are covered after they happened	○	○	○	○	○
How easy it is to get around in the site	○	○	○	○	○

Create follow-up questions. When technologically possible, ask questions that further expand on a given answer. Ideally, follow-up questions should appear only after a specific answer for a given question. This is technologically possible with some online survey systems. When it's impossible, it should be clear that the follow-up questions are related to a given answer and that they should not be answered otherwise.

If one question asks

Check all the sites that you read regularly.

A follow-up can then contain a list of sites that were marked as being read regularly.

> Rate how important each of the following sites are to you, from "Crucial" to "Unimportant."

Note A list of common questions is provided in the Appendix. However, don't hesitate to experiment with new questions and question types. Much online research still shows its roots in the paper survey world, with online questions essentially the same as their printed ancestors. Using the technology offers a lot of possibilities for innovative questions. A simple example: rather than asking people for the size of their Web browser window (something that many people may not know), it's possible to put a picture of a ruler on-screen and ask "In the image above, what's the largest number you can see without scrolling?"

Include an opt-out option. Always include an option for people to signify that a question does not apply to them or that none of the suggested options are appropriate. These are typically phrased as variations on "None of the above," "Don't know," or "No Answer," depending on what's appropriate for the question.

Leave space for comments. Although most people won't use them, you should include a space at the end of the survey for people to provide comments about it.

Edit and Order the Questions

The first thing you need to do is to pare down the survey size. One way to maximize the number of responses to a survey is to keep it short. Most people should be able to complete your survey in 20 minutes or less. Surveys that take more than 20 minutes begin feeling like a burden, and respondents have to schedule time to do them. Since reading the instructions takes about 5 minutes and each question takes 30 seconds or so to read and answer, this limits you to about 30 questions total. Keeping a survey to 20 questions leaves you with a safe margin. Besides, as the old game implies, you can find out almost anything about anyone in 20 questions, provided you choose the questions carefully.

Once you've written and culled your questions, it's time to edit and organize them. The question order is as important as the wording. A survey is a dialogue, with every question revealing something to the person taking the survey and providing information to the person receiving the results. Question order should pace, focus, and selectively reveal information.

In some ways, a survey is like a short story. The beginning grabs the readers' attention, drawing them in. As they read the survey, they begin to get an idea of what kind of information the survey is trying to find out. In the middle, big ideas are explored and "twists" on the basic plot are introduced as certain avenues of inquiry are followed. Finally, loose ends are tied up, and the survey ends. Admittedly, even at their best, surveys do not make exciting stories, but writing them with even a small narrative arc can make them more interesting for the participants, which reduces the number of people who drop out due to boredom.

As in a story, you can gradually reveal what the survey is about, not explaining too much up front in order to get people's responses about general topics. Earlier topics may influence people's expectations and thoughts. If your survey is trying to understand how people buy toys online, you may not want to reveal that your survey is about toys until after you've gotten a general picture of their buying behavior.

For example, a survey is trying to understand the relationship between people's food-buying and toy-buying habits. The following two questions are logical ones to pose:

A. What was the total price of groceries you bought last year?
B. How carefully do you track your purchases?

If question A is asked before question B, then people may think B applies only to groceries, which they may track very carefully, but the survey is more interested in people's general purchasing behavior. By asking B before A, the survey collects people's general impressions without constraining their perception of the survey's scope.

A typical survey has the following four parts:

- An *introduction* that presents the purpose of the survey, instructions for filling it out, the duration of it, and contact information in case questions arise.
- A *beginning* with teaser questions. These questions should be interesting to the person taking the survey, drawing them in. They should not be demographic questions, which are considered boring and, at this early stage, could be construed as intrusive.
- A *middle,* where it's a good idea to keep things moving by alternating questions that are likely to be interesting to the respondents with questions that are not. Questions are grouped

thematically, such as "General News Reading Behavior," "On-line News Reading Behavior," "Quality of News Sources," and "Unmet Needs and Desires."

- The *end,* which concludes with all the remaining demographic questions, provides an open-ended field for general response, and reiterates the contact information.

Within this structure, the survey should be flexible. When there isn't a logical progression in a list of answers to a multiple-choice question (best-to-worst, most-to-least, first-to-last, etc.), the list should be randomized whenever possible. This reduces the chances that the order of the answers will affect how people choose. Some online survey software products do this automatically, but it's also possible to create several versions of the survey with answers in a different order and randomly assign people to them when creating invitations.

Write the Instructions

There are two different kinds of instructions in a survey: *general instructions* and individual *question instructions.*

The *general* survey instructions should be brief and straightforward. They should run a paragraph at the longest and contain several pieces of information:

- *That the survey is important.* "We want to make vFork a better service for you. Your participation in this survey is very important to us."
- *What it's for.* "The survey is to help us understand the needs and desires of the people using vFork."
- *Why people's answers are safe.* "All of your answers are confidential and will be used strictly for research. There will be no sales or marketing follow-up because of your participation in this survey."
- *What the reward is.* "By completing this survey, you will have our gratitude and a 1 in 100 chance of winning a Palm personal digital assistant."
- *Who is responsible* for the survey, if not the company in question. "This survey is being administered for vFork by Adaptive Path LLC."

Warning Many places, such as most of the United States, have laws governing sweepstakes (which is what a survey offering a "one in X" chance to win something becomes). Sweepstakes require that their rules be clearly posted along with the survey description. You can get most of what you need by copying the rules from another sweepstakes, but you should absolutely have a lawyer look at what you've written before you launch your survey to the public.

Likewise, many places have rules about interviewing children. You should make it clear that the survey should be taken by people 13 and older. If your target audience contains a lot of kids, you should consult with a lawyer about how to allow them to take the survey (often this requires written permission from their parents).

- *How long the survey is running.*" This survey will run from July 17, 2003, until July 24, 2003."
- *Who to contact with questions.* "If you have any questions or comments about this survey, you may enter them into the form at the bottom of the survey or email them to Mike Kuniavsky at mikek@adaptivepath.com." This also personalizes it (the survey is no longer an anonymous form), which tends to increase the response rate.

Question instructions should likewise be simple and straightforward. Most close-ended questions won't need special instructions, but open-ended questions should say exactly what kind of answers you want. Rather than writing

> List your favorite Web sites.

the instructions could say

> Make a list of the URLs (Web addresses) of sites that you go to often or that you really like. Write up to 10 addresses.

For questions where you want a single answer, but people may feel that any of several options may be adequate, make it clear that they have to select what they feel is the strongest option.

Likert scale grids generally need a couple of sentences of explanation.

> The following is a list of features that can be found on vFork and other online fork sites. If you believe that you have used one of these features on vFork, please rate how important the service is to you when buying forks online. If you have never used a feature on vFork please select "Never Used." If you don't know whether you have never used it, select "Don't Know."

You should also make additional instructions visible whenever it's appropriate, such as for error pages or for sections of questions that resemble other sections, but function differently. For example, if a page is reloaded because of an error, the reasons for the reloaded page and any new instructions should be clearly highlighted on the first screen people see after the new page appears.

Lay Out the Report

The report? But we haven't started yet! That's right, lay out the report. One of the best ways to know what questions to ask is to make a list of the answers you want.

The data you collect should be dependent on what analysis you want to perform, what questions you want to answer. You should never ask questions "just in case" (although it's OK to ask exploratory questions for which you don't have a good idea how people will answer).

Your report should begin with your goals and your methods. Writing as if the survey has already been completed, describe why you've run this survey, your goals, and the design of your research. Include information about your estimates of the size of the total population from which you sampled, your sampling method, the size of the sample, the completion rate, and how you analyzed the data. Then write your conclusions. Of course, before you start analyzing your data, you won't know what your real conclusions will be, so these will be your hypotheses, but you will have some idea of what kinds of conclusions you want to have. So write those down.

Sixty-five percent of the people who bought forks in the last month buy forks three times a year or more.

This tells you that you need to collect information about when the last fork was bought and how many times people buy forks a year, and the people who bought forks in the last month need to be large enough for analysis based on it to produce statistically significant results.

Once you've written down your placeholder conclusions, you should make all the tables and graphs you're going to use to back up your conclusions. As the following example shows, the tables should say exactly what variables are being plotted against what other variables and what's being displayed.

OPINION OF FEATURES BASED ON LENGTH OF TIME ON THE WEB				
Features	Length of Time on the Web			
	< 6 Mo.	6 Mo.–1 Yr.	1–2 Yrs.	2+ Yrs.
Fork Finder				
Shopping Wiz				
Main Catalog				

Because the process of writing the report can affect the content of the survey, make sure you budget enough time to write the report beforehand. That way you can make changes to the survey method or the kind of data you collect.

After you've run your pilot survey, use your report mock-up and run all the pilot data through the same processes you're planning for the real data, making the same tables and drawing conclusions as you would with the real thing. This will help shake out issues with your analysis procedure.

Web Survey Tips

Now you're ready to build the survey on the Web. I won't go into the technical aspects of creating a survey for the Web since the process will depend on your existing systems if you're using a software package that does much of the presentation and tabulation work. However, the basic structure of all Web surveys is the same: an HTML page containing a form and a backend CGI program or email-based script to collect the results. Tabulation is accomplished via a custom program, a statistical program, or for simpler surveys, a spreadsheet.

Free Web Survey Tools

As of 2002, in addition to a myriad of commercial products, there are several free online survey presentation and tabulation services that, though not as fully featured as a commercial product, address most of the needs of simple survey research.

- Sparklit *(www.sparklit.com)* is an ad-based polling service that allows you to ask basic multiple-choice questions and then tabulates the results as simple tables.
- Zoomerang *(www.zoomerang.com)* offers a larger set of question types, a selection of premade surveys, and the option for more sophisticated analysis tools for a fee.
- Survey Monkey *(www.surveymonkey.com)* similarly offers a larger selection of question types and more survey options.

In addition, there is phpESP *(phpesp.sourceforge.net)*, an Open Source survey construction and tabulation package that runs on Web servers that have the (likewise Open Source) PHP server-side scripting language installed.

There are some things to keep in mind when building any kind of Web-based survey.

Error checking. The backend system can check how people responded. If any are missing or incorrectly filled out (for example, if someone checked a checkbox for a specific choice *and* "None of the Above"), the page should be reproduced with the incorrectly filled-in responses clearly flagged.

Functionality. Survey pages should be checked like any other page on your site for functioning HTML, even more than usual. The survey page should download quickly and look right on as many browsers, operating systems, screen sizes, and modem speeds as possible. If you expect a segment of your user base to be using AOL or to be behind a firewall, make sure you check the performance with those systems, too. If you use JavaScript in the page, make sure that it works on all browsers and that there's an appropriate error message for people who have JavaScript turned off (or can't interpret JavaScript at all).

Usability. Usability-test the survey just as if it were a new feature. This helps to make sure that everything works and that people's experience of it matches their expectations.

Timing. Since you can keep track of when responses are returned, do so. This will help keep track of what responses arrived within the research period, and it provides another piece of information about the behavior of your user population. If a large group of your respondents claim to be in the eastern standard time zone and their responses arrived between 9 a.m. and 5 p.m. EST, you can hypothesize that they were accessing your site from work.

Mortality. Keep track of the people who drop out of the survey. Note at which points they dropped out, and try to draw some conclusions about how they differ based on the answers they completed.

Response rate. Similar to mortality, this is a count of people who were offered to take the survey versus how many actually responded. This is critical information when projecting your analysis to a larger population.

Form Tricks

Distinguishing between skipped responses and default responses in Web surveys can be difficult unless forms are set up to anticipate it. Create a difference by making the default option a space character. This doesn't sway people toward selecting a specific option and makes it clear when something is selected (and the space character makes sure that there's *some* response in the file, which makes it easier to process the data and exchange the data). The HTML for a blank pull-down menu is

```
<select name="news_quality">
   <option value="1"> Strongly agree
   <option value="2"> Agree
   <option value="3"> Neither agree nor disagree
   <option value="4"> Disagree
   <option value="5"> Strongly disagree
   <option selected value=" ">
<\select>
```

For radio buttons, don't define any options as "checked" by default.

```
<P>What is your gender?<\P>
<blockquote>
<P>
 <input type="radio" name="gender" value="M">
```

```
Male
<br>
 <input type="radio" name="gender" value="F">
Female
 </P>

As opposed to

<input type="radio" name="gender" value="F" checked>
```

Test the Survey

> *Take every opportunity to pretest each aspect of the study design under*
> *whatever testing conditions may be available.*
> —Earl Babbie, *Survey Research Methods,* p. 235

A survey can often only be run once. Rerunning a whole survey is almost as expensive as running the survey the first time; surveys shouldn't be changed on the fly. Pretesting the survey (also known as *pilot testing*) is a critical part of its development and can eliminate a lot of costly mistakes.

A pretest is run just like the real thing, using all the same software, the same recruiting methods, the same data collection methods, and the same analysis methods as the final survey. You should even make a pretest report using your report template, drawing conclusions just as you would with the final data. The difference is in terms of sample size. A pilot sample contains 5–10 responses from people who are, ideally, representative of the group who will be responding to the survey (if you can't get people who match that profile, it's OK to use people who may match only some of the key criteria). Don't tell the participants that it's a pretest. Use the same invitation materials you would use for the regular test, and see if the answers they provide are what you had expected.

Afterwards, or simultaneously, do two or three in-person user tests of the survey, watching people as they take the survey. Keep track of how long it takes them to take it and what problems and questions they have about it. You can also follow up with an email to the pilot participants, asking them to discuss how the survey went, what kinds of problems they had, and so forth.

Note If you have the resources or if this is going to be a particularly involved survey, consider running a prepilot survey, where you present 5–10 people with the survey questions phrased in an open-ended way. If all of their responses fit within the responses you have written in your prepared survey, you can be pretty sure you've covered the appropriate ground.

The Incentive

Unless your survey is extremely short, you should provide an incentive for people to take it. You will want to provide an incentive that's related to the complexity of your survey and the interests of your audience. Knowing your audience is important to picking the right incentive. The incentive for a site for teenagers and one for middle-aged millionaires will have different incentives, but the goal is the same: it's a reward for giving up a portion of their time and personal information. An online gaming information site offered a chance to get *one* Microsoft XBox in exchange for its visitors' participation in a survey. Ninety-five percent of the people visiting the site took the survey, a proportion that beats many censuses.

The way you present your incentive is important. If you're offering something that's worth $2 for a completed response and your survey takes half an hour to complete, many people may not think that it's worth their time to fill out. However, if you offer a 1 in 100 chance to win something that costs $200, you're likely to get more responses. Although the end costs to you are the same, it's been shown that people would rather gamble with their time for something that's worth more than take a sure thing that's worth less. Why? Who knows.

Fielding the Survey

Fielding a survey is the process of inviting people to take it. It sounds simple, but it's not. Surveys are neither censuses, which attempt to get responses from the entire population, nor questions answered by a haphazard group of people. They attempt to contact a randomly selected, evenly distributed subset of the population in a controlled way.

So before thinking about how to field your survey, it's important to discuss what it means to pick a sample from a population.

The Sample and the Sampling Frame

The group of people who fill out your survey is called a *sample,* but what is it a sample of? It's a randomly chosen subset of the group of people your sampling method can put you in contact with. This group is called the *sampling frame* (see Figure 11.1). In other words,

Note Since a large amount of survey analysis is understanding the uncertainty of the collection method, one of your chief goals in survey design should be to reduce the number of variables that need to be considered and controlled. Everything can influence how people respond to the survey, from who sees the survey to how fast the description page downloads. Thus, as you're creating the survey and the mechanisms for gathering respondents and collecting responses, continually think of ways of reducing the number of unknown variables.

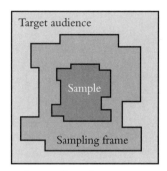

Figure 11.1 Sample and sampling frame.

out of the universe of all of your users, there's a subset your methods allow you to contact and a subset they don't. The subset you can hypothetically contact is your sampling frame; a random selection of people from your sampling frame is your sample.

Ideally, the sampling frame matches the whole population of people you're interested in. If it doesn't, then your results can be inaccurate and misleading since they will not represent the views of your entire audience. For example, if you field a survey only to the people who have complained about your product, you're not likely to get a good representation of your whole audience's opinion. Likewise, if you talk only to people who have signed up for a mailing list or who have purchased something from your site, you're talking only to a group of people who have expressed an active interest in your product, and those people likely form a minority of all the people who may be interested in what you have to offer.

Sampling frame mismatches can come in all kinds of flavors as well. If a survey is run only on Monday and Tuesday for a ski conditions site that gets the majority of their users on Thursday and Friday, the results will not be representative since the weekend ski audience is likely to be different from the midweek audience. Likewise, just running the survey on Thursday and Friday may miss a key market of hardcore ski enthusiasts. Knowing the composition of your sampling frame is critical to knowing how valid your results are. Unfortunately, there are many, many ways to sample badly and get the wrong sampling frame.

First, define the groups of users you're most interested in. Usage frequency is a good place to start. Are they regular users? (How do you define "regular"? Every day? Every week?) First-time users? Infrequent users?

Now add other characteristics that are important and that can affect the way you recruit people for your survey. Are they people who have bought products from your site? Are they from a specific geographic region? Are they students? People who are thinking of switching from your competitors' products? Power users?

Your survey may end up being the combination of several subgroups (power users and frequent users, European purchasers, and others).

Having decided who your users are, you will have to create a way that will comprehensively invite the people who make up your target audience, without missing or overrepresenting any groups. Each characteristic will create a different method of inviting people and a different set of potential problems in terms of data collection.

For example, say you're interested in the usability problems of frequent users, so you'd like to profile people who use your site all the time. Although it may be interesting to know if there's an observable difference between people who visit often and people who visit and buy your products, you need to stay focused on your target audience choices. So, for example, you decide that your target audience is "users who visit the site at least once a week and who have bought something."

So how do you contact these people? You could use a tracking cookie and ask questions of people whose cookies are less than a week old. But that's dependent on people not having switched machines, deleted their cookies, or changed browsers. What's more, it assumes that you have tracking cookies. It may be easier to randomly invite users and filter out the responses of anyone who doesn't say they visit at least once a week. Moreover, you will need to run your survey for at least a week or in week-long increments, so as not to overrepresent the visitors who show up on any given day. But is that still guaranteed to target all the users who fit your target profile? No. Some of them may be on vacation; others may skip a week and miss your survey. However, since people do these things randomly, it's unlikely that this will affect your results. There may also be other groups of users—say, people who shop infrequently but buy a lot—who are also important to you, but you're not aware of their existence. Missing these people can really affect your results.

So how are you going to know about and contact *all* these people? You won't and you can't, but you should strive to contact enough people that their responses can make a positive change in your product.

All this is to say that the more you know about your population and their habits, the better you can choose your sampling frame. However, if you know little about your audience, don't panic. Your first survey can be fielded to reveal a lot about your audience's profile, and qualitative research (contextual inquiry, focus groups) can reveal things about their behavior so that subsequent surveys can be more accurately targeted.

Sample Size

So how many people do you invite? Surveys always contain some amount of uncertainty. There always is a possibility of error in a sample since you're not asking every single member of the population the same questions in the same way. The size of the uncertainty can be estimated mathematically, but the amount that's acceptable will have to be decided by you.

Ultimately, surveys depend on the variation in your population. If all of your users are identical, then you need to ask only one of them to understand how all of them would respond. But all of your users aren't identical, so you have to estimate how many to ask based on how varied the population is. This is a classic chicken-and-egg problem: you can't find out how varied your audience is without surveying them, and you can't survey them unless you know how varied they are. Fortunately, it's possible to estimate how many people to invite by assuming that your population has a pretty "standard" variation and then adjusting future surveys if the estimate turns out to be too low (asking too many people is rarely a problem, other than the extra work it involves).

Let's start with the assumption that your entire user population has 10,000 people in it. That means that if you count everyone who has ever used your site or is ever likely to use it (within reason, say, within the next year), you'll get 10,000 people. Now you want to find out how many of them you need to survey in order to be able to get an idea of how all (or the majority) would answer your questions. You'll never get the "real" values unless you survey all 10,000 people, but (without going into the math—that's covered later in this chapter) by asking 300 of them, you can be 95% confident that the answers you get from them will fall in a 10% range ("plus or minus 5%," as they say on TV) of what you'd get if you asked everyone. What does "95% confident" mean? It too is explained later in the chapter, but for now you can read it as "pretty darned confident."

Three hundred people is fine, it's not such a big number, but what if your audience has a million people in it? Thirty thousand is a lot of people to have in a survey. Fortunately, the relationship between the number of people in your population and the number of people you need to talk to is not proportional in that way. The way the math works, you need to sample only 2000, which is significantly easier. So, without consulting a statistician, you can use the following table to estimate the number of people you need in your sample.

APPROXIMATE SAMPLE SIZES (ASSUMING 5% STANDARD ERROR, 95% CONFIDENCE, AND NORMAL VARIATION)

Population	Sample Size
1000	150
10,000	300
100,000	800

These numbers are a very rough minimum number of responses necessary for you to be able to extrapolate a survey statistic to the population at large. Statisticians will chastise me for butchering the statistics involved (and, believe me, they are butchered), but the numbers are close enough to make some educated guesses.

To complicate things a bit more, these numbers don't apply to your whole sample size, but to any single group you're going to be studying. If you're going to be segmenting your audience into subgroups (such as by gender or by experience or by region) and doing calculations on the subgroups, then *each subgroup* needs to be that big. For example, if your product has 10,000 unique users and you're planning to analyze frequent users separately from infrequent users, *both* sets of data must have at least 300 entries. This means you'll need to have at least 600 responses in your total sample.

Bias

Sampling bias is the Great Satan of survey research. It's clever, insidious, omnipresent, and impossible to eradicate. It's when the people who you thought would respond—the members of your sampling frame—are not members of the population that you're trying to sample (as illustrated in Figure 11.2). This is very dangerous.

For a sample to provide useful information about the population as a whole, it needs to resemble that population and their views. If it does not, then certain subgroups or views will be overrepresented while other groups and views get shortchanged. When the data from a biased survey are tabulated, the results don't describe the population. Since the purpose of a survey is to describe your users, misrepresenting elements of your audience undermines the whole endeavor.

To some extent, you are always going to exclude certain people. Just by fielding your survey on the Web, you are cutting out people who are not on the Web. By writing your survey in English, you are cutting out those who don't read English. The keys are to know whom you are excluding (or misrepresenting) and to make sure that they are not members of your target audience and that you do not include them in your analysis.

One of the most common and important kinds of bias is *nonresponder bias.* Some number of people will always ignore your invitation, but if there's a pattern to those who do, it's bias. If your

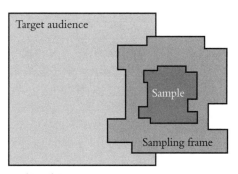

Figure 11.2 Sampling bias.

survey is repelling a certain group, then they'll never be represented in your research. For example, if you're surveying people about their time use, and your survey takes 45 minutes to complete, you may be missing the most important segment of your market simply because they don't have time to fill out your survey. There are many other different kinds of nonresponder bias.

- *Timing bias.* Does the time you invited people affect the way they answered? If you ask people about how much they enjoy shopping for gifts on the day before Christmas, you may get a different response than if you ask at a time when people aren't frantically grabbing toys off the shelf.
- *Duration bias.* Some behavior is cyclical: it consistently peaks during a certain part of the day or week or month. If your target audience consists of commodities traders and you run your survey from 9 a.m. to 5 p.m. when most traders are too busy to fill out surveys, you will likely miss a large portion of your audience.
- *Invitation bias.* How did you invite people to participate in the survey? The places, times, incentive, and wording all affect who is going to respond. If you're trying to invite skateboarders and you begin your invitation with "Dear Sir or Madam, you are cordially invited to . . ." you likely lose much of your audience (unless the invitation is obviously ironic). If you offer T-shirts as an incentive to senior managers, you're not likely to get a representative group.
- *Self-selection.* A special kind of invitation bias and a common mistake in Web surveys is the practice of letting people choose whether they want to participate in a survey without explicitly inviting them. "Click here to take our survey!" is often how this is presented. Who is going to take that survey? Why will they take it? In an opt-in situation like this, you have no idea who the people who aren't clicking on the link are. They could be the same kind of people who click on the link, but it's doubtful. Opt-in surveys tend to attract people who have extreme opinions and specialized interests, which is rarely the only group that you want to attract. It's better to have people have to opt out of a survey than opt in. That way you know that a random distribution saw the invitation, how many people were invited, and how many chose not to take it.

- *Presentation bias.* The way you present the survey, the survey's look and feel, also determines who feels interested in answering it. Technologically, if you use JavaScript to perform a certain key function and a portion of your key population has JavaScript turned off, they won't be able to take your survey. Esthetically, if you present the survey with a bunch of cute cartoon characters around it, businesspeople may be reticent to take it (conversely, if you present a plain black-and-white screen full of text to a group of teenagers, they may think it's too boring to pay attention to). The visual polish of surveys should match that of the sites they're being linked from. If a slick site links to a survey that is stylistically drastically different, it may cause confusion (and, if the shift is too harsh, it may even affect people's perception of the site brand).
- *Expectation bias.* People have expectations of what a survey is going to be about and why they should take it. If those expectations are not met during the course of taking it, they may abandon it. In a pretest of a survey, one user said "Oh, I thought that this was going to be about me and it's asking all these questions about how I change the oil. I don't care about that."

The art of survey design is in tracking response rates to minimize and understand all the preceding factors while maximizing participation. Tabulating results and drawing conclusions are pretty straightforward in comparison. Typical online survey response rates vary between 20% and 40% (which means that between 20% and 40% of the people who are offered to take the survey take it and finish it). Much less than 20% and the results of a survey are highly dubious. As Joshua Grossnickle, co-author of *The Handbook of Online Marketing Research,* says, "a survey with a 1% response rate is worthless data." Testing your survey and understanding the implications of your design in terms of the groups that it is excluding are key ways of minimizing the amount of bias.

Invitation

After bias reduction, the next task to consider is how to randomize your sample. Finding a truly random sample can be tough and depends on how you invite people. There are a number of common ways of inviting people to take your survey, and each method has its own benefits and carries its own problems.

Invitation Link

This is the easiest but least accurate survey invitation method. It consists of a link from a key page (generally the home page) inviting people to participate in a survey. Its benefits are that it's cheap and unobtrusive, but it suffers heavily from self-selection bias. There's no guarantee that a random selection of users to the site sees it, and there's no attempt to distribute the invitation among visitors, so the people who take it are likely to be people who want to communicate something about the site. These groups are likely to be experienced users who have strong opinions. Their views are useful, but are rarely representative of the typical user's views.

If you do use a front-door invitation link, keep track of all the unique visitors to that page and compare it to the number of people who responded. This will give you some idea of how many have seen the invitation versus how many filled out the survey. If the response rate is small (say, 5% of the number of people who have seen the site), then there's a high chance that the responses are not representative of your audience. The survey may still produce useful information, but it's unlikely that the conclusions can be extrapolated to the population at large.

Email

Warning When using tracking identifiers, make it clear that the survey software possesses this capability so that respondents who expect the survey to be anonymous know that it's not. Also make it clear that even though it's not anonymous, responses will still be confidential.

If you have a list of known users, you can select a random subset of them and invite them to take the survey. Such an invitation list won't reach users who aren't in your database (and therefore haven't used the services of your site that get them into your database), and it won't reach people who have opted out of having email sent to them, but it will let you contact people who almost certainly use your site. More important, it lets you issue explicit invitations so that you know that all potential users were exposed to the same invitation (thus reducing the problems of self-selection), and it lets you track exactly how many invitations resulted in responses.

There are two basic kinds of email survey invitation: one that's just an invitation to visit a Web-based survey and one that results in an email-based survey. Although email-based surveys can reach a wider group of people, they involve more work on the data collection side since the responses have to be parsed (either by hand or with software). Web-based surveys are generally preferred.

Ideally, each email survey invitation will have a unique identifier that will allow you to track which and how many people responded.

Interruption

An interruption invitation works by inviting random users to take a survey as they are visiting your site. Every user has an equal chance of being invited (either every time they visit the site or once per user), and the invitation interrupts their experience of your site such that they have to actively accept or decline the invitation to continue using the site. This tells you exactly how many people were invited, ensures that they were all equally aware of the survey, and guarantees that they are a random sample of all users.

Random interruptions can be done either by *probability* or *systemically.* Sampling by probability involves choosing visitors according to a probability that will make the total amount of visitors that meet that probability roughly equal to the expected number of responses. In practice, this generally involves picking a random number for each visitor; if the random number matches a predetermined "magic number," then the person is invited to take the survey. Otherwise, they experience the site normally, never knowing that a survey is under way for others. So if you have determined that you need 1000 responses for a week-long survey and the site gets about 100,000 unique visitors per week, then each visitor during that week should have a 1 in 100 probability of being invited to take the survey.

Random Selection JavaScript

A useful way of creating a consistent probability sample is to include a piece of code on every page. This code snippet performs the necessary calculations about whether the current visitor should be offered the survey and leaves a cookie in his or her browser so that the visitor isn't considered for invitation more than once per survey (unless, of course, the survey is measuring behavior per visit, rather than per visitor, but those types of surveys are considerably rarer).

Here is a piece of JavaScript written by Joshua Grossnickle and Oliver Raskin, authors of *The Handbook of Online Marketing Research.* It works in most situations (though, of course, not if the recipient's browser has JavaScript turned off).

(Continued)

```
<script language="javascript">
//<!—
//the variables sLocation and sRate
//are set to the location of your survey and
//the desired sampling rate

var
sLocation="http://www.adaptivepath.com/survey.html";
var sRate = 15;
var cookieName = "SurveyCookie";

var cookieValue = getCookie(cookieName);
if (cookieValue == null) {
  setCookie(cookieName, "Sampled");
  var sampled = Math.random();
  if (sampled < sRate) {
  window.open(sLocation,'sWindow','scrollbars,resizable');
  }
}

function getCookie(Name) {
var search = Name + "=";
if (document.cookie.length > 0) {
  offset = document.cookie.indexOf(search);
  if (offset != −1) {
      offset += search.length;
      end = document.cookie.indexOf(";",offset);
      if (end == −1);
      end = document.cookie.length;
      return
  unescape(document.cookie.substring(offset,end));
    }
  }
}
```

```
function setCookie(name,value,expire,domainname) {
document.cookie = name + "=" + escape(value) +
((expire == null) ? "" : ("; expires=" +
expire.toGMTString()) + "; path=/"
}


//—>
</script>
```

In order to accurately measure all visitors, not just those who visit the home-page, the code needs to be inserted into every page that someone can get to by typing in a URL. This is easiest with dynamically generated sites, or sites that include a uniform navigation header (in which case the code can be inserted as part of the header), but even sites that are "flat," made with plain HTML, should still have it inserted at all the likely entry points into a site.

Systemic interruptions are sometimes simpler. A systemic sample works by inviting every *n*th visitor. In our example, this would equate to picking a random number between 1 and 100 and then taking every 100th visitor after that person until 1000 visitors have been invited. This is more of a traditional paper survey technique, where it has the advantage of being simpler to implement, but it's not as flexible.

Telephone, In-Person, and Standard Mail Surveys

Traditional survey techniques such as telephone, in-person, and paper mailed surveys are beyond the scope of this book, but they should not be forgotten because they're the most effective ways to get a truly random sample of the population. These are the typical survey techniques used by political and market research. One typical tool is the random phone call: a machine randomly dials phone numbers within a certain area code and telephone exchange until someone answers, then a person takes over and begins reading a telephone survey script. However, users of a specific software product or visitors to a certain Web site are likely harder to find by randomly dialing phone numbers than people who belong to a certain political party or who buy a certain product, so the technique isn't as efficient for finding users. Although collecting data in person seems to defy the global nature of the Internet, if your audience is easily accessible—such as for a site that's serving the teachers in a local school district—then the flexibility and information-gathering potential of an in-person survey is hard to beat. These methods are generally more time consuming and expensive than Web-based surveys, but they should not be forgotten just because they're not digital.

Warning The world abounds with bad survey research that's bandied about just because it contains numbers. Do not be deceived by numbers, and do not try to deceive with numbers. Just because there are numbers does not mean that a rigorous process has been used to arrive at those numbers.

How to Analyze Survey Responses

Survey analysis and interpretation is as much of an art as a science. Although it deals with numbers, proportions, and relationships, it also measures statements, and the relationship between statements and actions is notoriously difficult to understand. From the ambiguities of recruiting bias, to misunderstandings in question wording, to the tendency of people to exaggerate, the whole process involves approximations and estimates. Ultimately, every person is different, and the final analysis will miss the subtleties of any single person's perceptions, behavior, or experience. However, this is all right. In most cases, results can be valuable and useful without complete certainty, and often it's important to only know the odds in order to make an informed decision.

Thus the analysis of survey data should strive for accuracy and immediate utility. Although sophisticated techniques can sometimes extract important subtleties in data, simpler analysis is preferable in most cases. Simpler methods reduce the possibility of error and labor and are sufficient to answer the majority of questions that come up in typical product development situations.

The two common analysis techniques can be summarized simply as *counting* and *comparing*.

Counting

The easiest, and often the only, thing that you can do with results is to count them (to *tabulate* them, in survey-speak). When basic response data are counted, it can reveal simple trends and uncover data entry errors. It consists of counting all the response values to each question.

You should start by looking through the raw data. The raw information can give you ideas of trends that may be present in the data before you start numerically abstracting the results. How are the results distributed? Is there an obvious way that some responses cluster? Are there any really clearly bogus or atypical responses (such as teenagers with $150,000 personal incomes or skateboarding octogenarians)? Spending time with the raw data can give you a gut-level feeling for it, which will prove useful later.

Once you've looked through the raw data, a simple count of all the answers to a given question can be useful. For example, adding up the answers to the question "Which of the following categories includes your household income?" could yield the following table:

Less than $20,000	0
$20,001–$29,999	2
$30,000–$39,999	3
$40,000–$49,999	10
$50,000–$59,999	12
$60,000–$69,999	20
$70,000–$79,999	25
$80,000–$99,999	28
$100,000–$119,999	22
$120,000–$149,999	17
$150,000 or over	5
No answer	10

Displayed as a simple histogram, this reveals some interesting information about how your audience's income is distributed.

From Figure 11.3, it looks like the audience's income peaks somewhere between $80,000 and $100,000, and that people with incomes between $60,000 and $150,000 make up the majority of the users. If your site was aimed at lower-middle income participants, then it's clear that your site isn't attracting those people in the way you had hoped.

Taking the data from the table, it's possible to calculate the *mean* and *mode* of the data. The mean is the average of the values, in the traditional algebraic sense. It's calculated by adding all the values of the responses to a given question and then dividing by the number of responses. In the case of ranges of numbers, such as the one above, you can use the midpoint of every range as your starting point. For this example, the mean would be about $86,000, calculated as such:

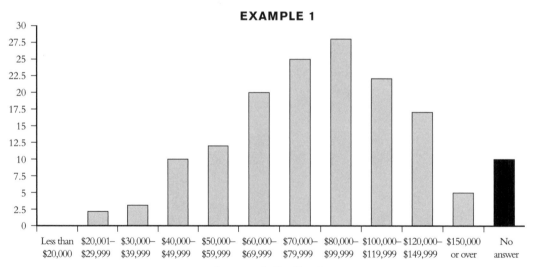

EXAMPLE 1

Figure 11.3 A normal distribution.

$$= \frac{(25,000 \cdot 2) + (35,000 \cdot 3) + \dots + (150,000 \cdot 5)}{144}$$

$$= \frac{12,425,000}{144}$$

$$= \quad 86,285$$

It is "about" $86,000 because the ranges are broad, and the highest range of "$150,000 or over" is unbounded at the upper end (the lower bound was used in calculations). For practical purposes, this is generally enough.

The mean, however, can be easily skewed by a small number of extreme results. It's the "billionaire" problem: if you're sampling the actual values of annual salaries and you happen to survey Bill Gates, your "average" value is likely to be significantly higher than what the majority of people in your sample make. This is where looking at the raw data is important since it will give you a gut-level expectation for the results. Your gut could still be wrong, but if you looked at a bunch of responses where people had $40,000 and $50,000 incomes and your mean turns out to be $120,000, then something is likely pushing the value up. You should start looking for *outliers,* or responses that are well outside the general variation of data since a few extreme values may be affecting the mean.

The *mode,* the most common value, can be compared to the mean to see if the mean is being distorted by a small number of extreme values (in our example, it's "$80,000-$99,000," which has 28 responses). When your responses fall into a *normal distribution,* where the data rise up to a single maximum and then symmetrically fall off (forming the so-called bell curve), the mean and mode are the same (as they are in the example). The larger the sample, the more likely you are to have a normal distribution. However, sometimes you don't. If for some reason, your site manages to attract two different groups of people, the mean and mode may be different numbers. Take, for example, a site that's used extensively by practicing doctors and medical school students. The income distributions may look something like this.

Less than $20,000	20
$20,001–$29,999	17
$30,000–$39,999	14
$40,000–$49,999	6
$50,000–$59,999	10
$60,000–$69,999	12
$70,000–$79,999	18
$80,000–$99,999	22
$100,000–$119,999	20
$120,000–$149,999	15
$150,000 or over	9
No answer	3

The mean of incomes based on this table is about $70,000, but the mode is about $90,000. This is a large enough difference that it says that the distribution of responses is not a balanced bell curve (in fact, it's what's called a *bimodal* distribution), so it's a tip-off that additional analysis is necessary. A histogram (Figure 11.4) shows this clearly.

Since it's important to know whether you have a single homogeneous population or if you have multiple subgroups within your group of users, looking at the difference between the mode and mean can be an easy, fast check.

Likewise the *median,* the value at the halfway point if you sort all the results, can also tell you if your mean is being affected by extreme values. The median of Example 2 is about $75,000 and the mode is $90,000, which tells you that the mean value of $72,000 is being affected by a large cluster of lower numbers, which the histogram clearly shows. Because it's less affected by outliers than the mean, the median is the standard typically cited and compared when discussing standard demographic descriptors such as income and age.

EXAMPLE 2

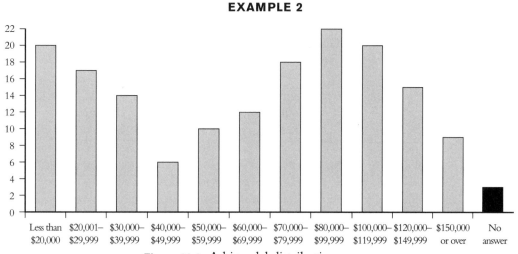

Figure 11.4 A bimodal distribution.

How to Deal with Missing Data

Not everyone will answer every question. How should you deal with that? The simplest common method is to report the missing elements when tabulating variables and eliminate those responses from calculations that use those variables in comparisons. Elimination creates the problem that different calculations and conclusions will be based on different numbers of responses. If the sample is sufficiently large and the number of eliminated responses is relatively small, the calculations should still be usable and comparable, but it becomes an issue when the amount of missing data overwhelms the margin of error. Regardless, when the number of responses differs, always list the actual number of responses used. This is generally reported as N = *x*, where *x* is the number of responses used in the calculation.

Comparing

Tabulating single variables can be informative and useful, but the real power of survey research lies in comparing the contents of several variables to each other. For example, you may be interested in how the frequency with which people use your site affects what kinds of features they use. Do people who use the site all the time use a different set of features than people who use it occasionally? Knowing this could allow you to better emphasize features and create introductory help. Just looking at the data, this type of relationship is difficult to discern, so you need to start using a comparison technique. The most common comparison technique is *cross-tabulation*. Cross-tabulation uncovers the relationship between two variables by comparing the value of one to the value of another.

Although there are a number of ways to create a cross-tab, a typical technique works as follows:

1. Start by identifying the *independent* variable. This is the factor that you feel is doing the "affecting" and the one that is the subject of your question. In "How is the frequency of visitation affecting the kinds of features our users use?" the independent variable is the frequency of visitation since that is likely affecting the features that people are using (rather than the other way around, where using certain features causes people to visit the site more—this is possible, but not as likely, based on what you know of people's use of the site).

2. Group the responses to the question according to the values of the independent variable. For example, if your question asked, "How often do you use [the site]?" and the multiple-choice answers were "less than once a month, once a month, several times a month, and so on," then grouping the responses according to the answers is a good place to start.

3. Tabulate the answers to the other variable, the dependent variable, individually within each independent variable group. Thus, if another survey question said, "Which of the following features did you use in your last visit to [the site]?" then people's answers to it would form the dependent variable. If the answers to this question were "the Shopping Cart, the News Page, and the Comparison Assistant" you would tabulate how many people checked off one of those answers for each group.

4. Create a table with the tabulated values. For example, the following table compares the features that various groups of people report using in their last visit to the site:

	Less Than Once a Month	Once a Month	Several Times a Month	Etc.
Shopping Cart	5%	8%	20%	
News Page	20%	25%	15%	
Comparison Assistant	2%	10%	54%	

At this point, it should be possible to see simple relationships between the two variables, if any are there to be seen. For example, people who use the site multiple times a month use the Comparison Assistant significantly more than people who use the site less frequently, which likely means that the more people use the site, the more that feature becomes valuable to them. (Why? That's a question that surveys can't easily answer.) Likewise, the News Page seems to be somewhat less important to frequent users than to others, which isn't surprising considering they visit enough so that less is new to them with each visit. Additional relationships can be found by comparing other variables to each other (for example, length of use to frequency of use: do people use the site more frequently the longer they've been using it?).

The following table compares the answers to the question "How often do you visit this Web site?" with "Why are you visiting this site today?" in order to understand whether frequency of visitation affects the reasons why people come to a site. It summarizes only the responses to "Why are you visiting this site today" that have 500 responses or more (because that was determined as the minimum number necessary to be statistically significant).

	This Is My First Time	Less Than Once a Month	Once a Month	Once a Week	More Than Once a Week	Row Total
Looking for information about a specific radio program	260	229	167	129	115	900
Other	220	159	104	56	78	617
Want to listen to a radio program	344	245	251	298	630	1768
Want to read news or information	140	120	106	96	109	571
Column total	964	753	628	579	932	3856

Displayed as percentages, it's a little more informative.

	This Is My First Time	Less Than Once a Month	Once a Month	Once a Week	More Than Once a Week	Row Total
Looking for information about a specific radio program	29%	25%	19%	14%	13%	100%
Other	36%	26%	17%	9%	13%	100%
Want to listen to a radio program	19%	14%	14%	17%	36%	100%
Want to read news or information	25%	21%	19%	17%	19%	100%
Mean response	25%	20%	16%	15%	24%	100%

A proportion chart, shown in Figure 11.5, however, tells the most complete story.

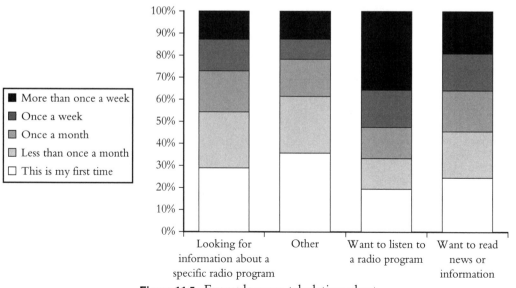

Figure 11.5 Example cross-tabulation chart.

Just glancing at the chart reveals several observations.

Note If you are using Microsoft Excel for tabulation, much of the grunge work of doing cross-tabs is eliminated by PivotTables. PivotTables allow you to take lists of raw survey data, one complete set of responses per row, and automatically cross-tab one variable against another. This can be a great time-saver, but be careful: it's easy to get lost in comparisons and easy to compare things that—logically—should not be compared.

- Regular visitors visit to listen more than more casual visitors. This implies that one of the driving "stickiness" factors may be the fact that the site offers audio streaming capability.
- Infrequent users tend to look for program information more than regular users. Maybe this is because they don't know that there's more there. If so, this could impact both the site's design and its marketing. Such users also have a tendency to look for "other" things, which may be a further indicator that the site insufficiently communicates what is available since that value drops only a small bit for people who have visited more than once.

Of course, there are other conclusions that can be drawn and many more sophisticated ways of manipulating and displaying relationships between variables, but these topics are beyond the scope of this book (for that see the excellent information visualization books by Edward Tufte).

When constructing the table, you should always make it clear how many total responses there are to each independent variable group. The customary way to do this is to add a "total" column (though that's less useful when discussing percentages, in which case the total is usually 100%; in those cases, use the $n =$ notation, where n is the number of responses).

This is also the time when the calculation for a minimum number of responses comes into play. If the total number of responses in any independent variable group is less than the minimum sample size you calculated at the beginning of the survey, you should not draw *any* conclusions about that variable. The results are insignificant and should be marked as such, or left out of the report entirely. You can, however, merge groups to create larger groups that have the requisite sample size. When you do that, you should label the new "supergroup" clearly. Thus, if there weren't enough results in "18–24 years old" to draw any conclusions, you could leave it out of the report entirely, or you could merge it with "25–30 years old" and create an "18–30 years old" group. This, of course, works only with groups where it makes sense to combine the categories.

Estimating Error

Since every survey uses a sample of the whole population, every measurement is only an estimate. Without doing a census, it's impossible to know the actual values, and a lot of confusion can come from the apparent precision of numerical data. Unfortunately, precision *does not* mean accuracy. Just because you can make a calculation to the sixth decimal place does not mean that it's actually that accurate. Fortunately, there are ways of estimating how close your observed data are to the actual data and the precision that's significant. This doesn't make your calculations and measurements any better, but it can tell you the precision that matters.

Standard error is a measurement of uncertainty. It's a definition of the blurriness around your calculated value and a measure of the precision of your calculations. The smaller the standard error, the more precise your measurement—the larger, the less you know about the exact value. Standard error is calculated from the size of your survey sample and the proportion of your measured value to the whole. It's calculated as

$$\sigma = \sqrt{\frac{PQ}{n}}$$

where P is the value of the percentage relative to the whole, as expressed as a decimal, Q is $(1 - P)$, and n is the number of samples.

So if you sample 1000 people, 400 of whom say that they prefer to shop naked at night to any other kind of shopping, your standard error would be calculated as the square root of $(0.4 \times 0.6)/1000$, or 0.016. This means that the actual value is probably within a 1.6% spread in either direction of the measured value ("plus or minus 1.6% of the measured value"). This is sufficiently accurate for most situations.

Standard error is also useful for figuring out how much precision matters. Thus, if your calculation is precise to six decimal places (i.e., 0.000001), but your standard error is 1% (i.e., 0.01), then all that precision is for naught since the inherent ambiguity in your data prevents anything after the second decimal place from mattering.

The easiest way to decrease the standard error of your calculations is simply to sample more people. Instead of sampling 1000 people, as in the example above, sampling 2000 gives you a standard error of 1.1%, and asking 5000 people reduces it to 0.7%. However, note that it is never zero—unless you ask everybody, there will always be some uncertainty.

Standard deviation is a measure of confidence. It tells you the *probability* that the real answer (which you can never know for sure) is found within the spread defined by the standard error. With a normal "bell curve" distribution, the numbers are standard: the real value has a 68% chance of being within one standard deviation (one standard error spread) on either side of the measured value, a 95% chance of being within two standard deviations, and a 99% chance of being within three.

The range that a standard deviation specifies around the measured value is called the *confidence interval* (see Figure 11.6). It's how standard error and standard deviation are related. Standard error defines the width of the range where you can expect the value to fall, whereas standard deviation gives you the odds that it's in there at all.

Say, for example, a survey measures that 50% of the population is made with a 3% standard error. This means that you can have 68% confidence (one standard deviation, as shown in Figure 11.7)

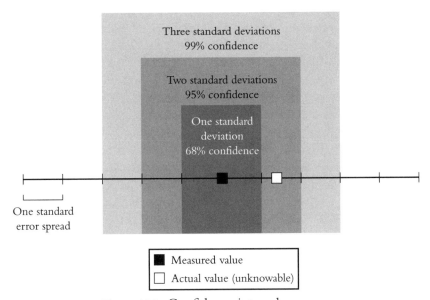

Figure 11.6 Confidence intervals.

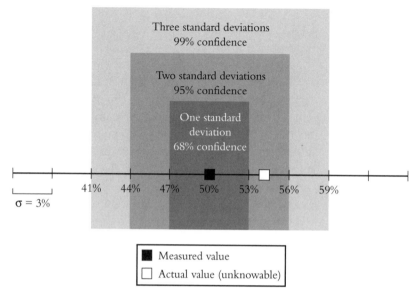

Figure 11.7   Confidence interval example.

that the actual male percentage of the population is somewhere between 47% and 53%, 95% confidence that the actual percentage is
between 44% and 56% (two standard deviations), and 99% confidence that it's between 41% and 59% (three standard deviations).
You can't know where in that range it is (maybe it's 54.967353%),
but if you need to make decisions based on that amount, at least
you'll know how close your guess is to reality.

Measurement Errors

By calculating the standard error and confidence level of a sample,
you can get some idea of how close your measured data are to the
(often unknowable) objective truth. That doesn't mean, however,
that your data actually represent what they're supposed to represent. It's still possible to systematically collect data in a logical, careful, statistically accurate way and still be completely wrong.

As an example of problems that cannot be compensated or predicted with statistics, witness the crash of NASA's Mars Climate
Orbiter. The Orbiter was a state-of-the art piece of equipment built

by some of the smartest people in the world. It was launched from Earth in December 1998 and was scheduled to reach Martian orbit in the fall of 1999. The margin of error for such a trip is exceedingly small since the craft carries almost no fuel for corrections should something go wrong. For most of the journey, everything looked great. It flew the whole way flawlessly, its systems regularly reporting its position and velocity back to Earth. The last critical phase before it began its scientific mission was its entry into Martian orbit, which was to be carried out automatically by its systems. As it approached the planet, it began its automatic deceleration sequence. At first it got closer and closer to the planet, as it should have, but then it began to go lower and lower, dropping first below its designated orbit, then below any moderately stable orbit, then below any survivable altitude, and finally into the atmosphere, where it disappeared forever. In the investigation that followed, it was discovered that although one development team was using the English measure of force to measure thrust, pounds per second, another was using the metric measure, newtons per second, which is four times weaker. So, although both sets of software were working as designed, the spacecraft thought that it was using one measurement system when, in fact, it was using another, causing a multi-hundred million–dollar spacecraft to crash into Mars rather than going into orbit around it.

Something similar can easily happen in survey research. A financial site may want to know how often people make new equity investments. The question "How often do you buy new stocks?" may make sense in light of this, but if it's asked to a group of shopkeepers without first preparing them for a financial answer, it may be interpreted as referring to their inventory. So although the analyst thinks it's a measurement of one thing, the participants think it's a measure of something entirely different.

This is called *systematic error* since it affects all the data equally. The Mars Climate Observer suffered from an extreme case of systematic error. No matter how accurate the measurements were made, the measurements weren't measuring what the engineers thought they were. However, there is also *random error*, the natural variation in responses. Measurements of standard error are, in a sense, a way to compensate for random error; they tell you roughly how much random error you can expect based on the number of samples you've collected. Since random errors can appear in any direction, they can cancel each other out, which is why standard error shrinks as the number of samples grows.

Drawing Conclusions

The conclusions you draw from your results should be focused on answering the questions you asked at the beginning of the research, the questions that are most important to the future of the product. Fishing through data for unexpected knowledge is rarely fruitful.

Before you begin making conclusions, you need to refresh your understanding of the tables you put together at the beginning and that you are filling out as part of the analysis. What variables do they display? What do those variables measure? Why are those measurements important? Redefine your tables as necessary if your priorities have changed over the course of your analysis.

When you are comparing data, you may want to use numerical tests to determine whether the differences in responses between two groups of responses are significant. In the radio example, the difference between people who came to read news once a week and those who came to read news more than once a week is 2%. Is that a significant difference? *Chi-square* and the *Z-test* are two tests that can be used to determine this, though explaining the math behind them is beyond the scope of this book.

When making conclusions from data, there are a number of common problems that you should avoid.

- *Confusing correlation and causation.* Because two things happen close together in time does not mean that one causes the other. A rooster crowing at dawn doesn't make the sun come up though it does usually precede it. This is one of the most commonly made mistakes (look for it and you'll find it all over the media and in bad research) and is probably one of the strongest reasons for surveys and statistics getting a bad name. It's a simple problem, but it's insidious and confusing. Just because a group of people both like a product and use it a lot doesn't mean that liking the product makes people use it more or that frequent use makes people like it better. The two phenomena could be unrelated.

- *Not differentiating between subpopulations.* Sometimes what looks like a single trend is actually the result of multiple trends in different populations. To see if this may be the case, look at the way answers are distributed rather than just the composite figures. The distributions can often tell a different story than the summary data. For example, if you're doing a satisfaction survey and half the people say they're "extremely satisfied" and the other half say they're "extremely dissatisfied," looking only at the mean will not give you a good picture of your audience's perception.
- *Confusing belief with truth.* Survey questions measure belief, not truth. When you ask, "Have you ever seen this banner ad?" on a survey, you'll get an answer about what people believe, but their beliefs may not have any relationship to reality. This is why questions about future behavior rarely represent how people actually behave: at the time they're filling out the survey, they believe that they will act in a certain way, which is rarely how they actually behave.

Even if you draw significant distinctions between responses and you present them with the appropriate qualifications, there are still a number of issues with the nature of people's responses that have to be taken into account when interpreting survey data.

- *People want everything.* Given a large enough population, there's going to be a group of people who want every possible combination of features, and given a list of possible features abstracted from an actual product, everyone will pretty much want everything. And why not? What's wrong with wanting it cheap, good, *and* fast, even though you may know it's impossible? Thus, surveys can't be used to determine which features no one wants—there's no such thing—but a survey can tell you how people prioritize features and which ones they value most highly.
- *People exaggerate.* When presenting ourselves—even anonymously—we nearly always present ourselves as we would like ourselves to be rather than how we actually are. Thus, we exaggerate our positive features and deemphasize our failings. Taking people's perspectives on their opinions and their

behavior at face value almost always paints a rosier picture than their actual thoughts and actions.

- *People will choose an answer even if they don't feel strongly about it.* There's a strong social pressure to have an opinion. When asked to choose from a list of options, even if people feel that their feelings, thoughts, or experiences lie outside the available options, they'll choose an answer. This is one of the failings of the multiple-choice survey, and it's why the choices to a question need to be carefully researched and written, and why providing "None," "Does Not Apply," or "Don't Care" options is so important.
- *People try to outguess the survey.* When answering any question, it's common to try to understand why the person asking the question is asking it and what he or she expects to hear. People may attempt to guess the answer that the author of the survey "really" wants to hear. This phenomenon is why it's important to avoid leading questions, but it should also be kept in mind when interpreting people's answers. Pretesting and interviewing survey respondents is a good way to avoid questions that exhibit this kind of ambiguity.
- *People lie.* Certainly not all people lie all the time about everything, but people do exaggerate and falsify information when they have no incentive to tell the truth or when they feel uncomfortable. For example, if you ask for an address that you can send a prize to, it's unlikely that people will lie about being able to receive mail there, but if you ask about their household income and they feel that it doesn't benefit them to answer honestly, they're less likely to be as truthful.

Ultimately, the best way to analyze a survey is to hire a professional statistician who has appropriate survey research experience and to work with him or her to answer your questions about your product. Ideally, you can begin working with the statistician before you even write the survey. The more you work with a statistician, the more you will realize what kinds of questions can be asked and what kinds of answers can be obtained.

But don't shy away from running surveys if you don't have access to a statistician. Without a pro, it's still possible to field surveys that produce valid, useful, significant results, but it's important to stay with straightforward questions and simple analyses. A limited survey with a small number of questions fielded to a well-understood group of customers can reveal a lot about your user base, enough to form a foundation from which you can then do other research.

Follow-Up and Ongoing Research

Once you've run one survey, you should not consider your surveying complete and the survey process over. As your site grows and changes, so will your audience and your knowledge of them. Following up with qualitative research and tracking your audience's changes can help guide your other research and predict the needs of your audience rather than just reacting to them.

Follow-Up Qualitative Research

Survey research tells you what people feel and think about themselves, their behavior, and your product, but it's too limited a technique to say much about *why* they feel that way. For that, you need to follow up with qualitative research.

When trying to understand people's values and their causes, one of the best tools is the *focus group* (described in detail in Chapter 9). For example, if you are running a satisfaction survey and your audience says that they're unsatisfied with a certain feature or features, it's almost impossible to understand why they're unsatisfied. Is it the idea of the feature? Is it the implementation? Is it the way that it interacts with other features? It's difficult to understand this without asking people directly, but without first running a survey, a focus group series may concentrate on a different, less important, feature set than what really matters to the audience.

To understand people's actual behavior, rather than how they report their behavior in the survey, direct observation is important. *Contextual inquiry* (Chapter 8) can reveal the situations in which people make certain decisions, whereas *log analysis* (Chapter 13) reveals the pure patterns of their actions. If, in your survey, people say that they read online news two to three times an hour, it's possible to get an idea of the accuracy of that by actually observing a group of people for a couple of hours during the day. If only a few follow the "two to three times an hour" pattern, then you may take that fact with a grain of salt when interpreting the results.

Usability testing (Chapter 10) and other think-aloud techniques can reveal people's decision making and what functionality leads to their perceptions of the product. If they don't like it, maybe it's because they can't use it. Or maybe they like it because it's fast. Or maybe the speed doesn't matter and they don't like it because the button text is red on black or they can't find what they're looking for. It's difficult to know what causes opinions from a survey, but once you know what those opinions are, it helps focus the questions of later research.

Tracking Surveys

By running the same survey in the same way at regular intervals, it's possible to track how your site's audience changes. So, for example, as a certain kind of service becomes more popular, it's likely to attract more and more mainstream users. But how many more? What defines "mainstream"? Repeatedly presenting the same survey to a similar number of people who are invited in the same way reveals whether the profiles change and, if they do, in what ways.

Refined Surveys

If you determine a set of "core" characteristics that define your audience, you can field additional surveys that ask additional questions that deepen your knowledge. So if you determine that the most important factors that define your audience are the level of their computer experience, the frequency of their computer use, and what software they use, you can field surveys that—in addition to asking these questions—ask further questions to probe their preferences, their satisfaction, the common ways they use your product, and so on. Asking all this on one survey may be impossible for purposes of length, but spreading the "noncore" questions among similarly sized groups with a similar composition can give you deeper knowledge than you could acquire otherwise.

Pre/Post Surveys

There are times when you want to know how your audience changes in reaction to a specific change. It could be a major interface change, or it could be an advertising campaign. Identical surveys conducted before and after a significant change in a site or its marketing can reveal how the users' opinions or how the makeup of the users' population changes because of the product changes.

A *pre/post survey* is, as its name implies, run before and after a certain event. The results are compared to see what, if any, effect these changes had on the population. Was a new demographic group attracted to the product after an ad campaign? Are the users more satisfied since the redesign?

Before running a pre/post survey, it's important to determine what variables you will be observing. What do you expect will change as a result of the changes you're about to implement? What do you not want to change? Write your survey with those issues in mind, making sure to include appropriate questions that will address these issues.

It's also important to try to understand the effects of timing on these surveys so that the "pre" survey is fielded before the effects of the change have affected the audience, and the "post" fielded when the effects are greatest. When do you expect that the most significant change will happen? Will it be immediate, or will it take a while to affect the population? Do you expect there to be a buzz around the changes you're about to make? Taking these things into consideration well ahead of the change can minimize the "noise" in observations between the two groups.

In general, multiple surveys can monitor not just what changes happen in your audience, but *how* the audience changes. Ideally, you should run two surveys *before* the change and compare them to give you an idea of some of the natural variation in the way people respond to your survey (the natural bias in people's answers). Several surveys after the change can help you track how the changes progress. For example, running one survey a week after your change and then a second one several months later may tell you which changes were short term and which were more long term. Even a postsurvey a year after a presurvey is possible if the product does not change in a way significant to what you're testing.

When fielding multiple surveys, the most critical thing is to keep the surveys as similar as possible. Don't change the wording, the presentation, or the way that people are invited to take them. Analyze them the same way. Then, compare the analyses with an eye for the element that you think changed between the two surveys. Say your changes were made to capture a different market—was your market in fact different? Was it different in the ways you had expected?

Again, the most important thing when analyzing the data from multiple surveys is to make sure that you have set out your questions in advance and that you've focused your whole survey effort on answering those questions. Otherwise, you risk snow blindness in the whiteout of data that surveys can generate.

This chapter merely scratches the surface of what surveys can do. The possible combinations of survey methods are limitless. When used carefully with supporting research, they can provide insight into who your audience really is and what they think.

Example: News Site Survey

This is a survey that was written to profile the users of a radio network's Web site and to find out the general categories of information that are driving people to go to the site. It was designed to reveal visitors' expectations in order to optimize the presentation of the content and to provide constraints for subsequent qualitative research. Secondary goals were to prioritize site functionality and to perform a basic analysis of the competitive landscape.

Question	Answers	Reason
1. How often do you listen to a news radio station? [Pop-up]	○ More than once a week ○ Once a week ○ Once a month ○ Less than once a month ○ Never	For consistency with previous survey To verify news radio listenership

Question	Answers	Reason
2. How often do you visit this Web site [site name]? [Pop-up]	○ This is my first time ○ Less than once a month ○ Once a month ○ Once a week ○ More than once a week	Comparison with previous surveys Cross-tab vs. functionality Cross-tab vs. reason for visit
3. Why are you visiting the site today? (Choose only one) [Radio buttons]	○ Want to read news or information ○ Want to listen to a radio program ○ Conducting research ○ Looking to purchase a tape or transcript ○ Looking to purchase an item other than a tape or transcript ○ To see what is new on the site ○ To chat with other listeners ○ To communicate with staff and on-air personalities ○ Other (specify): _____	Find out general reason for visiting
4. If this is not your first time visiting the site, are these typical reasons for your arrival? [Pop-up]	○ Yes ○ No ○ Not applic... first visit... ○ Not...	

Question	Answers	Reason
5. If you're looking to read news or information, what did you come here to find today? (Choose only one) [Radio buttons]	○ Not looking for news ○ Current headlines ○ Information about a specific current news event ○ Information on a current news story heard on the radio ○ In-depth analysis of recent news events ○ Commentary or opinion ○ Newsmaker profile ○ In-depth research on a specific topic ○ Cultural or arts news coverage ○ Entertainment ○ A broadcast schedule ○ Information about a specific radio program ○ Other (specify): _____	If general reason is news- or information-related, find out more specific information about cause of visit
6. If you came to listen to a specific radio program on this site, please choose which one you came to hear from list below.	○ [list of program names] ○ Not applicable (did not come to listen) ○ Other (specify): _____	To see which programs people are explicitly coming to see To see which programs appear in "Other"

Question	Answers	Reason
7. Check which of the following topics you actively seek out information about regularly. (Check all that apply) [Checkboxes]	○ Politics ○ Entertainment ○ Sports ○ Current events ○ Business ○ Science and technology ○ Interesting people ○ Local cultural events ○ Local news ○ In-depth reporting about your region ○ Travel ○ Fashion ○ Other (specify): _____	To find out the general topics of interest
8. Select any Web sites that you get news or information from at least once a week. (Check all that apply) [Checkboxes]	○ www.npr.org ○ www.cnn.com ○ www.nytimes.com ○ www.news.com ○ www.bloomberg.com ○ news.yahoo.com ○ www.msnbc.com ○ www.ft.com ○ www.wsj.com ○ www.usatoday.com ○ www.espn.com ○ www.salon.com ○ www.slate.com ○ Other (specify): _____	Competitive analysis

(Continued)

Question	Answers	Reason
9. How valuable have you found the following kinds of content when reading news online or (where applicable) in a newspaper? [Radio button grid with "not valuable," "somewhat valuable," and "extremely valuable"]	○ Maps showing specific locations mentioned in a news story ○ Charts, tables, and graphs summarizing and illustrating information in a news story ○ Photos displaying events described in news or feature stories ○ Photo galleries that walk you through a story visually ○ Photos showing individuals featured in stories ○ [etc.]	To get an idea of the desirability of different kinds of content offerings
10. Please rate the following site functions based on how often you think you would use them when visiting [site name]. [Radio button grid with "never," "sometimes," and "often" buttons]	○ Lists of the top 10 stories read or listened to by [site name] users today, this week, or this year ○ Lists of books related to a given story or topic ○ Polls or surveys of [site name] readers ○ Online chats with a reporter, host, or newsmaker ○ Online discussions on a topic ○ Lists of links to other sites relating to a given story ○ The ability to email a story to friend	To get an idea of the desirability of different kinds of site features

Question	Answers	Reason
11. Please rate how important the following characteristics are in stories you read on [site name]. [Radio button grid with "not important," "somewhat important," and "very important" buttons]	○ That they have the latest breaking information ○ That they provide enough background information to help me understand what the news really means ○ That the stories are original and the angles on common stories are unexpected	What qualities do people value in stories? Timeliness Background Original perspective
12. What is the resolution of the monitor you use to surf the Web? [Pop-up]	○ 1600 × 1200 ○ 1280 × 1024 ○ 1024 × 768 ○ 800 × 600 ○ 640 × 480 ○ Other ○ Don't know	
13. Do you own or regularly use a PDA such as the Palm Pilot, iPaq, or PalmPC? [Pop-up]	○ Yes ○ No	
14. Which of the following describes how you usually connect to the Internet? [Pop-up]	○ 28.8Kbps modem ○ 56Kbps modem ○ ISDN (128K) ○ DSL (128K+) ○ Cable modem ○ T1 or higher ○ Other ○ Don't know	

(Continued)

Question	Answers	Reason
15. Are you male or female? [Pop-up]	○ Male ○ Female	All demographics questions for advertising profiling to compare with previous survey research, both online and offline
16. What age group are you in? [Pop-up]	○ Under 18 ○ 18–24 ○ 25–34 ○ 35–49 ○ 50–64 ○ 65+	
17. What is the highest level of education you've completed? [Pop-up]	○ Grammar school ○ Some high school ○ High school graduate or equivalent ○ Some college ○ College graduate ○ Graduate/postgraduate degree	

CHAPTER 12
Ongoing Relationships

Most Web sites are used more than once. They continue to be useful to their customers over periods of months or years. People's use of a product and their relationship to it change with time. They grow accustomed to how it works; they learn what to focus on and what to ignore; and while their understanding of it deepens, they develop habits with it. If all goes well, loyalty and comfort increase rather than resentment and frustration.

In nearly all cases, you want people to get comfortable with your product and learn its more subtle facets. However, in order for the product to support long-term use, the development team should know how and when people's relationship to it and understanding of it changes. Most of the techniques in this book are not designed to support such understanding. They give an understanding of people's experience *right now,* a point on the curve. Knowing a point on the curve is valuable, but it doesn't define the curve. Knowing the shape of the curve can help you predict what people will want and help you design an appropriate way to experience it.

Thus you need techniques that help you understand the behavior and attitude changes that appear over time and the patterns embedded within those changes.

At first, the solution to this seems pretty straightforward: once you've recruited users one time, just invite them back on a regular basis and observe how their use and their views change. Unfortunately, it's not so simple. With the common methods—usability testing, focus groups, surveys—when you run the same kind of research with the same people, they start to lose their objectivity and the process starts to lose its validity.

Moreover, user research is generally done in an artificial, intense environment. The process of being in such an environment changes the way that people look at a product in their daily lives. They learn things about the product and themselves that they would not have known otherwise. Increased familiarity changes their ability to respond as they would have had they never been tested. Long-term feedback needs to be approached using different techniques from the regular feedback processes in order to compensate for this effect.

This chapter reviews several techniques—diaries, advisory boards, beta testing programs, and research telescoping—that provide an understanding into the long-term effects a product has on people's experiences, and how those experiences change with time.

Background

As people use a product for extended periods of time, their understanding of it and its place in their environment changes. The exact nature of these changes in perspective varies with the person, the product, and what they're doing with it. A home office user looking through an office supplies site for a replacement toner cartridge is going to have a different perspective on the content of the site than the office manager who is continually purchasing products there. Although the office manager probably started with a perspective much like the home user, his or her long-term use of it is profoundly different.

During the progression from *newbie* to expert, several things happen.

- *Mistakes are made.* Many (probably most) people learn software products by puttering around. They guess at functionality and features. Sometimes they're right. Often, they're not. These mistakes are informative and frequent. As people learn, they make different kinds of mistakes.
- *Mental models are built.* Products are black boxes. As people learn to use them, they create models of how the boxes operate so that they can predict what the boxes will do in unex-

pected situations and how they can make the boxes do what they want.

- *Expectations are set.* As familiarity grows, people learn to anticipate the experience the product provides. Certain areas of the screen are expected to have certain kinds of content. Situations are expected to follow a particular pattern.
- *Habits are formed.* People get used to doing things in a certain way. They find patterns of commands that work even if they're inefficient or not how the product is ideally supposed to function.
- *Opinions are created.* Products are rarely accepted or rejected outright by people who have used them. Some parts they like; others they don't. Sometimes, things that seem confusing or unnecessary at the beginning become elegant and useful as experience grows. At other times, minor irritation builds into outright hatred for a feature or subsystem.
- *A context is developed.* The relationship that a product takes to its users' goals, job, and the other tools they use changes with time. Some products become indispensable; others are marginalized.

All these changes affect the user experience of the product and are difficult to capture and understand in a systematic way unless you track their progress.

Note All these effects happen in the context of people's entire experience. As they use various similar products, these kinds of knowledge develop for the whole class of products, not just yours. Systemwide effects are difficult to track and even more difficult to compensate for, but they are no less important than people's experiences with a single product.

Diaries

Directly observing people as they use a product over time is difficult, time consuming, and likely to affect how they use it. *Diary studies* are, as the name implies, based on having a group of people keep a diary as they use a product. They track which mistakes they make, what they learn, and how often they use the product (or anything else that is of interest to the experience researchers). Afterward, the diaries are coded and analyzed to determine usage patterns and examined for common issues. Even with minimal analysis, they can provide a source of feedback that reveals patterns that would be difficult to identify otherwise. They are best done on fully functional products.

For practical reasons, indirect observation can provide good knowledge at a much lower cost. Diary studies are one of the least expensive ways to track how use of your site changes over time for specific users (*virtual usability testing,* described in Chapter 16, and *clickstream log analysis,* described in Chapter 13, are other ways, but they both involve a lot more data processing, labor, and expense). Letting people track their own progress can give you a view into their experience without actually having to stare over their shoulders—literally or metaphorically—for months at a time.

Diaries are also one of the only geographically distributed qualitative research methods. You can have people fill out diaries around the country (or the world, for that matter) without leaving your office. This allows you to perform research into internationalization and into how cultural and geographic differences affect people's experiences of your product. Before beginning a diary study, you need to determine several things based on how often people use your product.

- The *duration* of the study. There should probably be at least a half dozen diary entries for trends to be observable (though this of course depends on many factors). If the product is used once a week, the study will need to go on for about two months to be able to measure a change. However, if the product is expected to be used every day, then a week may be sufficient to see changes in people's use.
- The study's *sampling rate* determines the levels of detail of the trends that you can observe. The more frequently people fill out diary entries, the more subtle changes you can notice in their experience. However, changes happen at all levels of detail, and there are important monthly and yearly trends even in products that get used many times a day.

Since people aren't diary-filling machines, picking a sampling rate and duration that won't overly tax their time or bore them is likely to get you better-quality information. For example, a study of how moderate search engine users learn a new search engine started by recruiting people who searched roughly once per day (with a different search engine than the one being researched). Picking daily searchers defined the maximum sampling rate since asking them to fill out more than one diary entry per day would not have produced any additional information.

There are two kinds of diary study: *unstructured* and *structured*. *Unstructured diary studies* are participant driven. Within a loose structure, the "diarists" relate their everyday experiences, tracking their learning and the problems they encounter as they encounter them. *Structured diary studies* resemble extended surveys or self-administered usability tests. Under the remote guidance of a moderator, diarists perform specific tasks and examine specific aspects of the product, reporting their experiences in a predetermined diary format.

Five to ten participants should be enough for a small research group (or even a single researcher) to manage. Participants should be recruited for their availability throughout the testing period, their willingness to commit to regular participation, their ability to articulate their experiences, and—in most cases—a similar experience level among all the participants. Punctuality is also nice, but difficult to screen for.

Note Recruiting people who are dedicated enough to fill out diaries over an extended period of time will likely bias the kinds of people you find. The diligence that comes with such willingness may also bring along other qualities that are not representative of your general user population. However, the value you get from conducting diary studies will likely offset this bias, though you should be aware of it when analyzing your results.

Unstructured Diaries

Completely open-ended diary studies are rare. Even so-called unstructured diary studies have some structure to focus on issues that are important to the developers.

After being recruited, screened, and invited to participate, diarists are instructed in what's expected of them. The instructions should be specific, brief, and complete. They should give the diarists a set of guiding principles about what kind of behavior should be recorded while encouraging active participation.

Sample Diary Email Instructions

Thank you for participating in our evaluation of HotBot, Wired's search engine. We are in the process of evaluating it for redesign, and we would like your input so that we can base the design changes on people's daily experiences with it. For the duration of this research, we would like you to use HotBot for as many Internet information research needs as you can. Your thoughts and experiences are very valuable to us.

For the next month, you will receive this instruction sheet along with a diary form twice a week (on Mondays and Thursdays) in email.

It's a good idea to remind people of their obligations and to set some expectations. Attaching the instructions to every email reminds the participants of how they should think about filling out the diaries.

> We would like you to fill out the diary form and email it to
> *diary@adaptivepath.com* before the next one arrives (mailing it on
> the same day is fine). We estimate that it will take 20–30 minutes
> to fill out completely.
>
> If you can't email the diary to us by the time the next form arrives,
> contact us *as soon as possible.* Contact information is at the bottom of
> this sheet.

Contact information should be easily accessible and people should be reminded it's there whenever appropriate.

> The form is designed to help you describe your experiences while using
> HotBot to look for information. You don't have to fill it out at any specific
> time, and you can write as much as you want. But we would like you to
> fill out as much as you can.
>
> Here are some things to keep in mind while you're filling out the form.
>
> - Relate as much as you can about your experiences, positive and
>   negative, big and small. We are interested in all of it, no matter
>   how minor it may seem at the time. We are especially interested
>   in experiences that were surprising or unexpected.
> - Our goal is to make HotBot work better for *you.* If you can't get
>   some feature to work, *it is not your fault.* Please describe any
>   such situations in detail.

As with all situations where people report their experiences, they should be assured that they're not the ones being tested, it's the product, but that it's their responsibility to accurately report such failings.

> • Whenever you try a feature of HotBot that you have not used before please tell us about it, whether or not you were able to get it to work. Describe the situation in which you used it in detail.

People may not know when they're using something new, but it doesn't hurt to encourage them to look for and record novel situations.

> • If you have a problem with HotBot, but are then able to solve it, please describe the problem and your solution in detail.
> • Please include the specific search terms you used whenever possible.

Encourage specifics when possible. Search terms and products are relatively easy to note down, so it's feasible for people to record them, but more abstract or labor-intensive tasks should be avoided. If people are asked to write down everything they clicked on and every checkbox they selected, they're likely to spend all of their time writing about the minute elements of their experience instead of the more important issues.

> • If you're not sure about whether to put something in the diary or not, please put it in.
> • If you have not performed any searches by the due date of the form, please mark it as such and return it.
>
> If you have any questions, please don't hesitate to contact Mike Kuniavsky at *mikek@adaptivepath.com* or (415) 235-3468.

After the instructions are sent out, it may be useful to review them with the diarists either in person or through some other real-time method (the phone, instant messaging, etc.) so that subtleties can be clarified.

Sample Unstructured Diary Email Form

HotBot DIARY

Please return this diary entry on or before *Thursday, June 22, 2003*

Today's date: _____   The current time: _____

1.   Approximate number of searches since your last diary entry: _____

2.   Of those, the approximate number of searches using HotBot: _____

3.   Please describe your experiences while searching with HotBot. Your description may include

     •   what you were searching for.

     •   your search procedure.

     •   whether you found it.

     •   any difficulties (if you were able to find a solution, please describe how you solved it) or unexpected incidents (describe what you had expected and what you got).

4.   How well is HotBot working for you? _____
     (Please rate your experience from 1 to 5, where 1 means that it's not working at all and 5 means that it's working very well.)

5.   What is your opinion of HotBot as a service?

6.   Has your opinion changed since the last diary entry? If so, how has it changed and was there a specific experience that precipitated the change?

7.   Other comments. Are there any other issues you'd like to tell us about or questions you'd like us to answer?

When you've completed this form, please email it to *diary@adaptivepath.com.* Thank you very much for helping us make HotBot a better product.

If you have any questions or comments about this form, please contact Mike Kuniavsky at *mikek@adaptivepath.com* or (415) 235-3468.

Along with the instructions, there should be a standardized form for reporting experiences. The form of the diary research is quite flexible, in general, and you should feel free to experiment. The form's goal is to give the diarists a relatively open-ended forum while encouraging them to share their goals, problems, and insights. The forms can be distributed as plain text email, as HTML email (only if you know that all of your participants can accept HTML email), or as URLs that point to individual HTML forms.

The specific content of the diary forms will depend on the product and your goals for the research. The forms should be first tested for coherence and timed not to take too much of the diarists' time (a typical diary entry should take 20 minutes or less to write, 30 minutes at the longest).

As with all experience research techniques, setting out specific goals at the beginning of the study is key to the study's success. As the responses start coming in, they should be carefully read. If it appears that the kinds of responses being received will not meet the goals of the research, the format of the study should be adjusted. Fortunately, this is pretty straightforward since the diary forms can be easily changed and the instructions adjusted (though all changes should be prominently noted in the instructions to avoid confusion). Even diary studies where people are given no specific instructions will probably provide some interesting results (although few studies give no guidance at all).

Structured Diaries

Adding structure to a diary is a way to make sure that specific aspects of the experience are examined. An unstructured diary can produce great information about aspects of the product that you don't care about and never touch on ones you most need to research. Explicit instructions to diarists give you a better chance that they comment on what's important. However, that same structure can bias the responses. The participants may look at parts of the product they have not looked at before, describe it in ways that they normally wouldn't, or use it in novel ways.

There are three different kinds of *structured diaries:* diaries that are structured like surveys, diaries that appear like usability tests, and diaries that resemble problem reports.

HotBot DIARY

Please return this diary entry on or before *Thursday, June 22, 2003*

Today's date: _____   The current time: _____

1. Approximate number of searches since your last diary entry: _____

2. Of those, the approximate number of searches using HotBot: _____
   Please describe what you searched for most recently, providing the search topic and the exact
   search terms you used, along with any + or − modifiers.

3. How successful was this search? _____
   *(Please rate the search from 1 to 5, where 1 means that it was unsuccessful, 3 means that the in-
   formation you found was adequate, and 5 means that you found exactly what you were looking for.)*

4. How well is HotBot working for you? _____
   *(Please rate your experience from 1 to 5, where 1 means that it's not working at all and
   5 means that it's working very well.)*

5. In your recent searches, did you use any of the search options in the left-hand margin of the
   main search page (the first page you see if you go to *www.hotbot.com*)? If so, which ones?

6. If you used any of the tools in the left margin, how well did they work? _____
   *(Please rate their effectiveness from 1 to 5, where 1 means that they did not help your search
   at all and 5 means that they were critical to its success.)*

7. Please describe your personal strategy for narrowing your search, if at first it is unsuccessful.
   Has this changed in the recent past?

8. Have any of your views about HotBot changed since the last diary entry? If so, how have they
   changed, and was there a specific experience that caused the change?

9. Other comments. Are there any other issues you'd like to tell us about or questions you'd like us
   to answer?

10. When you've completed this form, please email it to *diary@adaptivepath.com.* Thank you very
    much for helping us make HotBot a better product.

If you have any questions or comments about this form, please contact Mike Kuniavsky at
mikek@adaptivepath.com or (415) 235-3468.

Survey-Structured Diaries

One kind of structured diary is more like an extended survey, with a set of questions that the diarists answer to complete each diary entry. Questions can repeat in order to measure directly how the diarists' experience changes or focus on different areas of the product with every entry.

For example, a more survey-structured version of the HotBot diary form could look like this.

As described earlier, asking people for the specifics of their actions is worthwhile as long as it's not burdensome. So instead of asking for all the things the participant may have searched for since the last diary entry, this form asks for just the most recent search.

Open-ended questions give participants the opportunity to explain their experiences in depth. Asking people to present a narrative of the changes in their experience, although prone to the bias of selective memory, can compress the analysis process, providing direct insight into how people's views and thoughts are changing.

This form adds several questions about a feature cluster on the front door interface. This allows the researchers to get feedback on a specific part of the product.

Usability Test Diaries

Another kind of diary study is more like a remote usability test, where the diarists are asked to perform specific tasks that exercise certain features or expose them to certain content. They are asked to evaluate these parts of the site and describe their use of it. Over time, you can track which of the features participants have been introduced to they actually use. This type of study is most useful when studying how the use of specific features changes over time.

HotBot DIARY

Please return this diary entry on or before *Thursday, June 22, 2003*

Today's date: _____   The current time: _____

1. Approximate number of searches since your last diary entry: _____

2. Of those, the approximate number of searches using HotBot: _____

3. Please describe what you searched for most recently, providing as much detail as possible about your search procedure, including approximately how long it took.

4. How well is HotBot working for you? _____
    (Please rate your experiences from 1 to 5, where 1 means that it's not working at all and 5 means that it's working very well.)

Please examine the Advanced Search page for 2–3 minutes. This can be found by clicking on the "Advanced Search" button in the left margin of the main search page (the first page you see if you go to *www.hotbot.com*). Read through the options on this page then go back to the main page.

5. Find a photograph of a Silkie chicken. This is a kind of fluffy white Bantam hen with bluish feet and a blue beak. We are aware of several photos on pages belonging to agriculture schools.

    *   You do not have to use any of the advanced options, we just wanted you to be aware of them.
    *   Don't spend more than 5 minutes looking for the chicken.
    *   Whether or not you can find a picture of the chicken, please describe your search process in detail.

6. Please describe your personal strategy for narrowing your search, if at first it is unsuccessful.

7. Have any of your views about HotBot changed since the last diary entry? If so, how have they changed, and was there a specific experience that precipitated the change?

8. Other comments. Are there any other issues you'd like to tell us about or questions you'd like us to answer?

When you've completed this form, please email it to *diary@adaptivepath.com*. Thank you very much for helping us make HotBot a better product.

If you have any questions or comments about this form, please contact Mike Kuniavsky at *mikek@adaptivepath.com* or (415) 235-3468.

Again, it's useful to set people's expectations for what kind of information they are expected to provide and how they should approach the task in order to make it easier for them to provide the information you need and not to feel bad if they can't do it. (Loosely based on Reiman, John, "The diary study: A workplace-oriented research tool to guide laboratory efforts." In *Proceedings of INTERCHI, 1993 Amsterdam, ACM, New York.)

This form introduces the participants to a specific set of features and creates a task that can be more quickly accomplished using those features. By examining the diarists' descriptions of their search process, it's possible to see whether or not the Advanced Search interface is understandable and whether people use it after an initial introduction. Question 3 is also modified to request information about the timing of recent searches in order to see if people's search duration changes based on exposure to additional features (of course, this is too coarse of a measure to see anything but the most extreme behavior changes).

Problem Report Diaries

Still another kind of diary form resembles a problem report or a critical incident report. It's filled out whenever the diarists have problems or insights. Although this does not have the focus or depth of a remote usability testlike diary, it minimizes the amount of bias that the study has on the users' behavior, and it highlights the most painful parts of the interface. Such problem report studies can be run continuously throughout the product lifetime to document the kinds of problems people have. Although somewhat "soulless," they're easier to deploy on a large scale, thus increasing the total rate of feedback. They're not as good for tracking use systematically since they depend on people remembering to fill them out when they have problems or insights.

Sample Problem Report Diary

HotBot DIARY

Diary start date: _____

Please make an entry in this diary whenever
- *HotBot fails* to perform as you had expected or intended.
- *You have an insight* into how to better use HotBot to find content.

Please describe the situation in detail.

You do not have to describe the same problem more than once, but please enter it into the diary every time it happens.

a) Date of entry: _____
   Search strategy description:

   Problem feature name/description: _____
   Problem:

   Severity (1–5): _____
   (A severity of 1 means that it's an annoyance or an observation, and 5 means that it's a catastrophic problem that prevents you from accomplishing your goal.)

Insight/Solution:

b) Date of entry: _____
   Search strategy description:

   Problem feature name/description: _____
   Problem:

   Severity (1–5): _____
   Insight/Solution:

   Etc.

Please email this form to *diary@adaptivepath.com* on *Thursday, June 22, 2003*, even if it's blank. Thank you very much for helping us make HotBot a better product.

If you have any questions or comments about this form, please contact Mike Kuniavsky at *mikek@adaptivepath.com* or (415) 235-3468.

Depending on diarists' diligence and their perception of what a problem or an insight is, filling out this form can become a big chore. Defining the specific parameters that the development team is looking for, communicating that to the diarists, and creating a strong incentive (whether material or in terms of reminders) reduces the no-response rate somewhat. Some amount of ambiguity will always remain, but the scope of what the participants need to write down should be specified as closely as is reasonable.

Continually evaluate how well the diary forms are working to address the goals of the research. If they're not working (if the diarists are not discussing what you had hoped, if they're not responding as completely as you'd like, etc.) try to identify the problem and change the forms appropriately.

Managing Responses

One of the keys to a successful diary study is the management of responses and respondents. Since much of the content is self-initiated, it's easy for people to treat the diaries as optional. To maximize response, you have to give people incentives and remind them of their obligations.

If participants are not sufficiently encouraged, there will be a high dropout rate, which is equivalent to a high self-selection rate and skews the responses. The people who finish an underencouraged diary study will likely not be representative of your target audience.

Incentives should be proportional with the amount of time that it takes participants to complete the work. Six diaries may well take a total of three hours to complete, with an extra hour of overhead spent managing them. They should be paid at a rate somewhere between 60% and 100% of what you would pay participants who came to your lab. Assuming a standard rate of $60 per hour, this means that each participant in a two-month study that requires two diaries per week should receive roughly $200 as an honorarium at the end of the study. It is possible to do this less expensively (one diary study I was involved in paid $50 and a T-shirt), but you risk high dropout rates—only one person out of eight finished that study. You may want to encourage completion with additional surprise incentives (T-shirts, restaurant gift certificates, etc.) placed throughout the process. When working within a company where incentives may be inappropriate, consider asking the participants' managers to allocate time to fill out the diaries.

Reminders can be important tools in bridging the gap that happens when you're not doing research face to face. Reminding the participants of their commitment *and* of the importance of that commitment to the product can inspire them to provide better feedback—and to put the diary on their to-do list. Prompt telephone follow-up to missed entries tells the participants that you're still there and that their feedback is important to you. Regular email communication thanking them for their responses and answering their questions also reinforces this, but don't spam them with a dozen "keep up the good work!" messages a day.

How to Analyze It

Analyzing diaries is similar to analyzing focus groups. The techniques discussed in Chapter 9 mostly apply here and will not be repeated. Starting with the goals of the research, the contents of people's responses are systematically examined for common themes. These themes are then pieced together into trends.

The first part of analysis is simply reading the diaries. This should start as soon as entries begin coming in. Don't wait until the end of the research. Read the entries and begin comparing the responses between the participants. Compose hypotheses about people's behavior and address the initial goals. Note what other trends appear. As more diaries come in, test and modify these hypotheses based on the new information.

Diary analysis can stop with careful reading, but there are more rigorous techniques that can be applied. Formal analyses, although more time consuming, can reveal use patterns that are not obvious in regular analysis, and they bring rigor to generalizations made from the data. Rather than saying "most people learned about the advanced options after roughly a month" after a formal analysis, you can say "four out of six participants were regularly using the advanced options five weeks into the study."

Rigorous Trend Extraction

To make trends clearer, issues raised by the diary entries can be abstracted so that the same kinds of phenomena are called by the same name, regardless of who wrote them or when.

Note Follow up with an email or a phone call if a diary entry is ambiguous. The responses will, of course, be filtered through the person's memory, but a specific question (or asking them to look at the Web page or section of the product under discussion) can cut to the root of a problem or provide a nugget of insight, saving you guesswork.

Coding the diaries, as described in Chapters 9 and 13, is an organized method of tagging observations with consistent labels. Once a workable set of codes is established, each diary entry is examined and tagged with codes that represent categories of comments that occur in the entry. You may want to code for items that support or oppose your hypotheses. This is also a good time for pulling out representative quotations.

Once you have all the entries coded, start organizing the entries. The themes along which you group responses will depend on the questions you want to answer, and there is an infinite number of ways it can be done. There may be interesting groups of comments in a single person's experience, such as when he or she learns to use the tool better and notes down ever more sophisticated comments, or clusters could appear across several people's experiences if everyone learns at the same rate. Similarity between behavior can be found in the content of what people say, in the relationship between people's comments, when they say it, and which features the comment refers to (some features may have lots of comments about them, others few).

Timelines can often immediately show you a number of interesting patterns that would be otherwise difficult to observe. For example, the HotBot study could map the amount of times "Advanced Search options are mentioned" (one of the coding categories) against time in order to see whether people mention the advanced options more as they use the product.

The process of coding and organizing should be enough to give you an idea of what kinds of trends are apparent in the data. Once you have a list of information clusters, however, you have to relate them to people's behaviors somehow.

Some relationships are obvious. Lee, in Figure 12.1, doesn't discuss Advanced Search options often. However, as the research progresses, he discusses them more and more. Likewise, even though the users didn't discuss Advanced Search options at first, by the fourth week four of the five talked about them at least once.

List as many of these trends as you can find. Some trends may be obvious, and your confidence that they represent an actual behavioral pattern may be high. Others may be more difficult to pick out (do people use HotBot Advanced Search options more by the 12th week than they did at the 6th week? Maybe, but it's hard to tell

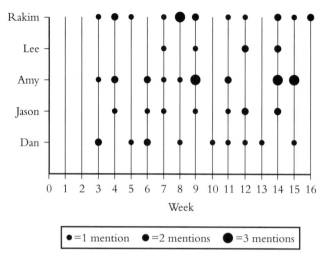

Figure 12.1 Mentions of Advanced Search options in HotBot diaries.

for sure). You should label the various trends ("The Third-Week Effect") in order to differentiate them and discuss them later.

Make Hypotheses

Once you have your list of trends, it's time to try to understand their causes. Since this isn't pure science (it's *highly* applied), certainty in the absolute truth of your hypotheses doesn't have to be complete. In order to make product development decisions, it's often enough to make guesses that are pretty likely to be right.

Thus, it's time to make hypotheses. Why does Lee's discussion of advanced options seem to grow with time? It could be the fact that he becomes more comfortable with the options the more he uses them. It could also be because he's searching more. A quick check of his diaries can show which is the case. If it *is* because he's growing more comfortable with the options, then that could point to a learning curve that could be researched by looking at the other diaries.

If you couple your diary study with follow-up focus groups or interviews, you can then check your hypotheses against people's actual experiences. Working together, you and the diarists can isolate the most important parts of their experience with the product.

Self-Reporting

When you ask people to report on their own experiences, you ask them to step outside their normal perception of themselves and comment on their behavior. Some people have no problem with this, providing accurate, honest answers. Others have more difficulty. Even if they want to help you and think that they're telling you everything, they may not feel comfortable admitting failure or revealing that they don't know something. This needs to be taken into account when reading *any* self-reported information such as support comments, survey questions, or interview responses, but it's especially important in diaries. Often the diary entry is your only contact with the person, and there's no way to know the objective reality.

As in journalism, self-reported actions should be independently verified whenever possible. Ask for clarification of important statements. Follow up with additional interviews or research. If you're *really* ambitious, compare one diary entry to another from a different day to see if the reported behavior matches. And always keep a grain of salt handy.

Advisory Boards

A popular way of getting user input into the software development process is to create a *user advisory board* (sometimes called a user "panel," "team," or "committee"). The advisory board consists of a group of users who are tapped by the development team whenever the team feels that they need input from end users on changes to the product.

Theoretically, this provides an easy way for the development team to bounce product ideas off the people who directly benefit from them (or are harmed by them if they're a bad idea). Members of the advisory board quickly become familiar with the functionality of the product, with the issues that the product and the company are trying to resolve, and with the members of the development team. Such familiarity can cut out the process of familiarizing participants with the product and the company: everyone knows the ongoing issues with the product, and the focus can remain only on the new ideas. On the one hand, this is a great time-saver. On the other, the same familiarity that makes this method so attractive is also its biggest problem.

The more that users discuss a product with the development team, the more they start thinking like the development team. When their views converge with that of the development team,

Warning An advisory board made up of people who are primarily buyers—especially large buyers—rather than users can create tensions between the development staff and the sales and marketing staffs. Sales and marketing will naturally want to present new product ideas to the board to sell those ideas, while the members of the board may expect to be treated preferentially in the sales cycle. It's a tricky balancing act not to bias the board or lose their business. In such situations, explain the purpose of the board to both groups and set appropriate expectations. Say up front that there will be no selling to the board members while they're "wearing their board member hats"—and say it to both the board and the sales staff. Another good technique is to meet off-site, after hours, over food. That reduces the likelihood that participants will expect to be sold to and reduces the opportunities for them to be sold to.

which will happen soon enough, they are no longer outsiders. They can no longer provide the perspective of an impartial user. In effect, they've joined the development team as expert consultants.

Thus, this relationship can be extremely valuable, but the advisory boards' perspective should not be treated as representative of any but a small group of domain expert insiders.

That warning aside, it's probably a good idea for any product that has a stable, long-term user base to maintain some form of advisory board. The board can be formed soon after the product is launched (and even beforehand, if there is a sizable prerelease user base). After the group has become established with a working product, it's possible to introduce more abstract product ideas. Introducing abstract what-if ideas too early in the process can lead to a lot of wish lists, little follow-up, and a disappointed advisory board.

Members of the Board

How you choose the members of the advisory board will depend on your current relationship with your users. SAP, the software company, lets each branch of its (self-organized) user groups choose a representative to the company's advisory board. Most are voted in, making the whole process somewhat akin to choosing senators. However, most companies don't have such an organized user community, so they won't have this option. They'll have to find people some other way.

One common method is to invite representatives of large customers. This can be effective, but runs into the fact that most large customer contact is with the people who specify or buy the product rather than its actual end users. These people (MIS managers, for example) are the target market, not the *user market*. Moreover, inviting large customers tends to overlook the needs of smaller customers, whose needs are often quite divergent from their bigger cousins.

It's also common to invite people from the "friends and family" of current employees. This makes for easier recruiting, but it can run into the problem that the board members won't have an impartial perspective on the development. If my friend Lucie knows I spent four months working on a new feature that doesn't work, she may not be as vocal about its deficiencies as if she didn't know me at all.

A relatively impartial board recruiting method is to treat the board as a focus group. The participants are invited and screened according to the description in Chapters 6 and 9, except that their commitment is ongoing rather than for a single group. This maximizes the impartiality of the board, but if the recruiting isn't done carefully, it can lead to a weak or ineffectual board since the people recruited may not have as much involvement or interest in the future of the product.

While the recruiting process may be similar to the one for focus groups, there are specific qualities that board members need to have that don't apply to most focus groups.

- They have to *know the task*. They don't have to know the specific software or the company, but they should be advanced users in the domain that your product addresses.
- They need to be *end users,* at least some of the time.
- They should be *articulate.* A good moderator can work around one or two inarticulate people in a focus group, but an advisory board's lifetime is significantly longer, so it's especially important that the participants be able to communicate their thoughts, experiences, and feelings.
- They should be *available.* Consistency in the board helps it maintain momentum and preserves the connections that are established with the development team. The participants should be able to commit to at least a year (or three or four scheduled meetings).

The size of an advisory board should be about the same as the size of a focus group. There should not be more than 10 people total.

To preserve the freshness of perspective, new boards can be formed at regular intervals. Inviting all new people once a year is typical, though some boards last for years, and some rotate through board members on a schedule.

Working with the Board

The meetings of the advisory board can resemble either board of directors meetings or focus groups. Some meet monthly; others meet

Note Set appropriate
expectations for the board.
They are in a privileged
position as users, but their
input is—or should be—
only one of a number of
end-user research projects.

only a couple of times a year. The purpose of the board determines the frequency and the topic.

For an established product with an extensive research docket, it may be appropriate to meet a couple of times a year and discuss the "big picture" strategic issues facing the product.

For a fast-moving product with a light research strategy, it may be appropriate to schedule frequent meetings and discuss the product in detail. The group can discuss current problems, their desires, and the specific functionality of the product.

In all cases, the purpose and structure of each meeting and the group as a whole should be carefully determined ahead of time. This is the group's "charter" or "mandate." The charter doesn't have to be extensive, but it should be specific about the board's role and goals. Computer Consultants Corporation, for example, has a user advisory board with the following charter:

CCCORP USER ADVISORY BOARD CHARTER

Mission Statement

The User Advisory Board (UAB) is an important organizational component of Computer Consultants Corporation's (CCCORP) client services commitment. The UAB strengthens CCCORP's position within the credit union Information System services marketplace by helping to plan our joint futures for mutual success.

Values

The UAB pledges to provide honest and complete input on subjects of relevance to the future of the company or its present or future clients.

UAB members volunteer their time in the interest of all User Support Group members with the understanding that CCCORP desires and plans to provide the best possible value to its clients.

UAB members may derive personal benefits and their credit unions may also enjoy advantages from this participation, but members pledge to represent the best interests of the User Support Group as a whole, setting aside personal or particular credit union interests in discussion and decision making.

Discussions, debate and dissent within the Board are considered private, not to be discussed with others without the Board's prior agreement.

Policies and Procedures

1. The members of the UAB of CCCORP must be from Credit Unions who are current members of the CCCORP User Support Group.

2. The CCCORP Executive Team nominates UAB members. CCCORP shall determine the need to add members and present their nominees to the UAB. The UAB shall meet with the nominees and present their recommendations to CCCORP. CCCORP shall choose their candidate(s) from the UAB recommendations. The candidate(s) shall then be confirmed and installed by the UAB at an official meeting.

3. Members may serve until such time as they resign or are unseated by Procedure #5 (below). Current members and their date of appointment are as follows:

[Member list removed]

4. The Board shall elect officers of its choice at the winter meeting. Officers shall be, at least, a Chairperson and a Secretary. Duties of officers may be set by the Board; as a minimum, they are to assure that at least one Annual Meeting should occur and that Minutes are kept and recorded.

5. Members are subject to recall for cause or may be removed by the Board for any reason upon majority vote to unseat.

6. A quorum is required for all Board action and is defined as a majority of the seated members.

7. At a minimum, the Mission Statement, Values, and Policies and Procedures shall be reviewed annually, at the winter meeting, and may be amended by a two-thirds majority of all UAB current members.

The U.S. Department of Agriculture also has a user advisory board with a charter. Their "users" are users of their broad range of services, rather than a specific software product, but the charter is still an instructive contrast. It's more specific about duties and membership, but doesn't specify as much procedure.

RESPONSIBILITIES AND STRUCTURE OF THE USDA USER ADVISORY BOARD CHARTER

The National Agricultural Research and Extension Users Advisory Board (UAB) is a statutory committee established by the National Agricultural Research, Extension, and Teaching Policy Act of 1977 and reauthorized in the 1981, 1985, and 1990 Farm Bills.

The Board has general responsibility for preparing independent advisory opinions on the food, agriculture, and natural resource sciences. Board members:

- Review policies, plans, and goals of research, teaching, and extension programs within USDA, other Federal agencies, State agencies, and colleges and universities.

- Assess the extent of agricultural research, teaching, and extension activities conducted within the private sector and the nature of the private sector's relationship with federally supported agricultural science and education.

- Assess adequacy of resource distribution and funding for research, teaching, and extension and make relevant recommendations.

- Identify emerging research, teaching, and extension issues.

- Recommend programs and technology-transfer solutions for use by the public and private agricultural science and education institutions.

- Make evaluations and recommendations in two annual reports.

- Serve as consultants to the President, Secretary of Agriculture, and House and Senate Agriculture and Appropriations Committees.

- Brief the Secretary of Agriculture orally on adequacy of resource distribution and future program and funding needs for research, extension, and teaching.

The Board's membership is purposely diverse so that a composite view can be formulated by those whom the programs are expected to benefit. There are 21 UAB members from the following 13 sectors of the agricultural community:

- Production (8): Four members represent agricultural commodities, forest products, and aquaculture products; one represents farm cooperatives; two represent general farm organizations; and one represents farm suppliers.

- Consumer interests (2): One member must represent a nonprofit consumer advocacy group.

- Food and fiber processors (1).

- Food marketing interests (1).

- Nonprofit environmental protection organizations (1).

- Rural development work (1).

- Animal health interests (1).

- Human nutrition work (1).

- Transportation of food and agricultural products (1).

- Agriculturally related labor organizations (1).

- Private nonprofit organizations/foundations (1).

- Private sector programs for developing countries (1).

- USDA agencies without research capabilities (1).

Beta Testing

Beta testing is a time-proven quality assurance (QA) technique. When software has been debugged so that all the critical metrics are met, a limited number of end users are invited to use it. As they use it—presumably in a realistic way in their actual environment—other problems occur. Using a structured feedback system, these users then report the circumstances under which these problems occurred to the software's developers.

Eventually, no more critical functionality bugs appear and the software ships.

Although this is a great technique for understanding the problems of software, it's not such a great user research technique. Admittedly, the line can get fuzzy between QA and user research, but there is a line: on one side are the user's needs, desires, and abilities; on the other side are the software's. There are two primary differences: when the research takes place and who participates.

Beta testing is generally done at the very end of a development cycle, right before the site is supposed to go live or the final CDs get pressed. By that point, all functionality has been agreed on, interface decisions have been made, and the identity long decided. Additional knowledge about the users is unlikely to be able to make any fundamental changes in the product. At that point, it's assumed that what is being made is what people want, and what is most important is that it is bug-free. If there are fundamental questions about the product or its users, then it probably isn't ready for beta testing.

Moreover, the people who are invited to test software are not typical users. They're at minimum early adopters and power users, people who are drawn to new functionality, even at the expense of stability. In video game development, for example, there are legendary *professional* beta testers, experts at breaking other people's software. They serve a very important purpose in making quality software, but not as representative users. Their experiences and perceptions are unlikely to resemble those of any but a small fraction of actual users.

All that said, user researchers should not ignore feedback from beta testing and should work with the QA group in developing beta testing materials. Much like customer support comments (as discussed in Chapter 13), beta testing effectively provides "free" additional information about your user population. It may not be of a typical population using the product in a typical way, but it's part of the population, regardless, and useful insight can be had from the process.

From a user research perspective, several things can be learned from examining beta testing feedback.

Note A great way to gather information about users' mental models and expectations is to create a "support" mailing that all the users are on and to encourage them to share their experiences and help each other on the list. These interactions will reveal how people are expecting to use the product and how they're using and misusing it. An unexpected shortcut or workaround by a user can be slightly changed to become a legitimate feature for the product as a whole.

- *The makeup of the advanced members of your user population.* Who are your bleeding-edge power users? Beta testing programs rarely survey their population and compare it to their "average" population. Using a standard survey, it's possible to understand who the beta population really is.
- *What features they use.* Tracking the features where the beta comments cluster, and the kinds of problems that are being reported, can tell you something about the interests and habits of power users, who are often an important segment of the population.
- *Questions about the needs of the population at large.* The feedback from beta testing can be used as a trigger for other user research topics. For example, if a lot of HotBot beta feedback refers to the "related page" links, when it wasn't considered to be an important feature even for power users, maybe it's time to research how desired—and understood—that function is for other kinds of users.

Telescoping

For a variety of reasons, there will be times when you can't maintain a long-term relationship with users. Your development cycle may be too short, your users may be too mobile, or you may be unable to sustain relationships with them for some other reason. Regardless, there will be situations where you want to know how people of different experience levels and lengths of usage experience your product over time.

One way to collect such information is to *telescope* your research. An optical telescope flattens out perspective, making distant items appear right next to closer ones. Telescoped research compresses time by bringing users of different experience levels together simultaneously.

Normally, when recruiting for a research study, you may get participants with a range of experience. Some may be newbies and some old hands. This is desirable in general since you get a perspective on the kinds of issues that affect people through their use of your site. By inviting a range of people, you can see which issues affect everyone across the board and what users value regardless of how long they've been using your product. Sometimes you may intentionally skew the recruit list in favor of one group or another.

Telescoping takes this idea one step further. If you keep track of the experience level of the people you invite, you can recruit people specifically for their expertise or for the amount of time they've been using your product. By keeping track of the problems and perspectives that people have based on their experience level, you can deduce the kinds of changes that people are going to go through as they use your product for long periods of time.

For example, running a focus group series with people who have been using your service for a month and a second series with people who have used it for a year will tell you how people's desires for the service change with time. It won't tell you *when* those changes happened or the context in which they happened, but you can see how people's visions differ.

Taking the Longer View

The field of user experience research is sufficiently new that there are not many established techniques that allow you to study the change in people's experiences over time. Most research focuses on the initial experience or the typical experience, not on how that experience changes over time. That's unfortunate since it flattens out a complex terrain of user abilities and perspectives. It's important to know how products change and how people's relationships to them shift as time goes on so that the products can be designed to grow with the knowledge and needs of its users.

CHAPTER 13
Log Files and Customer Support

Much user experience research is geared toward understanding how people *could* experience your site or estimating how they would *want* to. But it's difficult to understand how they *are* experiencing it. Satisfaction surveys can get at what people feel is working and not working, but people's predictions and preferences are not good predictors of their behavior. Contextual inquiry can reveal issues in the way people use your site, but only one person at a time. Usability testing can uncover many likely problems, but suffers from the problem of projecting people's behavior in a laboratory environment versus real life. None of these actually tell you how people are currently using the site, what problems they're *really* having with it "in the wild." Knowing users' actual behavior closes the loop that started with the research and profiling you did before beginning the development of the site. Without it, you never know whether your designs really work.

Fortunately, there are two sources of information you probably already have that reveal your users' current experiences: customer support comments and Web server log files. Merging knowledge of people's behavior and opinions with your other understanding of your users and your company can reveal deep patterns of behavior and help you make their use of your product more efficient and profitable for everyone involved. Unfortunately, both of these sources feature large data sets that need analysis before they can be useful. While they're a gold mine of information about user behaviors and interests, gold usually doesn't lie around in nuggets. It requires energy to extract, but it's energy well spent.

The first place to start gathering information about users' experiences is their self-generated comments. Customer support comments are a direct line into the thoughts, interests, identities, and problems of your users. It's one area of research for which the researcher doesn't have to ask the questions, the answers come to you.

If customer feedback were objective and representative, there would be no need for any other kind of user research. People would tell you exactly what they want, what's wrong, and what's right. But customer feedback is not objective. The reasons that people contact customer support are many and varied, but they're overwhelmingly negative, and so it's impossible to get a balanced view of the experience your product provides just by looking at user comments. Nonetheless, customer feedback is an asset that needs little cultivation and should not be ignored. It provides insight into several key aspects of the user experience.

- It helps you see how people think about the product as a tool and to learn the language they use. This helps you understand their mental model of the task and the product.
- It reveals a lot about people's expectations and where those expectations are met and where they're not.
- It underscores the perceived "points of pain," which helps prioritize issues to determine which features to concentrate on.
- It gives you specific questions to ask in your research plan and directions for guiding future research.

In other words, these findings help to guide your research toward issues that are perceived as most important by your users, and the place to start understanding customer support comments is to understand the support process.

The Customer Support Process

Every service has a support process, whether formal or not. When people have problems or when they want to ask a question, they contact *someone*. That someone is customer support, regardless of whether they have that title. Sometimes the process is more formally organized than at other times, but there's always a process in place so that people's questions get answered (or, at least, collected).

In the best of situations, there's an organized system that collects questions and answers and produces statistics about them (how often a typical question is asked, the certainty of the answer, links to additional information, etc.). In the worst cases, it's just the memory of someone who is in the unlucky situation of having an accessible email address. Regardless of the system, there's a way to collect and categorize support comments.

It's instructive to follow the process by which people leave feedback to locate ways in which the process can affect the kinds of feedback that are left. What is the tone of the invitation? Is every comment followed up? Is there an automatic response mechanism? How are responses created? Is additional information collected or encouraged? Every feedback collection process biases the kinds of comments it collects. If it's really difficult for someone to leave feedback, then the feedback that is collected will only be from the most driven, persistent, clever and (by the time they figure out how to leave it) upset users, which will affect the kind of feedback they leave.

Collecting Comments

In automated systems, the comments should already be collected, which makes this part of the process easy. If it exists, a database of questions and answers is a good starting place. Such databases may have data going back a long time and over many versions. For a user support organization, this archival data is effectively free, so they keep it around just in case, but it's not all that useful when trying to figure out what's going on right now. Recent issues, from the last couple of weeks or months, are generally enough to provide a list of topics and features to focus on.

If there isn't an automated system, collecting the data may be more challenging. You can begin by interviewing the support staff about how questions are answered and gathering their "stock" answers to frequently asked questions. This gives you a top-level idea of what kinds of issues arise.

In addition, it's important to look at people's actual comments. Looking at all the comments, not just the ones that have been deemed important enough for replies, gives you a much fuller picture of the users' experiences. Gathering reams of feedback data is unnecessary. A randomly selected sample of 100–200 comments from across the previous month should provide a decent idea of people's problems and responses, though if the content is particularly diverse or if volume is particularly heavy, it may be necessary to gather more. When possible, preserve any additional information that's available, such as the section from which the comment was sent or if there's a clickstream associated with the session.

Reading Comments

The fastest kind of analysis is simply reading the comments. I print out large groups of comments (again, 100–200 should be sufficient) and go to a quiet cafe for a couple of hours, marking and pulling ones that have good quotations or clear examples of behavior. When reading them, I keep a couple of things in mind:

- *Read from the user's perspective.* They don't know everything I know about the product. They don't use the same words. They don't have the same emotional attachment. Try to read feedback as it was written.
- *Focus on the facts.* What is wrong? How is it wrong? What part of the product is being referenced? Some comments will be made in the throes of anger or euphoria. When they're angry, they should not be discounted, nor should they be given extra weight because they're laudatory. However, what makes people happy or angry provides insight into a powerful part of their experience.
- *Don't jump to conclusions.* A couple of messages doesn't necessarily define a trend, but even a single message can contain a useful idea. Just because a couple of people have said that they like or don't like something doesn't mean that they're representative of a sizable segment of the population.
- *Don't make the list of common problems into a list of must-have fixes.* Complaints are pointers to problems, not problem de-

scriptions. Complaints from people not finding the "fork" link don't mean that there immediately needs to be a bigger "fork" link. It could mean that the way silverware is divided is incompatible with the target audience's expectations, or that they don't understand how that structure is being communicated. Resist the urge to solve problems as you learn about them.

- *Take comments with a grain of salt.* There's a reason why the term *silent majority* exists. There are many people who do not feel or behave the same way as those who send comments. Don't trivialize the feedback, but don't treat it as gospel either. Sometimes gripes are amplified versions of common problems, and sometimes they're just unjustified gripes.

As for analysis, I keep track of several facets of the audience's experience and try to notice patterns in them.

Note It's tempting to ignore the flames ("U STINK!") and pay extra attention to the compliments ("My kittens and I LOVE you!"). Don't. Hover above the personal nature of the feedback and use it to understand the audience's perspective, first as facts, then in the context in which they're made, and only finally as emotional responses.

- *Who the users are.* People can give a lot of information about themselves while they're explaining a problem or a request. Different groups of people may have different kinds of comments.
- *What they're trying to do.* Are there common goals they're trying to reach? What are the intermediate goals (as described by the users, not as part of the interaction model)?
- *How they approach problems.* Despite having different specific problems, there may be common strategies that help people understand how to use the system. Similar descriptions and problems at analogous places in the process provide insight into the mental model people build.
- *The problems they're having.* Are there similarities to the kinds of problems people are having? Are there obvious bottlenecks?

Organize and Analyze Them

If the system keeps statistics, start your exploration by looking there. This can set your initial expectations and give you some quick insight into what your users feel is worthy of comment. The numbers and proportions of comments should not be taken as a literal representation of the severity of the problems they describe, but they begin to give you a flavor for your audience and their concerns.

Formal comment analysis begins with organization. Organization is the process of grouping comments by the subject of the comment. The clusters allow you to reduce the flurry of people's words to something more manageable.

One quick way to organize comments is by the *subject* of the comment and its *severity.* The subject is the part of the service that the comment is directed toward, whereas the severity represents the analyst's judgment of the impact that the comment's subject has on the user experience. A more formal way of organizing comments is by *coding* them.

Coding Comments

Coding any kind of content is a process for creating an organizational scheme for a list of relatively unstructured information. The process described here is based on one described by Carol A. Hert and Gary Machionini in their work for the Bureau of Labor Statistics *(ils.unc.edu/~march/blsreport/mainbls.html)*. It requires the participation of two people.

1. One person begins by working through the messages and creating categories until no obviously new categories appear. This will probably not require the whole set of comments. Comments are generally categorized "at the sentence level" so that the analyst looks each sentence in the comment. Categories can be anything—the subject of the comment, the nature of the comment (a question, a feature request, etc.), its tone ("anger," "praise," etc.), or whatever else makes sense for the analysis. There can be multiple categories inspired by a single sentence. Each category is then assigned a name, which is its *code.*
2. Using the list of codes, the first person and a second person independently categorize *the same* subset of the messages. The subset should be fairly large (several hundred messages would be a typical size for customer service analysis).
3. The two people then compare their categorizations. Did they interpret the code names in the same way? Are there any that are too general? Too specific? Are there some that don't make sense? Do two codes mean the same thing? In comparing the

way that the two subsets were coded and discussing the codes, the two people define the meaning of the codes and their scope. Once decided, the two people should create guidelines for using the codes.

4. When the coding scheme has been established and documented, the rest of the comments—however many there are—can be divided and categorized by as many people as necessary.

Coding Software

There are several pieces of software specifically designed to assist in coding interview data. These allow you to tag specific passages in a transcript with codes and then treat the coded document as a database, extracting content based on specific codes and combinations of codes. This can be useful if you have huge quantities of text or if you're doing fine-grained analysis.

A guide to the available products can be found in *www.textanalysis.info/ qualitative.htm*.

The U.S. Center for Disease Control (CDC) provides a free piece of analysis software, EZ-TEXT *(www.cdc.gov/hiv/software/ez-text.htm)*.

Tabulating Comments

When the comments have been coded and organized, they should be tabulated.

Counting the number of items that fall into each code shows you where there are areas of interest or friction. In addition, once a coding scheme has been established, you can apply it to groups of comments collected over a certain period of time or from a group of people, and compare how different groups perceive your service or how perceptions change over time. For example, if the number of complaints the month after a change to the product is double that of the month before the change, there's probably a qualitative change in the experience of a sizable chunk of the audience. The doubling doesn't mean that twice as many people are unhappy across your whole user base, but it's an indicator that there is a change and that the change is for the worse.

Analyzing the Comments

Once support comments have been analyzed and an organizational scheme created, then it should be shared with the people who are in the front line of collecting user feedback. If customer service has an existing classification for their questions, these content-based categories may help organize future comments, while insights into user profiles and mental models can help them formulate answers. Once the analysis has been done one time, regularly revisiting support comments makes it easier to keep tabs on how the audience changes and how they react to site modifications.

But people's perceptions of the problems they face may not reflect the actual core problems in their experience. Knowing how they actually behave, and comparing that to how they're expected to behave, can expose the places where things are *really* going wrong. For this, you can turn to *log files*.

Log Files

Whenever someone gets a page from a Web site, the server makes note of it. In a traditional store or office, the management can only guess where people go and what they look at, but Web servers know exactly who is looking at what when (though, of course, looking doesn't guarantee understanding or interest). A Web site visitor has to ask to see every piece they're interested in, like in a jewelry store. This is different from a supermarket, where he or she can spend all day squeezing every tomato, and no one would ever know. This is why a clerk at a jewelry store is likely to have a much better understanding of customers' behavior than a supermarket cashier.

Web servers have the ability to collect a surprisingly large amount of information. For every request (including every page, every image, every search), they store the address of where the request came from, what was requested, when it was requested, what browser was doing the requesting, what operating system the browser was running on, and a number of other facts about the connection. This produces a lot of data, and it's not unusual for busy sites to produce gigabyte-sized log files on a daily basis.

So how is this data mountain mined? Carefully. Up-front planning can reduce the vertigo that comes from confronting the task of data mining. As you answer initial questions, you discover what other information should be examined, collected, and processed.

What's in a Log File, and What's Not

A log file is a raw record of everything that the programmers felt warranted being recorded. It's like the program's stream of consciousness. Web servers are capable of logging all kinds of information and interacting with all kinds of software, so it's possible to have a lot of different log files. Some may be lists of purchases, some may be records of authenticated logins, and others are litanies of internal software errors. The type of log file that generally provides the most user experience information is the *access log*. This file contains a record for each item requested from the server with as much information about the user's browser as the Web server is able to gather.

Here are some elements that are found in many Web log files.

TYPICAL ACCESS LOG ELEMENTS

- The *IP address* of the computer that made the request (most servers can be set to resolve these numeric addresses such as 192.0.34.72 into human-readable DNS names such as *www.example.com*).
- The *date* and *time* the request was made.
- The *kind of request* made (whether to get an HTML page, post a form response, etc.).
- The *name of the file* that was requested. This takes the form of everything in the URL that was requested that comes after the domain name and often includes query strings to dynamic pages generated by content management systems.
- The *server status* code. This is a numeric code that represents whether the server was able to deliver the file or whether it was redirected or produced an error. The infamous "404 File not found" is one such error.
- The *user agent,* information identifying the browser and operating system used by the client.
- *Cookies* sent by the client. Cookies are ways that a client program (such as a browser) sends the server its identity.
- The *referrer.* The page and site that the client viewed immediately before making the current request.

For example, here is a typical access log entry requesting a page called example.html.

    192.0.34.72 - - [05/Apr/2002:04:50:22 -0800] "GET /example.html
    HTTP/1.1" 200 18793

(Continued)

And here is a referrer log entry that says that the last page visited (likely the page that linked to the current page) was a Google search result page for the word *adaptive* and the page that was fetched was /adapt.html.

http://www.google.com/search?hl×en&q×adaptive -> /adapt.html

There are several excellent articles on understanding and interpreting log files on Webmonkey.

http://hotwired.lycos.com/webmonkey/e-business/tracking/index.html

With all this information, it's theoretically possible to get a precise idea of who asked for what when. However, log files are not without their problems.

First of all, when a browser requests a Web page with graphics, it doesn't make a single request. It requests every element on the page separately. Each graphic and HTML segment is asked for and logged separately. Thus, what looks like a single page can produce a dozen or more requests and log entries. Similarly, when a page contains frames, the browser typically asks for the frameset (the document that defines how the frames are visually displayed) and the HTML files (and all of their contents) individually. This can potentially create a score of log entries and a confusing interlacing of framesets, navigation, and content pages, all in response to a single click by the user.

Server logs also don't record whether a browser stopped the transfer of a file before it was completely delivered. When looking at a standard log file, it's impossible to tell whether people are abandoning a page because there's too much content or if they're bailing because the server is too slow. Without a packet sniffer (a piece of equipment that monitors all information coming in and out of the server), you know a page was requested, but you don't know whether it ever arrived.

Dynamically generated sites (typically database-driven or content management system–driven sites) can also produce confusing log files since the logs may only contain the fact that a certain piece of software was invoked, not what the software returned. Unless the software is set up appropriately, all access to the dynamic content of a site can look as if it's going to a single page.

The most severe problems come from the *caching* of Web pages. Caching is the process of storing files in an intermediate, quickly accessible location so that they don't have to be downloaded from the server again. This improves the user's browsing experience immensely since clicking a back button does not cause the previous page to download again because the files get fetched from the local hard disk instead. Though great from a user perspective, this introduces a level of complexity into analyzing site logs. When someone clicks the back button to get to a previous page or uses his or her browser's history mechanism, the browser may get the page from a cache and never contact the server when showing the page. From the perspective of the server, it may look like someone is spending a long time looking at one page, when in fact he or she is in a completely different section of the site.

There are two kinds of caching: *personal* and *institutional* (see Figure 13.1). All common Web browsers have some sort of personal caching mechanism built in: they save the last several days' or weeks' worth of browsing into a cache on the local disk. Modern browsers have a setting that allows them to check for updated versions of pages, and most have it set on by default, so they'll often do a quick check with the server to make sure that the HTML page they're about to load hasn't been updated since they put it into their cache. This solves the most severe of the problems though there are still situations where the browser never gives the server any indication that the user is looking at a different page.

Institutional caches are more problematic. These are caches maintained by computers that sit between a user's machine and the Web server and intercept browser requests before they get to the server. They make local copies of Web site data that the browser requested. When another request comes along for data they have stored, they serve it directly rather than passing the request along to the server where the information originally came from.

From a user's perspective, this saves bandwidth and can improve the apparent speed of a site, but it circumvents any way for the site's server to track usage, and adds an element of uncertainty to all log analysis. For example, AOL has a large institutional cache for all its users. When an AOL user requests a page that was requested by someone else in the recent past, the AOL cache will serve the page to the user directly, bypassing the "home" server. The site's original server may *never* know that someone is looking at their content since it will never have been contacted. Hundreds of AOL users may be

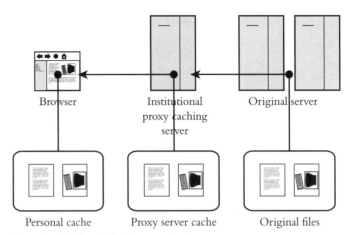

Figure 13.1 How Web files are cached.

looking at your site, but your Web server will have registered only a single visit, the original one that got its content into AOL's cache.

This is not to vilify caching. It provides many benefits in terms of the user experience, and it creates a more efficient Internet, but it does make getting perfect statistics about usage impossible since some amount of traffic will always be obscured by caches. This quality makes log analysis more of a qualitative analysis technique than a quantitative one.

For a sales rep who needs to know how many AOL users clicked on an ad banner, exact numbers are important, but fortunately when it comes to understanding the user experience, exact counts are not strictly necessary. Treating log files as a random sample of your users' behavior is generally sufficient: you need to know how people behave and how their behavior is affected by changes to the site, and a random sample can tell you that. Knowing the *exact* number of people who behave in a certain way is rarely useful for drawing general user experience conclusions.

Logs and Cookies

If only anonymous use logs are collected, it's impossible to say anything particularly subtle about people's behavior. Because the logs just collect information about which files were requested, it's only possible to tabulate conglomerate statistics about the overall popularity of pages. To allow deeper insight into information such as the order people visit pages, how long they spend on each page, and how often they visit the site, it's necessary to isolate individuals in the log files and to track those individuals across visits.

Originally, individuals were tracked by keeping a note of unique IP addresses, but by using this method, it's difficult to track different individuals. Even if people are identified, it's almost impossible to track the same person over different sessions. So Web cookies were invented. A Web cookie is a token—generally, a tiny file—that's exchanged by a browser and a Web server, and every time the browser connects to the server, it sends the file. For most cookies, a unique identification code embedded in the cookie identifies it as belonging to a specific visitor's browser. Cookie identification is commonly used for personalization (Amazon, for example, uses them to identify you so that it can make recommendations) and order tracking, but they're also useful for tracking user behavior. The same cookie that lets Amazon give you a personalized experience can be used to see how often you visit their site, what you've looked at, and what you've bought.

Like their edible namesakes, cookies have expiration dates. These dates can range from the short term ("10 seconds from now") to several years. Although primarily a security feature, expiration dates can be used to maximize their utility as tools for understanding how users use the site. One trick that makes user behavior analysis easier is to use two different kinds of cookies with two different expiration times.

- *Session cookies,* with expiration times between a couple of minutes and several hours, identify an individual session. If no page has been fetched at a search engine site in 10 minutes, for example, it's likely that the user has finished using it. Likewise, a newspaper site may want to give people 30-minute session cookies, whereas an online game might give ones that last several hours.
- *Identity cookies* have much longer expiration times, on the order of months or years. These cookies identify a single user and can be used to track that person's behavior over multiple sessions.

Note Cookie-based session tracking is built into both Apache and the Microsoft IIS server, and just needs to be turned on for cookie information to start appearing in your log files. Please see your server software documentation to see how to do this.

Information about the Apache user-tracking module (which uses cookies) is available at *http://apache.org/docs/mod/mod_usertrack.html.*

An article describing Microsoft IIS 4.0 user tracking is available at *msdn.microsoft.com/library/default.asp?url=/library/en-us/dnw2kmag01/html/EventLogging.asp.*

Using this technique, every user will have two cookies from a site at any given time: a short-term session cookie identifying the current session and a long-term identity cookie identifying the computer. Using a session cookie with a list of pages in an access log allows you to extract the order of pages in a session to produce a *clickstream*. Clickstreams tell you the order of pages visited in a session, which specific pages were accessed, and how much time was spent on each page. They are the molecules of the user experience and the cornerstone for many of the arguments that claim the Web contains the potential to produce unprecedented experiences for its users (and unprecedented profit for the companies that know how to understand them). But more on clickstreams later.

Log Analysis Ethics

People get the willies when you start talking about tracking them. This is natural. No one likes being followed, much less by salespeople or the boss. When people feel they're being followed, you lose their trust, and when you've lost their trust, you've lost their business.

Thus, it's critical to create and follow a strict user privacy policy and to tell your users that you're doing so. Here are some guidelines.

- Keep confidentiality. Never link people's identities to their behavior in a way that is not directly beneficial to them (and determine benefit through research, not just assuming they're interested in your sales pitch).
- Never sell or share behavior information that can reveal individual identities.
- Protect behavior data. Personal information is top-secret information to your company, on par with its intellectual property, and it should be protected with the same rigor.
- Keep all results anonymous. Never produce reports that can associate a user's identity with his or her behavior.
- Maintain an analyst code of ethics. Publicize the code. Make everyone agree to abide by the code before granting him or her access to the data.
- Tell your users which information is collected about them, and give them the option to refuse to supply it.
- Join and follow the guidelines of a user privacy organization such as TRUSTe and the Electronic Frontier Foundation.

Also see the Interactive Marketing Research Organization's Code of Ethics, *www.imro.org/code.htm,* and TRUSTe's site, *www.truste.org.*

Some Useful Metrics

Before formulating a plan to analyze a set of log files, it's useful to decide how the site is underperforming or where the development team believes it can be improved. A list of problems and their hypothetical causes helps constrain the questions asked of the data (see Chapter 5 for suggestions on collecting research goals and problems). This focuses the process on solving the most pressing problems and avoids the morass of data analysis that can accompany log mining.

Here are some typical open-ended questions.

- Do the recent changes in the interface make it easier to buy?
- How many people do we lose before they find what they're looking for? Where are we losing them?
- Where do people spend the most time?
- How many visitors eventually become purchasers?
- How does the behavior of various groups of users differ?

A more systematic way of formulating their questions can come from looking at the kinds of analysis that can be done. Four different types of analysis are relevant here: aggregate measurement, session-based statistics, user-based statistics, and path analysis.

Aggregate Measurements

The easiest questions to answer are those that cover the largest windows of information. Looking just at the most crude measure of site traffic, composite page view tallies create a kind of "50,000-foot" view of how people use the site. These tallies include the following:

- The total number of *pages viewed in a given period*. "How many page views were there in December 2000 versus June 2000?" Be careful not to compare page views before and after a redesign since that's like comparing two different sites and tells you little.
- The distribution of *page views over a specific time*. "Are there more page views when people are at work than when they're not?"
- The distribution of *page views over the whole site*. This is a breakdown of total page views over a section of the site. It could be as fine as individual pages or clustered by content type.

These are crude measures and should not be taken literally. For example, when looking at a time-based distribution of pages the page views may be consistently lower on Wednesday and Thursday than on other weekdays. Although this is interesting, it doesn't really provide any information about why the cause of the drop-off. It may be because of users' behavior, but it could be that your ISP is busiest during those two days and some people can't even get through.

Other conglomerate statistics include the following:

- *Operating system and browser proportions.* These reflect the popularity of operating systems and browsers in the site's user population. From a user experience perspective, this information is most useful when determining how much to tailor a site to browser idiosyncrasies.
- *Client domain.* For most sites, the hits will come from either .net or .com sites. This says little since ISPs anywhere on earth can have addresses in those domains. Once those are removed from the equation, it's possible to use the proportions of remaining country domains to get an idea of the size of the site's international audience or the audience from a single ISP (such as Earthlink or AOL).
- *Referrer sites.* These are the pages and sites outside yours that were visited immediately before a given page was requested. In most cases, these are the ones that linked to your site, and knowing how people get to the site can help in understanding the context in which they're using it.
- *New/repeat users.* A problematic statistic when looking for absolute numbers (because of the fallibility of cookies), it's still possible to use new/repeat users to understand long-term user behavior. If the proportion of returning users to new users is consistently low, the users may not be finding sufficient value in the site to return.
- *Search engine referrals and key words.* The referrer log contains the URL of the last page visited. Many search engines keep the keywords that generated a results page in the URL to that page, so it's possible to see which search engines directed traffic to the site and the keywords that brought up the site on the results page. That can help the marketing department target search engine advertising.

Session-Based Statistics

The most useful metrics are ones that can use session information when creating conglomerate results. These reveal a richer set of user behaviors than simple conglomerate stats.

Some of the more useful are as follows:

- Average number of *pages per session*. The number of pages in a typical session is a measure of how broadly people explore the site. For example, if most sessions consist of only one or two page views (as is often the case for a search engine), then all navigation and the whole information architecture needs to be focused on these "short-hop" navigation elements. However, if people see five pages on average, then the navigation needs to support a different kind of usage. A slight variation on this is a measurement of the number of *different* pages per session: if there are 20 pages per session on average, but all the visits are confined to 3 pages, it says that people are having a different kind of experience than if all 20 pages were different.

- Average *duration of session*. Page timing is an underused branch of log analysis, primarily thanks to the confusion created by caches and the back button. Even with these limitations, time-based metrics are still useful when compared to each other. Breaking out the *time per page* can also be quite fruitful when trying to see which pages are used as content pages and which are transitional.

- *First and last pages.* These are sometimes called "entry" and "exit" pages, and they can tell you if people are moving through the site as you anticipated. The first page people see determines a lot about how they relate to a site. If people enter this site in unexpected ways, you may want to consider how and where you present information.

User-Based Statistics

Identity cookies can give you a further level of information about individual aggregated user behavior.

Some of these metrics are as follows:

- *Number of visits.* The number of times users come to a site is an important measurement of their loyalty and their trust.
- *Frequency of visits.* How often people visit can determine how often content needs to be updated. If the content is updated five times a day, but the majority of visitors visit only once a week, it may not be as important to have such frequent updates.
- *Total time* spent on the site. The amount of time people spend on the site over the course of a week, a month, or a year is another indicator of loyalty or utility. If the average time on a site is 5 minutes a month, but competitors' users average 40 minutes, then your site is either much more efficient or much less interesting.
- *Retention rate.* The number of people who come back after their first visit. This, too, can be measured over the period of weeks, months, or years, depending on the purpose of the site and the horizon of typical usage.
- *Conversion rates.* The proportion of visitors who eventually become purchasers (or frequent users or whatever is important for the site's success). This is measured by calculating the proportion of all new users from a given point in time who eventually became purchasers and comparing it to users who weren't "converted." It's the best direct measurement of a site's success.

In addition to measuring the behavior of the whole user population, it's possible to couple identity cookies with clickstream analysis and segment users by their behavior. For example, a person who goes more frequently to the fork section of a kitchen site than other sections can be labeled a "fork aficionado." Fork aficionados' behavior can then be compared to that of spoon lovers and cup fans. These, in turn, can be compared to the user profiles defined at the beginning of the development process. This is a powerful technique for understanding behavior and for personalization, though it is still in its infancy.

Clickstream Analysis

In addition to the general metrics, there are other measurements that get at the user experience. Of course, as with all indirect user research, none of these methods can tell you *why* people behave the way they do (for that you need the direct user contact that contextual inquiry, usability testing, and focus groups provide), but they can certainly narrow down the possibilities of *how*.

One of the most useful of these synthetic techniques is *clickstream analysis*. This is the process of analyzing the paths people followed through your site to uncover commonalities in the way people move through it. Clickstream analysis can produce such interesting results as

- The *average path*. This is an analysis of a "typical" path through the site. Of course, as with all these metrics, what is considered to be typical depends on the quality of the data and the algorithm used to determine "typicality," but it can still provide useful insights.
- *"Next" pages*. This statistic gives the proportion of pages that were the immediate successor to a given page. For example, you could look at the "next" links from a search engine results page and see how many people went to a page with specific information versus how many people went back to the search page. This could tell you how effective your search results were in helping people find what they were looking for.

More specialized analyses are possible for products that have a niche focus. For example, ecommerce sites can define several specialized types of clickstream analysis.

- The *purchase path*. This is the average path people followed when buying something. It's typically calculated by figuring out the average path from entry pages to the "thank you for shopping with us" page.
- *Shopping cart abandonment*. The common form of this finds where in the purchase path the process typically ends, when it doesn't end at the "Thank you" page. This bailout point can

then be studied for usability issues (are people just changing their minds, or is there something that's preventing them from completing their purchase?). In addition, when abandoned paths are joined with the shopping cart database, it's possible to see how many people never buy what is in their cart and thereby determine value of lost sales.

Another good technique is *content clustering*. The pages of a site are abstracted into chunks by topic ("silverware," "dishes," "new products," etc.) or function ("navigation," "help," "shopping," etc.). These clusters are then used in place of pages to get results about classes of content rather than individual pages. For example, looking at the traffic to all the silverware on a kitchenware site may be more useful than the statistics for the spoon page. It's then possible to investigate how effectively the "Fork of the Week!" link drives silverware sales by comparing the proportion of silverware traffic to dish traffic before and after the link was added.

Extracting Knowledge from Data

If it's easy to measure, it's probably not useful. If it's useful, it won't be easy to measure.
—"A Web Statistics Primer" by Teresa Elms on builder.com

Once there are logs to analyze and questions to answer, the process of answering the questions with the contents of your logs begins. Regrettably, this is difficult.

Log analysis is generally too time consuming to do by hand. Therefore, the two options are to write analysis software yourself or buy an off-the-shelf solution (or, of course, to let someone else do it). Top-end analysis packages can cost tens (or even hundreds) of thousands of dollars, but cost-effective solutions exist that can satisfy the needs of many small- or medium-sized sites.

DIY

Starting completely from scratch is not recommended. There are a number of inexpensive or free products that can provide basic conglomerate statistics (path analysis or behavior segmentation software is complicated, and as of this writing, I don't know of any inexpensive products that do it with any degree of sophistication).

When working with low-end products, it's useful to prefilter the data to reduce noise in the results. There are four classes of hits that can be removed to improve the final statistics (check the documentation of the package you're using because some packages do some of these for you).

- *Hits from search engines.* Search engines regularly send out spiders to gather site content. These spiders don't act like users. They follow links in the order they appear on the page, not in terms of what's interesting or useful. Thus, they fill up logs with data that have nothing to do with how your site is used. Fortunately, most of them use a distinct user agent field so that it's possible to quickly extract them from a log file. A list is available from *info.webcrawler.com/mak/projects/robots/robots.html.*
- *Offline browsing agents.* These are programs that download all the files from a site so that it can be viewed offline at a later time. They act like spiders and have the same problems. A list is available at *www.jafsoft.com/misc/opinion/webbots.html#offline_browsers_and_other_agents.*
- *Outliers.* Outlier is the name given to a value that lies far outside the majority of collected values. Outliers can skew compound statistics, such as average times and path lengths by skewing the mean (they're described as part of the "billionaire" problem in Chapter 12). To test if your statistics are being skewed by outliers, compare the mean of your data to the median. If the two are drastically different, then you may have a large number of outliers, which should then be removed and the results recalculated (again, the general ideas behind this are described in more detail in Chapter 12).
- *Your site.* Since much of the traffic on your site comes from inside your own company, it can annoyingly skew your referrer statistics.

A list of free or cheap log analysis products is available from *www.uu.se/Software/Analyzers/Access-analyzers.html* and Yahoo!'s

Computers and Internet > Software > Internet > World Wide Web > Servers > Log Analysis Tools category. The majority of these produce conglomerate statistics. Though they generally don't do much with session or user tracking, several of them allow drill-downs to the clickstream level.

Once the basic statistics have been examined, more usage information can be gleaned by looking at individual clickstreams. Even without automated path analysis, it's possible to get a gut feeling for how people use the site. By looking at a relatively large number (50–100) of random clickstreams and taking notes, it's possible to get an idea of how often people followed one path or another, how deep the paths were, and the entry and exit pages.

However, manual log analysis is time consuming and inaccurate. Commercial tools get deeper, more certain, more consistent knowledge.

Big Tools

Kirk to computer: "Correlate all known data."
Computer: "Wor-king . . . ."

At heart, they work similarly to the low-end tools, but industrial-grade analysis products kick this process into a whole other realm. By correlating information from multiple databases, such tools produce a more complex picture of users and their "consumer life cycle" than is possible with less sophisticated, run-of- the-mill tools. One such product is described by the Aberdeen Group as being able to "process Web logs, customer buying histories, demographic information, and other data to create a view of a customer's visits and proclivities. It will then map that customer behavior to the business's categories and analyze the intersections, ultimately segmenting customers into groups and explaining the rules that created those segments." This, in effect, allows the company to create a highly personalized experience (and marketing plan) for the people who match their segments.

The kinds of products that do this level of data integration and analysis can generally be found when looking for Web "data mining" or CRM information. As of this writing, some companies that make these products include TeaLeaf, NetGenesis, Accrue, Web-

Trends, Coremetrics, Limelight, and Personify. There is a lot of overlap between all of them, though each has some unique features, and several are geared toward experience personalization, so they tend to be more experience focused than advertising or strategy focused.

Most of these packages are primarily designed for assisting strategic marketing and business decisions, but their tools can also be used by developers and designers to understand user behavior and gauge the effectiveness of changes to the user experience. For example, knowing that a large proportion of people who look at forks also look at napkin rings can help adjust the information architecture of a site. Extending that kind of analysis to the relationships between all the categories can tune the whole site more finely than can qualitative research methods.

Moreover, tools that integrate bottom-line financial information with user experience data can help resolve tensions between usability and business needs. For example, a search engine moved the banner ad on its results page so that it was more prominently displayed. This was intentionally more distracting to users and produced the expected higher click-throughs and higher revenues. However, it was important to know whether the additional revenue was a short-term effect that would be undermined by users growing annoyed at the new ad placement and never returning. Analyzing user retention rates before and after the change, it was discovered that retention did not perceptibly change—people were not running away any more than they had before the change—whereas revenue went up significantly. The search engine decided to keep the change. Later, the same search engine made a change that made the advertising even more prominent, but retention rates began falling while revenue did not significantly increase, and the change was rolled back.

These large tools can be expensive (typically, it costs tens or hundreds of thousands of dollars to integrate one with your existing databases and then analyze the results), so they need to be chosen carefully and with specific research goals in mind. As you're evaluating them, often with a consultant from the company providing the service, ask which of the questions in the research can be answered by the package, and with what level of certainty it can be answered.

Regardless of the level of sophistication of your analysis, people's existing experiences should not be ignored. Customer support and log analysis are powerful tools that can be used at almost any time in a product's life to expose valuable, immediately actionable information. They should be used in the context of a complete research program, but they should not be forgotten.

A Note About CRM

This chapter merely scratches the surface of customer relationship management (CRM), a rapidly growing field that attempts to track customers throughout all of their interactions with the company. It begins with things like customer comments and log files, but includes deep quantitative user/customer behavior analysis and attempts to relate user behavior to the company's products and revenue streams. For example, Mattel's Tickle Me Elmo doll was a popular and expensive toy when it came out. It worked reasonably well, but when it broke there was little support for its repair (at least from the perspective of the parents I spoke with). Many buyers became quite upset when they discovered their toys weren't fixable. Mattel was clearly not meeting customer expectations for a certain group of people, but how many? What effect did this have on these people's opinions of and behavior toward Mattel and Sesame Street? How did this affect Mattel's bottom line in the short term? The long term? The point of CRM is to understand the relationship between the customer and every facet of an organization.

Many of the ideas and quantitative techniques of CRM overlap with user experience research, and there will certainly be a lot of fruitful cross-pollination between the two fields in the future.

CHAPTER 14

Competitive Research

Products don't exist in a vacuum. For any given service or consumer niche, there is a whole ecology of competing products. Each has a different approach to how it attends to the needs of its users. But which differences matter? Small differences in functionality, presentation, or identity can sometimes make a big difference in how people perceive a product. And sometimes they don't matter at all.

Understanding which of your competitors' strategies work and which don't is critical to understanding what will work with your product and where to focus your development energy.

Traditional competitive analysis is performed by the business development group or by independent auditors. The goal is to look at a company's offerings and analyze them from a financial or marketing perspective. By examining public documents and doing field research, they can understand things such as how much their competitors' products cost, who buys them, where their customers live, and what aspects get emphasized in advertising. This is valuable information that helps executives make strategic decisions about the general direction of the company and its products. However, it doesn't do a whole lot for understanding which parts of a product people actually use, what they like about it, or what keeps them coming back. That's the realm of competitive *user experience* research.

Most of the techniques discussed in this book can be applied to your competitors' work nearly as well as to your own. They can reveal your competition's strengths and weaknesses, and help you identify opportunities and threats. In some sense, competitive research is the purest user research of all since it ignores the assumptions or constraints under which the other products were constructed and concentrates purely on the user's perspective. This makes it some of the most useful research of all.

When Competitive Research Is Effective

[Competitive research] is one of the first things you should do. It can define *your world for you and make your life a whole lot easier.*
—John Shiple, user experience architect, Yahoo! Inc.

Competitive research can be done at any point in your product cycle. Whether previewing the landscape at the beginning or comparing your finished product to the competition's, it always provides useful information. Picking the perfect moment to do it is less important than doing it regularly and thoroughly. For the most benefit, you should check on your competition repeatedly and continually throughout the lifetime of your product. Whenever you're not testing your own work, you should be researching your competitors'. Even when you have a full testing plan for your product, it makes sense to occasionally put your work aside and investigate your competition.

That said, there are several points where competitive research can really affect your development process.

- *When gathering requirements.* Research into what the competition's customers find useful, what they find attractive, and where those products fail can guide selection and prioritization of features for your own product.
- *Before you redesign.* As your product develops and evolves, competitive research can answer questions about design directions since your competition's products can be treated as functional prototypes of some of your own ideas.
- *When your competitors make major changes.* Researching those changes on people's perceptions and behavior provides insight into their effectiveness, helping you know how to react to the changes.

Competitive Research Methods

Competitive user experience research focuses largely on how people use and perceive a product without focusing on its popularity, business model, or revenue stream. Traditional competitive analysis or brand analysis tries to understand what makes companies successful by looking at their revenue and other "fundamentals." Such analyses rarely focus on the consumer's or user's view apart from the occasional feature grid or brand perception study. User experience research can work in concert with more traditional competitive analyses, of course, but its focus is from the bottom up rather than from the top down.

Apart from this fundamental difference, the process is quite similar to traditional competitive analysis. In both cases, the analyst must determine who the competitors are, what aspects should be compared, and how to compare them. The general sequence of steps is largely the same one that a financial analyst would follow when understanding the competitive landscape.

- Identify the competition.
- Profile them for the key attributes that make them competitive.
- Compare them to each other (and to your product).
- Use the comparisons to create "actionable intelligence."

Identify the Competition

This may seem obvious, but before you can start competitive analysis, you need to know who your competitors are. Unfortunately, this is harder than it may first appear. Although the obvious competition is from companies and products that are in the same sector as yours, the exact definitions of that sector are often fuzzy.

You can start researching potential competitors by looking in online directories. If your product is listed in a category in Yahoo! or the Open Directory, look at the other sites in the same category. They're probably your competitors. Go one level up in the hierarchy. Take a likely competitor and search for it in the directory. What other categories does it appear in? The members of these categories are probably your competitors, too. Look at the sister categories at the same level as the one where you would put your product. These may contain competitive products, too.

Moreover, as discussed in Chapter 8 on contextual inquiry, the obvious competition may make up only part of the competitive landscape. There may be other competitors in other media. A bicycle touring site's competition (at least for someone's leisure time) is not just other bicycling information sites, but bicycling itself, since the site user's end goal is not just to find out information about bicycles, but to go out and ride. A health advice product competes with the *Physician's Desk Reference,* the family doctor, and even grandma. Likewise, although Barnes and Noble is an obvious competitor to Amazon, so is the corner bookshop. What does the corner bookshop have that Amazon doesn't have? How is the bookshop's user experience better or worse than Amazon's? Take into account what other tasks people could be doing instead of using your product. Unless they're being paid to use it, if it's not more useful, more fun, or more informative than competing tasks, they're not going to do it.

Make a list of your competitors. List the most likely ones from the directories, and brainstorm ones from other media and in other situations. If you want, you can write them on index cards or Post-it notes to make them easier to organize.

Then sort them. You can sort them any way you want, of course, but the following is a typical organization that I have found useful:

- *Tier 1 competitors* are those whose product most directly competes with yours. Barnes and Noble competes directly with Amazon's bookselling business, Yahoo! Auctions competes directly with Ebay. These products try to capture the same audiences in the same way, offering the same (or very similar) service, and these are the primary targets of your analysis. There should be no more than five of these in your list. There may be more than that in actuality (there are a lot of places that books are sold, for example), but five is probably enough to give you a good idea of the competitive landscape. There will always be a competitor. Even if you perceive your product as completely new and innovative, it's still competing for your audience's time with *something.* That something is the competition. Cars and horses look and work differently, but in the early 20th century, they were tier 1 competition for each other.

- *Tier 2 competitors* are products that are from the same category as the tier 1 competitors, but either they are not as directly competitive as those or they are so similar that researching a tier 1 analogue is sufficient. They're products you should look at to check your understanding of the tier 1 products, but understanding them is not as critical. There shouldn't be more than five or ten of these. For example, Half.com and Alibris.com both sell used books online, and they may be competitors for each other, but they're not really direct competitors to Barnes and Noble.
- *Niche competitors* compete directly with part of your product, but not the whole thing. In the 1880s, horses and trains competed on long-distance travel, but not in terms of local transport. As of summer 2002, Barnes and Noble's site doesn't carry toys so it doesn't compete with Amazon's Toys and Games section. It does, however, sell books, so its book and music offerings compete with Amazon, and the only aspect of its toy section that it needs to worry about are its children's books.

Profile the Competition

To focus your competitive research, you need to know something about whom you are dealing with. A complete competitive analysis will begin with *competitive profiles* of all the competitors. These consist of two elements: a description of the product and a profile of its audience.

Product Description

A product description should not just be a list of features. It should be a statement from the users' perspective of the *value* it brings them. From a user perspective, Amazon's primary value does not lie in big discounts, huge selection, fast access, and its highly relevant recommendations. Few of those boil down to single features or precise quantities.

Product descriptions should not be more than a paragraph long. How would a user describe it at a cocktail party to someone who had never heard of it? For example,

> ZDnet is a daily technology magazine. It offers hardware and software reviews, the latest news on the high-tech world, in-depth analysis, and columns written by insightful industry commentators. Its articles provide an in-depth understanding of the changes in the technology world and are written in a direct and lively style. It provides a number of email newsletters on popular sectors of the technology world.

Audience Profile

Chapter 7 lists attributes that your user profile can have. Using this list, look at the competitor's product and try to assign values to as many attributes as you can, creating separate profiles when you feel that the product serves multiple audiences. As with your own product, you may want to create three or more different profiles that represent the different kinds of customers. Highlight the differences between these people and your audiences. If they're direct competitors, the profiles could be quite similar to yours, but each of them will have at least one key difference: they don't use your product. Why not? What makes the competition's user market different from yours?

Identify Features and Attributes

The most important step in profiling your competition is creating a list of things to compare. These can be specific features, or they can be abstract qualities. Feature identification should come from the user's perspective. Your product may run on state-of-the-art hardware in a climate-controlled data center, whereas your competitor's runs out of a dusty closet on 10-year-old Amigas, but your users don't care. They care about things such as how quickly they can get their work done and whether they can find what they're looking for.

There are two ways to collect lists of attributes: by asking users and by looking for yourself. You should do a combination of both.

The users' perception of what constitutes a feature may be different from yours, so you may want to start by doing some light contextual inquiry or a small focus group series. Identify what people consider to be the key qualities of your service and what they consider to be the important functionality. These may be as complex as "I like the way the features are integrated so that my numbers carry over from one section to another," or as simple as "The search button is easy to find."

In addition, do a *feature audit*. Sit down and make a list of the prominent features of your product. From a user's perspective, what does your product do? What are the prominent functions? Then look at each of your competitors' products and check which ones have the same or similar features (but, again, similarity is measured from the perspective of the user, not how you know the site works). As you run into new features that your competition offers, add them to the list. You can also look at product reviews to see which features reviewers highlight and what they have to say about them.

A list for a search engine could look like this.

- Fast response.
- Provides category and specific site matches.
- Corrects simple spelling errors.
- Sorts results by relevancy.
- Compatible with AltaVista search language ($\pm$, link:, etc.).
- Etc.

Next, combine the two lists and *prioritize the features* into tier 1 and tier 2 lists. Prioritization is important when concentrating your research. Prioritize based on the areas that mean the most to the product's functionality, to the company's success, or to the users' satisfaction. You will probably want to discuss the competitive research plan with management since they may have questions of their own that your process can answer.

While you are collecting features, you should also be collecting the important *attributes* of the competitive products. Attributes aren't necessarily related to functionality, but they are things that make a product memorable, likable, or interesting. They are the adjectives that people use to describe the product to friends or co-workers. Although not as important to the usability of a product as the actual features, attributes describe the feeling and environment of a user experience. A product's vibe can change the way people experience and use it; it should not be ignored. For example, the user experience of a product that is perceived as "bland" and "boring" will certainly be affected by people's opinion even if they are not directly related to how well it works. Form may follow function, but it shouldn't be ruled by it.

Competitive Analysis Techniques

The same techniques that provide insight into your product—usability tests, focus groups, surveys, and the like—work as well when applied to your competitors as when done for your own products. The major difference in approach is the amount of focus you place on creating a balanced perspective. When researching your own products, it's common to focus on the problems that the product is having—after all, those are more immediately actionable than knowing where change is unnecessary—but in competitive research it's as important to understand what your competitors have done *right* as it is to know where they've faltered. In addition to knowing where their failings are, which parts of their product do users have *no* problems with? What aspects do they *like?*

Recruiting

Just as you should recruit real users (or potential users) when trying to understand how people perceive your product, you need to recruit real users when working competitively.

The process of recruiting is the same as that described in Chapter 6, but with the additional consideration of the target audience's experience with your competitors' products. Whether such experience is important depends on the kind of research you plan on doing. If you're usability-testing advanced features, you'll probably have

Warning Keeping the identity of your company anonymous is important when competitively recruiting. People will almost certainly behave differently if they know that the research is for the purpose of comparison. Some feel defensive about their choices; others choose to use the testing opportunity to vent their frustrations. Both cases are an exaggeration of how they really respond and should be avoided.

to find people who have experience with the more common features, so it's not necessary to familiarize the participants with basic functionality. Likewise, focus groups of current users can tell you a lot about what attracts them to the product. However, research with inexperienced users—with people who have no experience with your product or your competitors'—often provides some of the most valuable competitive information because the first experience with a product determines a lot about users' future relationship to it and understanding of it.

The logistics of recruiting people who match a competitive recruiting profile is no different from the process described in Chapter 6, but how do you find your competition's users?

One method is to do a broad public invitation and include in your screener for it a list of products that includes both your product and your competitors', but does not reveal that you (or the recruiter) represent one of them. The list should contain your product, your competition's product, and several others. Invite those who use your competition's products but don't use yours.

Competitive Contextual Inquiry

One-on-one interviews with users of a competitive product can reveal much about what makes that product functional and where it fails. Watching people use your competition's product reveals usage patterns that your product can emulate or avoid.

For example, while watching people reading news online for a technology news competitive analysis, a researcher observed that frequent news readers would first go to CNN or CNBC and read a couple of stories, then they would jump to a smaller news site. When questioned, they consistently said that they use the major news sources for general headlines and the specialized news site for a comprehensive view of the topics that most interested them. The specialized sites provided better views of their favorite topics, whereas the general news sites were better for "hurricanes and stuff." The technology news site was planning to carry general news content from a news wire, but seeing this they decided that a wire feed was unlikely to compete with CNN on the "hurricanes and stuff" front, so they decided to highlight breaking technology news instead.

Focus Groups

Inviting the users of a competitive product to participate in a focus group can reveal *why* they use it and which aspects of it attract and repel them. Such groups can also reveal people's views of the brand and the identity of the product, and the qualities they assign those brands. Anecdotes collected during the focus group can be analyzed to see what the initial impetus for using product B (the leading brand) versus product A (your product) was.

For example, several focus groups with the users of a furniture sales site were invited to talk about how they buy furniture online and offline. The goal was to understand what information they found most valuable and what presentation most compelling. Quickly and consistently, it was seen that there were certain classes of furniture that most participants would buy only through a trusted name. Unfamiliar with most manufacturer brands and unable to touch the furniture, they needed the assurance of a reputable seller. They complained about the quality of the navigation and pictures on the site, but the trust they placed in the name overrode their apprehension.

More than one product can be discussed in a competitive focus group. Introducing several products and actively comparing them with a group helps further reveal what people value and find interesting. These groups can be made up of people who have experience with one of the products or with people who have no experience with any of them (though it's probably not a good idea to mix the two groups). When presenting multiple products, the order in which they're discussed should be varied so as to minimize the bias that can come from having the same product shown first every time or having the same two products appear in the same order every time.

Note For the record, both of the furniture sites—the one discussed in the focus group and the one for which the research was done—failed. The focus groups also revealed that people weren't likely to buy much furniture online at all, but both sites clearly thought that this would change. It didn't.

Usability Tests

Competitive usability tests are one of the more useful competitive research techniques. Watching people use your competition's product can show you where its functionality differs from yours (something that's not always apparent when examining the interface), where it succeeds, and where it fails.

The features you concentrate on will drive the development of the script and the tasks. Focus on the features that most differentiate your competition's product from yours, and isolate the features that will best describe whole classes of functionality. For example, it may be more valuable to investigate how well your competitor's navigation tabs work than whether people understand the icons used in the shopping cart. Even though the icons may be a flashy differentiator, the tabs are more likely to affect more people's experiences with the site.

The tasks you create will likely differ little from those you use when testing your own products. In fact, you can use the same tasks. In addition to being less work, this lets you compare how different interface organizations can create different usage patterns.

An occasional problem occurs when you don't have access to your competitor's product. For publicly available sites, it's easy to just point a browser at them or pay the nominal registration fee for an account or two. But for products that you don't have access to or for which the registration costs are outside your budget, testing them can be challenging. In such situations, many questions can be answered by prototypes that you build or, in the case of software, demo versions (which are often freely downloadable, though you should carefully read the demo's user agreement to make sure that competitive analysis is an appropriate use of the product).

It's also possible to test multiple products at the same time. Compare approaches by giving evaluators the same task on several different interfaces (but only if the tasks are actually doable on all the interfaces). Again, you can reduce bias by changing the order in which you present the competing products and not recruiting users who have experience with any of the products under examination.

For example, a general-purpose Web directory wanted to understand what worked in its competition's interfaces. Many of the category-based directories were based on Yahoo!, and that site had already been studied, so it was decided to choose two of the lesser-known directories. LookSmart and snap.com were chosen because they offered similar services to similar audiences (at the time). People who had not used either site were asked to search for similar things with both services. Localization features (either by specifying a zip code or a region) were considered to be of tier 1 importance

Warning Bias easily creeps into the testing process. A subconscious nod toward a preferred solution or a moderator's slip of the tongue can skew a participant's perceptions. Although this can happen in any research situation, it's more likely to happen when the moderator has strong competitive allegiances. Focusing on behavior and current usage, rather than opinion, reduces the chances that an opinionated moderator will skew the results.

Bias is also the reason third-party consultants are particularly useful when doing third-party analysis.

and were the primary focus of the usability test. Most of the participants said these features were interesting, and everyone understood the two sites' different methods of communicating this functionality (in snap's case, it was an "Enter Zip Code" field, in LookSmart's, a "My Town" navigation tab). However, the ability to use the two sites' implementations of the features was different. LookSmart's "My Town" tab attempted to anticipate people's local needs, almost always incorrectly, whereas snap's option dropped people into a different directory, which was treated by the users as a separate service and understood as well as they understood the general snap interface. The Web directory decided to go with a snap-like model.

Surveys

Before you run special competitive surveys, look at the customer and user research you already have. Useful competitive information can often be extracted from surveys not specifically designed for it. You can filter responses to pull out users of competitors' products and tabulate the responses of just those users, treating them as a subset of the whole survey population. Although the results will likely not be significant relative to the general user population, analyzing them may be able tell you something about what differentiates your users from your competitors'.

The process of writing a survey specifically to understand your competition follows the same steps as for a regular survey. Create reasonable objectives about what your survey is to accomplish, focus most of the questions on the tier 1 issues, and present the features in a neutral way. From the respondent's perspective, the questions should read as if an impartial third party wrote them.

Some popular topics of competitive investigation in surveys include

- *Other products your users use.* This question allows you to estimate the popularity of your competitors and, using published third-party audience numbers, can give you a ballpark figure for the total size of your market.
- *How much they use the products.* If you are using dynamic survey generation software, leverage its capabilities for creating customized follow-up questions to ask in-depth rating ques-

tions about your competition. How often do people use their product? For how long do they use it? When did they start using it? Have they ever switched between competing products? How often? Why?

- *Their loyalty to the competition.* What attracted your respondents to your competitor in the first place? How satisfied are they? You can create a grid of Likert rating scales that lets the respondents quickly fill out their views about specific features and attributes of the products (see Chapter 11 for more information on Likert scales).
- *The features they use.* These questions can be generated from a database of known competitor features, or it can be free text, letting people discuss how the product is useful to them. It can also include a feature satisfaction component.

Surveying just your competitors' users is difficult. You don't even necessarily know who they are. Unlike surveying the users who come to your door, you have to actively find your competition's. You can either field the survey to your own users and filter out those who use competitive products or you can field it to a broad range of users (say, through a banner ad on Yahoo! or a site that you feel will attract a lot of competitive users) and hope that enough of the respondents will be competitive users to justify the cost. Of course the best way to get a representative survey is to do a random telephone survey, but those are cost prohibitive in most cases.

Like other kinds of competitive research, surveys can be easily biased if they're revealed to be competitive. The knowledge that they're discussing one product for the benefit of another can change the way that people respond to questions, especially satisfaction and preference questions. It's probably OK to reveal your identity at the end of the survey (or at the end of any of these procedures), after they've submitted their responses, but it's generally better to do the whole thing as a third party.

Analyzing Competitive Research

The goal of traditional competitive analysis is to create a side-by-side, feature-for-feature comparison grid. The assumption in creating such a matrix is that point-by-point matching of features is important for competitiveness. This isn't always the case from the user's perspective. There is usually a core set of functionality that needs to be similar for two products to be considered competitive, but beyond that the actual feature set can vary broadly and two products can still compete. Many online companies compete directly with brick-and-mortar companies, for example, though the actual user experiences are drastically different.

Competitive user experience research should reveal the fundamental strengths and weaknesses of the competition, not create a scoreboard.

The comparison begins with the research reports you produced in the data collection phase. Taking the report, enumerate the *advantages* that the competition's product gives their users and the *hindrances* it places in their way. Again, these should be from the users' perspective. Even though it may be in your best interest to have people stay on your site longer, a site that lets people get in and out quickly may be preferable. Similarly, although new daily content may be positioned as an advantage of one product, it may make little difference to users, and, in fact, a frequently changing page may be seen as a hindrance if it requires them to relearn the navigation.

Looking at the results more closely, what do they say about the company and its development process? Where does it provide consistently strong experiences? What are the characteristics of those experiences? How does it regularly falter? Business analysts call the collection of a company's strengths their *portfolio of core competencies.* Likewise, it may be useful to maintain a *portfolio of frequent foibles* that lists consistent weak points in the competition's approach to creating experiences.

CNET, for example, were masters of brand identity and design cohesion. With all of the distinguishing marks removed, people who had seen a CNET site could immediately pick out a different CNET site from a lineup. Users considered this to be a benefit because they trusted the company and felt comfortable navigating its products. However, CNET's navigation was less consistent than its branding. When researched competitively (by me while working for Wired Digital), its users felt that they knew how to use a CNET site because it resembled other CNET products, but they actually had more trouble navigating some CNET sites than ones made by CNET's competitors. When researching a number of CNET sites, it was seen that both the strong branding and the bad navigation were consistently present in many of their products.

Traditional competitive analysis can, of course, also be revealing. It shouldn't be the only kind of analysis, but it can provide a useful shorthand. If, for example, users clearly value a certain set of features, then it may be appropriate to create a feature comparison matrix with those features. Such side-by-side comparisons, however, need to be between actually *comparable* items. Thus, a site map *somewhere* on a site should probably not be compared with one that has a map front and center on the homepage.

Benchmarking

In the interest of creating a shorthand by which to evaluate competition, some competitive analysis techniques introduce numerical or letter grade competitive ratings. You can, for example, give each feature in a feature matrix a score—say, 0–5, where 5 means the product does something well and 0 means it doesn't do it at all. Adding up all the scores gives you a total for the competitiveness of the site. This allows you to quickly see which ones are, theoretically, most competitive because relative to the others they are the most successful at what they do.

Such techniques are useful when new competitors are constantly entering the field and you need to evaluate them quickly, but it obscures important information about which aspects of the competition influenced the final score, which may actually be more important than the overall value. However, the exercise can be useful when figuring out which strengths are serious threats and which weaknesses are important opportunities.

Acting on Competitive Research

Finally, once you've collected all the data, analyzed the responses, and performed all the comparisons, you need to do something with it. To make the research usable—to create *actionable intelligence*—you need to refocus on your work. Take your list of advantages and hindrances and reflect them back on your product. For every item on the list, explain its relationship to your product. Every advantage that a competitor's product provides can be seen as a *threat* to yours, and every problem as an *opportunity*. Everywhere the competition's product is more effective than yours reveals a weakness in your product, and vice versa.

Warning Don't use your own results in your advertising. Although it's tempting to use the results of your internal competitive research in your ads, it's generally not recommended. People won't give it a lot of credence, and your competitors may decide to sue if they think your results are incorrect. If your internal research shows, for example, that four out of five people prefer your product over its competitors, and you're *convinced* that this is an accurate proportion of the population at large, hire an independent research agency to replicate your research. An independent agency is likely to use much more rigorous standards in their research, and their results will carry much more weight in consumers' (and judges'!) minds.

Then create a theory explaining the motivation behind the design choices that were made by your competition, both good and bad. Why was the product made the way it was? What were the constraints? What was the likely rationale? Which choices do you agree with? Which do you not? Which are inexplicable? Concentrate on the *whys* of your competitor's decision-making process, not necessarily on *what* was done.

The final outcome of competitive research is a deeper understanding of what makes a good user experience, admiration for your competitors' ability to solve problems, pride in your own product, and a plan that allows you to use this knowledge to your advantage. These are all worthwhile lessons, and there are few other ways to learn them.

Example: A Quick Evaluation of ZDNet

The following is an excerpt of a rapid competitive usability test done of ZDNet for an online news site. In the interest of saving space, the description of the research process and the way that these results feed into the larger list of core competencies have been omitted.

- *The general perception is that ZDNet is mostly for software and hardware reviews, not for cultural information. When asked to categorize what they thought the site was about, the evaluators generally focused on the technical review aspects of the site. They did not feel that this was a site to go to for information about how technology would affect their world in a broad sense, but appeared to feel that it was a comprehensive site for information about what's happening now in terms of new mainstream hardware and software.*
- *Because of email newsletters, many people never go to the front door (shown in Figure 14.1). At least one of the evaluators said that he had been to the site in the recent past, yet when shown the ZDNet front door—which has been redesigned for several months—he was surprised by the design. Therefore, depending on how much traffic comes through the front door directly versus links from other sites or from newsletters, the navigation and information on deep pages may be as equally important as or more important than that presented on the top page.*

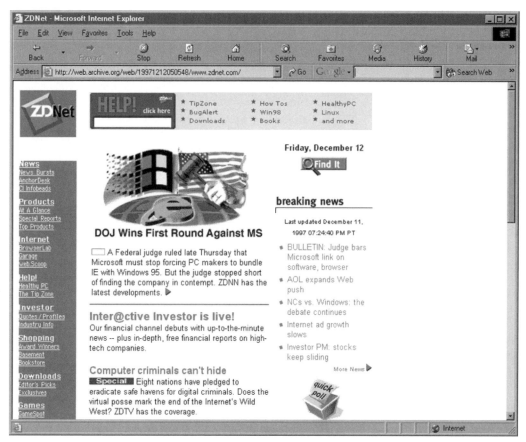

Figure 14.1 The ZDNet interface (circa 1998).

- *Section naming was confusing and didn't invite exploration. "CI" is a reference to Computer Intelligence, a ZDNet property. The abbreviation was not known or recognized by any of the participants. "Infobeads" and "Garage" were picked out as especially confusing. "Help!" was possibly the most egregious example of this (even verging on deceptive) since people took it to be help with the site, when in fact it was a site for tips to use with other software. In fact, even after surfing around the "Help!" section for a while and looking at the actual content, the expected content was sufficiently strong to continue to confuse users since they were still trying to align reality with expectations.*

- *Evaluators did not see the navigation bar because it was placed between an ad and the top headline. One evaluator thought that it was an ad at first. The confusion between advertising and content because of proximity and shape has come up before and could be one of the reasons for evaluators' dismissal of the suggested words at the top of Excite's results pages.*
- *Navigation to specific stories was confusing. One evaluator said, "[This site has] exactly what I would have wanted, if I could ever find it again."*
- *Stock quote navigation was almost impossible to figure out and made an almost perfect example of how to design an interface that was consistently misunderstood. Everyone (including me) made exactly the same sequence of mistakes with the stock quote interface when trying to find a quote for Netscape (NSCP).*
   a. *When typing into the provided type-in box, everyone typed in the actual ticker symbol. However, because the interface did not understand ticker symbols, it just brought back a blank page.*
   b. *Everyone then, seeing the line of numbers and letters above the type-in box, clicked on the "N." This brought them to the top of the "N" list of companies, showing 20 at a time.*
   c. *Everyone then clicked on the "Next" button, bringing them to the next "NA" portion of the database.*
   d. *Realizing that this was a large data space and that getting to the intended information would involve a lot of clicking, everyone then typed "Netscape" into the type-in box, generating the intended information.*

   All this (roughly 30 seconds' worth of work) could have been solved by a single line underneath the type-in box reading "Company name, NOT ticker symbol."

- *Search is a major method of site navigation. When asked to locate an article on a specific topic—though not for a specific article—people universally used the site search engine. Fortunately, the "Find" pop-up button was memorable, and people quickly gravitated to using it.*

However, for one evaluator there was a little confusion between it and the Search page, as listed on the navigation list on the left (which searches the whole site).

- In the downloads section, users appreciated the rating system, but didn't know what the system was rating. Since shareware is so numerous and overlapping, people appreciate an "expert" opinion about the quality of the shareware. However, the metric of that quality may be an important piece of information to educate people on since they would like to know how a four-star program differs from a three-star and why.

CHAPTER 15

Others' Hard Work: Published Information and Consultants

Not all research has to be done from scratch. You can find out about important aspects of your audience without resorting to doing research from first principles. The judicious use of published information and consultants can save time, energy, and (occasionally) money when trying to know your audience and understand how they experience your product. It's even possible to get information that would not be feasible to collect on your own.

There are a number of reasons for going outside your company walls to acquire audience knowledge. Obviously you can often save money and time by going to external sources if the information you're interested in is readily available, but it's not just economic reasons that justify outsourcing your research. By going outside your immediate development context, you can quickly acquire a high level of perspective that you probably wouldn't be able to re-create in-house. You probably don't have the resources to do a broad survey of all of your possible target audiences to find out whether they have the basic needs and meet the basic requirements to use your product, but a market research company does. And although it may involve some amount of interpretation and extrapolation, a perusal of high-level data may quickly focus your research by eliminating some obvious problems. Moreover, a different organization is likely to see things with a different perspective. Approaching the same audience with a different set of goals and assumptions produces results that are different from what you can collect. This can be invaluable in giving depth and understanding to your own results.

But this is not a trivial process. Finding trustworthy and appropriate information is hard, and interpreting it correctly is even harder. And consultants aren't the cavalry coming over the hill either. For all of their value, their efforts need to be managed as carefully as you would manage your own research. External research is an important resource, but like all powerful tools, it has to be used carefully.

Published Information

There are many kinds of published analysis for you to choose from. Even if something doesn't *exactly* apply to your problem, maybe it's useful enough for you to base a decision on. Maybe it gives you some information about where to start looking for problems or who your audience isn't. Or maybe it just gives you a better perspective on how to approach your own research.

Keep in mind that published information is not the same as research done in-house. It's broader and shallower than research that you would do, and it doesn't have the quality controls that you would put into your research. It may turn out to be more rigid than is necessary for your purposes or, alternatively, too unfocused. However, buying others' research is often much faster than doing it yourself, which means that, in the long run, it can be cheaper.

Independent Analysis

The business model for most research companies is pretty simple: they do independent in-depth analysis on a specific topic or a specific industry, and then they sell reports to companies from the industry they just analyzed. These reports are not cheap, but they often represent a lot of comprehensive thinking by a group of industry experts (or, at least, research experts).

As an outgrowth of the marketing research industry, these companies tend to focus on the financial health of specific markets, industries, or companies. As part of this, however, they often research the needs and desires of those markets' target audiences. Much of the knowledge necessary to sell to a target audience is the same as what is necessary to give that audience a good experience, and such marketing-focused information can be immediately valuable when creating user profiles or setting expectations for contextual inquiry.

Some companies that specialize in this kind of research include

- Jupiter Communications, *www.jup.com*
- Forrester Research, *www.forrester.com*
- Zona Research (a subsidiary of Intelliquest), *www.zonaresearch.com*
- IDC, *www.idc.com*
- The Gartner Group, *www.gartner.com*

Additionally, some other firms create research that's focused on evaluating the user experience presented by companies or industries rather than just their business metrics. These companies include

- Nielsen Norman Group, *www.nngroup.com*
- User Interface Engineering, *www.uie.com*

Although these reports present a ready-made trove of potentially useful knowledge, it's important to read them closely. The researchers who write them will often not know the industry as well as insiders; they may misjudge the behaviors of users and the motivations of companies. A careful reading of the research methodology is important.

Traffic/Demographic

By knowing who is using your competitors' products, how much they use them, and what they use them for, you can avoid your competitors' mistakes and capitalize on their strengths. Unfortunately, as great as it would be to have access to your competition's log files and survey data, this is rarely a legal option. Fortunately, services exist that collect some of these data independently, reporting the conglomerate information and selling access to specific slices of the data. By using these services' data and tools, it's possible to gain insight into the makeup and behavior of your competition's users.

Some companies that provide this kind of research include

- ComScore, *www.comscore.com*
- Nielsen/Netratings (a subsidiary of AC Nielsen), *www.netratings.com*
- NUA, *www.nua.com*
- WebSideStory, *www.websidestory.com*

Interpreting these results and how they apply to your product is more difficult than reading an analyst's report, and the sheer amount of data received from one of these services can be daunting. There are typically two kinds of data in one of these reports: the participants' behavior, as it was tracked by the company, and the participants' profile, as it was reported to the company. Linking these produces a powerful set of measurements. For example, you can (hypothetically, not all services allow you to do this directly) get data about the most popular sites in a given market and then get a profile of the people who use those sites.

Of all the data that's possible to extract, often the most immediately interesting information is the demographic makeup of your competition (or of companies in a parallel industry) and their technological and Web usage profile. You can immediately see how old, how experienced, and how affluent their audience is (among many other variables). These are, of course, aspects that you probably considered when creating your own audience profile, but a set of independent data can confirm your assumptions or cast them in doubt.

Like all research, the process by which the data were collected needs to be carefully examined since that aspect is least under your control. Sometimes the data collection methods can introduce subtle biases, which need to be taken into account. For example, Comscore Media Metrix requires its participants to install a piece of software on their computer; the software tracks what sites they visit and when they visit them. Although they can get a mostly representative sample of users this way, this approach misses a key group of people: those who are unable to install this software on their work computers because it violates their company's software installation rules. This means that the data collected by the service is skewed toward home-based computers and companies with lax internal security standards. For many situations, this bias does not affect the applicability of the final data; for instance, the data would be insufficiently representative for a B2B sales site targeted toward Fortune 100 companies. It would be important to track B2B users at work, but it would be impossible under the MIS security rules of most of the target audience.

Marketing Research

As is obvious from many of these descriptions, the tools of marketing research can be used for user experience research. The marketing department of your company is interested in what will make people want to go to your site and use your product. The reasons that they will want to go to your site and will be able to use your product are directly related to the user experience.

There is often research that marketing has done that can be immediately applied to understanding your user population. For example, the following is a portion of an audience profile developed as part of researching the primary market for a service targeted at 20- and 30-something-year-old women:

PARTIAL TARGET AUDIENCE PROFILE

Demographic

Women, aged 24–34

Education: college educated

Income: $30,000–$70,000

78% are online

Motivation

Socializing with household members and family

Visiting with friends

Keeping up with current events

(Continued)

Priorities

Puts relationships before work and career

Households

Mid- to late 20s: typically share a household with one other individual

Early-to-mid 30s: most likely have kids

Internet Behavior

Women 25–34 make up highest percentage of new Internet users

Spend 3–10 hours online per week

Don't surf the Web, but rely on others for Web site pointers

Primary motivations in life are same as those of women without Internet access

Approximately 50% go online via AOL

Email is the primary online tool

Email Usage

Use email to stay in touch with the most important people in their lives

91% primarily use email when using the Internet

78% get excited about opening their emails

Use email like a telephone to communicate with family and friends

Favorite Web Activities

- Seeking health information
- Playing games
- Hunting for spiritual or religious information
- Looking for job information
- Also like fun Web activities, such as chat rooms and hobby sites

Top Web and Digital Media Properties (for Women 18+)

- AOL networks
- Microsoft sites
- Yahoo! sites
- Google
- About.com sites
- Amazon
- NBC Internet

Of course not all this research is equally useful. The income doesn't really tell us how people are going to be using it, though it hints at what kind of computer system they may be using. Likewise, the favorite sites may be interesting as models of the kinds of architecture and interaction the users are accustomed to, but it's not critical information. And what exactly does "use email like a telephone" mean? For a marketer that may be enough to define the site's market positioning (say, for an advertisement), but it doesn't say much about the experience that the product is supposed to provide. Does it mean that the interaction should resemble a telephone or that it should be instantly available like a telephone? Maybe there should be a mobile phone interface option. The marketing document doesn't answer this, but it is an important question that can be investigated from an experience standpoint.

Other information, however, is immediately useful. Because these women are the fastest-growing Internet audience, a large percentage are likely to be relatively new to the Internet, which implies certain things about experience, expertise, and expectations. Similarly, their favorite Web activities can influence the information architecture, emphasizing the aspects of the site that fall in line with what we already know this group prefers.

Publications

Familiarizing yourself with the publications that affect your field is probably a good first step in any kind of user research. Time spent at the library (or with a search engine) is rarely wasted and often reveals sources of information that would otherwise take a lot of work to replicate. Books and trade magazines are obvious candidates for perusal, but there are also some unexpected sources of potentially valuable information: you may want to consider the decidedly old-fashioned method of hiring a newspaper clipping (also known as "media monitoring") service to find periodical articles that analyze your competitors' products or your audience and then mail them to you.

White papers are essentially analyst reports, but from a biased source. They're often written to justify a particular company's perspective and explain their technology, but that doesn't mean that they're not useful. In defending their perspective, they often contain valuable information, though it should always be examined with attention to the bias inherent in its source.

Finally, a number of user experience pundits maintain daily diaries called weblogs, or *blogs*. Although there's often a lot of fluff in these sites, they can contain important (although unedited) insights into user experience design and research long before it formally appears in any publication.

Some Free Internet Resources

General

Usable Web (Keith Instone's usability directory), *www.usableweb.com*

Usability.gov (the National Cancer Institute's site focused on Web site usability), *usability.gov*

Information Architecture Resources (Jesse James Garrett's information architecture directory), *www.jjg.net/ia/*

Boxes and Arrows Journal, *www.boxesandarrows.com*

Nielsen Norman Group (includes links to frequent essays by Jakob Nielsen, Don Norman, Bruce Tognazzini, and others), *www.nngroup.com*

IBM ResearchDeveloperWorks usability research papers and essays, *www.106.ibm.com/developerworks/usability/*

Microsoft Usability Research publications, *www.microsoft.com/usability/*

CyberAtlas (a compilation of Web use statistics run by internet.com), *cyberatlas.internet.com/*

Adaptive Path's publications, *www.adaptivepath.com*

Usability Blogs

WebWord, *www.webword.com*

Louis Rosenfeld, *louisrosenfeld.com*

Challis Hodge, *www.challishodge.com*

Gleanings (Christina Wodtke's blog), *www.eleganthack.com/blog/*iaslash, *www.iaslash.org*

Black Belt Jones (Matt Jones' blog), *www.blackbeltjones.com/work/*

Warning Full disclosure: I am a partner in a user experience consulting company, Adaptive Path *(www.adaptivepath.com).*

Some of these links are likely to be obsolete by the time this book is published. The Open Directory Project's Web usability category should have mostly up-to-date links.

dmoz.org/Computers/Internet/Web_Design_and_Development/Web_Usability/

Mailing Lists

sigia-l@asis.org, an information architecture mailing list. Subscription information and archives available on *mail.asis.org/mailman/listinfo/sigia-l*

CHI-WEB@acm.org, a Web-specific mailing list for the ACM SIG CHI community, but open to everyone. Subscription information and archives available on *sigchi.org/web/*

UTEST, a usability testing mailing list maintained by Dr. Tharon Howard. Subscription information is available by contacting Dr. Tharon Howard at tharon@hubcap.clemson.edu

Hiring Specialists

There are times when resource constraints do not permit you to build the necessary expertise in-house to do something yourself. For nearly every task described in this book, from recruiting participants to competitive research to setting up video cameras, you can hire a professional to do it for you. For a price, experts can immediately bring nearly any knowledge and experience that you need.

But working with a professional is not simply writing a check and forgetting about the task. To use specialists effectively, they need to be hired at the right time, with the proper set of expectations, and then carefully managed.

Timing

Note I'm including consultants, contractors, and consulting agencies in my definition of *specialist*. Although a large consultancy (of the Accenture/ KPMG/IBM Global Services model) works differently from a single contractor, their relationship to your product and your company is similar. They are called in to solve specific problems, and they work as an adjunct to your team, interacting when necessary, but keeping their responsibility to the one aspect of the development that they were hired to do. Your team's work may range all over the product as needs warrant it, but specialists will rarely leave their specialty to solve a problem they were not hired to solve.

A key to using specialists well is calling them in at the right moment. Often, consultants get the call to produce a perfect solution late in the game, after all in-house methods have failed and a deadline is approaching. More often than not, this is asking for a miracle. Unfortunately, despite the way some advertise themselves, consultants are not saints.

The work that hired specialists do is not all that different from what your in-house staff can do, and it needs to be scheduled just like in-house work. Actually, it needs even a little more time than what you give your in-house projects since the specialists will need to learn about your product and the task that's involved.

I have been asked a number of times to "do a little user testing a couple of weeks before launch." I regret telling the caller that this is not unlike looking up to see where the moon is after you've already launched the rocket. The kinds of results that testing a completed product will reveal may help with tiny course corrections, but no amount of testing and adjustments will help if the rocket was pointed in the wrong direction. This holds for any other kind of specialty.

In addition, consultants, as opposed to other kinds of specialists, need to be called in especially early. Technical specialists don't teach you; they do it for you. They don't know your business before they come in and, most likely, won't after they leave. Good consultants, on the other hand, absorb enough of your business to recommend solutions *and* strive to transfer some of their expertise to you. Good consultants will leave your company in a state where you won't have to go to them with the same problem again. Good technical specialists will do their job quickly and accurately, but if it has to be done again, you'll probably have to call them back in.

Fortunately, it's hard to call user researchers in too early, but it's still important to do the right research at the right time. As discussed in Part 1 of this book, a good iterative development process involves user input at nearly every iteration. The responsibility for picking what research is needed is as much the project developers' as it is the researchers'. For example, if a product's interaction is usability-tested before the feature set has been defined, much of the information may go to waste since people's use of it will likely change based on the options available to them. Likewise, testing a product that's been built without first researching its audience's needs will result in a lot of unnecessary effort: if the product's audience has no interest in it, then they have little motivation to understand how it works or to use it in a realistic way.

Find a Specialist

For tasks with relatively straightforward needs, such as a single round of contextual inquiry or some focus groups to set feature priority, the procedure is similar to finding a carpenter for your house.

1. Write a description of your research needs and goals. What kind of research do you want to do? Why? How are you going to use the results? This is similar to how you would prepare for your own research, as described in Chapter 5.
2. Make a list of specialists to contact. Ask colleagues for recommendations or contact one of the usability professional organizations, all of which maintain lists of consultants and contractors. Some prominent organizations are
   - Usability Professional's Association, *www.upassoc.org*
   - American Society for Information Science and Technology, especially their Information Architecture special interest group, *www.asis.org*
   - Association for Computing Machinery's special interest group on computer-human interaction (ACM SIGCHI), *www.acm.org/sigchi/*
   - BayCHI, the San Francisco Bay Area's chapter of SIGCHI, which maintains a list of consultants that includes people in many geographic areas, *www.baychi.org/general/consultants.html*
3. Check qualifications. The specific experience of the research companies should be investigated before you hire them. You probably don't want a carpenter who specializes in houses to make furniture or a furniture builder making a house. A user experience specialist may not have any experience doing marketing research even though the techniques are quite similar (and vice versa).
4. Get quotes and an explanation of philosophy and techniques. If possible, get a sample results document from all the consultants under consideration. Read the results for an explanation

of techniques and look for a sensitivity to the needs of the product and the client.

5.   Ask for references to several recent clients and follow up the references. Inquire into the quality and timeliness of work, but also the quality of service. Did the consultant follow through on what was promised? Did they listen? Were they responsive?

The Formal Method: RFPs

For more complex tasks (large focus groups, surveys, multiple iterations with different techniques), the procedure is more like that of building a house from scratch. Because of the size of the tasks and their interrelationships, the process of finding the right group of specialists can get quite complex.

1.   Write a request for proposals (RFP). An RFP is a description of your problem and a structured request for a solution. It's useful not just to set the parameters for evaluating a consultant's bid, but as the first step in managing and organizing a project. It sets out, in specific terms, what you believe your problems to be and what you want to gain from an outside solution.

2.   Broadcast the RFP. You can send the RFP to certain consultants that you've first contacted, or you can post it to a larger group. Don't spam, but certain mailing lists and bulletin boards allow you to post such requests (ask the moderators of lists about their RFP posting policies).

3.   Evaluate the responses. The consultants should respond quickly with specific solutions rather than sales pitches. Watch out for proposals that subcontract key work to another firm; if that's the case, then evaluate the subcontractor with the same rigor as you evaluate the primary contractor.

The following page has a sample RFP for a very large, long-term, multipart project. RFPs for smaller projects do not need all the sections and details of this one.

SAMPLE RFP

Request for Proposal

User Experience Research for a B2B Surplus Industrial Products Web Site

January 12, 2003

Responses due: February 12, 2003

Part 1: Project Summary

We represent one of the world's leading raw surplus materials trading Web sites, which is undergoing a systemwide redesign. We are committed to using the best practices of user-centered design as part of this re-design and on an ongoing basis thereafter. With this RFP we hope to find a vendor who can fulfill the full complement of user research needs the project requires.

This RFP will outline for you our vision for the project, our selection criteria, and our expectations for your response.

Background

Our company runs one of the world's largest online industrial raw materials trading services. With over a billion dollars in transactions in FY2001 and 30,000 active users, we are one of the most prominent surplus materials trading services in the world. Our users count on us for the livelihood of their business and entrust us to deliver. We continually strive to improve our service for the benefit of our users and for our profitability.

Project Description

In the interest of improving the user experience of our service, we have launched a major redesign program, creating the service from top to bottom with an eye on the needs of, and input from, our users.

The redesign will be done in a series of phases. Each phase will involve the reexamination of the current product and a refinement of the product vision for the next design. User experience research will be a major component of each phase, and each phase will contain a major research project that will be appropriate for the goals of that phase.

The project will take place Q2–Q4 2003.

(Continued)

Part 2: Elements of Your Proposal

We would like your proposal to be in a specific format, containing all the sections described below. You may add sections if you feel that these do not sufficiently address your core competencies.

Questions

We would like to understand how you are thinking about this project. Please use the information contained in this RFP to answer these questions.

1. One key to the success of this project will be to implement the users' needs as determined by the research, but those needs may not necessarily align with the business needs of the service. What process will you use to solve that challenge?

2. Another key to a successful product is the transfer of knowledge from the user research staff to the production staff. In your view, what are the chief barriers to transferring user knowledge within a company, and how would you address them?

3. What do you see as the most challenging barriers to the success of this project, and what should we do to ensure the best possible results?

Case Studies

Please present up to three case studies that highlight the strengths your company shows in managing projects such as the one described here. Present final deliverables and appropriate collateral.

Core Competencies

We seek a partner, or partners, that have demonstrated achievement in the following areas. Please give us specific examples, if possible, of your experience in these areas.

- Analysis of complex information research and purchasing tasks
- User experience–oriented focus groups
- User testing of Web sites
- Researching the needs of business Web site users, ideally large industrial and manufacturing users
- Understanding the needs of new or occasional users and frequent long-term users

Your Process with Deliverables

Please describe the process your company would use to accomplish this project. Include a description of research, spec development, production, integration, Q/A, and methods of building consensus and sign-off at each stage.

Schedule

The schedule for the entire project is 220 days. Please provide a specific development timeline for this project. Break down your process by deliverables, and be specific about the timing for each section.

Client's Role

Please describe what, if any, expectations you have or deliverables you will need from our company for the project. Describe what sorts of resources you are expecting at each phase, and who from our company you will want to meet with.

Your Team

Please describe the specific roles of the individuals who would be assigned to this project. How many individuals would you assign to the project? To the extent possible, provide background and contact information on the individuals who would be assigned to the account and describe their specific responsibilities. Please identify key projects that each member has worked on in this capacity. Please also indicate the percent of their time that would be allocated to this project.

Budget

Please provide us with a detailed budget proposal. You may present your budget in any format that is familiar to you, but do include cost per milestone, hourly cost per team member, and anticipated expenses.

Also include a description of how cost is typically communicated during the course of a project, and how overages are managed and presented for approval.

(Continued)

References

Please provide us with names and contact information for three references from relevant recent projects that can comment on your services.

Process

We have invited several organizations to make a proposal on this project. Based on the quality and nature of those proposals, we will invite up to three companies to make presentations to us.

You will be given 1.5 hours to make your presentation and answer questions to the management team. Be prepared for detailed, specific review of budget and process. Please plan to bring the specific team members who will be assigned to this account, including the leads for project management, quantitative research, qualitative research, and analysis.

[Based on a template created by Janice Fraser]

The Casual Method: Email and Phone Call

Most user experience research and design work, however, is not sufficiently complex to warrant the RFP process.

For most of our work at Adaptive Path, we prefer a short (several paragraph) email description of needs and problems, followed by a one- or two-hour conference call where we delve into details. This procedure saves both parties time—neither RFP nor RFP response need be written—and can focus quickly on the most relevant elements rather than trying to predict them ahead of time. We consider our role as consultants to begin at the first phone call, and we try to help clients understand and formulate their needs immediately rather than just responding to what they believe their needs to be. However, in situations where a project is huge and there are potentially many companies vying for it, a comprehensive RFP can be the best option.

Set Expectations

Going into a relationship with a specialist, especially a consultant or a consulting company, requires setting appropriate expectations on both sides.

As a client, *you know your business better than they do.* If they knew what you know, they'd be your competitors. Even if you tell them everything that you know, you will still know your business better than they will. You have more experience and should frame what you expect specialists to do from that perspective. The role that they play is not as replacements, but as information sources and tools.

Moreover, user experience researchers are, on the whole, better at uncovering problems than they are at creating solutions to those problems. It's tempting to want to go to a single source and have them tell you what your products' problems are and then give you the solutions to those problems. And consultants will happily give you what they believe is the best solution for a given problem, but it will still be coming from the perspective of someone who has limited experience with your business. The responsibility for taking their advice, understanding what it means in your situation, and applying it correctly is still yours.

Specialists provide perspective based on experience. Because of their experience, they know some general solutions that work better than others, and they can tailor those solutions to your problem. What they tell you may not match your perception of the world, but it's important to listen to them. Inside your development process, you come to conclusions based on a certain set of assumptions. No matter how honest and forthright you and your staff are, eventually you're all going to see the problems from much the same perspective, based on the same information. Outsiders come in with an entirely different set of assumptions and information, so their conclusions can be much different from yours. This does not mean that they are right and you are wrong, or vice versa, but the perspective they bring enriches yours. Allow them to ask fundamental questions and reintroduce topics that you may have already decided on.

One way to think about consultants is that they are people who know now what you will find out in two to three months if you don't hire them. That's it. Think of them as people who are a couple of steps ahead of you, and by hiring them you are shaving a couple of months off your development schedule. A couple of months of development time is really expensive, so bringing in specialists is generally worth the money. But what you're buying is time, not magic.

These expectations can be distilled into a series of guidelines for managing specialists.

GUIDELINES FOR MANAGING SPECIALISTS

- *Know what you want.* If you familiarize yourself with the basic ideas and methods of the industry, you can be a much more informed consumer of consulting services. Calling a user test a focus group is more than just a faux pas in a meeting with a consultant; it creates confusion as to the goals of the research and of the project as a whole. Once you know what's available, know what questions you want to get an answer to. Determining the goals of the research ahead of time based on the business needs of the company and the proposed product makes the results more meaningful and useful.

- *Schedule carefully.* Research needs to address the needs of the company when it's delivered. When it comes too early, the project will likely have changed by the time it's needed. When it's too late, the time to fix the identified issues may have passed.

- *Provide lead time.* As with any topic, the more preparation time the specialist has, the better the results are going to be. To recruit just the right audience may involve multiple iterations to get the screener right. To ask the right questions, the researcher needs to understand the research goals and your product. Analysis is always a time-consuming process, so the more time that is left for it, the better it's going to be. Consultants always benefit from an appropriate amount of lead time.

- *Be open to suggestions.* Specialists may not know your business as well as you do, but if they suggest things that challenge your assumptions about the product or its market, their perspective should still be evaluated and considered. One product, for example, was supposed to be used by teenagers on PDAs while skateboarding. User testing revealed that although the teenagers could use the product, they were unlikely to bring their PDAs skateboarding. The consultant recommended that the information be made available in an easily printed format because paper is more portable and less valuable, but the client said, "we can't put ads there; paper is not where the money is."

- *Observe the process.* Although reports and presentations are valuable summaries, the amount of information that can be put in them is a small fraction of the knowledge that can be collected by directly observing the consultants' process. Whenever possible, have members of the development staff watch the research live. If direct observation is impossible (as in the case of most contextual inquiry research), ask for copies of the videotapes and notes and study them. Since you as the client are more familiar with the product and the problems it's trying to solve, you're likely to notice things that the consultant would not.

- *Get a presentation.* It's tempting to get a consultant's written report and skip the presentation. After all, the thinking goes, the presentation consists of the consultant reading the report to us, which we can do on our own. A good presentation goes beyond that. It allows the consultant to prioritize and emphasize issues, elaborate on points, and answer questions.

- *Treat the consultants as a resource after the initial research is over.* Once they've done the research, consultants have a level of expertise that should not be neglected. If you have questions about their work after they've completed it, don't hesitate to ask them about it (but pay them for their time!). Sometimes it's even valuable to keep consultants on retainer for a couple of hours a month in between major research projects, bouncing ideas off them and clarifying observations. Over time, they may lose some objectivity, but they'll gain a deeper understanding and commitment to your product and its audience.

The relationship between a specialist and client can be a valuable one. When it works, both parties benefit and learn from each other, while making the development process a bit more efficient. When it doesn't, it can be broken off easily, and neither is much the worse than before. In the long term, the most valuable aspect of reusing knowledge and experience is it makes the whole industry more efficient and gives everyone a reason to think about the things that really matter. Don't reinvent the wheel if you don't have to.

CHAPTER 16

Emerging Techniques

Every technique described in this book is designed to provide a different insight into people's perceptions, desires, and abilities. Usability testing gives you fine-grained information about people's abilities and expectations. Surveys broadly paint your users' desires and hopes. Contextual inquiry helps you understand the full environment in which the experience happens.

As described here, the methods work at specific times using a set of common techniques. However, what's written here is not gospel. There are many situations that call for drastically different approaches than I have described. Please do not feel constrained by the methods described in this book. Invent, experiment, and explore the possibilities of the methodologies. Adjust them to your situation.

In addition, although each technique can be used alone, it's not a single all-purpose entity. Just as a sawmill makes planks with attention to the strengths and needs of hammers and nails, the tools of user research exist symbiotically. Each tool is drawn from an array of many tools and should be used with them in mind. Combining the information you gain from various techniques lets you leverage the strengths of each technique and hone your understanding in specific, targeted ways.

Variations on Techniques

The chapter for each technique describes some alternatives and some flexibility that's built into each technique. You can do usability tests with 3 people or 30. You can survey random users to your site or just the people who've signed up for your mailing list. Focus groups can discuss large, abstract issues, or they can tightly focus on specific topics. There are many ways that you can make these methods fit the needs of your research. In addition, there are a number of popular variations that take the techniques in significantly different directions while still gathering valuable data.

Virtual Focus Groups

Focus groups don't have to have all the participants in the same room together. A group of people can be brought together through any of the "telepresence" technologies currently available. The simplest is the conference call. *Telephone focus groups* have the advantage that you don't have to get everyone in a room together, and the participants' time commitment is limited to the duration of the actual group. In-person focus groups have to take factors such as travel time, traffic, availability, and waiting time into account when figuring out who can make it and when. This limits participants to people with large chunks of time who live or work near the meeting location and makes recruiting more difficult while also biasing the group somewhat. Conducting group interviews over the phone eliminates these geographic constraints. You can run a focus group over the phone with every member in a different part of the country, speaking from where it's most convenient for them.

Telephone focus groups, however, are more challenging than in-person groups. It's more difficult for strangers to bond and have uninhibited discussions when they can't see each other. It's also more difficult for them to read each others' intentions and meanings when they can't read body language. Visual illustrations, which are often used as triggers in focus groups to start and maintain discussion, are also more difficult to introduce. Moreover, in an in-person focus group, you know that the participants are focused: you can see them and they have little stimuli other than what you've presented them. You don't have that kind of control over a focus group. Although you can encourage people to pay attention, you can't prevent them from checking their email or buying their groceries when their attention should be on the group.

Still, in situations when you can't get people with specific skills to participate otherwise (say, busy executives) or when you want a wide geographic reach, telephone focus groups can be invaluable.

A second common virtual focus group is the *online focus group*. These are group interviews that are conducted using chatrooms (often with specialized software). Participants sign on to the focus group and instead of speaking to each other and to the moderator, they type. This has many of the same advantages as telephone focus groups in terms of the geographic and time availability of the participants. In addition, online focus groups provide a level of distance and anonymity that other methods don't. This is a two-sided issue. On one hand, it allows people to say things that they may not normally feel comfortable saying, or in ways that they wouldn't normally say them. On the other hand, it makes it still harder for people to feel like they're part of a group, which may make them less likely to speak their mind. Thus, some participants may become much more open while others clam up.

Moderation of such a situation—especially in the context where there are no intonational or physical cues about a person's attitude—is significantly more difficult than moderating a standard focus group. Additionally, the constraint that all the participants have to be able to type their thoughts in real time can really limit the potential audience.

In situations where the audience is appropriate (say, teenagers or heavy Internet users), the technique can work great. Web sites and software can be presented in the most natural environment—people's own monitors—and topics can be discussed that wouldn't be otherwise.

With higher bandwidth and more powerful desktop systems, the near future may also present new technologies for remote focus groups. High bandwidth may allow Internet telephony applications to be much better integrated with presentation software than current conference calls, thus allowing for much richer telephone focus groups. There may even soon be streaming video focus groups direct from people's desktops, which will eliminate many of the problems of chatroom- and phone-based interviews.

Nominal Groups

Focus groups are generally structured to get at the underlying values and desires of the participants. By having the participants discuss issues in depth among themselves, it's possible to understand what those issues are. However, it's difficult to understand their relative importance. Often, the most discussed or contentious issue appears to be the most important, when it could actually be of relatively minor importance compared to an issue that everyone agrees on. In order to minimize this, Delbecq, Van de Ven, and Gustafson devised the *nominal group technique* in the late 1960s and early 1970s. It's a highly structured group interview that mixes focus group and survey techniques.

Nominal groups are based on one primary idea: that people will be most honest about their feelings and most committed to their views if they're asked to write down their thoughts before group discussion begins. This reduces the possibility of group-think and the possibility of charismatic participants swaying the other participants' views.

The method is as follows:

- First, a topic is introduced. This should be a topic that people can succinctly reply to in a short time. For example, "The qualities of silverware that you consider to be important."
- The participants write down their responses to the topic.
- Everyone reads and explains their responses, one at a time, while the responses are listed in a central location (like a whiteboard). There's no discussion of the responses, only clarification. The responses are then given unique identifiers (numbers or letters).
- The participants then rank the responses by writing down the identifiers of responses they find important and rating each with a Likert scale (see Chapter 11).
- The choices and ranks are then shared and discussion begins, using the ranking as the center point. (Discussion, which is the key in traditional focus groups, is even sometimes skipped or truncated in nominal groups.)

The method minimizes the amount of participant bias at the expense of depth. Since people can generally write a lot less in a given amount of time than they can say, this method produces less information about people's values and needs than a traditional focus group. Its benefits are that it's straightforward, needs little analysis afterward, and can prioritize issues. It can be used to set the agenda for a larger discussion (since the interpersonal interaction is limited, it can even be done via email before the actual focus group), but it's somewhat anemic when it comes to in-depth understanding.

Friction Groups

When focus groups are recruited, careful attention is paid to make all the participants similar in key ways so that they can feel comfortable with each other and draw from similar experiences. Keeping a specific slice of the population homogeneous reduces a number of variables that the researcher has to consider when attempting to understand what affects their perspectives and the breadth of their experience.

Picking people who see the world the same way has some drawbacks. A discussion with a group of similar people may miss fundamental issues completely since everyone involved is speaking from a common set of assumptions. Moreover, when people feel that they have become members of a group, they may be less reluctant to deviate from it and voice dissent. This leads to group-think, which is always dangerous in a focused interview situation.

Some marketing research companies have started to experiment with the focus group form in order to reduce these effects. One technique is called *friction groups,* and it's (somewhat) the evil twin of traditional focus groups. Instead of screening all the participants for the same values, participants are recruited to intentionally include divergent perspectives. The participants are then encouraged to discuss and defend their views.

When recruiting, the participants should be the same in every way with a single *differentiating factor.* This reduces the possibility that the differences in people's perspectives are caused by something other than the factor under research. A differentiating factor can be a view ("Real estate is a better investment than stocks") or a choice ("Dell versus Acer").

An equal number of people should be chosen to represent any given view so that no one feels that the others are ganging up on

Warning Friction groups are a relatively new idea. There is not a lot of experience with them and plenty of places where they can go really wrong since people's divergent opinions cause them to retrench their views rather than try to defend them. Thus, they should be done with extreme care.

them. Thus, if you include two different views in an eight-person focus group, there should be four representatives of each. If you decide you want three views, schedule nine participants, with three representing each perspective.

The recruiting is the same as for a regular group, but with extra care paid to verifying that all the key variables are met by all the participants, in terms of both their differences and their similarities.

Moderation of friction groups is sure to be especially tough. The goal of a friction group is to understand people's values by seeing how they defend those values without becoming offended or angry. To create such a situation among a group of strangers needs to be done carefully and with a thorough understanding of the motivations and mental models of the participants.

Virtual Usability Tests

It's not necessary to watch people over their shoulder to get an idea of whether they can do a task or what problems they have with a product. The basic idea of a usability test is to gauge a users' success with a product while allowing them to step back and comment about their experience with it. In standard usability tests, this is done by a moderator who gives users tasks to do and asks them questions as they're using the site. This technique works for any kind of product, whether it's a piece of software or a toaster. Web sites, however, allow the easy creation of this kind of "cognitive distance" without having someone nearby. Since they're downloaded from a central server, it's possible to create a kind of "mental wrapper" around the site using frames or another window and provide the kinds of tasks and questions a moderator would ask in the lab. Furthermore, it's possible to automate this process so that the testing can be done not with 6 or 10 people, but with 60 or 100 (or 6000 or 10,000). These data can lead to compound usability metrics that are formed from a much broader base than traditional usability tests.

Virtual usability tests (sometimes called "remote usability tests" by companies such as Vividence and NetRaker who offer the service) are more than merely a usability test performed "virtually"; they're a cross between a survey, a usability test, and log analysis. In these systems, a separate frame (or dialog box) contains questions and tasks. As the people perform the tasks, the system automatically tracks their progress (like a log file) and presents questions about their experience at appropriate times (such as when they feel they've finished a task or if they give up on it). In addition, it measures the speed at which they do the tasks and their success rate with those tasks.

In the end, the data are automatically analyzed, and various metrics are computed based on the collected data. Vividence, for example, can compute the proportion of people completing a task compared to the first item they clicked. This can lead to a deeper understanding of the effectiveness of the site navigation. They also offer a clickstream map with successful and unsuccessful paths highlighted.

Although such a system can measure success rate and ask basic questions—the foundation blocks of usability testing—it lacks the flexibility and in-depth anecdotal data that a true usability test has. When analyzing usability testing videotapes, most analysis will do a lot more than just measure the success rate for tasks and note down people's comments. A good moderator will observe problems as they happen and probe into their causes, focusing the usability test on the subjects that matter the most to the participant and the product. The analyst will be able to use these probes to try to understand the participants' mental models and assumptions, which can lead to a more fundamental and wider-ranging understanding of the user's experience.

This makes such systems great for straightforward questions ("How do people fail when they try to log in?") but fails to address more complex issues ("Why are people looking for knives in the fork section?"). Answering the basic questions is important and can highlight a lot of issues, but only goes part of the way to understanding the reasons behind a site's interaction problems. Moreover, it's difficult to understand users' reasoning or build mental models based on their answers to multiple-choice questions and their task successes. Although these systems also offer the ability for open-ended questions, they can't be tuned to the specific user's experience, so the replies (much as with open-ended survey questions) tend to be negative rants and of marginal utility.

It's also possible to conduct usability tests using the same kind of telepresence technology that allows for virtual focus groups. Video-conferencing facilities coupled with remote computer control technologies such as Netopia's Timbuktu Pro *(www.netopia.com)* or WebEx's desktop conferencing products *(www.webex.com)* allow for the moderator and user to be in different parts of the world and still maintain the spontaneity and depth of a face-to-face usability test.

Eye Tracking

Although it seems like a pretty low-level way to look at experience, knowing where people are looking at a given point in time can reveal a number of higher-level phenomena. Human eyes have the property that only the fovea, the center, can resolve fine detail. This means that whenever we want to examine something, we need to look directly at it. For example, try reading something on your right while looking left: you can still see the thing you want to read, but you can't read it because your eyes just don't have enough resolution there. In addition, the amount of time that people's eyes spend on a given object is pretty much proportional to how much time they spend thinking about it. Using tracking equipment (such as that made by EyeTools, *www.eyetools.com*), it's possible to create a map of where someone looked and for how long, to a fine granularity. When this is mapped to what they were looking at (e.g., the Web pages they were looking at), it's possible to see what dominated their thought processes.

When eye tracking is used in a usability test, it can reveal how certain behaviors and mistakes are based on the visual emphasis and organization of interaction elements.

A basic analysis of eye-tracking information can be done visually. The patterns of use can be examined to see which parts of the interface inspired the most traffic. This provides immediate feedback about how people's attention is distributed among the interaction elements. Did the participants pay any attention to the ad banner on the left or to the navigation bar at the bottom? Understanding the reasons for differences in attention is tougher. Did people spend a long time looking at the navigation list because they were really interested in it or because they were confused by it and were trying to figure it out? Did they not look at the links on the left-hand side because they didn't see them or because they knew that section well and didn't need to look there? Eye tracking can't, in general, answer these questions and needs to be coupled with a technique that can.

The biggest problems with eye tracking are that the equipment to perform the technique is expensive and cumbersome, and any interpretation besides the most basic ("the person looked at this spot the most") requires trained operators and analysts, which adds to the expense. That said, it could well become a powerful tool as the technology becomes more affordable.

Parallel Research

Any research process is susceptible to some kind of bias, whether it's in the way that participants are recruited, how questions are asked, or how the results are analyzed. Ideally, the people running a research study can understand where the biases can occur and can compensate for them (or at least warn about them). However, it's impossible to avoid them entirely.

The people who run studies often introduce idiosyncrasies into the process, and it's difficult to know where these biases occur, especially for the people who are responsible for them. One way to expose research skew is to compare the results of several studies on the same topic. Different groups of people will implement techniques in slightly different ways. These differences are likely to skew the results in different directions since the groups are not likely to include all the same biases. When the results are compared, it may be possible to see where they diverge.

In some cases, it's possible to compare your results to other research (as discussed in Chapter 15). If you're collecting geographically organized demographic information, it's possible to compare it to data produced by the U.S. Census. This can be a quick and straightforward way to check your data, but it rarely gets at biases that are specific to your product or to the questions that are being answered.

The best way to see how your own research and product skews is to run your own parallel research studies. This doubles the cost of doing the research (and the amount of data that need analysis), but it can provide a valuable perspective.

A simple parallel research technique is to run two studies simultaneously in-house. Such studies are carried out by two (or more) teams who use a "clean room" approach to the research. The teams do the research entirely independently of each other, not discussing their methods or results, but working from the same set of general questions. Each team will likely use a different technique and will analyze the data in a different way. It's also possible to have each team analyze the other team's data, as well as their own, and compare the results afterward.

If there aren't resources to run two sets of research in-house, it's possible to run one set of research in-house and hire a consultant or specialist research firm to run another set of research. Or two firms can be hired and their results compared.

The technique requires having the resources for several completely independent research teams, which can become quite expensive. Moreover, although it increases the certainty of the results, and doubles the amount of anecdotal evidence and pithy stories, it does not double the quantity of findings.

A different use of parallel research attempts to find phenomena that apply to all (or most) users versus ones that are specific to a group or a task. Comparing the results of identical research with intentionally divergent groups of users or tasks can show what's common to most users versus the ones that appear in only a certain group's perspective or behavior.

Participatory Design

As much a philosophy as a set of techniques, *participatory design* was developed in the 1970s in Scandinavia as a means to democratize product design, and developed further in the 1980s as a complete design method (see the June 1993 special issue of *Communications of the ACM* for an in-depth examination of the topic).

At its core, it's an iterative design process that uses focus groups to outline needs, task analysis to distill those needs into specifications, and user advisory boards to maintain user input throughout the development process. Brainstorming, prioritization exercises, and frequent end-user review make up a big chunk of the rest.

IBM's Joint Application Design (JAD) and Edward Deming's Total Quality Management (TQM) are methods that extensively use participatory design ideas. A common element that appears throughout most of these methods is the day-long workshop. During the workshop, representatives of the various *stakeholders* in the product development (people who are directly affected by or affect the product), including users, develop a consensus about the vision for the product and its needs. This is usually done through a focus group style of meeting that features a number of needs analysis and prioritization exercises. After the issues have been outlined, task analysis is used to decompose these issues into specific problems. These are then used as the basis for a group-written solution specification, which is then given to the development staff to implement.

At regular times thereafter, the process is repeated with prototype solutions, and the focus shifted to other products and problems.

The technique is excellent at creating solid solutions to the functional needs of users. Its weaknesses are similar to those of advisory boards: the users who participate will come to think like the members of the development team after a while, no longer being able to think outside the constraints of the development process. Moreover, it's quite easy for the process to limit itself to views expressed by user representatives, who are often not representative of the user population as a whole. And the techniques provide little guidance for determining the product's identity and financial responsibility. A participatory design panel with a narrow vision can easily miss the key elements that can make a product popular or profitable.

Combining

By themselves, all the techniques described in this book are useful and informative, but they can be even more powerful when used together, when the output of one becomes the input of another. Using multiple techniques to understand the answer to a question allows you to triangulate on a problem from different perspectives or delve deeper into issues.

Focus Groups and Diaries

One of the most useful ways to use diaries is in a hybrid with a series of linked focus groups or interviews. The diaries serve as the trigger for discussion, and they maintain context in between the focus groups.

For example, a group of users was recruited for a series of four focus groups over the course of three months to study a search engine. The goal of the focus groups was to understand the issues that experienced search engine users would face as they learned to use the search engine. At the time many of the product's users were "defectors" from other search services that they had used for a long time. The company was interested in attracting more such users, but it was important to know what kinds of issues they experienced in order to be able to maximize the value of their experience and increase their retention (search engines were considered to be a commodity by most users, and when one failed just once, the user was likely to abandon it immediately for another one).

During the first meeting the group was introduced to the concept of the research. The object of the focus group was to understand the problems that the users experienced with their current search engine choices and to uncover what they valued in search services in general (since this would be tracked throughout the study). They were then instructed on the diary system being used (a relatively unstructured format that would be emailed to them twice a week) and asked to keep diaries in between the meetings.

A month later, the second meeting convened. Throughout the process, the research team kept track of the surveys and the issues that appeared. Discussion of these made up the bulk of the second focus group. The participants clarified their thoughts and shared greater detail about their experiences in the previous month.

The third focus group, a month later, was designed to concentrate on the ongoing learning that had happened. Reading the second month's diaries, the researchers saw how the search engine was used and got an idea of what the participants had learned. The meeting focused on clarifying these issues and understanding the mental models the people had built about how the service worked and what they could expect from it. The desirability of proposed features was probed and other search services were compared.

Between the third and fourth meeting, the diary frequency dropped to once per month, and the diary forms became more usability-testlike in order to expose the participants to specific features. The fourth focus group concentrated on summarizing the participants' experiences with the various features of the service and introducing mock-ups of several feature prototypes that were specifically designed to address issues that had been discussed in the previous focus groups.

The back-and-forth play between the focus groups and the diaries gave the developers a richer understanding of the issues faced by a transitional user experienced with other systems.

It's similarly possible to combine diaries with interviews. Using the knowledge of people's experiences to structure follow-up interviews can target the topics of the interviews better than just using a standard script.

Observational Interviews and Usability Tests

Traditional usability testing is almost exclusively task based. The process is driven by the desire to have people perform tasks and then to use their performance on those tasks as the basis for understanding interaction and architecture problems with the product. This works fine, but underutilizes the potential of interviewing an actual (or potential) user of your product. These are people who can tell you more about their experience than just whether they have trouble saving their preferences. What attracts them? How well do they understand the product's purpose? Which features appear useful to them? Why?

Combining usability testing with in-depth attitudinal questions such as those that could be found in a contextual inquiry process or an observational interview can create a richer set of data to analyze. The description of a *hybrid interview* in Chapter 10 is one kind of such interview. In that process, the participants are asked for their impressions of the site as a whole before they are asked to use it. By allowing for a subjective, impressionistic component, it's possible to uncover more than just what people can't use and what they can't understand; it's possible to understand what attracts them and what their values are. Motivation can be a powerful force in user experience. Desirability and affinity are linked to motivation. A technique that allows the researcher to simultaneously understand what is comprehensible, functional, desirable, and attractive can uncover why a product "works" for the audience, or why it doesn't.

For example, an online furniture site was interested in how their prototype would be accepted by potential customers. Time was of the essence, and little other user research had been done. Since the prototype was already in development, it was too late to research the target audience's needs and desires in detail. A group of potential customers had already been invited to usability-test the prototype. This created an opportunity to do some research about people's desires, experiences, and expectations before they were exposed to the ideas or implementation of the product. The participants were recruited without revealing the product or the research criteria, and the research was held in an anonymous rented office space.

The first half hour of every 90-minute session was devoted to a series of general interview questions. All participants were asked to discuss their experience buying furniture, the difficulties they encountered, and the criteria they used in choosing a furniture retailer and furniture. This interview, though brief, provided a perspective on the customers and the product that had not been seen before and instituted profound changes in the positioning of the product (though it didn't prevent the eventual failure of the company).

Unfortunately, the process of asking people to examine and vocalize what attracts them can bias their use of the product. They may concentrate more on the interface and notice aspects of the product that they would otherwise pass over. This can lead to a skewing of the results: what was initially confusing could become understandable, or what was attractive at first blush may become overdone with extended exposure. Thus, combining usability testing and interviews does not replace rigorous usability testing, but it adds a valuable element when time and resources are short and when rapid, deep (if not as accurate) research is needed.

Surveys and Focus Groups

The classic marketing research mix is an interrelated series of surveys and focus groups. Surveys answer the "what" questions about your audience, whereas focus groups answer the "why." By interleaving them, it's possible to use one technique to answer questions posed by the other.

Surveys reveal patterns in people's behaviors. The causes for these behaviors are then investigated with focus groups, which in turn suggest other trends to be verified with surveys. It's a circular pattern that alternately flushes out interesting behaviors and attempts to explain them.

- First, a general demographic/technographic/webographic survey is fielded to provide the basic audience profile.
- Focus groups then recruit people based on this profile. The focus groups research their general values and their experiences relative to the problems the product is supposed to solve.
- The focus groups bring up questions about functionality and competition, which are then investigated by another round of surveys.
- And so on.

This is a tried-and-true technique, and it has been used for many years to create the products and advertising that you're familiar with. Companies like Clorox have a never-ending cycle of surveys and focus groups, each folding into the next, with the results then applied to the products. The downside of these techniques is that they reveal little about people's abilities or actual needs. Marketing and consumer product development is often more about perceived needs than real needs, which is what these techniques are best at uncovering. But people's views of themselves are not necessarily accurate and need to be tempered with a more objective understanding of their actual state. Thus, the output of this type of research needs to be seen as a valuable component to understanding people's motivations and desires, but it should be coupled with ability- and need-assessment techniques, such as usability tests and contextual inquiry.

Log Files and Usability Tests

Usage data analysis can be one of the best pointers toward interaction problems, which can then be examined and analyzed with usability testing. Log files provide a direct means of understanding how people behave. It's possible to use them to reveal where there are certain unexpected behaviors. For example, a task requires submitting information to a script that produces an error page if the information does not fit the required format. If a large proportion of users are shown the error page, it implies that the task is not defined clearly, the options are not presented well, or the users are misunderstanding the process. Log files by themselves may not uncover the prevalence of these three situations in the users' interaction with the product, or complex analysis may be required in order to extract any relation-ship. Instead, a usability test that concentrates solely on that single feature may quickly reveal the comprehension/interaction issues.

Likewise, it may be possible to examine log files based on in-formation collected in usability testing. A hypothesis about how people behave can be formed by observing them using an inter-face, and then tested by analyzing log files to see if people actually seem to behave that way "in real life."

Both techniques help you understand the low-level interaction that people have with an interface. Usability testing is the less ob-jective, more explanatory technique, whereas log analysis is objective and descriptive, but can provide little information about ability, un-derstanding, or motivation. They complement each other well.

Task Analysis and Usability Tests

Task analysis is the process of decomposing how a task is done. Us-ability testing reveals how someone actually performs a task. Thus, a task analysis can serve as the "ideal" model that is verified by us-ability testing. Likewise, the format and goal of usability testing can be based in the model defined by task analysis.

For example, task analysis revealed that in auto repair shop se-lection, the lists of possible shops were determined by momentum ("we've always taken all our cars there"), location ("it's near my of-fice"), authority ("I always take it to a Ford dealership"), or recom-mendation ("the insurance company recommended it"). Choices were few: people would have one, maybe two candidates, and they would choose the one that was generally considered first. More-over, once people chose a shop, they stuck with it even if problems arose. A literal implementation of this in a claim management site initially presented these four options in a repair shop selection mod-ule. However, even though these were the criteria by which people chose repair shops, they did not think of it in those terms. Usabil-ity testing revealed that presenting these as options confused the participants. They understood the system as something more of an authority than they were, so they preferred to always let it recom-mend a shop.

These kinds of effects are difficult to predict when decompos-ing a task into its components, but they're critical to the functionality of the product. These effects can be investigated with talk-aloud usability tests of prototypes, and existing products can quickly zero in on the most prominent issues affecting people's ability to complete a task and so can verify the accuracy of the task analysis in general.

Ultimately, each of these techniques is really just a starting point. They're all different ways of observing and interpreting many of the same phenomena. By using these techniques and changing them, you get a better perspective on the goals and needs of your research and the strengths and limitations of the techniques. When you know what you want to find out and you know how the methods work, you can tune your research so it gets at exactly the information you need.

PART III
Communicating Results

CHAPTER 17

Reports and Presentations

Results are the product of research, and like any product, they need to be useful to their audience in order to be successful. A good report of results should consist of more than just a list of a product's problems; it should enable the development team to make changes to the product and educate to avoid similar problems in the future. Structuring the presentation of results—in effect, *engineering* their delivery—is one of the most important steps to making research useful since the best research is useless if it's misunderstood or ignored.

The audience's needs determine the best way to present a given piece of research. It could be a simple email message or an elaborate 100-page thesis. It could be a phone call or a day-long presentation with highlight videos. It could be a bug database. Fortunately, regardless of the complexity of the final product, the process is the same. Whether it's a song-and-dance number or a short chat, the steps to make it are pretty much identical; what varies is how long each step takes.

Because written reports and in-person presentations are the two most prevalent methods of reporting results, this chapter will primarily focus on them. Most of the ideas here can apply to any delivery medium. Moreover, much of the advice in this chapter is not unique to user experience research; it's true about nearly any business-oriented presentation.

Preparation

Preparing a report is different from analyzing the data. The content of the report should be mostly done by the time the report writing begins (as described for surveys in Chapter 11). The report is the presentation of that information, a structured experience of the knowledge, and depends on the completed content. Thus, before the report and presentation writing begins, the audience and the data analysis process need to be understood.

Know Your Audience

An audience profile helps define what words to use, what level of detail is appropriate, and the order in which conclusions should be presented. This doesn't have to be a formal profiling process, but establishing several things about the audience really helps focus the writing of the report. Here are several questions to ask.

- *Who is getting the report?* The composition of the report's audience can change the emphasis of the content. CEOs will certainly need a shorter and more high-level report than the QA team. A large group of nontechnical people will need a different set of information from a small group of programmers. In certain cases, even the needs of specific individuals in the audience should be considered. If the vice president of production is driven by specifics and wants lists of quick fixes for her product, she's going to expect that. However, if usability testing shows that the product had systemic problems that needed more than just a list of repairs, the report should be prepared to satisfy both needs. For example, each quick fix can be introduced as a symptom of larger systemic problems, thus both the vice president's preference and the larger issues can be addressed.
- *What are their goals?* How are they going to use the information? Sometimes all that's required is an explanation of existing problems and a set of development targets. In other cases, the audience may need justification to argue for certain changes. Still others need an external perspective to evaluate how well *they* understand their users.

- *What do they know?* What's the level of technical sophistication in the group? This applies not just to the technology under consideration—though that should be taken into account, too—but the methods you are employing. If they've never been involved in user experience research, they may need more explanation of the reasoning behind your methods. If the presentation is to marketing research, the audience will likely not need to be told the difference between a focus group and an interview, but if they're engineers or designers, they may need an explanation.
- *What do they need to know?* Why are they getting this report? How is it going to make their jobs easier? The research project has a series of goals, which are based on a list of needs. Meeting those goals is the primary purpose of the report, but there may also be other information that should be communicated. During the process of conducting the research, the project's focus may have shifted, or a secondary class of information may have been revealed. These may need to be communicated. For example, when doing a contextual inquiry series for a kid's Web development site, it became apparent that the parents' level of technical sophistication wasn't much greater than the kids'. This insight was outside the goals of the original research (which was only to research the usage patterns and needs of kids), but it was very valuable to know.
- *What are they expecting?* Anticipating the audience's reactions to the information in a report helps you structure an effective presentation. The report should be written with an understanding of the audience's expectation of its contents. If the conclusions of the report go completely against the current belief of the development staff, then the report will likely need to contain a more thorough explanation and justification for the conclusions. Likewise, if many of the findings are in line with the staff's understanding of the issue, then the report may place greater emphasis on the aspects that differ from the common understanding.

If the restrictions on your audience are too constraining—you have to deliver information to nontechnical executives *and* the core programming staff, for example—it may be necessary to break up the audience. Presenting different aspects of the same information as different presentations may be preferable to everyone involved: the audience won't feel either lost or patronized, and the presenters will have to field fewer questions.

Know Your Process

There are limitations to even the most carefully conducted research. When considering how to present findings, keep these in mind. Acknowledging the limitations in the process helps the audience understand the results, believe in them, and act on the recommendations. The questions to ask about the process are the same that should be asked of any research.

- *What are the data collection problems?* The limitations and potential distortions in the data collection method should be acknowledged. Actual data collection problems should be mentioned in the report ("We were only able to speak to one of the two user audiences"), but potential problems with the method should be considered during its preparation ("We chose to focus on one user group because we believe that, given our limited resources, they will give us the best feedback"). If a member of the audience points out a potential flaw, it should have been anticipated and addressable.
- *What are the limitations of the analysis?* There are many ways to analyze a given set of data, and only a subset of them will have been used in your analysis. A videotape of a user test can be analyzed by watching it once and taking notes, or by doing a frame-by-frame analysis of every single utterance, keystroke, and mouse click. The strengths and limitations of the chosen analysis method should be known and acknowledged. So, for example, although tabulating survey results is fast and easy, it may not reveal as much as cross-tabulating the results of several of the variables, but that's a trickier procedure and requires more responses. Likewise, a focus group can tell you

what people want, but not whether they need it or would be able to use it if it was given to them.

Understanding the biases in all facets of the research process helps when trying to explain it. The recruiting process, the participants' perspective, the research conditions, the analyst's experience—each can subtly skew the information collection process. Preparing for these biases and knowing about them helps minimize them and lets the truth of the situation shine through.

The Report

The written report is the primary deliverable of most user experience research. Its structure is the basis for how the presentation will flow and what other material, such as video, is necessary.

Pick a Format and Organize

Before the report is written, the report format should be discussed with its audience. When time is pressing, it's often fine to deliver the report in email. Other situations, such as a presentation to an executive board, may require a more formal paper report with illustrations and a fancy cover. Still others may be best served by HTML reports where observations are linked directly to problem areas. Show a sample report to its intended recipient and see if the format meets his or her needs.

Once a general format has been decided upon, arrange the findings in the most effective way for the audience. Secondary findings are clustered with primary results and ordered to support "big" ideas. Your results can be prioritized according to the three classic priority levels. "Nice-to-know" information is included only in the most complete version of the report, "should know" is in the general report, while "must know" is the kind of stuff that's put in email to the project lead when time is critical. Once prioritized, quotations are pulled from transcripts to support or elaborate on the findings.

Newspaper Style

Regardless of the format, all reports should be structured like newspaper stories. They're written with the assumption that some people will only have time to read the first couple of paragraphs, some will read a page or two, some will skim the whole thing, and some will closely read every word. Each of these audiences needs to be satisfied by the report's contents.

In classic newspaper style, the first sentence tells the most important fact ("The stock market rose dramatically today in spite of signs of weak consumer confidence," for example). The first paragraph tells the basic facts, the next couple of paragraphs elaborate on several key elements mentioned in the first paragraph, and the rest of the story provides background, finishing with a historical summary of the story.

Thus, when writing a report, *never* "save the best for last." Save the least important for last.

Example Report: A Usability Test for an Online Greeting Card Company

Executive Summary

Six Webcard users with a range of experience were invited to look at the existing Webcard interface and a prototype of the Gift Bucks interface. In general, people found Webcard to be easy to navigate and to contain many desirable features. The Gift Bucks interface was quickly understood, and the feature was exciting to most of the participants. Most of the problems with the site had to do with feature emphasis and information organization rather than navigation or functionality.

In this case, the most important observation is that the site interaction was basically good. People could use it and found the features interesting. It's followed by a short summary of the problem findings. If someone reads only this paragraph, he or she will have an idea of the most important discovery. This is followed by a short, clear explanation of each of the general problems. Since the goal of the project was to uncover deficiencies in the interaction, rather than the reasons people like it, the problems with the product are elaborated.

- **People had little interest in finding specific cards.** They were interested in categories and were willing to change their mind to accept what was available. Even when they could not find a specific card, they still had a good browsing experience. This is good. Although the participants consistently failed to find specific cards because of the organization of the categories, they had little trouble navigating between the categories themselves. Specific card location was further hampered by the search interface, which was difficult to understand and was not a full-text search, as all the participants had expected.
- **Several desirable front door elements were ignored** because people's attention was not drawn to them.
- **Most people didn't know what My Webcard was,** or what benefits it held for them, even though they expressed interest in some of the benefits when presented individually.
- **The Gift Bucks interface was quickly understood** and seen as straightforward although people wanted more information about the process. They often didn't see the links that would have led them to some of that information.

Desirable additional features included the ability to synchronize Microsoft Outlook with the Webcard address book, the ability to enter arbitrary Gift Buck amounts, and more options to organize cards.

The executive summary tells the whole story in broad strokes. The next section sets expectations and provides the necessary background to understand the subsequent observations. If the audience is well versed in the technique, it may only be necessary to sketch it out in a couple of short sentences. This audience had not been exposed to the technique, so a more thorough description was appropriate.

Procedure

We invited six people with electronic greeting card experience to evaluate the Webcard interface and comment on a prototype of Gift Bucks. They were selected from Webcard's user lists based on their recent usage of the site (they had to have used it in the past month), their online shopping activity (they had to have bought a present in the last two months), and their availability to come into the Webcard offices during working hours on January 20 and 21.

Each 90-minute interview began with a series of questions about the evaluators' Web usage, their experiences with online shopping, and their experiences with online greeting services. The moderator then showed them the current Webcard site and asked for their immediate impressions as they moved through it. After looking at it for a few minutes, the moderator asked them to search for an Easter greeting card for a friend. After several minutes of searching, the moderator asked them to return to the main page and go through the interface thoroughly, discussing every element on the front door and most of the catalog and personalization page elements. Their next task was to find a card with a picture of San Francisco. After spending several minutes on this task, they were shown a prototype of the card personalization interface with Gift Bucks attached and asked to discuss the new interface elements found therein.

The moderator concluded the interviews with an exercise to help the evaluators summarize their views of the product and brainstorm on additional features.

Throughout the process, they were asked to narrate thoughts aloud and were occasionally prompted to elaborate on specific actions or comments. In addition, they were prompted to discuss feature desirability and additional functionality when appropriate.

All the interviews were videotaped. The tapes were examined in detail for trends in participants' behaviors, beliefs, and statements. Partial transcripts were made of interesting or illustrative quotations. The observations were then organized and grouped. These groups provided the material from which more general trends were distilled.

This type of explanation may be useful in any case since the specifics may vary from one project to another, but it'll be most useful when the report audience needs to understand how the results were obtained.

Next, a weakness in the process was called out.

Evaluator Profiles

NOTE: Because of the short recruitment time and the requirements for a weekday downtown San Francisco visit, the evaluator pool is biased toward professionals working in downtown businesses, with several in ecommerce-related positions.

Describing participants isn't critical, but it's effective for reinforcing the reality of the research to people who did not observe it and provides context for interpreting their statements. Although everyone knows that real people were interviewed, details of the interviews bring home the participants' perspectives, their differences, and—most important—the realness of their existence. At least there should be a table summarizing how the participants fit the recruiting profile, or there can be a more extensive description.

Leah

Works in the marketing department of an ecommerce art site. Spends 10 or more hours on the Web per week, half of which is for personal surfing. Spends most of her online time investing, shopping, and finding out about events. Buys something online once a month, more often during holidays. Has bought wine, books, CDs, "health and beauty aids," about half of which are gifts (especially the wine). Doesn't often buy gift certificates. Likes electronic cards because they're spontaneous, they're good for casual occasions, and you can send one to a number of people at the same time. Would have balked at sending sympathy cards

(Continued)

electronically, but recently got one that changed her mind. Sends electronic cards more based on the recipient than the sentiment: some people aren't online or (she feels) wouldn't have a positive reaction to electronic cards. Has only used Webcard and sends at least one card a month.

Etc.

Once the context has been established, the results are presented as directly and succinctly as possible, avoiding jargon.

The first two entries in this report describe user behavior that affects the product on a deep level and across a number of features. When the data support it, it's appropriate to generalize underlying causes, but overgeneralization or unsupported conclusions should be avoided.

Warning To protect your participants' privacy and confidentiality, be extremely careful when revealing any personal information—especially names—in a report. When recruiting people from the general public who will likely never participate in research about this product again, it's usually OK to use their first names in the report. However, when reporting on people who are in-house (or who are friends and family of people in-house), it's often safest to remove all identifying information. Rename participants as "U1," "U2," and so forth.

Likewise, be wary when creating highlight tapes with people who may be known to the viewers. If someone is likely to be recognized, they should generally not be shown, and a transcript of their comments should be used instead.

Observations

NOTE: These observations were made based on a videotape review of the interviews. They are organized by topic and importance. Severity should not be inferred by the length of the entries; some things just take more words to explain than others.

General

1. People don't appear to look for specific cards or show any attachment to specific cards. They browse for cards in a category and either find something that adequately matches what they're looking for or change their strategy and look for something else. Their criteria are loose and often defined by what they're not looking for. When initial directed attempts fail, the evaluators start looking at all the cards in a given category to see what grabs them. When nothing fulfills their basic level of acceptability, they tend to adjust their expectations until something does. There seems to be some amount of acceptance for sending somewhat inappropriate cards, as long as they're "close."

"If I wanted to do a greeting and thought 'wouldn't that be cool if it was a San Francisco greeting?' and I didn't find it, I'd come up with some other idea."

"I usually don't go past page 1. I don't want to spend a lot of time looking. I find something I like, click on it, send it, I'm done."

"If I didn't find what I was looking for, I'd probably change my mind about what I wanted to send her."

2. The participants spent no more than ten minutes looking for a card, averaging about five minutes per search. During that time, most change their strategy repeatedly to accommodate their desires based on the available inventory.

Note Attaching severity ratings to observations ("1 means it's a showstopper, 2 means that it greatly impacts the user experience, etc.") is common practice, but I prefer to let the audience decide the importance of observations. What may be a blip in the user experience may have deep impact for the product and company. People scrolling a banner ad off the top of the page is a minor event in their experience of the product, but not if the ad represents the entire revenue stream for the product and raising clicks on it by 0.5% represents a 20% increase in revenue. It's possible that only people intimately familiar with the company's business model will appreciate the importance of observing that users behave this way and presumptuous that an outside consultant will know otherwise.

It's appropriate to describe the severity of problems, but don't equate severity with priority. Some problems may be quite severe but may play only a small role in the user experience if they're used infrequently. This should be taken into account when describing a problem.

3. No one found the search page in under a minute, by which point most would have given up looking for it. When asked whether there was a search feature, several people said that there wasn't one. When pressed, everyone scanned the entire interface looking for it, examining every element until they found it. Additionally, despite the participants' extensive Webcard experience, no one appeared to have ever used it. However, as described in 1, none of the participants expressed much interest in finding specific cards, and all were happy simply browsing through the categories.

"If there is a search page, I don't know where it is."

"If there was a search box, that's how I would find that card."

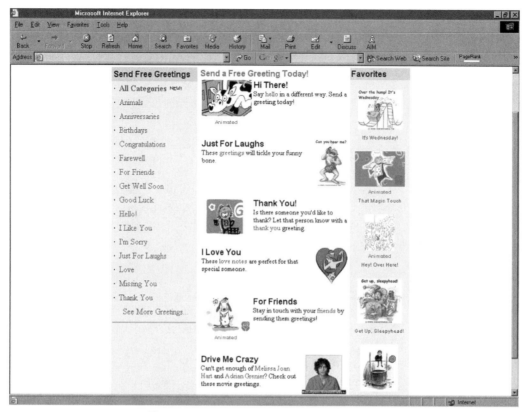

Figure 17.1 The Webcard homepage.

For the following observation, there are some obvious solutions that can be recommended. However, the decision of whether to suggest solutions alongside problems depends on the composition of the audience and the expertise of the analyst. This report's audience are the product's interaction designers and production staff, who know more about the task domain and the design constraints than I do. Since they're responsible for creating appropriate solutions, I chose to thoroughly describe problems and provide recommendations when appropriate, but let the design staff create appropriate solutions.

4. Three of the evaluators said that some of the smaller text was too small. Specifically, the text in the expanded subcategories in the catalog page and the informational links on the Gift Bucks pages were said to be too small (and, in the case of the links on the Gift Bucks, often ignored when looking for assistance).

5. Several of the people did not find the "home" link at the top of the page when asked to "go to the front door of the site" and preferred to navigate using the back arrows on their browser.

6. When asked to "go to the front door of the site" without using the back button, more people chose to click on the "home" link rather than the logo to go to the homepage.

Sometimes it's as important to note what expected events do not occur as it is to note unexpected ones that do.

7. Most of the left-hand side of the front door was ignored. After looking at the features in the top left-hand corner, most evaluators' attention quickly focused on the main menu, causing the features along the left-hand margin to go unread, even if they had been noticed in the initial scan of the page. The lower on the page the features were located, the less they were noticed, with the items near the bottom—"Make your own Valentine," "Sound Cards," and "What's new"—universally unnoticed and unread.

    "This is probably some of the most interesting stuff, but I didn't see it." [links at the bottom of the left-hand side]

    "This is a great a idea and it's lost!" [Make your own Valentine]

Once all the observations have been made, the report should wrap up with a conclusion and useful background information. The conclusion is a good place to discuss the larger issues raised by the research and to recommend broad-based solutions. It should help the audience pull back from the details and understand the product and research process as a whole.

Conclusion

The Webcard service is considered useful and generally well done by its audience. Although people's inability to find specific cards was ameliorated by their light attachment to any given card, this does not eliminate the problems with the search functionality and the information structure. As people's performance in the task to find a San Francisco–themed card shows, whole sections of the site are inaccessible because of an information structure that doesn't match people's expectations. We recommend using card sorting and observational methods to research users' expectations and "natural" organizational schemes and simplifying the search process by using a full-text search interface and carefully chosen keywords.

The Bonus Bucks addition was easy to use, but the actual functionality received a lukewarm response. We hypothesize that the denominations offered are too high. To the users, a Webcard is a quick, free way to express a lightly felt sentiment. A $25 or $50 gift is not seen in the same light and would likely not occur to most users. In fact, the larger denominations may put people off entirely. We recommend reducing the Bonus Bucks denominations to $10 maximum.

Etc.

Any additional information should be included in support of the main points. It's tempting to include every scrap of information that you've collected just in case it'll be of use to the readers, but don't inundate the audience with information.

Interesting Quotations
(full transcripts available upon request)

Leah
"I would have said that I would not have sent a sympathy message [with Webcard], but recently someone sent something to me and it was a beautiful greeting, so now I'm more open to that."

"It's not occasion based, it's more recipient based. There are people who are really open to electronic communication, and other people who are not."

"I already have a place I buy CDs online, I already have a place I buy books online. I don't need another place to buy those. If I was going to buy a gift on Webcard, I would want it to be something else that I might not already have a place to buy online."

Etc.

Once the report has been written, it should be tested. Like any product, it needs to be checked to see if it fulfills the needs of its audience. Maybe the development staff wants screen shots with problem areas explicitly marked. Maybe they would like the problems broken out by department or by user market. Sounding out the audience before the report is complete can verify that it's useful to them.

A couple of people from the report's audience should be shown a "beta" version of the report. A 10–15 minute interview after they've had a day or two to look at the report reveals a lot about how well it addresses the audience's needs. Does it cover the topics that they had expected? Does it prioritize the results appropriately? Do they expect other staff members to have any issues with it?

The Presentation

The way results are presented is nearly as important as the report that summarizes them, maybe more important. The complexity of a product's user experience is often difficult to understand from a description, and functionality details are often easier to explain with a careful demonstration than with a text description.

But presentations are more than just readings of the report. Creating and delivering effective presentations is an art to which this book can do little justice. From high school speech classes to motivational executive speeches, there is a lot of presentation advice in the world. That said, there are a couple of points that are particularly appropriate to user research presentations.

- *Prepare your audience.* Before talking about specifics, the audience should be put into a mind-set that helps them understand the information they're about to get. Apart from giving a quick summary of the procedure, I usually give a variation of the following speech: "The results of this user research will not make your product problem-free and universally loved. They are issues that we observed while talking to people and watching them use your product. By fixing these problems, you will be making an incremental change that we believe will make your product more in tune with the needs and abilities of your audience. But that doesn't change the fundamental nature of the product or the business model that it rests upon. If it's something that people don't want, then they won't want it no matter how likable or easy to use it is."
- *Pick your points carefully.* Carefully choose the observations you're going to highlight. For an hour-long presentation, one or two major themes backed up with five to ten important points and another five or so secondary points is a lot of information for most audiences and gives little time for digressions or questions. This means that generally only the "must know" topics get covered.
- *Use real examples.* Seeing a problem "live" is much more effective than having it described. The closer the audience gets to seeing the exact behavior or attitude, the better. A videotape of several groups of people saying the same thing or

people making the same mistake over and over is much more effective than a description. When that's not possible, a quick demo of the problem using the actual product is also pretty effective. If that's not possible, then a description using actual participant names and quotations might be used. For example, "Jim spent three minutes examining the front door before he gave up and said that there must not be a search interface. When it was pointed out to him, he spent another minute apologizing for being 'so stupid' despite the moderator's statements that it wasn't his fault." Any such description or demonstration, however, should not last more than a minute or two.

- *Emphasize the user market's perspective.* Whenever people start creating solutions, or even when they try to understand the nature of problems, they naturally begin with their own perspective. Since this is almost never the same perspective as the users', this can lead to erroneous or distorted conclusions by the development team. When results are presented, they should be presented with a strong emphasis on the user perspective. There should be a thematic thread throughout the presentation underscoring the differences between the users' ideas and the ideas of the development team.

- *Use terminology sparingly, and only after defining it.* When people hear a lot of words they don't understand, they feel either out of touch or condescended to (or both). Sometimes, however, it's useful for the audience to know a term for a technical concept because it's important in understanding the report. A single sentence defining *information architecture* as "the discipline of categorizing and organizing information in a way that makes sense to a given audience" can make its use much more palatable. In addition, know the audience's terminology, and highlight differences between their definition and that used in the report. A group of radio editors, for example, considered the word *headline* to refer only to the title of an important breaking news story, whereas the designers used it to refer to a text presentation style. There was a lot of confusion about the implications of the experience research before the terminology difference was discovered.

- *Use numbers carefully.* Humans tend to see numbers as objective and absolute, even when it's explained that they're not. Numbers, histograms, and pie charts look good in presentations, but unless they're backed by hard data, try to avoid them. Otherwise, the audience may fixate on the numbers as an exact measurement rather than as a presentation of ideas.
- *Leave a third of your time for questions.* If a presentation ends early and there are no questions, no one will complain, but if an audience has questions and no time is left for discussion, they are likely to be upset. Anticipating what an audience is going to ask and producing "canned" answers can be quite beneficial.
- *Always practice.* Do the whole thing from beginning to end by yourself at least once, and at least once in front of someone else.

Presenting to Specific Groups

Different audiences require different approaches when presented information. The exact needs of each audience are going to be unique, but there are some generalizations that can be made about certain specific groups.

Engineers

The software engineer's traditional role is as a problem solver. The waterfall development process is completely geared to this, and it's difficult to think about development otherwise. Engineering time spent investigating the underlying causes of problems is seen as more wasteful than time spent creating solutions to ameliorate them. In most cases, problems are assumed to have been understood in the specification stage and need no further research by the time they reach engineering. This perspective creates an engineering culture that's almost entirely focused on solutions, not problems.

When presenting to engineers, this solution-focused perspective should be expected. It's important to prepare the group with instructions on how to understand and interpret the results. Early on in the presentation, I usually say something like, "This is not a laundry list of fixes that should be addressed and forgotten, it's a group of symptoms that point to underlying problems. Sometimes you can cure the problems by treating the symptoms, but often you need to understand the root cause in order to effectively treat the problem." This is intended to get the audience thinking about the larger context of the product's problems rather than sketching code in the report margins.

The "larger context" philosophy can be taken too far, however, and can cause people to conclude that making any change is futile unless the whole product is revamped from scratch (which, in most cases, will never happen). Explanations of wide contextual issues should be balanced with short-term changes that can immediately improve the user experience.

Engineering is a fairly scientific discipline, and engineers are often better versed in the procedures and philosophies of the natural sciences than the social sciences. Thus, they are often dubious of the nonstatistical methods used in much user experience research. Explaining the procedures and why they are valid can anticipate and address many engineers' reservations. Likewise, it's useful to focus on facts rather than introduce hypotheses or opinions since concrete facts will tend to carry more weight with the audience.

Be especially careful about presenting suggestions that have already been discussed and discarded by the engineers, unless your recommendations are derived from a drastically different way of examining the problem. For example, an interface development group discarded creating a portion of an interface using Macromedia Flash because they felt that their users' computers and network connections would be too slow even though it would have provided for an easier development environment and a more elegant experience solution. A survey of the site's audience showed that the vast majority of their primary user base had high-speed network connections and late-model computers. They would likely have the technical capabilities to use Flash, but since the engineering group had already discarded Flash as a solution, its reintroduction required an additional explanation of why it would work.

Engineers also tend to want to solve the problem for all possible cases, which tends to encompass all possible users and uses. "What about users with text-only browsers?" is often heard as a typical example of this perspective. Of course they're right, and it *is* bad to intentionally cut out any portion of the user population, but the constraints imposed by attempting to satisfy all possible audiences usually require expending more resources than the rewards of catering to those audiences. Telling the engineering audience the reasoning behind the user profile and that user research is merely a prioritization of needs, not a complete list, can help them accept it as a subset of "all possible users."

Visual Designers

Designers tend to fall asleep as soon as you show them a task analysis, so I try to keep them awake at all costs.
—Victoria Bellotti, senior scientist at Xerox PARC (personal email)

Even though visual designers would seem to be of the opposite temperament to engineers, their perspectives overlap in one important aspect. The designers' role has also traditionally been defined as a problem solver. They create solutions to a different class of problems than engineers, but based on specifications nonetheless. They're likely to sketch in the margins, too, but they'll be scribbling identity and interface elements rather than object hierarchies.

Note If e. e. cummings and William S. Burroughs are brought up as counterexamples, point out that the purposes of their art were different from that which most Web sites are designed for. In this literary analogy, most Web sites are more like the Sharper Image catalog than *Naked Lunch*.

In addition to being solution oriented, many visual designers have moved into interaction from identity design (often from print). The problems facing identity designers more often involve creating a strong initial impact and communicating a single message rather than the sustained series of interrelated messages that software design often requires. Friction can arise because good design of the latter does not imply good design of the former. Preparing an audience of designers may require first explaining and emphasizing the distinction between the identity of a product and its functionality. I sometimes use a writing analogy: the style of the writing and its grammatical correctness are not at odds with each other. Grammar is the functionality of a document, whereas style is its identity. Spell-checking a document does not affect meaning, and user research is like spell checking.

Once this distinction has been established, designers often need to be reassured of their role as problem solvers in this interactive domain. One of the most painful things for a designer (or any other solution-oriented profession) is to work by committee. When created by a group, a solution often ends up with the lowest common denominator, the least elegant option. User experience research does not replace—and should not imply that it is going to replace—any of the designers' problem-solving creativity or their visual authority. Research is not a method of creating solutions, but a method of prioritizing problems. I sometimes say, "It's likely that none of the problems you see here are new to you. What this process does is help prioritize problems before you start solving them. Even if nine of ten users say they hate the bright green background color and love earthtones, that does not mean that you need to make the interface brown. What matters is that users pay attention to color, not their choice of colors."

Designers, in general, are not as concerned about the scientific validity of research as much as its face validity (it feels correct) and consistency. Thus observations and recommendations should immediately make sense and fit into the general model under which a site is being designed.

Whenever possible, use visuals and interactivity to support your observations. Ideally, the designers would actually observe some of the research in real life. Video highlights and live demonstrations of phenomena are also effective, as are screen shots. Jeff Veen, a user experience researcher and designer, prefers to create a workshop environment in the presentation, instead of a lecture. As Jeff says, "It's hard to sit in a conference room and write code, but you can sit in a conference room and move things around." Problems can be examined, and rough functionality can be mocked up quickly. It's possible to iterate quickly based on the results of the research, giving designers concrete things to work on while presenting the results of the research.

Marketing

The practice of marketing is focused on understanding desire. Marketing involves satisfying a target audience's desires by letting them acquire or use a product or service.

The tools used by marketing researchers are often quantitative and comparative. Surveys are used to create lists of competitors and competitive attributes. Since user experience research often focuses on the reasons behind choices, rather than just the choices themselves, it can inform marketing researchers trying to understand the data they've gathered. Marketing communications staff can find the information useful in crafting the image of the product they want to present.

Thus, when user research results are presented to a group of marketers, they should be focused on the reasons behind people's choices. Why are they attracted to the product? What drives them away? What keeps them coming back? What can drive them away forever? User experience research presents a cohesive, consistent mental model that helps explain users' existing behavior and expectations while helping to predict future behavior and uncovering barriers that prevent them from purchasing the product (or joining the service, or whatever is important to the short-term business success of the product). A summary of the mental model should probably be the most important point you make in the presentation.

Upper Management

As an audience, management's perspectives can be greatly varied. Some managers are concerned only with the long-term, large-scale issues that affect their companies and products. Their concerns are strategic, and only the topics that affect their perspective (their "50,000-foot view") are important. Others are much more involved in the minutia of how their product works and how their business is run. They feel most comfortable when they know the gritty details of how their customers perceive their product.

Effective presentations are geared toward the interests and perspectives of the participating executives. Their agendas (as far as you know them) should be taken into account when crafting your presentation. As the expert source for information affecting the product, you should be aware of what's really important to them.

The easiest way to find this out is to ask them. Arrange for several short phone calls with the key stakeholders who are going to be in the meeting. Introduce the subject of the discussion, and ask them if there are any topics that they're particularly interested in or questions that they've wanted answered. A frequent request is for numerical metrics (as described in Chapter 18); these are used to gauge success and to investigate the value of the research. Finding out which metrics are most critical to management (is it the number of new leads, the number of new people signing up for the service, the amount of resources expended on support?) can set the cornerstone for the report and presentation.

In structuring the actual presentation, don't gloss over or simplify important findings, but present the information in such a way that it can assist managers in decisions that they make. Punctuating discussions of general trends with examples and recommendations is often more effective than presenting lists of recommended changes or completely abstract discussions.

Allow plenty of time for questions. Even with background research on your audience's interests, it's often difficult to predict what information people will need, and since company executives have a broad range of responsibilities and interests, their concerns are especially difficult to predict.

Common Problems

A number of problems regularly occur in presentations that can lead to all kinds of uncomfortable stammering and hedging by the presenter. Anticipating these and preparing for them can reduce a lot of on-the-spot consternation.

- *"This is not statistically significant!"* This is often heard when presenting qualitative results from focus groups, user tests, or contextual inquiry. It's true, the results in these research methods are most often not statistically significant, but that's not the purpose of the research. The goal of qualitative research is to uncover likely problems, understand their causes, and create credible explanations for their existence, not to determine the precise proportion of problems within the population at large. Another way to counter this objection is by showing that different kinds of research—say, usability tests and log file analysis—show the same behavior. If several different research techniques show people behaving in the same way, it's much more convincing that that's how they actually behave.
- *Conflicting internal agendas.* Sometimes there are conflicting agendas in the company that get revealed through user confusion. For example, there might be friction between the online sales group and the dealer support groups. One is trying to

increase the company's direct sales effort while the other is trying to appease a dealer network that feels threatened by the direct sales. The site may reflect the designers' attempts to relieve this tension by creating a bifurcated interface, but this shows up as a major point of confusion to the users. In such a situation, describing the user confusion may trigger a surfacing of internal tensions, with the research results serving as a catalyst. If you do not work for the company, it's best to stay out of the discussion and serve as an impartial resource to both camps. However, it's also important to make sure that all sides understand the meaning and limitations of the research. Defend your findings and clarify the facts of your research, but let the two groups decide the implications of those facts. If you're part of the company, however, then it's especially important to defend the impartiality of the research.

- *"This user is stupid."* This can be stated in a number of ways: "the user is unsophisticated," "the user doesn't have the right amount of experience," and so on. If the research has been recruited based on a target audience profile that was accepted by the project team, then the users are members of the target audience and either their experience needs to be respected as the experience of the target audience or the target audience needs to be specified further.

- *"User X is not our market."* Similarly, if the target audience was rigorously defined at the start of the research and the recruiting followed the definition, then User X should be a member of the target audience. If the audience feels otherwise, then it's important to discuss the definition of the target market and how the user does not fit that. It's also useful to discuss whether the observed problems are caused by the specific individual or whether they can occur in a larger segment of the market.

- *"User X did Y; therefore, everyone must do Y"* (often followed by a variation of "Told you so!"). This is overgeneralization. Although trends observed in the behavior of several users underscore issues to be studied and phenomena to be aware of, a single data point does not qualify as a trend. Thus, one user's behavior (or even several users' behavior) could be interesting and could point to a potential problem, but it doesn't represent the experiences of the population at large.

If there's an internal debate about the prevalence of a certain phenomenon, a single instance one way or another will not resolve it (but it may be a good thing to research as part of a future project). As Carolyn Snyder, principal at Snyder Consulting, says, "From one data point, you can extrapolate in any direction."

- *"They all hated the green, so we need to make it all white, like Yahoo."* People, especially solution-oriented people, often tend to tangent off of a superficial observation, assuming that solving it solves the underlying problem. It's the old "treating the symptom, not the disease" problem and should be avoided. Steer discussions away from specific solutions while stressing underlying issues.

- *Be aware of stealth problems.* These are frequently severe problems that affect the user experience but that participants don't complain about or are so fundamental to the idea of the product that they're never discussed, by either the developers or the research participants. These problems can be difficult to uncover and discuss without questioning the basic nature of the product. One site, for example, consolidated the process of contacting and donating to nonprofit organizations, yet was itself a for-profit company. People universally rejected its for-profit nature, and the shadow of that rejection was cast over the experience of every user's examination of the site's feature set even though it was rarely mentioned outright. Any discussion of readability or navigation paled in comparison to the importance of discussing how to present the site's fundamental nature such that the audience did not reject it.

Understanding the desires and expectations of the presentation audience is not very different from understanding the needs of a software product's audiences. The media are different, but the issues are the same. In general, the best strategy to overcome people's doubts and answer their questions is to understand them and anticipate their needs. Sometimes, this can be in the form of expectation setting, but mostly it's in preparation. Knowing your audience's agendas and questions is more than just good showmanship; it's critical to moving a research project from being considered interesting information to being seen as an indispensable tool.

CHAPTER 18

Creating a User-Centered Corporate Culture

Researching the users of your product is extremely important in making it more popular, more profitable, and more compelling. But companies make products, not user research teams. A company needs more than data about its users; it needs to be able to take that knowledge and act on it. Unless the benefits and techniques of user-centered design and research are ingrained in the processes, tools, and mind-set of the company, knowledge will do little to prevent problems.

A user-centered development process means making an overall shift in perspective from how products are made to how they are used. Development processes are focused on making a product, not satisfying needs. This is a major gap between how a company and their customers think about its products, a gap that's often revealed by user research. The difference between the capabilities of a product and the unsatisfied needs of the users reflects deficiencies in the development processes as much as in the product itself. This is where a solution that's based solely on research can fail. Merely knowing what the users need is often not enough to continue making products that people will want to use and that will serve the company's needs. For research to have a sustained impact on the customer experience, the whole organization needs to understand it, value it, and know how to act on it.

That's a hard sell. The benefits of a user-centered development process are seen as intangible and long term, as an abstract "nice to have" that can be written off when it's time to squeeze out a profitable quarter. But making a user-focused customer experience is not just a long-term strategy that may save a penny here or there; it is a vital short-term process that can create immediate value. Good user experience research takes both the user experience and the company's needs into account, creating a set of needs and constraints that make it more likely to produce a successful, and therefore profitable, product.

Unfortunately, this reticence is not unfounded. Creating an effective user-centered corporate culture is difficult. It's straightforward to have everyone agree in principle to make products "with the users' needs in mind," but it is undeniably difficult to create a development process that is steeped in an understanding of the user while still balancing the needs of the company. Creating a process by which the developers' perspectives are secondary to the users' *at every point* requires letting go of our innate preference for our own perspective. That's difficult and needs to be done carefully, introducing changes and justifying them at the same time.

Note Karen Donoghue's book, *Built for Use,* covers the relationship between business goals, features, and the user experience, and many of her thoughts are directly related to the ideas in this chapter.

Integration

The assumption that user experience is just another add-on is fairly consistent across the industry.
—Don Norman, "The Invisible Computer"

Initially, it may seem easier to rip everything out and start over again because traditional processes seem so different from user-centered ones.

Don't do that. That may seem easier, but it isn't. The momentum in a company's existing development process is usually so strong that a complete restructuring requires a huge, disruptive effort. Questioning the basic fabric of a company's life cycle is a big gamble, and big gambles can fail spectacularly. Thus, when first introducing user-centered thought, pick the right place to start.

Know the Current Process

Note Much of this section is indebted to the work and thinking of user experience consultants (and my business partners) Janice Fraser and Lane Becker.

There's a process by which products are created now. Sometimes it's formal, established, and closely followed. At other times, it's ad hoc. Before you begin introducing user-centered processes into your company, you should know how development is supposed to work, how it actually works, and how you can manipulate it so that it works better.

The starting point to introducing new ideas is *internal discovery,* the process of understanding how and why products are created inside a company and the constraints that shape their creation. Put simply, this is the process of answering three major questions.

- Why is it being done?
- What does it do?
- Who cares about it?

Answering these questions in a broad way about any single project will help you understand how to introduce change into the development process as a whole. Like "follow the money" for journalism, each question is designed to lead to other questions rather than a pat answer.

Why Is It Being Done?

What is the fundamental business case for the product? The reasons for creating or updating an offering are rarely simple. They conceal assumptions and expectations. There are reasons the company wants to make the thing. What are they? If it will generate revenue, then exactly how is it expected to do that? If it will improve the company's image, then how is it going to do that (and what's wrong with the image now)? If it will fulfill someone's personal agenda, then what are they hoping to gain from it, and why are they pushing for it?

What Does It Do?

The functionality a company wants to include reveals much about its understanding and prioritization of user needs. Why are these features more important than others? What makes them critical now? Why not do more? Why not do less?

Who Cares About It?

Introducing user-centered ideas means first identifying who makes the decisions about a product and what their responsibilities, needs, and agendas are. When someone is a *stakeholder* in a product, its success is their success, and changes to the process of making it will affect how comfortable they are with it and how loyal they are to it. The person who most wants it to happen and who is in the best position to make it happen is its *sponsor.* Who is the project sponsor? Who are the other stakeholders, the other people who care about or can influence it?

Profiling the stakeholders is the first step to knowing how to present to them, and identifying them ahead of time helps you know who to talk to when it's time to create a strategy for introducing user-centered ideas in the company. In some situations, it may be as simple as convincing the chief operating officer that there's a bottom-line benefit to making a more usable product (which is, of course, harder to do than say). In other cases, you may need to work a grass-roots campaign to win over the engineers by showing them how few grubby support tweaks they'll have to make if they get the user's mental model right ahead of time. In many cases, you need to do both, gaining strong support at the top and allies at the product team and director levels.

Internal Discovery

All this is to say that understanding the impetus for a product involves learning to understand the current position, self-image, and political structure of the company. These details are present, if unacknowledged, in every company. Uncovering them is the process of *internal discovery,* which consists of asking the preceding questions in a systematic and consistent way.

It begins with a list of the major questions based on the general categories defined earlier. Some common ones are

- Who are all the stakeholders?
- How are decisions made and scoped?
- What are the current business mandates?
- How are key terms and concepts defined?

Expand the questions as appropriate. For example, the following questions may help you identify key stakeholders:

- Who are the people who are clearly interested in this project?
- Who are the people who should be interested in it?
- Who are the people whom it's dependent on?
- Who can roadblock it? Who is likely to do so? Why?
- Who is likely to want to help it?

This will give you a first-order understanding of whom you should talk to when doing internal discovery. They may be people who are already on your team, or they may be in adjacent departments. They may be top executives. They may be opinionated engineers.

Once you have an idea of who is important to the project, the company's business mandates, and the reasons for its scope, you have the building blocks for creating a strategy. In a sense, corporate cultures are games. By uncovering the rules and players and playing with a sense of ironic detachment, you play better.

Start Small

In some companies, it's best to start reforming the process from the top, with an executive evangelizing and pushing until the whole company has changed. In another, it may be appropriate to create a "skunk works" that exists outside the rest of the company. Still in others, it may be more appropriate to disseminate abstract ideas first, letting the ideas filter in over the course of months or years before introducing additional methods.

In many cases, starting small works best. When they fail, small projects are not seen as severe setbacks. When they succeed, they can be used as leverage for larger projects. Moreover, they educate everyone in the methods, goals, and expectation of user experience research and user-centered design.

How small is small? Initial targets should be short term, doable, and straightforward. They should also be things that the success of your project doesn't hinge on. A first project can be the redesign of a small section with known problems: a registration page, for example. John Shiple, former director of user experience for BigStep.com, suggests shoehorning user experience research into Web site front door redesigns. Front doors are redesigned on a regular basis, and they serve as entryways and billboards for the company. They are important parts of the user experience, but their design often affects presentation more than functionality, so unsuccessful designs can be rolled back easily. This gives their redesign scope and importance, but without the weight of core functionality redesign.

For example, a news site decided to redesign their front door to improve retention and repeat visits. The designers were working from assumptions based on their own experience when they decided to integrate some user research into the process. It was a month before their relaunch, so there wasn't enough time to research fundamental audience needs or make detailed profiles, but they could test whether their plans to increase content density and emphasize subsection navigation made sense to their potential users. They recruited eight people who matched their audience profile, and wrote a user test to profile their users and test several prototypes.

As they interviewed the participants, they discovered several things they had not expected: increasing the density of data on the front page made it clear that the site contains a lot of information, but overwhelmed a number of participants, several of whom called it "cluttered." Moreover, most of the participants didn't use the navigation bar at the top of the screen, but chose to type keywords into the search box instead. The team realized that their search engine was much more important to the success of the site than they had previously thought.

Likewise, although they weren't studying people's attitude toward their brand, they observed that a number of their users were fiercely loyal, but would never be daily users. Until this point, they had assumed that everyone would be looking at the site every day. This result was, in effect, asking a fundamental question about the design of the product and how the company defined customer retention and success.

Prepare for Failure

Prepare to stumble as you start bringing user-focused techniques in-house. You may do the wrong research at the wrong time with the wrong part of the product. You may ask all the wrong questions in all the wrong ways. You may be asked to do something that's inappropriate, but you have to do it anyway. The research results may be useless to the development staff, or they may completely ignore it. Management may ask for hard numbers that are impossible to produce.

This is one of the reasons to start small. This is also an occasion to be philosophical. Bad research happens to everyone, but every piece of user research, no matter how flawed, provides insight even if it's only into how to structure the research better next time. Recognizing failure greatly reduces the likelihood of such failure in the future. Set appropriate expectations for yourself and for those who may be receiving the results, use problems to make further plans, get feedback from your interview subjects, and examine how well the research is going even as it's still under way.

Involve Stakeholders Early

A heuristic evaluation—or, thoughtful criticism—often does not convince partners that such and such sucks. A live event—with donuts—behind one-way glass can, however. That's sad, but true.
—Dave Hendry, Assistant Professor, University of Washington Information School, personal email

A process is truly customer centered when customers can change designers' initial understanding of the work.
—Beyer and Holzblatt, *Contextual Design,* p. 54

Making people observe and participate in research is one of the most effective ways to sell them on its value and effectiveness. Observing users failing to use a product is an incredibly powerful experience. It communicates to the observers that their perspective may be entirely unlike the way their users think.

The development team and key stakeholders need to be involved in research, but they need to be involved in different ways.

The Stakeholders

Those who make decisions about a product need to see the value of the process firsthand. The best way to accomplish that is to make

them watch research firsthand. They don't have to actively participate, but if they can be in the same room watching people struggle
and listening to the kinds of ideas that these struggles inspire in the
development team, they are much more likely to support such efforts in the future.

The Development Team

Those who are directly involved need to see the research process
and its results. For them, participation in the research should involve
direct participation in developing the research goals, creating research prototypes, and analyzing the results. Once they've participated, they are much more apt to support the process and to integrate it into their future plans.

Including everyone in every bit of research is often difficult,
however, and developers need to be directed toward research that
will be most meaningful for them. For example, people from marketing and business development are more likely to be interested in
ideas that speak to broad, strategic issues with the product. These are
often embodied in focus groups or contextual research studies and
less so in usability tests. Technical writers and trainers benefit from
knowing which concepts people want explained better, issues that
are revealed during task analysis or usability testing interviews. Engineering and interaction design absolutely need to be included in
usability testing, but participating in contextual research may not be
as immediately useful to them (that said, these two groups should
probably be in as much research as possible since they are in the best
position to apply bottom-to-top knowledge of the user experience).

Warning Respect your development team. Just as there's a tendency in developers to write off users who don't understand their software as "stupid," there's a tendency in user experience researchers to write developers who don't understand user-centered design processes as "stupid" or at least "clueless." Take an active part in development, explain processes, and listen for suggestions. If a development team seems clueless at first, it's surprising how quickly they appear to wise up when engaged as partners in a research project.

Show Results

Almost as important as involving people in research is showing results in such a way that stakeholders see its value. It's most important
to present it in a way that is immediately useful, but the ideal research also *convinces*. Every report can serve as another platform
from which to discuss user-centered development.

Presentations should be tailored to specific audiences, as discussed in Chapter 17. For example, the vice president of online ser-

vices of a media company did not have time to attend any user research, or even to sit for a full presentation of the results. However,
he was an important person to convince of its value. So the research
team asked him for ten minutes of one of his notoriously quick
lunchtimes. There was no time to describe the findings in detail,
but it was enough to expose him to important concepts. The
presentation focused on the process and showed him a couple of
factoids showing improvements in the product. This told the vice
president that his staff were thinking in original ways about the customer and introduced him to some new ideas about the development process.

Even as you're writing your report for the developers, think
about how to make it a good lever when changing your corporate
culture. Present changes in small groups to encourage rapid iteration
and discussion. With every report, highlight unanswered questions
and future research possibilities to encourage more research. Discuss the interaction of the needs of users, advertisers, and the company's identity to get people thinking about the product as a meld-
ing of the three.

Be Patient, but Persistent

> *You need to be stubborn, committed, and shrewd, but know when to back off*
> *and when to barge into the senior VP's office.*
> —Chauncey Wilson, Director, Bentley College Design and Usability
> Testing Center, personal communication

Software development cultures attempt to schedule their revolutions. In such an environment, it can be difficult to convince
people that an evolutionary approach is worthwhile. But that's exactly what needs to happen when introducing user-centered methods within an organization. A carefully chosen pace will keep the
momentum of innovation going, but without unduly stressing the
development process or the people in it.

Sometimes, though, the response to research will be lukewarm.
Reports can sit unread on managers' desks or be discounted by engineers who see insufficient scientific rigor in them. In these situations, continuing the research is especially important, showing that

results are real, valuable, and consistent. For example, if you once had ten minutes with a vice president, request a similar amount of time after every piece of research on a regular basis, presenting the highlights of the research once a month. Even though he or she may not be interested in the specifics of each research project, the stream of interesting tidbits of information will be a useful reminder of the process and its value. Schedule lunchtime seminars on user-centered design and invite people in from outside your company to talk about successful projects. Buy some pizza. Having an outside voice discussing situations similar to those your group is encountering can be quite convincing.

Encourage Specific User Experience Roles

When the value of user experience research and user-centered design begins to be acknowledged in the company, it's useful to start pushing to create positions that take charge of the process. When someone is responsible for the process, they can serve as both spokesperson and evangelist.

In reverse order of seniority, here are a few sample job descriptions.

User Experience Specialist

The User Experience Specialist is responsible for evaluating, tracking, and designing an effective user experience within a development team. The specialist will monitor the development process for situations that require managing the execution of the research and working with the development team to interpret the results.

Usability, marketing research, experimental psychology, or real-world cultural anthropology experience required. Design and software development or project management experience preferred. The ideal candidate will be able to manage research projects and interpret research for design, engineering, and technical writing audiences in addition to moderating research and analyzing results.

Director of User Experience

The Director of UE is responsible for all user experience research within the company. Responsibilities include managing all in-house research projects, communicating results to management, training junior research staff in basic techniques, and transferring knowledge across all research projects as appropriate.

Familiarity with common user experience research methods (usability testing, task analysis, contextual inquiry) is required, and all candidates should have at least three years' experience conducting frequent research studies from beginning to end. Specific experience should include creating user profiles for research and development, recruiting participants, moderating research, and analyzing and presenting results. Experience working closely with interaction designers and software developers required. Information architecture experience preferred.

In addition, candidates should be able to train others to conduct user experience research and be able to adjust research methods in response to the needs of the product or the development team.

Chief Experience Officer (CXO)

The Chief Experience Officer is a senior management position in charge of the entire user experience for all classes of users under all circumstances. This position encompasses any design, marketing, and customer support effort that affects the way people interact with the company. It requires familiarity with all facets of user experience and marketing research. In addition, the CXO should have extensive experience with the design end-user interaction, whether from a visual, creative standpoint, an interaction standpoint, or as part of a customer relationship management system.

In concert with ensuring the best possible experience for the users of a company's products, the Chief Experience Officer is responsible for introducing and maintaining a culture that integrates user input and user research at all key points in the development process. The CXO should be familiar with user-centered management. Finally, the CXO has the responsibility for balancing the needs of the users with the needs of the company, reporting first and foremost to the users, but also to the stockholders and board.

Justification

Without justification, there is no incentive to integrate. Improving the quality of the user experience is treated as a long-term investment. It's easy to forsake long-term strategies in a world driven by financial quarters and shaky valuations, and when budget compromises have to be made, user research is rarely considered relevant to the current crisis. It gets lumped in with other goody-goody endeavors such as preserving rain forests and adopting stray cats.

User-centered development needs to be positioned as a solution that makes immediate financial and corporate sense. It needs to be shown that it is a "must have" and not a "nice to have." How to do that requires having arguments and methods that justify its existence.

Reasons for User-Centered Processes

It's often necessary to keep arguing and debating throughout the introduction of user-centered methods into a development process. Since these are usually new ideas and new ways of working, they meet resistance and their benefits require clarification.

Though the actual emphasis will vary from situation to situation, several basic arguments have met with success in the past.

- *Efficiency.* Products that people actually want don't have to be remade. Products that are designed around the way people work don't need to be changed. When there's a model of how people use a product, there will be fewer disagreements, less ambiguity, less development delay, and you'll know just where to add functionality (and where not to).

  All in all, it's a process that uses your company's resources more efficiently: it creates a clearer road map before launch; after launch it reduces the amount that servers and support staff are taxed.

- *Reputation.* Users who have a positive user experience are more likely to keep using your product and to tell others to use your product. Products that match people's needs, desires, and abilities will create a level of satisfaction that goes beyond mere complacency and acquires an aura that extends beyond functionality. People associate themselves emotionally with the product, creating a bond that's much stronger than one that's merely based on rational functional trade-offs.

- *Competitive advantage.* The more detailed the user model, the more easily it's possible to know which of their needs your product satisfies. This makes it possible to identify needs that are unfulfilled by the competition and drive innovation not based on technological capabilities (which may or may not have practical applications) but on real needs (which certainly do). Rather than reacting to user behavior, you can anticipate it and drive it.
- *Trust.* When a product behaves according to people's expectations and abilities, they trust it more. Trustworthiness, in turn, leads to loyalty, satisfaction, and patience.
- *Profit.* Ultimately, when a product costs less to make, costs less to maintain, attracts more customers, and provides better value to business partners (all things that are explicit goals of user experience research and design), it makes more money. This is discussed in greater detail in the "Pricing It" section.

These general improvements in turn imply specific short-term advantages that directly affect development.

- The number of prelaunch redesigns is reduced.
- There are fewer arguments between departments and between individual members of the development team.
- Schedules are more likely to be met because surprises are reduced and development time can be more accurately predicted.
- It's easier to share a vision of the product with the developers and the company as a whole.
- It is easier to communicate product advantages to the end users.
- The customer service load is reduced since fewer questions have to be answered.

- Equipment load is more predictable because feature popularity can be estimated.
- Quality assurance needs are reduced since typical usage patterns determine where to focus attention.

All these things can come together to save the company money, extend the value of its brand, and make it more responsive to market conditions. They are all excellent reasons to warrant creating a user research pilot program, and provide an intermediate step between the CEO's proclamation that the company is "Dedicated to customer service!" and a rigorous, comprehensive program of user-centered development.

Measuring Effectiveness

Eventually, if the arguments are met favorably, these methods will begin to be integrated into the development process. Ideally, the results are obvious, and all the products and processes are so improved that it's unnecessary to convince anyone of the effectiveness of these ideas. Otherwise, it's necessary to be able to demonstrate the effectiveness of the processes. Even when change is obvious, some measurement is always required to determine how much change has occurred.

That's where *metrics* come in. Metrics abstract aspects of the user experience in a way that can be measured and compared. In an environment of speculation and opinion, they can clarify gray areas and verify hypotheses. They can play an important role in understanding the magnitude of problems and evaluating the effectiveness of solutions.

Choosing Metrics

It's like a finger pointing away to the moon. Don't concentrate on the finger, or you will miss all the heavenly glory.
—Bruce Lee, *Enter the Dragon*

A metric is something that can be measured that (it is hoped) is related to the phenomenon that is being studied. All energy should not be focused on measuring and affecting the metric while ignoring what it represents. As they say, the map is not the territory.

Warning Many important aspects of user experience cannot easily be measured. It's tempting to try and quantify the effects of good user experience design with lots of quantitative metrics, but trying to attach numbers to the effects of design can often cloud understanding by appearing to be objective (numerical) measurements, rather than revealing little about the phenomena they're supposed to be measuring. Satisfaction and trust, for example, can only be hinted at in surveys, but survey numbers are often presented as precise "scientific" measurements of them. Repeat visits, which are measurable in log files, are only part of loyalty though they're often used to stand in for it.

Metrics begin with goals. The ultimate goal is to evaluate the quality of the user experience that the product is providing. A secondary goal is to understand how much of a change the new techniques are making. The basis should be in the same goals that were defined when writing the research plan. Goals are problems with the product. Defining metrics is part of the process of understanding where the experience is failing. Just as some goals affect the end user's experience while others address the company's interests, certain metrics will be more important when tracking the effectiveness of changes, while others will convince stakeholders.

For example, one of the questions asked about shopping cart use in Chapter 6 is "What is the ratio of people who abandon the shopping cart versus those who complete a transaction?" This is a metric. Although it could be measuring several things (how fickle people are, how much they're willing to experiment with the product, etc.), it primarily measures how much they get frustrated.

SOME TYPICAL WEB SITE METRICS

The percent of visits that end on a "leaf" page (a page with information)

The ratio of people who start a shopping cart to the number who reach the "thank you for shopping with us" page

The duration spent on the site

The number of times the search feature is used in a single session

The number of times that top-level navigation pages are loaded (i.e., the number of times people back up)

The number of critical comments per day

The number of visits per month per visitor

All these, of course, have to be used with an understanding of the reasons for users' behavior. For example, an increase in the number of leaf pages could represent more interest in the material or more errors in finding what they're looking for.

A more systematic approach is to list the goals for the current project and cross them with general categories of the user experience, creating a metric at each intersection. This ensures that the major questions are examined from the important perspectives. So the Sport-i.com example given in Chapter 5 could look like this.

SOME SPORT-i.COM METRICS

	Efficiency	Effectiveness	Satisfaction
Conversion of viewers to shoppers	The length of the clicktrace leading to a purchase	The ratio of visitors to purchasers	The ratio of positive comments to negative ones in surveys
Improved navigation	The frequency with which navigation pages are consulted	The number of different navigation pages consulted	The ratio of positive navigation comments to negative in surveys
Timeliness of information	The number of daily users	The ratio of casual visitors to daily users	The ratio of "timely" comments to "not timely" in surveys

As you can see, some of the metrics make a lot of sense in the context of the site and the data that can be collected, whereas others are more questionable. Regardless, doing the exercise with stakeholders forces everyone involved to think about the relationship of product goals to facets of the user experience, but that doesn't mean that you have to follow through and measure everything in the grid.

Note Metrics can have hidden problems. If page views represent success, but several pages are cut out of a typical task, then your metric may actually go down, even as your product becomes easier and more satisfying.

The exact metrics created will be an idiosyncratic mix of what needs to be tracked in order to understand the change's effectiveness combined with what's required to convince the company that the process is effective. Moreover, metrics don't have to be based on data collected in–house. It's possible to use external measurements. For example, because Google ranks the cost of keywords based on the frequency with which they're mentioned, it's possible to use Google prices as a metric of brand name penetration.

Collecting and Comparing Metrics

There are two primary ways of measuring performance with metrics, and both have been covered in other sections of this book. Clickstreams can reveal aggregate behavior among large numbers of current users. Obtaining the results of a new metric just means processing the log files a little differently.

Metrics collected through usability testing, however, are a different matter. Normally, the exact number of participants who react in a certain way doesn't matter in usability testing, which is concerned with broad trends. But when trying to answer questions about specific proportions ("the percentage of users who can find the new site map versus 47% before the redesign," for example), user tests have to be conducted differently.

Unless you interview hundreds of people, a user test is going to be statistically insignificant, and its results can't be projected to the entire population. They can, however, be compared to the results of other *tests*. Two carefully conducted user tests, one before a change is made and one after, can be compared to get some results quantitatively to see if a change has happened.

As with any experiment design, it's important to minimize the variables that change. Three main things can change between the tests.

- *The population.* There will likely be a different set of people in the second test. They should be a comparable group of people, recruited in circumstances that closely match those of the first test, but they won't be identical (even if they were the same people, they will have already been exposed to the product once, so they won't have the same reaction).
- *The test procedure.* A change in the way that a prototype is presented creates a change in people's experience of it. Even small changes in wording or order can affect perceptions.
- *The prototype.* Changes in the interface obviously change people's experience of the product. This is usually what's changed between comparative user tests.

Changing more than one of these factors usually introduces more change than can be effectively understood and managed in a test process, and renders any numbers collected to be highly dubious, if not meaningless. To maximize the validity of the process, it's also useful to test with more people than with qualitative usability testing. More people let you understand both the breadth of responses and their consistency. Jakob Nielsen recommends at least 20 people per test as opposed to 6 to 8 for a test without a quantitative component, and that's probably a good base number.

Compared to test management, measurements in user tests are pretty straightforward, if occasionally tedious. You count. Timing measurements used to understand the efficiency of an interface can be done using the tape counter on a video deck or a hand stopwatch. Error counts ("how many times the back button was used") can be done with simple hash marks.

For log files or surveys, the procedures are identical to those given in Chapters 11 and 13. The metrics need to be defined ahead of time, and the exact date and time when the experience changed needs to be known. In the case of large products, where many changes can happen simultaneously, knowing what else changed at the same time helps identify whether observed changes are incidental or caused by the interface alterations under scrutiny. For example, if a front door is redesigned and launched with great fanfare, a measurement of traffic to the homepage may be as much a measure of the marketing as it is of usability. In such a situation, a measure of completed tasks may be a more accurate assessment of the effectiveness of changes to the interaction.

Pricing Usability

Note The ideas in this section are heavily influenced by *Cost-Justifying Usability,* edited by Randolph G. Bias and Deborah Mayhew, 1994, Academic Press. It is a much more thorough and subtle presentation of the issues involved in pricing user experience changes than can be included here.

Using changes in metrics to calculate *return on investment* (ROI) is very convincing, but notoriously difficult. Many factors simultaneously affect the financial success of a product, and it's often impossible to tease out the effects of user experience changes from the accumulated effects of other changes.

That said, if you can make a solid case, bottom-line financial benefits are the most convincing argument for implementing and continuing a user-centered design process. On the Web, this is somewhat easier than for packaged software, where many changes may happen simultaneously with the release of a golden master.

Ecommerce sites have it the easiest. They have metrics that can be quickly converted to revenue.

- *Visitor-to-buyer conversion* directly measures how many visitors eventually purchase something (where "eventually" may mean within three months of their first visit, or some such time window).
- *Basket size* is the size of the average lump purchase.
- *Basket abandonment* is a measure of how many people started the purchasing process and never completed it. Multiplied by basket size, this produces a measure of lost revenue.

Each of these measures is a reasonably straightforward way of showing that changes have happened in the site that make it more or less profitable.

For other kinds of services, one whose function is to sell advertising or disseminate information to employees, for example, different measures need to be found. Since salaried staff answer customer support calls and email, reducing the number of support calls and email can translate to direct savings in terms of staff reduction. However, support is a relatively minor cost, and reducing it generally increases the bottom line insignificantly. What's important is to find ways of measuring *increases* in revenue because a product was developed in a user-centered way.

For example, a news site is redesigned to make it easier to find content. The average clickstream grows from 1.2 pages to 1.5 pages, which represents a 25% increase in page views, which translate to a proportional increase in advertising revenue. Seems pretty cut-and-dried, but say that a marketing campaign is launched at the same time. Both the usability and marketing groups can claim that their effort was responsible for the increased revenue. To justify the user experience perspective and separate it from marketing, the impact of usability can be estimated and ROI calculated. This creates a formula that can spark a discussion about the relative effects of advertising and usability, but at least the discussion can be on a relatively even plane.

Recently our site underwent a redesign that resulted in increased page views and advertising revenue. This came at the same time as a marketing campaign encouraging people to visit the site.

Our analysis of the usage log shows that the average length of a session was 1.2 pages for the 8-week period before the redesign. This means that people were primarily looking at the front door, with roughly 20% of the people looking at two or more pages (very few people looked at more than four).

Usability testing showed that users had a lot of trouble finding content that was not on the front door. One of the goals of the redesign was to enable them to find such content more easily.

For the 4 weeks after the redesign, the average clickstream was 1.5 pages, a 25% increase in per-session pages and page views. The marketing campaign certainly contributed to this increase, but how much was due to increased usability of the site? If we suppose that 30% of the increase was due to the greater ease with which people could find content, this implies that 7.5% of the increase in page views is a direct result of a more usable site.

Using the average number of monthly page views from the past year (1.5 million) and our standard "run of site" CPM of $10, this implies a monthly increase in revenue of $1125. If the marketing efforts were responsible for getting people to the site, but the new design was responsible for all the additional page views, the added accessibility would have been responsible for $3750 of the increase in monthly revenue.

However, deep use of the site is different from just visiting the front door and has an additional effect on revenue. The CPM for subsections is $16. At 30% effectiveness, this would imply an increase of $1800 in revenue per month, $21,600 per year, or roughly 10% of all revenue.

Our costs consisted of 80 hours of personnel time at approximately $50 per hour, or $4000 plus $1000 in incentive and equipment fees. Thus, the total cost to the company was approximately $5000. When compared to the annual return, this represents a 270% to 330% return on investment at the end of the first year.

In some cases, the ROI may be purely internal. If good user research streamlines the development process by reducing the need for postlaunch revisions, it could actually be creating considerable savings to the company that is impossible to measure in terms of direct revenue. Comparing the cost of revisions or delays in a development cycle that used user-centered techniques to one that did not could yield a useful measurement of "internal ROI."

What If It's Too Difficult?

None of this stuff is easy, but what if the entrenched corporate culture just doesn't allow integration of usability concepts? What do you do then?

First, identify the nature of the resistance. Resistance comes in two primary forms: *momentum* and *hostility*.

People fall into old habits easily. User-centered design takes time, energy, and commitment. Doing things "the old way" is almost always going to be easier, and may momentarily seem like a more efficient way of doing things. "Well, if we just did this the old way, we could do it in three weeks. You want us to do a month of research first? That'll just make us miss our deadline even more!" Using near-term efficiency as a pretext for abandoning proper procedures misses the point of the approach. Though gut-level decisions made in the "old school" style may end up being adequate, they are much more likely to cause long-term problems and ultimately create more work.

The way to counter momentum is to build speed in a different direction. As described earlier, a slow introduction of user experience research techniques can be effective when coupled with an internal "marketing campaign" documenting the process's effects on the product and the company (as described in Chapter 17). Likewise, an executive commitment to revamping the whole development process can be effective, although it requires more resources and commitment than most companies are willing to expend.

In some cases, though the company buys into the ideas, changing the process in any major way may be impossible in the short run. In such cases, user experience research efforts may need to be justified one at a time.

Hostility is more difficult to deal with, although in some ways an aggressive challenge can allow for a more radical, more rapid change in mind-set than a program of slow subterfuge. Then again, it can be really messy if it goes wrong.

Jeff Veen described the reaction he was met with from one company's staff about doing user research: "To the engineers, usability was a set of handcuffs that I was distributing; to the designers, it was marketing." Jeff's solution was to turn it into an event. He made it clear that something special was happening to the company and to the developers: that management was listening to them and really looking carefully at *their* product. He first arranged for the delivery schedule to be loosened, giving the developers more breathing room and alleviating their apprehension that this process was going to add extra work that they wouldn't be able to do. He then invited all of them to watch the usability research in a comfortable surrounding and with all meals included. As they all watched the interviews together, Jeff interpreted the test for them, emphasizing the importance of certain behaviors and putting the others in context. He also encouraged the developers to discuss the product. After a while, they noticed that they were debating functionality in terms of specific users and their statements rather than principles or opinions.

Warning *Research paralysis.* When user-centered processes start becoming popular and the development team has bought into the basic processes, there's a tendency to want to make all changes based on user research. This is an admirable ideal, but it's generally impractical and can cause development to grind to a halt.

Don't get distracted by research and forget the product. It's OK to make decisions without first asking people. Just don't make all of your decisions that way.

In certain cases, users threaten people. They call them "lusers," describe the process of making usable products as making them "idiot proof," and approach their users' demands or misunderstandings with derision. Such statements betray an attitude toward the product that's somewhere between arrogance and insecurity. When hostility is especially irrational and obstinate, there's little that can be done about it. However, direct exposure to users can help convince the doubtful. At first, seeing users fail at something can confirm the doubter's worst fears: that people are unable to use their product and that they're profoundly different and alien. This is really uncomfortable, but it brings home many of the core ideas. Extended exposure almost always reveals that as frustratingly different as users are, their problems and concerns are easier to alleviate than the developers may fear.

The Only Direction

However, even if it is difficult to implement this kind of process in your company and it becomes frustrating and demoralizing, it doesn't mean that it will never happen. The ideas behind user-centered design have been floating around for more than two decades, slowly penetrating even the most user-phobic, inward-focused companies. The pressure to create more successful products than your competitor will always be there and user-centered, user research–based methods are one of the best—if not *the* best—ways to do that. A user-centered company communicates better, makes fewer guesses, solves more pressing problems, and responds better to changes. It is, in short, a company that runs with less friction and a clearer vision.

Such companies may be few today, but there are more of them all the time because there have to be. As the Information Revolution—which only began in earnest in the late 1980s and early 1990s—penetrates societies all over the world, the habits of the Industrial Revolution melt away. With a world where it's no longer necessary to mass-produce and mass-market and mass-distribute products and ideas, it no longer makes sense to think of mass markets. It's no longer necessary to create one solution for everyone based on the limited knowledge of a few. And as economic times get tougher and the bite of competition more painful, companies everywhere learn that good business does not end with the end users of a product or service; it begins with them.

Appendix A:
The Budget Research Lab

A user research lab doesn't have to be extensive. Its primary goal is to provide a consistent, quiet, comfortable space to do research. Beyond that, investment in a lab is a game of diminishing returns. Million-dollar labs do little more on a day-to-day basis than can be done with a conference room. Nevertheless, it's highly advantageous to have a usability research lab. On a practical level, it allows for a consistent equipment setup, which greatly reduces the hassle of having to worry about audio and video quality in documentation.

Figure A.1 shows the physical layout of a usability testing lab, as described in Chapter 10 (focus group layouts are described in Chapter 9).

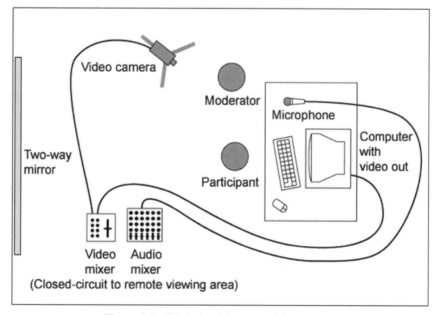

Figure A.1 A typical usability testing lab.

Here is the list of equipment for a budget setup, including closed-circuit observation equipment (which can be used in place of or in addition to a two-way mirror) and picture-in-picture imaging of what the participant sees.

Video Equipment

- Consumer-grade computer: $1500. Computer equipment used in research should resemble the kind of equipment that users are likely to have, which will rarely be state of the art. Moreover, one of the best ways to keep a computer setup neutral is to start with a generic setup.
- Scan converter: $300. Scan converters convert the signal from the test computer's videocard into a video signal, which is processed and recorded. Make sure that you pick one that can do the typical resolution that you're likely to be testing with (many low-end ones only do 640 × 480, which is unacceptably low resolution for most usability testing).
- Two miniDV video cameras with IEEE1394 (Firewire/i.LINK) interfaces and external video input: $800–$2000 apiece. It's useful to have two cameras: one to serve as the camera and one to serve as a video recorder, recording the output of the video mixer picture-in-picture image. The cameras don't have to be particularly fancy since even a basic modern camera will do most of what's required. The cameras don't have to be identical since only one is going to be recording at any given time, and that can be the higher-quality camera (in fact, the recording camera doesn't have to be a camera at all; it can be a VCR). But if you're going to build the lab from scratch, it's useful to buy two of the same one for redundancy. The IEEE1394 output makes it much easier to import the video into desktop video editing software for making highlight reels.
- Video switcher: $1000. In order to record both the image of the user and what the user is looking at on the same tape, it's useful to use a low-end video switcher.
- Professional video monitor: $700–$1000. This allows for playback without degradation in quality, which can be important during analysis.

- Two big TVs: $700. For closed-circuit observation, it's good to have a couple of big TVs. One has the picture of the person on it, and the other, a picture of what he or she is looking at. The TVs are also useful for playback of highlight tapes to larger groups.
- Video tripod: $150.
- Interconnect cables: $50.
- Closed-circuit cables: $200. These are long, shielded video cables that can run into another room without getting interference from various computer equipment. You could also buy a couple of the wireless "tv doubler" units, but they don't always work inside office environments.
- RF modulator: $30. This converts the component signal that high-end video equipment uses to TV-style antenna signal, but may be unnecessary with some TV models.
- miniDV tapes: $8–12 apiece.
- Transportation cart for mixer, deck, and monitor: $200.

Options

- Lapel microphone: $150 for better audio.
- Cardiod microphone: $150.
- Stand for cardiod microphone: $80.
- Microphone mixer: $200.
- Microphone cables: $50.

The Research Lab as Destination

However, more than the pragmatism for good video should drive the creation of a lab. A user research facility plays an important role in establishing the importance of user-centered development in a company. It creates a destination for people within the company to go and watch as users use their products. This makes the abstract ideas of integrating users into development much more real, transforms the idea of "the user" into a group of actual people, makes shaky solutions much less certain, and generally reinforces that good can come from such a process.

Appendix B:
Common Survey Questions

This is a list of the kinds of questions that can be asked in a survey, with some suggested answers. It is neither exhaustive, nor perfect for all situations since the goals of your survey will determine the actual wording of the questions and responses.

Demographic Questions

1. Which of the following categories includes your age?
   - ○ Under 18
   - ○ 18–24
   - ○ 25–34
   - ○ 35–49
   - ○ 50–64
   - ○ 65+
   - ○ Rather not say

2. What is your gender?
   - ○ Female
   - ○ Male
   - ○ Rather not say

3. Select the educational level you have reached.
   - ○ Grade school
   - ○ Some high school
   - ○ High school graduate
   - ○ Vocational/technical
   - ○ Associate degree
   - ○ University undergraduate graduate
   - ○ Masters degree
   - ○ Professional degree (JD, MD, etc.)
   - ○ Advanced degree (PhD, PsyD, etc.)
   - ○ Other

4. Which of the following categories includes your household's annual income?
   ○ Less than $20,000
   ○ $20,001–$29,999
   ○ $30,000–$39,999
   ○ $40,000–$49,999
   ○ $50,000–$59,999
   ○ $60,000–$69,999
   ○ $70,000–$79,999
   ○ $80,000–$99,999
   ○ $100,000–$119,999
   ○ $120,000–$149,999
   ○ $150,000+

5. What is your current employment status?
   ○ Employed full-time
   ○ Employed part-time
   ○ Not employed
   ○ Self-employed

6. What is your job title?

7. What is your company or organization's primary product or service?

Web/Internet Use Questions

1. How long have you been using computers?
   ○ Less than 1 month
   ○ 1–6 months
   ○ 6 months to 1 year
   ○ 1–2 years
   ○ 2–3 years
   ○ 3–5 years
   ○ 5 years or more

2. How often do you use a computer?
    ○ Less than once a month
    ○ Once a month
    ○ Several times a month
    ○ Once a week
    ○ Several times a week
    ○ Every day
    ○ Several times a day or most of the day

3. Where is the computer located that you use most frequently?
    ○ Home
    ○ Work
    ○ School
    ○ Library
    ○ Public computer lab
    ○ Wherever you are (laptop/PDA)
    ○ Other

4. How long have you been using Internet email?
    ○ Less than a year
    ○ 1–2 years
    ○ 2–3 years
    ○ 3–4 years
    ○ 4–5 years
    ○ 5 years +

5. How long have you been using the World Wide Web?
    ○ Less than 1 month
    ○ 1–6 months
    ○ 6 months to 1 year
    ○ 1–2 years
    ○ 2–3 years
    ○ 3–5 years
    ○ 5 or more years

6. How often do you use the World Wide Web?
    ○ Less than once a month
    ○ Once a month
    ○ Several times a month
    ○ Once a week
    ○ Several times a week
    ○ Every day
    ○ Several times a day

7. On average, how long do you spend on the Web in a given session?
    ○ 5 minutes or less
    ○ 5–15 minutes
    ○ 15–30 minutes
    ○ 30 minutes to 1 hour
    ○ 1–3 hours
    ○ 3–6 hours
    ○ 6 hours or more

Product Use Questions

1. How long have you been using *[name of product]*?
    ○ This is my first time
    ○ Less than one week
    ○ 1 week to 1 month
    ○ 1–6 months
    ○ 6 months to 1 year
    ○ 1–2 years
    ○ 2–3 years
    ○ 3 or more years
    ○ Don't know

2. Which of the features from the following list have you used in the last three times you used *[name of product]?* (Check all that apply)
   - ☐ Feature 1
   - ☐ Feature 2

   . . .

   - ☐ None
   - ☐ Don't know

Technological Capability Questions

Note Connection speeds and technologies change so frequently that the connection options available as this book is being written will certainly have changed by the time it's published.

1. What operating system do you use most frequently?
   - ○ Windows 2000
   - ○ Windows NT
   - ○ Macintosh OSX
   - ○ Linux
   - ○ Other
   - ○ Don't know

2. What is the CPU speed of your primary computer?
   - ○ Less than 500MHz
   - ○ 500–1000MHz
   - ○ 1000–2000MHz
   - ○ More than 2000MHz
   - ○ Other
   - ○ Don't know

3. What is the resolution of your primary monitor?
   - ○ 640 by 480 pixels
   - ○ 800 by 600 pixels
   - ○ 1024 by 768 pixels
   - ○ 1600 by 1200 pixels
   - ○ Larger than 1600 by 1200 pixels
   - ○ Other
   - ○ Don't know

4. What is the speed of your connection to the Internet?
    ○ Less than 56K
    ○ 56K
    ○ DSL or cable modem (144K–1.5M)
    ○ T1
    ○ T3
    ○ Other
    ○ Don't know

Appendix C:
Observer Instructions

Focus Groups

1. Listen. As tempting as it is to immediately discuss what you're observing, make sure to listen to what people are really saying. Feel free to discuss what you're seeing, but don't forget to listen.

2. Don't jump to conclusions. Use people's statements as guides to how they think about the topic and what their values are, but don't treat the specifics of their statements as gospel. If everyone in a group says they like or hate something, that doesn't mean that the whole world thinks that way, but it is a good indicator that there are enough people who do that you should pay attention.

3. Focus groups are not statistically representative. If four out of five people say something, that doesn't mean that 80% of the population feels that way. It means that a number of people may feel that way, but it doesn't mean anything in terms of the proportions found in the population as a whole. Nothing. Zilch.

4. Focus group participants are experts. The participants in a focus group know what they want to do and how they currently do it. Listen to their needs and their experience and treat them as consultants who are telling you what your customers need, not as the consumers of a product or the targets of a sales pitch.

5. Focus groups are not a magic bullet. A couple of good ideas from every group is enough to make that group worthwhile, but not every statement that the group participants make should be followed to the letter.

6. Feel free to pass questions to the moderator, but don't overdo it. Occasional questions to the group are OK, but there should not be more than a couple in a session. Write your question clearly and concisely, and phrase it as if you were talking to the moderator. Then give it to the assistant moderator, who will then take it to the moderator. When appropriate for the flow of conversation, the moderator will introduce the question. However, the moderator may decide never to introduce it if the timing or topic is inappropriate.

7. People are contradictory. Listen to how people are thinking about the topics and what criteria they use to come to conclusions, not necessarily the specific desires they voice. A person may not realize that two desires are impossible to have simultaneously, or he or she may not care. Two people may think they're agreeing, when they're actually saying the exact opposite.

8. Don't write people off. Sometimes, a participant may say things that indicate that he or she isn't getting it. Never assume that someone has nothing important to say just because he or she isn't interesting or insightful from the start. Understanding why one participant "doesn't get it" can hold the key to understanding the perspectives of everyone who "does."

9. Save some pizza for the moderator.

Usability Tests

1. Listen. As tempting as it is to immediately discuss what you're observing, make sure to listen to what people are really saying. Feel free to discuss what you're seeing, but don't forget to listen.

2. Usability tests are not statistically representative. If three out of four people say something, that doesn't mean that 75% of the population feels that way. It does mean that a number of people may feel that way, but it doesn't mean anything numerically.

3. Don't take every word as gospel. These are just the views of a couple of people. If they have good ideas, great, but trust your intuition in judging their importance, unless there's significant evidence otherwise. So if someone says, "I hate the green," that doesn't mean that you change the color (though if everyone says "I hate the green," then it's something to research further).

4. People are contradictory. Listen to how people are thinking about the topics and what criteria they use to come to conclusions, not necessarily the specific desires they voice. A person may not realize that two desires are impossible to have simultaneously, or he or she may not care. Be prepared to be occasionally bored or confused. People's actions aren't always interesting or insightful.

5. Don't expect revolutions. If you can get one or two good ideas out of each usability test, then it has served its purpose.

6. Watch for what people don't do or don't notice as much as you watch what they do and notice.

For in-room observers, add the following instructions:

7. Feel free to ask questions when the moderator gives you an explicit opportunity. Ask questions that do not imply a value judgment about the product one way or another. So instead of asking, "Is this the best-of-breed product in its class?" ask, "Are there other products that do what this one does? Do you have any opinions about any of them?"

8. Do not mention your direct involvement with the product. It's easier for people to comment about the effectiveness of a product when they don't feel that someone with a lot vested in it is in the same room.

Bibliography

This book isn't a scientific text, it's a how-to manual, so I am intentionally avoiding a long list of papers and documentation that's hard to obtain or too technical for daily use. This is a list of common books that make up a decent library of user research and user-centered development material. If you're interested in the more technical or historical aspects of each of these subjects, additional information can be found in the bibliographies of each of these books.

Qualitative Research

Beyer, H. and Holzblatt, K. *Contextual Design*. San Francisco, CA: Morgan Kaufmann, 1998.

Kirwan, B. and Ainsworth, L. K. *A Guide to Task Analysis.* London, UK: Taylor and Francis, 1992.

Krueger, R. A. *Focus Groups: A Practical Guide for Applied Research (3d edition).* Thousand Oaks, CA: Sage Publications, 1988.

Rubin, J. *Handbook of Usability Testing.* New York, NY: John Wiley & Sons, 1994.

Quantitative Research

Babbie, E. R. *Survey Research Methods (Second Edition)*. Belmont, CA.: Wadsworth Publishing, 1990.

Dillman, D. A. *Mail and Internet Surveys (Second Edition)*. New York, NY: John Wiley & Sons, 1999.

Grossnickle, J. and Raskin, O. *The Handbook of Online Marketing Research*. New York, NY: McGraw-Hill, 2000.

Kirk, R. E. *Statistics: An Introduction*. Belmont, CA.: Wadsworth Publishing, 1998.

Moore, D. S. *Statistics: Concepts and Controversies (Fifth Edition)*. New York, NY: W.H. Freeman, 2001.

Rosenthal, R. and Rosnow, R. L. *Essentials of Behavioral Research: Methods and Data Analysis (Second Edition)*. New York, NY: McGraw-Hill, 1991.

Design Philosophy

Brinck, T., Gergle, D., Wood, S. D. *Usability for the Web*. San Francisco, CA: Morgan Kaufmann, 2002.

Burroughs, W. S. *Naked Lunch (Reissue)* New York, NY: Grove Press, 1992.

Cooper, A. *The Inmates are Running the Asylum*. Indianapolis, IN: SAMS, 1999.

Garrett, J. J. *Elements of User Experience*. Indianapolis, IN: New Riders, 2002.

Nielsen, J. *Usability Engineering*. San Francisco, CA: Morgan Kaufmann, 1994.

Norman, D. A. *The Design of Everyday Things (Revised Edition)*. New York, NY: Currency/Doubleday, 1990.

Petroski, H. *The Evolution of Useful Things*. New York, NY: Vintage Books, 1994.

Veen, J. *The Art and Science of Web Design*. Indianapolis, IN: New Riders, 2000.

The Business of Usability

Bias, R. G. and Mayhew, D. J. (eds.). *Cost-Justifying Usability.* Boston, MA: Academic Press, 1994.

Donoghue, K. *Built for Use: Driving Profitability Through the User Experience.* New York: McGraw-Hill, 2002.

Software Project Management

Demarco, T. and Boehm, B. W. *Controlling Software Projects.* Englewood Cliffs, NJ: Prentice Hall PTR/Sun Microsystems Press, 1998.

Highsmith, J. *Agile Software Development Ecosystems.* Reading, MA: Addison-Wesley, 2002.

Mayhew, D. J. *The Usability Engineering Lifecycle.* San Francisco, CA: Morgan Kaufmann, 1999.

McConnell, S. C. *Rapid Development.* Redmond, WA: Microsoft Press, 1996.

Index

About the Author

Mike Kuniavsky is a founding partner of Adaptive Path, a user experience consulting company in San Francisco. He has been developing commercial web sites since 1994, and is the interaction designer of an award-winning search engine, HotBot. His design work and writing have appeared in many publications, including Web-Monkey, ID Magazine, Wired, Inc., *The Wall Street Journal,* and the *LA Times.*